KEY ISSUES IN
MENTAL RETARDATION
RESEARCH

KEY ISSUES IN MENTAL RETARDATION RESEARCH

Proceedings of the
Eighth Congress of the International Association
for the Scientific Study of Mental Deficiency (IASSMD)

Co-sponsored by the World Health Organisation

Dublin, Ireland   21–25 August 1988

Edited by W. I. Fraser

Professor of Mental Handicap
University of Wales College of Medicine
Ely Hospital, Cardiff

Technical Editor
C. G. I. Hussell

Editorial Board

R
ROUTLEDGE
London and New York

First published 1990
by Routledge
11 New Fetter Lane, London EC4P 4EE

Simultaneously published in the USA and Canada
by Routledge
a division of Routledge, Chapman and Hall, Inc.
29 West 35th Street, New York, NY 10001

Typeset by Columns of Reading
Printed and bound in Great Britain by Mackays of Chatham PLC, Kent

British Library Cataloguing in Publication Data

International Association for the Scientific Study of
Mental Deficiency, *Congress*; 8th
(1988: Dublin Ireland)
Key issues in mental retardation research.
1. Man. Mental handicaps
I. Title II. Fraser, William I. (William Irvine)
616.85'88

Library of Congress Cataloging in Publication Data

International Association for the Scientific Study of Mental
Deficiency. Congress (8th: 1988: Dublin, Ireland)
Key issues in mental retardation research: proceedings of the 8th
World Congress of the International Association for the Scientific
Study of Mental Deficiency (IASSMD): Dublin, Ireland, 21–25 August
1988 / co-sponsored by the World Health Organization; edited by W.I. Fraser.
p.   cm.
Includes bibliographies and indexes.
1. Mental retardation—Congresses.   2. Mentally handicapped—Congresses.
I. Fraser, William I.   II. World Health Organization. III. Title.
[DNLM: 1. Mental Retardation—congresses.   WM 300 I611k]
RC569.9.I57   1988
616.85'88—dc20
DNLM/DLC
for Library of Congress   89–10405
CIP

ISBN 0–415–01363–1

Contents

SECTION I
EPIDEMIOLOGICAL ISSUES

SECTION II
BIOMEDICAL ASPECTS

Contents

SECTION III
CLINICAL PRACTICE

SECTION VI
EDUCATIONAL ISSUES

SECTION VII
COMMUNITY INTEGRATION, ADJUSTMENT, EVALUATION AND COSTS

Preface

The Eighth Congress of the International Association for the Scientific Study of Mental Deficiency was held in Dublin, Ireland, in August 1988, the year of the City's millenium. The event was attended by 1300 registered participants and accompanying persons representing some 46 countries. 160 papers were submitted for publication, and read by at least one expert referee, in addition to the Editor and scrutiny by the Editorial Board.

We have been able to find space for only a selection of the many excellent papers presented at the Congress. In keeping with the name of the Association under whose aegis this book is produced, scholarly content constituted the principal criterion in the selection process, but we have attempted also to publish a representative collection of papers reflecting the theme of the Congress – "key issues". Each paper illustrates a key issue in this epoch of accelerating change – ranging from the effects of dietary patterns on the developing brain, the impact of new technologies, to consumer choice, and to the problems of ageing (so protean that they can only be summarised in this volume). I am particularly grateful to the Editorial Board and the following reviewers:

Dr. K. Aitken	Ms. D. Jackson
Dr. B. Andrews	Dr. P. Jackson
Dr. F. Anwar	Dr. F. James
Mr. P. Baker	Dr. J. Jancar
Prof. J. Berg	Dr. A. Kerr
Dr. A. Bernsen	Prof. C. Kiernan
Prof. P. Berry	Prof. C. Kremont
Dr. S. Bettison	Dr. W. Lindsay
Dr. R. Blunden	Dr. G. MacKay
Dr. K. Brown	Prof. I. Markova
Ms. B. Burford	Prof. P. Mittler
Prof. J. Campbell-Murdoch	Ms. J. Montague
Dr. S. Cheseldine	Dr. B. Monteiro
Prof. B. Cooper	Dr. P. Odor
Prof. C. Cullen	Dr. O. B. Pratt
Prof. C. Cunningham	Dr. J. M. Rao

Dr. H. Davies
Dr. P. Dickens
Prof. A. Dupont
Dr. D. Felce
Dr. E. Fischbacher
Ms. A. Van der Gaag
Ms. A. Green
Dr. J. Greenwood
Prof. R. Grieve
Dr. S. Hollis

Dr. N. Raynes
Dr. A. Reid
Prof. S. Richardson
Prof. C. Robson
Prof. L. Rowitz
Dr. O. Russell
Dr. P. Seed
Ms. J. Stansfield
Dr. T. F. Webb
Dr. D. Wilson
Dr. J. Wishart

In the preparation of this Volume I am indebted to The Technical Editor, Mr. C. G. I. Hussell, who has brought order out of chaos, and to my secretary Mrs. Dawn Doran.

In Dublin there were many memorable presentations, but the most unforgettable aspect of this Congress was the welcome from the Irish people.

W. I. Fraser

Authors' terminologies and English/American usage have been respected.

Officers of the IASSMD

Officers: 1988–1992

President	Dr. M. Mulcahy, Ireland (*assumes the position*)
President-Elect	Dr. T. Dolan, U.S.A.
Vice-President	Dr. A. Takahashi, Japan
	Dr. B. Hagberg, Sweden
Secretary	Dr. K. Day, England (*continues his term*)
Treasurer	Mr. J. O'Gorman, Ireland

Members of Council: 1988–92

Dr. M. Arima, Japan
Dr. B. Beck, Denmark
Prof. Blomquist, Sweden
Dr. R. Brown, Canada
Prof. B. Cantlon, Argentina
Prof. Ann Clarke, England
Dr. E. de Lorenzo, Uruguay
Prof. J. Grubar, France
Dr. S. Herr, U.S.A.
Mr. C. Magerotte, Belgium
Mr. A. Myhrman, Finland
Dr. H. Narayanan, India
Dr. S. Nemeth, The Netherlands
A/Prof. T. Parmenter, Australia
Prof. A. Rett, Austria
Ms. M. Rioux, Canada
Prof. L. Rowitz, U.S.A.
Mr. J. Tse, Hong Kong
Dr. K. Wilton, New Zealand
Dr. J. Zaremba, Poland
One member, to be arranged by Council,
    from the Middle East, Africa or USSR

Honorary Officers: 1988

Hon. President	Dr. Alan Clarke, England
Hon. Vice-Presidents	Dr. M. Begab, U.S.A.
	Dr. A. Dupont, Denmark
	Dr. C. de Jong, The Netherlands
	Dr. R. Andrews, Australia
Hon. Officers	Prof. S. Krynski
	Prof. B. Cohen
	Dr. J. Jancar
	Prof. J. Berg
	Dr. A. Bernsen
Hon. Secretary	Dr. D. Primrose

Committees: 1988–92

Constitution and By-laws

Chairman	Dr. C. de Jong, Netherlands
	Dr. D. Primrose, Scotland
	Dr. A. Bernsen, Denmark
	Prof. Alan Clarke, England
	D. J. Berg, Canada

Nomination and Election

Chairman/Vice-President	Dr. A. Takaahashi, Japan
	Four members to be appointed later by Council

Recognition and Awards

Chairman/Vice-President	Dr. B. Hagberg, Sweden
	Dr. J. Jancar
Secretary	Dr. K. Day
	Three members to be appointed later by Council

Finance and Membership

Chairman	Dr. R. Andrews, Australia
	Dr. D. Primrosc
	Mr. J. O'Gorman
	Prof. A. Dupont
	Dr. T. Mutters

Publications and Research

Chairman	A/Prof. T. Parmenter, Australia
	Prof. L. Rowitz
	Dr. M. Begab
	Dr. M. Janicki
	Dr. J. Hogg
	Prof. W. Fraser
	Dr. K. Wilton

Program Committee

Chairman/President-Elect   Dr. T. Dolan, U.S.A.
Secretary   Dr. K. Day
Three members to be appointed later by Council

Introductory Presidential Address to the Eighth IASSMD Congress

Throughout this Congress we are discussing KEY ISSUES IN MENTAL RETARDATION RESEARCH and also asking the questions: Is there a gap between knowledge and application of the knowledge? – and what is the size of the problem? How many persons do we speak about when we discuss the mentally impaired or the mentally retarded? The following figures are taken from the recent yearbook of the United Nations and cover the figures for the middle years of the 1980s. The total population of the world is about 5 billion persons; of the crude live birth rates we know that it differs enormously from country to country and from region to region; however of the 135 million newborn live births per year in the world at least about 1 million will be mentally retarded. This means that the population of the mentally retarded in the world increases enormously year by year, as it has been shown in many studies that the survival rate is increasing. And if we take a group well known to us all – Down's syndrome – there will be a new cohort born every year of at least 100,000 per year. It is difficult to grasp these figures, and if we consider the whole world population and how many of them will be mentally retarded at a given time, we know that it will be about 10–20 million mentally retarded in the total world, although also this figure is an average figure and of course with a great variation from country to country and from region to region. The figures I have mentioned make scientists speak about the rising pandemic of impairment in the world.

Now to *the topics* of these studies:
Although many of the topics for this Congress are the same as have been treated at nearly all the Congresses, the way it has been done and the results reached by the scientists are different, and show the progress of our scientific field. At the same time the persons we are speaking about, the mentally "retarded", the mentally "handicapped", the "disabled" or "impaired" persons are now living another life from when we started the IASSMD in 1964. However, some things have not changed. The field of mental retardation is still a Cinderella compared to many other fields in all the different sciences we could compare with. In medicine it is still the Cinderella of psychiatry and of cytogenetics etc. But general scientific study benefits from the experiences of our advances, for instance, in

Psychology, in Education, and in Sociology – and the organisation of our multidisciplinary teamwork has been an ideal for other fields of community care. At many of our Congresses community care has been discussed, but now – in the name of integration and normalisation – the reduction of special services earlier provided in the best of the special institutions. There is a great gap between knowledge and application of scientific progress for handicapped persons. For instance, if the general practitioners all over the world are to serve the mentally retarded of all degrees, all ages, with the many well-known additional handicaps e.g. cerebral palsy, epilepsy, different types of psychiatric symptoms and diseases, congenital malformations etc., then there is a need for intensive training of the medical students and the many groups of medical professionals. This has not taken place, not even in the most developed countries, and therefore there is still, if you measure the knowledge of the general practitioner taking care of the handicapped persons, a great gap between knowledge and application; it is a paradox that today with the very high standard of knowledge of the proper treatment, very few of the mentally retarded persons benefit from this knowledge. They are left with a cut-down of service in the name of normalisation and integration.

And what about prevention? In both the *primary prevention* of new cases and *secondary prevention* e.g. concerning early intervention, social service etc., there is only a fraction of application of our knowledge today. Time will not allow me to go through the very many areas of vaccination, nutrition and care of newborn babies and pregnant women, and treatment of the risk groups, prevention of traffic damage and brain injured children etc. or describe how the old traditions, ignorance and lack of resources, the growing pollution of food, air and water, block development in this field; and if we study the program of the World Health Organization with work for Health for All at year 2000, not much mention is made of mental retardation. However, the World Health Organization (WHO) which cosponsored the Congress, has produced to be distributed to the participants a directory of resources, and works with the IASSMD for the development of methods of assessing developmentally delayed people. In 1985 WHO and UNICEF stated that in the developing world about 10 infants die every minute of diarrhoea diseases – at the same time the very many survivors of infant diseases are at risk of developing mental impairment of varying degrees. We do not know the exact figures, but the pilot studies of the frequencies of disablements show that the problems of the developing countries concerning learning deficiencies and mental handicaps is about the same size as in the developed world although the predominant causes are different. Another important field is the prevention and control of iodine deficiency now in progress on a global program sponsored by International Organisations and Councils in order to prevent mental retardation and other disabilities in millions of children and adults. However, it was stated a few months ago that even in some European countries there is a persistence of severe iodine deficiency conditions. The Keyword of the International Council for control of these conditions is "to bridge a great gap between knowledge and application".

It is a misunderstanding that there is a lack of scientific activity in this field. On the contrary, take a look at the proceedings of our international congresses, and at the many international journals with news about different topics of our field. The program of this Dublin Congress demonstrates this. However, it is also necessary to evaluate the progress, the service and the results; this Congress shows that it is now possible to do this in a much more scientific way.

ANNALISE DUPONT
President

Section I

Epidemiological Issues

The Prevalance at Birth of Down Syndrome in 19 Regions of Europe 1980–86

H. Dolk, P. De Wals, Y. Gillerot, M. F. Lechat, S. Aymé,
R. Beckers, F. Bianchi, I. Borlée, A. Calabro, E. Calzolari,
A. Cuschieri, C. Galanti, J. Goujard, D. Hansen-Koenig,
F. Harris, G. Karkut, D. F. Lillis, M. S. Lungarotti, F. Lys,
M. Marchi, N. C. Nevin, A. Radic, C. Stoll, D. Stone, I. Svel,
L. P. Ten Kate, R. Zori
EUROCAT Working Group
EUROCAT Central Registry
Department of Epidemiology, EPID 30.34, Catholic University of Louvain,
Clos Chapelle-aux-Champs 30, 1200 Brussels, Belgium

A total of 1938 cases of Down syndrome were registered in livebirths, fetal deaths (20 weeks gestation and over) and induced abortions in 19 European regions covering a population of 1,414,805 live- and stillbirths in the period 1980–6. Of the total of Down syndrome cases, 87.7% were livebirths, 3.0% fetal deaths, and 9.3% induced abortions. Livebirth prevalence rates ranged from 5.8 to 20.8 per 10,000 livebirths in the 19 regions. Prevalence at livebirth was affected by the maternal age distribution of total births and the extent of utilization of prenatal diagnosis (leading to termination of pregnancy). There are large differences between regions and countries in these factors. The proportion of births to women over 35 varied from 5% to 18% in the 19 regions. The average proportion of induced abortions among total cases ranged from 0% to 27% and among cases with maternal age 35 years and over this proportion ranged from 0% to 48%. The combined effect of differences in maternal age distribution and in utilization of prenatal diagnosis meant that from 15% to 58% of livebirths with Down syndrome were born to mothers over 35.

INTRODUCTION

The most important known determinant of the risk of Down syndrome is maternal age. Models of risk which best fit population data describe a linear increase in risk up to age 30 and an exponential increase thereafter

3

(Hook, 1980). Over the last few decades, changes in the maternal age distribution of the birth population have led to changes in the total prevalence rate at birth of Down syndrome in many areas of the world (Luthy *et al.*, 1980; Mikkelsen *et al.*, 1983; Koulischer and Gillerot, 1984; Owens *et al.*, 1983). In addition prenatal diagnostic services are increasingly available (Luthy *et al.*, 1980; Mikkelsen *et al.*, 1983), the main indications for use being advanced maternal age or previous history of a Down syndrome birth.

Within Europe, large differences exist in both maternal age distribution and in availability and utilization of prenatal diagnostic services. The EUROCAT network of registration of congenital anomalies covered geographically defined regions in 11 countries of Europe between 1980 to 1986. The registration data was analysed in order to look at the relative contribution of maternal age distribution and termination of pregnancy following prenatal diagnosis to the prevalence at livebirth of Down syndrome in 19 regions.

MATERIAL AND METHODS

The system of registration of congenital malformations in EUROCAT registries has been described in previous publications (De Wals *et al.*, 1985). The present study concerns 19 registries in 11 countries during the period 1980–6 (Table 1).

In 8 centres (Odense, Florence, Groningen, Dublin, Glasgow, Liverpool, Northern Ireland and Malta) the registration covers all births to mothers resident in a geographically defined area. In 8 centres (West Flanders, Hainaut, Umbria, Galway, Emilia Romagna, Strasbourg, Paris and Marseille) the reference population consists of all births occurring in a geographically defined area, but in Paris and Marseille births to non-residents are excluded from analysis. The West Berlin, Luxembourg and Zagreb registries cover births in selected hospitals within a region.

Each centre obtained regional or hospital statistics, as appropriate, for the total births covered by the registry. However in Paris, the total birth statistics included non-residents, and an estimation was made of the proportion of resident births according to the proportion of all registered livebirths with congenital anomalies which were residents of Greater Paris.

Cases of congenital anomaly are ascertained among livebirths and fetal deaths and among induced abortions following prenatal diagnosis of malformation.

Fetal deaths included in this analysis are those with a gestational age of at least 20 weeks, but ascertainment of fetal deaths of 20 to 27 weeks gestation was not necessarily systematic, depending on the sources of information and legal limits of birth notification for each registry.

In some of the countries induced abortion is illegal (Belgium, Ireland and Malta). In countries where induced abortion is legal 4 centres do not have access to this information (Umbria, Luxembourg, Emilia Romagna and Zagreb). Only induced abortions performed following prenatal diagnosis of congenital anomaly or for other medical reasons are covered by the registration system.

The maternal age distribution of total births in each centre was used to calculate maternal age-specific prevalence rates in livebirths. The maternal age distribution in livebirths was approximated according to the distribution in total births, the resulting inaccuracy being very small when dealing with the prevalence of a rare event. Maternal age distributions were based on regional statistics for the complete study period for Luxembourg, Liverpool and Strasbourg, for all years except 1986 for Dublin, Glasgow and Belfast, for all years up to 1984 for Paris, Odense, and Galway, for 1981–4 in West Flanders and for 1981–3 in Hainaut. Denominators in Emilia Romagna were estimated from a 1% control population for years 1980–86. The remaining centres did not have access to adequate maternal age statistics for the study period.

Maternal age was recorded in more than 95% of cases in all centres except Emilia Romagna where the information was missing for 13.7% of cases. This results in a slight underestimation of maternal age-specific prevalence rates.

Information on karyotype was sought in all cases of Down syndrome but registration could be made on clinical diagnosis only. Separation of cases into free trisomy, translocation trisomy and mosaic was not done in the present analysis.

RESULTS

A total population of 1,414,805 live and stillbirths was covered by the 19 registries in the study period (Table 1).

A total of 1938 DS cases were registered in livebirths, fetal deaths and induced abortions. A karyotype was known by the registry to have been made in over 90% of cases in 7 registries (HAI, ODE, GRO, GLA, BEL, STR, MAR), in 75–89% of cases in 4 registries (LIV, ER, GAL, LUX) and in a lesser proportion in other registries except Paris where performance of karyotype examination was not recorded.

Fetal deaths accounted for 3.0% of total cases. The rate of DS fetal deaths among total fetal deaths was 55.3 per 10,000. The ratio of fetal deaths to livebirths did not vary significantly with maternal age ($X^2(3) = 0.57$).

Induced abortions (following prenatal diagnosis of chromosomal anomaly) accounted for 9.3% of total cases. Induced abortions were registered in 11 centres, representing 5% to 27% of registered cases in

Table 1. Total births covered by 19 EUROCAT registries and proportion with maternal age 35 (40) and over

Registry[a]		(Abbrev.)	Country	Study period	Total birth coverage	% Mothers 35 +	% Mothers 40 +
West Flanders		(WF)	Belgium	80–86	50,386	4.89	0.75
Hainaut		(HAI)	Belgium	80–86	57,352	4.57	0.75
Odense		(ODE)	Denmark	80–86	32,648	5.97	0.65
Paris		(PAR)	France	81–86	213,090	10.59	1.95
Strasbourg		(STR)	France	82–86	65,383	7.25	1.02
Marseille		(MAR)	France	86	24,503	–	–
West Berlin		(WB)	F.R. Germany	80–86	42,945	–	–
Florence		(FLO)	Italy	80–86	63,261	10.60	2.10
Umbria		(UMB)	Italy	80–85	45,709	–	–
Emilia Romagna		(ER)	Italy	80–86	136,961	11.84	1.94
Luxembourg		(LUX)	Luxembourg	80–86	16,628	6.62	0.82
Groningen		(GRO)	Netherlands	81–86	50,379	–	–
Dublin		(DUB)	Ireland	80–86	163,985	13.82	2.62
Galway		(GAL)	Ireland	81–86	19,293	17.75	3.91
Glasgow		(GLA)	U. Kingdom	80–86	91,359	6.23	0.90
Liverpool		(LIV)	U. Kingdom	80–85	122,351	6.85	1.02
Belfast		(BEL)	U. Kingdom	80–86	195,012	11.88	1.94
Zagreb		(ZAG)	Yugoslavia	83–86	18,703	–	–
Malta		(MAL)	Malta	86	5,310	–	–

[a] Where the registry is listed as the name of a city, the geographical area covered includes the surrounding region.

Table 2. Number and proportion of total Down syndrome cases (livebirths, fetal deaths and induced abortions) registered as induced abortions, 11 EUROCAT centres, by maternal age

Registry	Total		<30 Years		30–34		35–37		35–39 38–39		Total		40–44		45+	
	no.	%	no.	%	no.	%	no.	%	no.	%	no.	%	no.	%	no.	%
HAI	3	5.9	0	–	1	12.5	0	–	0	–	0	–	1	25.0	1	100.0
ODE	1	5.0	0	–	0	–	1	33.3	0	–	1	25.0	0	–	0	–
PAR	91	26.7	2	2.2	7	10.0	7	12.7	20	57.1	27	30.0	48	73.9	5	50.0
STR	10	13.7	0	–	0	–	2	20.0	1	16.7	3	18.8	5	50.0	2	66.7
MAR	4	11.1	0	–	0	–	2	14.3	1	50.0	3	18.8	1	50.0	0	–
WB	11	22.4	0	–	2	16.7	5	50.0	1	20.0	6	40.0	3	50.0	0	–
FLO	17	17.2	0	–	1	5.0	0	–	1	12.5	1	4.2	12	54.6	3	100.0
GRO	6	9.1	0	–	0	–	1	12.5	2	40.0	3	21.4	3	60.0	0	–
GLA	14	13.7	3	7.7	0	–	4	28.6	3	60.0	7	36.8	2	25.0	2	40.0
LIV	12	8.5	1	1.7	1	2.9	3	12.5	1	16.7	4	13.3	6	37.5	0	–
BEL	12	4.2	0	–	0	–	0	–	2	6.5	2	3.0	8	13.8	2	66.7

these centres (Table 2). In Paris, Florence, Belfast and Strasbourg, the proportion of induced abortions was increasing during the study period, reaching, in 1985–6, 36%, 24%, 7% and 21% of cases for these 4 centres respectively. The increase in the proportion of induced abortions with increasing maternal age is shown in Table 2. For Down syndrome cases with maternal age 35 and over, 9% (Belfast) to 48% (Paris) were induced abortions.

The majority of induced abortions were performed between 20 and 22 weeks gestational age (56.7%), 3.5% were performed before 16 weeks, 17.7% from 16–19 weeks, 14.5% from 23 to 27 weeks and 7.6% at 28 weeks and later.

The prevalence rate at livebirth of Down syndrome ranged from 5.8 to 20.8 per 10,000 in the 19 populations (Table 3). The percentage of DS cases born to mothers of 35 years and over ranged from 15% to 58%, including 0 to 29% born to mothers 40 years and over (Table 3). Maternal age specific rates are given in Table 3. They can be compared with published Swedish rates (Lindsjo, 1974) for a population of over 330,000 livebirths where 7.5% of mothers were aged over 35, including 1.6% over 40.

DISCUSSION

Large differences exist within Europe in the maternal age distribution of births. The proportion of mothers over 35 varies from 4% to 18% in the regions surveyed (Table 1) and this is reflected in the prevalence at livebirth of Down syndrome in the different populations.

The proportion of liveborn DS cases with older maternal age (Table 3) constitutes a rough guide to the extent of reduction in the frequency of DS that would result from a reduction in the birth rate in these age groups.

A potentially large influence on the livebirth prevalence rate is the availability and utilization of prenatal diagnostic services. Crude figures indicate that up to 36% (Paris in 1985–6) of total DS cases are diagnosed prenatally resulting in termination of pregnancy. A very small proportion of these terminations are to younger mothers seeking prenatal diagnosis for indications of increased risk other than maternal age (Table 2). The proportion of induced abortions becomes significant from the age recommended for prenatal diagnosis in regional or national policy: 35 years in Hainaut, West Berlin, Belfast and Glasgow, 36 years in Groningen and 38 years in France and Italy (Table 2).

The reduction in the prevalance rate at livebirth due to prenatal diagnosis for maternal ages 35–9 and 40–4 can be seen by comparison with the Swedish rates (Table 3) characterised by thorough and validated case ascertainment and established at a time when prenatal diagnosis was

Table 3. Down syndrome among livebirths, proportion of cases to older maternal ages (MA 35+, MA 40+) and population and maternal age specific prevalence rates per 10,000 livebirths

Registry	Total no. cases (LB)	% MA 35+	% MA 40+	Total rate (LB)	Maternal age specific rates			
					< 30	30–34	35–39	40–44
West Flanders	46	15.2	8.7	9.2	6.6	16.4	14.5	99.5
Hainaut	42	21.4	7.1	7.4	5.9	7.2	27.6	75.2
Odense	19	15.8	0.0	5.8	5.7	3.4	17.4	_a
Paris	232	33.6	8.6	11.0	6.6	10.2	26.0	38.7
Strasbourg	59	27.1	8.5	9.1	6.4	9.6	27.2	65.0
Marseille	31	41.9	0.0	12.7	–	–	–	–
West Berlin	38	31.6	7.9	8.9	–	–	–	–
Florence	82	40.2	12.2	13.0	7.2	12.0	43.0	75.8
Umbria	55	29.1	12.7	12.1	–	–	–	–
Emilia Romagna	180	38.2	12.4	13.2	8.5	10.8	33.9	78.0
Luxembourg	22	27.3	0.0	13.3	9.4	13.5	62.5	–
Groningen	60	21.7	3.3	11.9	–	–	–	–
Dublin	283	54.1	23.3	17.4	7.0	14.0	47.8	139.1
Galway	38	57.9	28.9	19.8	5.8	16.8	41.5	130.8
Glasgow	85	23.5	10.6	9.4	5.7	16.1	22.7	78.2
Liverpool	125	28.8	8.0	10.3	6.1	15.2	36.7	67.9
Belfast	269	42.4	18.6	13.9	7.3	14.9	34.5	116.9
Zagreb	28	17.9	7.1	15.1	–	–	–	–
Malta	10	40.0	20.0	18.8	–	–	–	–
Swedish livebirth prevalence rates[b]				13.2	7.8	14.5	37.4	149.6

[a] Maternal age specific denominators not available or concern less than 250 births over the study period.
[b] Lindsjo (1974), Acta Paediatrica Scan., **63**, 571–6.

not yet practised. Such a comparison assumes that there is no large variation in maternal age specific risk between populations (Hook, 1980). Although the EUROCAT maternal age-specific rates are subject to some statistical fluctuation, especially in smaller registries, and are partly influenced by the exact distribution of maternal ages within each 5-year interval, rates which are selectively low for the older maternal ages can be considered to reflect the extent of utilization of prenatal diagnosis. The correspondance between this comparison and the number of induced abortions registered by each centre (Table 2) is not exact. This lack of correspondance is due to three main problems in the interpretation of the reported number of terminations.

Firstly, reliable information about terminations performed within the registration area may be difficult to obtain and only 11 centres registered such cases. Secondly, due to regional variation in the availability of prenatal diagnostic services, pregnant women seeking prenatal diagnosis may not do so in their region of residence. Such cases leaving the area often escape the information network of the registration system. Conversely certain registry areas containing centres of expertise attract cases from surrounding areas and efforts to exclude non-residents may not be entirely successful. Thirdly, the spontaneous fetal death rate for Down syndrome is relatively high and by registering terminations a certain number of cases are counted which would otherwise have been fetal deaths incompletely covered by the registration system. It has been estimated that the survival of Down syndrome babies to mothers 35 years and over after the time of amniocentesis (16–18 weeks) is approximately 70% (95% CI 58%–81%) when no termination is performed (Hook, 1983). Fetal deaths with Down syndrome may not be reliably registered either because of low gestational age (many centres cover only fetal deaths of 28 weeks and over) or lack of karyotyping (especially in cases of macerated fetuses) so that the ratio of livebirths to fetal deaths in the total EUROCAT material 1980–6 was 96.6:3.4 rather than 70:30. This implies that if all terminations were performed at 16–18 weeks, their number should be reduced by 27.5% to be compared with the total number of livebirths and fetal deaths, or by 30% to be compared with the number of livebirths. Such correction is likely to be inaccurate however, due to the imprecision of the DS fetal survival estimate, and the generally later gestational ages at which pregnancies are actually terminated.

It will be possible to predict future trends in Down syndrome prevalence by demographic analysis, and investigation of factors determining utilization of prenatal diagnostic services (Adams et al., 1981; Hook and Schreinemachers, 1983). However, this analysis of the contrasting patterns in Europe shows also that in most regions in the 1980s, a majority of Down syndrome cases are born to mothers of less than 35 years of age.

The potential of new screening techniques and strategies which would include women under 35 is currently being evaluated (Cuckle and Wald, 1984). Most importantly, progress needs to be made in identifying causal factors which might lead to a significant level of primary prevention.

REFERENCES

Adams, M. A., Finley, S., Hansen, H., Jamiel, R. I., Oakley, G., Sanger, W., Wells, G. and Wertelecki, W. (1981) Utilization of prenatal genetic diagnosis in women 35 years of age and older in the United States, 1977 to 1978, *Am. J. Obstet. Gynecol.*, **139**, 673–7.

Cuckle, H. S. and Wald, N. J. (1984) Maternal serum alpha-foetoprotein measurement: a screening test for Down Syndrome, *Lancet* **i**, 926–9.

De Wals, P., Weatherall, J. A. C., Lechat, M. F. (eds) (1985) *Registration of Congenital Anomalies in EUROCAT Centres 1979–1983*, Cabay.

Hook, E. B. (1983) Chromosome Abnormalities and Spontaneous Fetal Death following Amniocentesis: Further data and Associations with Maternal Age, *Am. J. Hum. Genet.*, **35**, 110–16.

Hook, E. B. (1980) Down Syndrome Frequency in Human Populations and Factors Pertinent to Variation in Rates, in de la Cruz, F. F. and Gerald, P. S. (eds) *Down Syndrome*, Baltimore, University Park Press, 3–67.

Hook, E. B. and Schreinemachers, M. S. (1983) Trends in Utilization of Prenatal Cytogenetic Diagnosis by New York State residents in 1979 and 1980, *AJPH*, **73**, 198–201.

Koulischer, L. and Gillerot, Y. (1984) Epidemiology of Down's Syndrome in Wallonia (South Belgium) Recent Data (1979–1981), in J. M. Berg (ed.), *Perspectives and Progress in Mental Retardation, vol. II: Biomedical Aspects*, IASSMD, 39–45.

Lindsjo, A. (1974) Down's syndrome in Sweden, *Acta Paediatrica Scand.*, **63**, 571–6.

Luthy, D. A., Emanuel, I., Hoehn, M., Hall, J. G. and Power, E. K. (1980) Prenatal Genetic Diagnosis and Elective Abortion in Women over 35: Utilization and Relative Impact on the Birth Prevalence of Down Syndrome in Washington State, *Amer. J. Med. Gen.*, **7**, 375–81.

Mikkelsen, M., Fischer, G., Hansen, J., Pilgaard, B. and Nielsen J. (1983) The impact of legal termination of pregnancy and of prenatal diagnosis on the birth prevalence of Down Syndrome in Denmark, *Ann. Hum. Genet.*, **47**, 123–131.

Owens, J. R., Harris, F., Walker, S., McAllister, E., West, L. (1983) The incidence of Down's Syndrome over a 19-year period with special reference to maternal age. *J. Med. Genet.*, **20**, 90–3.

Prevalence of Mental Retardation: An Empirical Study of an Unselected School Population

K. Sonnander

University of Uppsala, Department of Psychiatry
Ulleråker S-750 17 Uppsala Sweden

The main purpose of the study was to investigate empirically the hypothesis of selective casefinding by administering the Wechsler Intelligence Scale for Children (WISC) to a total unselected representative school population aged 6–12 years. Another aim was to investigate the adequacy of the current Swedish standardization of the WISC. The test score distribution yielded in the study was normal or Gaussian in nature and differentiated across the population tested. However, the population mean had increased by one stanine point and the whole distribution had moved upwards making old norms for identification of mental retardation too lenient.

INTRODUCTION

Existing data on the prevalence of mental retardation in Scandinavia are inconclusive and in certain respects even confusing. In order to test some hypotheses of possible causes of different figures of prevalence reported in particular in mild mental retardation, ten Scandinavian studies conducted between 1961 and 1986 were compared and critically analyzed by Kebbon (1987). The theoretical definitions of mental retardation used were found to correspond well, that is a measured test score of two standard deviations below the mean of conventional intelligence tests constituted the inclusion criterion. In contrast, the operational procedures and measures used were much more varied and even more so the case finding methods: sampling, screening or other identification procedures. Kebbon concluded that methods of ascertainment could be one reason why prevalence figures in studies using a psychometric criterion varied between 0.67 to 2.2%. Among the studies compared there was a tendency to get higher prevalence figures where total populations had been individually tested.

12

Alternative explanations for the differences in prevalence figures yielded are suggested to be improved pre- and postnatal medical care and improved standard of living (e.g. Hagberg *et al*. 1981), that is a lower prevalence is thought to indicate that there are in fact fewer (mildly) mentally retarded individuals today than ten and twenty years ago and according to tests standardized at that time.

The fact that current (Swedish) test norms were standardized in the 60s is also considered a possible explanation why prevalence rates well below the 2 to 3% predicted from a normal distribution of IQs are yielded (cf. Flynn, 1985).

PURPOSE

The purpose of the study was to investigate empirically the hypothesis of selective casefinding by testing all individuals in a total unselected representative school population using a well-known intelligence test. Another aim was to investigate the adequacy of the current Swedish standardization of test norms.

MATERIAL AND METHOD

A school population of 416 children aged 6–12 years (classes 1–5) formed the group tested. They represented all pupils in that age span in one school district of a larger Swedish town. The school district was found to be representative of the town on the following variables: distribution of socio-economic status, number of households receiving financial aid from the community, performance on test of school readiness and the amount of extra-remedial resources available at the schools.

The Wechsler Intelligence Scale for Children (WISC) (Wechsler, 1949) was chosen as a suitable test as it is well founded, well known, and one frequently used in Swedish schools. The WISC covers the ages from 6 to 12 years and is composed of five verbal tests: information, comprehension, arithmetic, similarities and vocabulary; and five performance tests: picture completion, picture arrangement, block design, object assembly and coding. The latest Swedish standardization of test norms was made in 1968 (Psykologiförlaget, 1969).

Written information about the study was distributed to all homes. A child could only take part in the study if there was parental consent.

Two psychologists especially trained for this study did all the testing. They were blind with respect to marks or general school achievement of the children. The testing took place during the ordinary school day.

The Board for Provisions of Services to the Mentally Retarded provided case registration data on the children in the area administratively classified. Those children were not tested.

Table 1. Age, class, sex and reasons for non-participation in WISC test study (N=392)

Age		Class		Sex		Reasons for non-participation	
Years	Number of children	Class	Number of children				
6	7	1	76	Boys	194	Pupil refuses	2
7	78	2	65	Girls	198	Parent refuses	15
8	62	3	79			Moved	1
9	71	4	86			Abroad	3
10	88	5	86			Language difficulties (pupil)	2
11	79					Language difficulties (parent)	1
12	7						
Total	392	Total	392	Total	392	Total	24

Table 2. Wechsler intelligence scale for children (whole test): actual and expected stanine score distribution % (N=392)

Stanine score	Expected percentage	Actual percentage	Difference
1	4	0.25	−3.75
2	7	2.60	−4.40
3	12	5.66	−6.40
4	17	9.00	−8.00
5	20	19.00	−1.00
6	17	22.88	+5.88
7	12	18.50	+6.50
8	7	13.11	+6.11
9	4	9.00	+5.00

RESULTS

Complete test protocols were received for 392 children. Table 1 shows age, class and sex distribution and reasons for attrition for the population tested.

Attrition was 5.8% (24 children), where the majority was due to no parental consent.

The distribution of test scores

The distribution of test results in stanine scores, i.e. standard scores on a nine point scale with a mean value of 5, is shown in figure 1. Figure 1 shows a clear upward shift of the curve with a stanine score mean of 6,

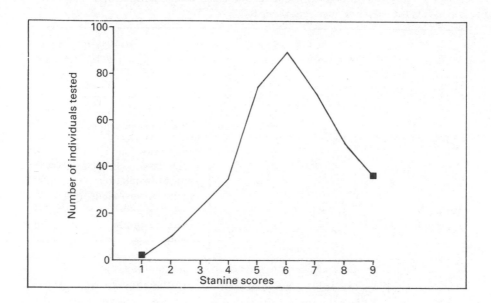

Figure 1. Wechsler intelligence scale for children (whole test). Stanine score distribution in an unselected school population aged 6–12 years (N=392).

i.e. one stanine point above the mean of the standardization population of the late 60s. However, the distribution of test scores is normal or bell-shaped and differentiates across the population tested. (The differentiating power might be less at the far right end of the distribution where there are too many scores. More important, there are no scores missing at the extreme far left end of the distribution, i.e. among lowscorers.

Table 2 shows the expected frequences in per cent for each stanine point level and the percentages yielded in this study. The figures illustrate the upward shift of the curve where there are scores overall missing at "the bottom half" and overall too many at "the top half" of the scale.

The WISC is composed of performance tests and tests of verbal character. It is a common experience that verbal tests are more easily influenced by cultural, social and time factors than tests of logic reasoning which show greater stability across populations and time intervals.

Table 3 shows IQ means and stanine point means for the whole test, the two test halves and the ten sub tests.

A difference, though slight, is found when verbal and performance test score means are compared. A higher figure is found for the verbal test half and generally for the verbal subtests. The means of the performance tests are closer to the standardized mean.

Table 3. WISC test study: IQ and stanine mean values across whole test, WISC-verbal, WISC-performance and subtests (N=392)

Test	IQ mean	Stanine mean	Subtests	Stanine mean
WISC (whole)	107.94	6.05		
WISC (verbal)	107.67	6.02	information	5.51
			comprehension	5.90
			arithmetic	5.47
			similarities	5.56
			vocabulary	6.52
WISC (performance)	105.85	5.76	picture completion	4.99
			picture arrangement	5.50
			block design	5.63
			object assembly	5.38
			coding	6.17

Further analyses of test score distributions and means of age groups, sex, testers and classes yielded the same pattern, i.e. a clear upward shift of the curve with a mean IQ of between 106 and 110 – or in stanine terms 5.8 to 6.4. The pattern of differences between verbal and performance tests is also comparable across groups.

Prevalance of mental retardation

The test study yielded only one child who scored IQ 70 or below, i.e. fullfilled the psychometric criterion of mental retardation. In order to establish the prevalence of mental retardation in this population the four children in this age span who were administratively classified as mentally retarded at the Board for Provisions and Services for the Mentally Retarded were added. The study then yielded a prevalence of mental retardation of 1.3% when a test score of IQ 70 and below (=stanine 1) and case registration data were used as methods of ascertainment.

CONCLUSIONS

From the results it can be concluded that, as expected, the test score distribution yielded in the study is normal or Gaussian in nature and differentiates across the population tested. However, the population mean has increased by one stanine point (or 8 IQ points). The whole distribution has moved upwards making current norms obsolescent and the estimated prevalence of mental retardation, based on the psychometric criterion, uncertain.

DISCUSSION

The psychometric definition of mental retardation is purely statistical and based on the assumption that mental ability is normally distributed when culturally relevant test items of varying difficulty are administered to a large enough representative population.

Tests were originally construed as instruments of selection, i.e. to identify those school children who performed significantly below the majority of their peers. A test score is always a relative measure and thus adequate norms are essential. The fact that test scores were normally distributed and differentiated across the population tested and perform-ance means showing a better stability indicates that the shift is in fact due to inadequate norms. A way of validating the results would be to actually test the registered mentally retarded not tested in this study as well as to retest the population with a comparable test of a more recent standardization. Such studies are planned. The shift upward of the curve in this study indicating an IQ gain *in relative terms* might be explained by effects of schooling or other knowledge experience or a secular trend making old norms too lenient (Emanuelsson, 1987).

Interpreting results solely in terms of an increased level of mental ability or a decline in numbers of mentally retarded individuals would be to abandon the statistical definition altogether.

Inadequate norms yielding a test score distribution with a stanine mean of 6 makes a psychometric criterion of IQ 70 too lenient. An approximation of the distribution downwards would yield nine individuals two standard deviations below the mean compared to the single score of IQ 70 actually found. The administratively classified mentally retarded in this population were four in number and should be included in the prevalence estimation. They represent 1% of the children of the district, a figure which should be compared to the national figure of 0.51% administratively classified in the age span 6 to 12 years (Swedish National Board of Health and Welfare, 1983, Statistics Sweden, 1988). The "corrected" total prevalence of mental retardation in this study is then estimated to 3.3% of the population, which should be regarded a high estimate.

The purpose of the study was to investigate empirically the hypothesis of selective case finding by testing all individuals in a total unselected representative school population using a well known intelligence test.

The fact that obsolete test norms blurred results considerably has of course implications for evaluating the findings. The conclusion one can draw are limited. However, if a total unselected representative popula-tion is individually tested, a low scoring group emerges.

In virtually all studies mental retardation is defined solely in terms of performance on intelligence tests. Definitions that consider social adaptation and/or associated disorders as well as IQ may well provide more accurate estimates of functional level.

To use old norms, whatever the test for identification of mental retardation makes the assessment unreliable. This study, above all, illustrates the urgent necessity of a re-standardization of the Swedish WISC.

ACKNOWLEDGEMENTS

This project is initiated and led by Asst Professor Lars Kebbon, Department of Psychiatry, University of Uppsala, Sweden. The Sävstaholm Foundation has generously provided financial support.

Gunilla Ringh and Lars Eriksson have been efficient and accurate test psychologists. This study would not have been possible without the cooperation of school staff, parents and the participating children.

REFERENCES

Emanuelson, I. (1987) Longitudinal studies of mental development. *Upsala, J. Med. Sci.*, suppl. **44**, 58–69.

Flynn, J. R. (1985) Wechsler Intelligence Tests: Do we really have a criterion of mental retardation? *Am. J. Ment. Def.* **90**, No. 3, 236–244.

Hagberg, B., Hagberg, G., Lewerth, A. & Lindberg, U. (1981) Mild mental retardation in Swedish school children I. Prevalence. *Acta Paediatrica Scandinavica*, **70**, 441–444.

Kebbon, L. (1987) Relation between criteria, case finding method and prevalence. *Upsala. J. Med. Sci*, suppl. **44**, 19–23.

Manual till WISC. (1969) (*Wechsler Intelligence Scale for Children*). Psyko-logiförlaget AB, Stockholm (in Swedish only)

Statistics Sweden (1988) *Statistical Abstracts of Sweden, vol. 74.* Liber. Stockholm.

Swedish National Board of Health and Welfare. (1983) *Statistics 21/1983* (in Swedish only)

Wechsler, D. (1949) *WISC manual.* New York: Psychological Corp.

Cause of Death in Mental Retardation: A Fifteen-Year Survey

M. P. Kent

Stewart's Hospital, Palmerstown, Dublin, 20. Ireland.

The cause of death over a fifteen year period (1973–1987) in a residential unit for moderate, severe and profoundly mentally retarded individuals was analysed. Sixty eight residents died. Autopsy examination was carried out on sixty individuals (88%) – forty one males (68%) and nineteen females (32%). In a number of cases the postmortem findings confirmed the clinical impression of the cause of death. However, there were some unexpected results demonstrating (a) interesting anatomical abnormalities that had not been diagnosed in vivo and (b) unsuspected cause of death.

INTRODUCTION

Limited information is available concerning the cause of death in mentally retarded individuals. In recent years Carter and Jancar (1983 and 1984) surveyed deaths over a fifty year period in a group of hospitals in England. Simila *et al.* (1986) reviewed the causes of death in mentally retarded children up to age seventeen years in Finland. Roy and Simon (1987) reported the cause of death with particular reference to intestinal obstruction, over a seven year period in a group of mental retardation hospitals in the West Midlands of England.

The present survey examines the cause of death over a fifteen year period (1973–1987) at Stewart's Hospital, Dublin. Stewart's Hospital, founded in 1869 has traditionally catered for the moderate, severe and profoundly mentally retarded and the multihandicapped. In the past, the occasional mildly mentally retarded individual was admitted for social reasons. The total complement of residents is, at present, three hundred and ten with a sex distribution of approximately two thirds male and one third female.

Kent

Table 1. Degree of mental
retardation

Mild	7	12%
Moderate	11	18%
Severe	11	18%
Profound	31	52%
Total	60	100%

METHOD

During the fifteen year period surveyed (1973–1987) a total of sixty eight residents died at Stewart's Hospital; autopsy was performed on sixty (88%). It is this group of sixty that has been studied.

The high rate of post mortem examination reflects the long tradition of clinical research at Stewart's Hospital. The majority of autopsies were carried out following reporting of the death to the Coroner who automatically arranges post mortem examination. The pathologists' reports together with comprehensive records from individual case files provided the necessary material for the survey.

RESULTS AND DISCUSSION

Sex

Of the sixty autopsies that were carried out the distribution between the sexes was: male forty one (68%); females nineteen (32%).

These figures reflect the sex distribution of the living population of Stewart's Hospital.

Degree of Mental Retardation

The degree of mental retardation as shown in Table 1 gives a fairly high (12%) incidence of mildly retarded individuals. This is due to the fact that these were older people who were admitted many years ago. The greatest number (31/60) of people (52%) who died were in the profoundly mentally retarded category as was found in other studies (Simila et al. 1986).

The Aetiology of Mental Retardation

The aetiology of the mental retardation is classified into five groups as used by Gustavson et al. (1977) and shown in Table 2.

Table 2. Aetiology of mental retardation

Prenatal			
Down's Syndrome	13	26	43%
Other causes	13		
Perinatal		13	22%
Postnatal		3	5%
Infantile Psychosis		9	15%
Untraceable		9	15%
Total		60	100%

Table 3. Age at death

Less than 20 years	15	25%
21–40 years	29	48%
41–60 years	9	15%
61–80 years	7	12%
Total	60	100%

Prenatal pathogenic factors were found to be the main cause of mental retardation as was also the case in the study by Gustavson et al. (1977).

This group which constituted 43% (26/60) of the cases was subdivided into two categories (1) Down's Syndrome and (2) other causes. Individuals with Down's Syndrome made up 50% of this group and just one person had a D/G translocation. The "other causes" in this group were made up of other conditions of prenatal origin including one with the XYY Syndrome, two with the Prader-Willi Syndrome and others with rare genetic conditions. Two had phenylketonuria – at the time of their birth the condition had not as yet been defined.

Fifteen per cent (9/60) were considered to be mentally retarded in association with infantile psychosis. Almost half of this group engaged in self injurious behaviour as did the majority of those included in the 'untraceable' category. This latter diagnosis was arrived at following review of history, in-depth investigations in vivo and autopsy findings.

Age at Death

Table 3 shows the distribution of ages at death in twenty year groupings. However, the youngest to die was only 5½ years old – a profoundly mentally retarded boy with epilepsy and spastic quadriplegia due to perinatal brain damage. He died suddenly: bronchiolitis was found at autopsy. The oldest to die was a 79 year old lady. She was a mildly retarded, non-epileptic, microcephalic person who had spent sixty (60) years in Stewart's Hospital. Post mortem examination confirmed the clinical cause of death of extensive bronchopneumonia with congestive cardiac failure. However, she was also found to have extensive necrotising papillitis with tubular atrophy of both kidneys – possible analgesic nephropathy.

The oldest person with Down's Syndrome who died was a 63 year old lady. She was severely mentally retarded and epileptic; the clinical diagnosis of Alzheimer's disease was confirmed at autopsy as was aortic stenosis and incompetence.

Causes of Death

The causes of death are grouped into four major categories as in Table 4.

Manner of Death

The manner of death was classified as sudden and non-sudden.

The category of sudden death was defined as occurring without warning within two hours of collapse as defined by Carter & Jancar (1984). Nineteen individuals (32%) died suddenly. One traumatic death by drowning is included in this group and this together with the other causes are listed in Table 5.

Respiratory Tract Conditions

As has been found by other workers (Carter and Jancar 1983; Simila *et al* (1986), the main cause of death was respiratory tract conditions – 40/60 i.e. 67%. The vast majority of these 35/40 (87%) were due to respiratory tract infections. This high incidence is hardly surprising in the group under study as 42/60 (70%) were in the severe and profound categories of mental retardation. One profoundly retarded young man died of tuberculous bronchopneumonia some months following admission to Stewart's Hospital.

A moderately retarded 71 year old lady who had been resident at Stewart's Hospital for 52 years died from a left bronchogenic carcinoma with carcinomatosis. A number of deaths associated with respiratory tract conditions were sudden and unexpected. Three disturbed individuals who were on large doses of major tranquillisers died suddenly. Similar cases were reported by Carter and Jancar (1984). In our patients, postmortem findings in two were of hemorrhagic pneumonia. The lungs of the third young man, who was a diabetic, showed necrotising bronchopneumonia due to Staphylococcus Aureus. Other unexpected findings at the autopsy of this latter moderately retarded, behaviourally difficult young man were granulomatous inflammation of lymph nodes, multiple endocrine abnormalities in addition to his moderately reduced in size pancreas –

Table 4.   Cause of death

Respiratory tract conditions			
Infection	35		
		40	67%
Other	5		
Carcinoma		5	8%
Cardiovascular disease		8	13%
Gastrointestinal		7	12%
Total		60	100%

Table 5.   Cause of sudden death

Pneumonia	7
Aspiration of food	4
Haemoptysis	1
Congenital anomaly of coronary arteries	1
Acute left ventricular failure	1
Small intestinal infarct	1
Haematemesis	1
Acute phlegmonous gastritis	1
Volvulus of colon	1
Drowning	1
Total	19

hypogonadism, lymphocytic thyroiditis and adrenal atrophy. The coronary arteries showed 95% stenosis at the origin of the left anterior descending and left circumflex artery due to a recanalised thrombus.

A profoundly retarded 47 year old lady with Down's Syndrome who died of pneumonia was found to have a papillary tumour of a vocal cord; in retrospect she had, for one week prior to death, been noted to emit a hoarse stridor-like sound.

The most rare and unexpected finding of all in the respiratory tract was that of microlithiasis alveolaris in an 18 year old profoundly retarded boy.

Two profoundly retarded individuals with a history of bolting food died from asphyxiation due to food in the bronchial tree. One lady with the Klippel-Feil Syndrome was at autopsy also found to have a split medulla. Two other also profoundly retarded people inhaled gastric contents in association with a meal. One was a twenty year old man who, in vivo, engaged in self-injurious behaviour and was found to have old subdural haematomata into which there had not been recent bleeding. The second was a 14 year old girl who had a tonic clonic seizure during a meal, inhaled gastric contents and asphyxiated. Her basal meninges round the optic chiasma and pons were found thickened and grey-white opaque. One profoundly retarded disturbed young man died from asphyxia in association with drowning.

One profoundly retarded youth with Down's Syndrome died suddenly following a large haemoptysis – bronchopneumonia superimposed on a lipoid pneumonia was found at autopsy.

Carcinoma

There were only 5 deaths due to carcinoma – a figure of 8% compared with 10% reported by Carter and Jancar (1983). One case of bronchogenic carcinoma has already been discussed. Two patients died from brain tumours – one was an 18 year old moderately retarded youth with severe epilepsy and a right hemiplegia considered to be due to perinatal brain damage. He died of a glioblastoma multiforme. The second patient to die of a brain tumour was an 11 year old severely retarded girl – also a severe epileptic. She had a Grade IV anaplastic astrocytoma; a left porencepahalic cyst was also found at autopsy.

A 72 year old mildly retarded man died from an intrahepatic carcinoma of the left hepatic duct.

A 47 year old moderately retarded man who presented with left shoulder pain and was found to have a pleural effusion died from metastatic colonic adenocarcinoma; in vivo he was completely free of gastrointestinal symptoms.

Cardiovascular Disease

Death due to conditions directly associated with the cardiovascular system accounted for 8 (13%) of the cases. Three of these caused sudden death.

One was a 15 year old boy with Down's Syndrome and epilepsy which latter did not contribute to his sudden death. Autopsy revealed congestive cardiac failure due to ischaemic heart disease consequent to coronary artery congenital anomaly. The left and right branches both arose above the aortic cusp area, on the anterior wall of the proximal aorta. The orifice of both branches was partly occluded by a thin web of tissue.

A 28 year old severely retarded severe epileptic man died from acute left ventricular failure due to myocardial ischaemia complicating status epilepticus; his brain showed petechiae within the cortex; there were no structural abnormalities.

A 45 year old profoundly retarded lady with Down's Syndrome and untreated tetralogy of Fallot died from a small intestinal infarct due to paradoxical thromboembolism.

The remaining individuals were considered to have died from cardiac failure, the older having degenerative heart disease. In two instances cardiac failure was deemed to have followed a single tonic clonic seizure in which cardiac arrest occurred with an ensuing shock-like state as has been described by Glaser (1983).

Incidentally 27/60 (45%) of those being studied were epileptic. This figure is considerably higher than the 30–33% usually quoted in other studies but, perhaps it is not unexpected, given the fact that such a large number in our series had additional neurological factors which are well known to contribute to the occurrence and chronicity of epilepsy. (Reynolds 1988).

A final interesting case in this group was a 56 year old moderately retarded lady who had cardiac failure due to a combination of ischaemic and rheumatic heart disease; she also had a cerebellar infarct.

Gastrointestinal Causes of Death

Seven deaths (12%) were due to conditions in the gastrointestinal tract, three of these causing sudden death. A 31 year old profoundly retarded man had a massive haematemesis. Autopsy revealed oesophageal erosions associated with chronic duodenal ulceration, neither of which had been diagnosed ante mortem.

A 22 year old profoundly retarded man collapsed and died and at postmortem was found to have acute phlegmonous gastritis; he had been on no medication. He was also found to have marked thickening of the skull with some degree of hyperostosis frontalis interna. He had thickening of the pia arachnoid and also extensive calcification of the falx.

A 41 year old mildly retarded disturbed man with a long history of varying gastrointestinal symptoms died suddenly. He was found to have a volvulus of the colon (Roy & Simon 1987). Sever ulcerative proctocolitis was considered to have caused bacteremic shock causing the death of a 52 year old moderately retarded lady.

Two young men died from peritonitis. In one case this followed perforation of the duodenum by an ingested piece of floor covering in a severely retarded very disturbed 22 year old. The second case occurred post-operatively. This was a profoundly retarded 21 year old man with Down's Syndrome who had been operated on for acute intestinal obstruction caused by a collection of twigs, leaves and paper. Roy and Simon (1987) have reported similar fatalities in severely retarded males with a history of dietary indiscretion as had the two individuals in this survey.

A 20 year old male with the Prader Willi Syndrome died from hyperglycaemia (blood sugar: 600 mg%).

Interesting Anatomical Abnormalities

Interesting anatomical abnormalities not already referred to included abnormalities of the genito urinary tract.

A 19 year old severely retarded, very disturbed, self mutilating, epileptic girl died from an empyema. At autopsy she was found to have a unilateral left kidney, ovary, fallopian tube and left unicornuate uterus; the urachus was present.

Duplication of the vaginal and uterine cavities were found in a profoundly retarded 18 year old epileptic girl who had congenital anomalies of both upper and lower limbs and trachea. She also had an internal hydrocephalus. Coincidentally, like the other girl she too died of an empyema.

One 58 year old mildly retarded lady with Down's Syndrome had cryptogenic hepatic cirrhosis in addition to Alzheimer's disease brain changes and extensive pneumonia.

A 76 year old mildly retarded man who had lived at Stewart's Hospital for 29 years died from pneumonia three days post operatively following pinning of a fractured neck of femur. He was, at autopsy, found to have lymphocytic lymphoma and in addition cervical spondylosis. As might be expected, the majority of interesting anatomical abnormalities were found in the central nervous system. Most have already been referred to. In addition the following were found at autopsy – marked atrophy and gliosis of the frontal and frontoparietal region of the right cerebral hemisphere. In the perinatal period this 7 year old profoundly retarded epileptic girl was diagnosed as having a right cerebral haemorrhage.

An 18 year old severely retarded boy with Down's Syndrome was found to have an osseous malformation of his skull with the odontoid process protruding into the foramen magnum and fused to the posterior surface of the basi-sphenoid with narrowing of the foramen magnum.

An 18 year old profoundly retarded, untreated phenylketonuric, epileptic boy had a subarachnoid hemorrhage over both parietal lobes.

Atrophy of the brain stem and cerebellum was found in a 35 year old profoundly mentally and physically retarded man. He was non-epileptic and was on no medication.

It is hoped that through the accumulation of data as presented here valuable clues to aetiology of mental retardation may be accumulated and thus reduce the relatively large numbers of cases that continue to fall into the 'untraceable' category.

As Cowie & Cole (1986) have suggested autopsies are systematically arranged in very few hospitals for the mentally retarded despite the opportunities they provide for comparing clinical observation with post mortem changes.

ACKNOWLEDGMENTS

I wish to thank Dr. Michael Mulcahy for his continuing encouragement and helpful comments and criticism during the preparation of this paper; the Dublin City Coroner (Dr. P. Bofin) and the Dublin County Coroner (Dr. B. Sheehan) for arranging the autopsies: Ms. Sally Moody for invaluable secretarial assistance.

REFERENCES

Carter, G. and Jancar J. (1983) Mortality in the mentally handicapped: a fifty year survey at the Stoke Park Group of Hospitals. *J. ment. Defic. Res.* **27**: 143–156.

Carter, G. and Jancar J. (1984) Sudden deaths in the mentally handicapped. *Psychol. Med.* **14**: 691–695.

Cowie, V. A. and Cole G. (1986) Neuropathology and clinical practice in mental handicap. *J. ment. Defic. Res.* **30**: 311–315.

Glaser, G. H. (1983) Medical complications of status epilepticus. In Delgado-Escueta A. V., Wasterlain C. G., Treiman, D. M., Porter, R. J. eds. *Advances in neurology, vol. 34.* New York: Raven Press. 395–398.

Gustavson, K. H., Holmgren, R. J. and Blomquist, H. K. (1977) Severe mental retardation in children in a northern Swedish county. *J. ment. Defic. Res.* **21**: 161–180.

Reynolds, E. H. (1988) The prevention of chronic epilepsy. *Elilepsia,* **29** (Suppl. 1): S25–S28.

Roy, A. and Simon, G. B. (1987) Intestinal obstruction as a cause of death in the mentally handicapped. *J. ment. Defic. Res.* **31**: 193–197.

Simila, S., von Wendt, L. and Rantakallio, P. (1986) Mortality of mentally retarded children to 17 years of age assessed in a prospective one-year birth cohort. *J. ment. Defic. Res.* **30**: 401–405.

Avoidable Death in a Cohort of Severely Mentally Retarded

A. Dupont & P. B. Mortensen

*Institute of Psychiatric Demography, Aarhus Psychiatric Hospital
DK-8240, Risskov, Denmark*

The aim of this study was to compare the cause-specific mortality in our cohort consisting of 9,891 severely mentally retarded (ICD-8 diagnoses 312–314) with that of the general Danish population. Furthermore, an attempt was made to evaluate the use of mortality statistics in special patient groups such as the severely mentally retarded, as a tool in the evaluation of the quality of medical care in these patients. This was done by comparing the so-called "avoidable mortality" from conditions that should not ordinarily lead to death if optimal medical care had been supplied.

The total mortality of the severely mentally retarded was found to be significantly increased in comparison with the general Danish population. The mortality from diseases of the lung, cerebrovascular disorders, gastrointestinal diseases and urogenital diseases were found to be increased both in the male and the female patients. Some sex differences were noted. The female patients had a significantly increased mortality from cancer while the male patients had a non-significantly reduced risk of death from cancer. The female patients had an increased risk of death from cardiovascular disease while the male patients' risk of dying from cardiovascular disease did not differ from that of the general Danish population. The male patients had a higher risk of death from accidents. Particularly, this was marked in the institutionalised male patients where especially falls, drowning accidents and choking contributed to this increased risk.

As regards the so-called avoidable mortality the risk of dying from these causes was about four times higher in the severely mentally retarded population than in the general Danish population. There were no differences between the male and female patients with respect to mortality from these causes. A possible explanation for these findings may be that the diagnosis of medical disorders in these patients is very difficult because of these patients' reduced ability to express their physical complaints. Still, the increased risk of death from accidents in institutions indicates that the increased mortality in this patient group probably could be reduced by further preventive measures.

From many parts of the world it has been shown that the excess mortality for the different groups of mentally retarded persons is changing with the new pattern of services. When Forssman and Åkesson in 1968 published the results from a study of 12,903 mentally retarded in Swedish institutions it was obvious that the excess mortality was specially high for the severely mentally retarded (with an IQ level below 50). The present publication is the third of three Danish studies on mortality and life expectancy of the mentally retarded: Dupont et al. (1986) and Dupont et al. (1987).

Few studies have been published with an analysis of the causes of death.

The aim of the present Danish study is to present a statistical analysis of the mortality of persons with severe mental retardation. The study is based upon all persons registered in the Danish National Service for the Mentally Retarded (DNSMR) with a diagnosis of ICD 312–314 (ICD-8).

MATERIAL AND METHODS

In the register of the Danish National Service of the Mentally Retarded (Dupont, 1975) 9,891 severely mentally retarded persons (ICD-8 diagnosis 312–314) were identified. This cohort consisted of all persons who had been included in the register with these diagnoses, either during the period January 1, 1976 to December 31, 1980 or had been included in the register before January 1, 1976 and were alive at this date. By linkage of the 10 digit number of each person to the personal identification number system (Danmarks Statistik, 1978), information of status (i.e. death, immigration etcetera) as at March 1984 was obtained. Through linkage to the registry of causes of death at the Danish National Board of Health, the information concerning cause of death was obtained. The total and cause-specific mortality rate of the cohort of the severely mentally retarded was compared to the rates of the Danish general population in the average year of death in this cohort, i.e. 1980 (Sundhedsstyrelsen 1982). The comparison was made for males and females separately and was adjusted for age using the method described by Breslow (1984). The calculations were made using the programme system developed by Juul (1984).

The so-called "avoidable mortality" was calculated using the above mentioned methodology. This method of describing the efficiency of a health care system using mortality from causes of death that potentially could have been avoided, if optimal medical care had been supplied, has been described by Rutstein et al. (1976). The causes of death and the age groups in which these causes are regarded as being potentially avoidable are listed in Table 1.

Table 1. List of diseases with ICD code and age group

Diseases	ICD 8th rev.	Age group
Typhoid fever	001	5–64
Tuberculosis	010–019	5–64
Whooping cough	033	0–14
Tetanus	037	0–64
Measles	055	1–14
Malignant neoplasm of cervix uteri	180	5–64
Malignant neoplasm, body of uterus	182	5–64
Hodgkin's disease	201	5–64
Diabetes mellitus	250	5–64
Chronic rheumatic heart disease	393–398	5–44
Hypertensive disease	400–404	5–64
Cerebrovascular disease	430–438	30–64
All respiratory diseases	460–519	1–14
Asthma	493	5–49
Appendicitis	540–543	5–64
Abdominal hernia	550–553	5–64
Cholelithiasis and cholecystitis	574–575	5–64
Maternal deaths	630–678	15–49
Osteomyelitis	720	1–64

RESULTS

The cause-specific mortality rates standardized for age (SMR) are listed in Table 2 together with the 95% confidence limits. (The SMR is calculated by dividing the observed number of deaths in the study population with the number of deaths that would have been expected if the mortality rate had been that of the general Danish population. Thus, e.g. a SMR of 2.0 means that twice as many deaths have occurred as should have been expected if the mortality had not exceeded that of the general Danish population. If the 95% confidence limit does not include 1.0, this means that the difference between the mortality rate of the study population and the mortality rate of the general Danish population is statistically significant at the 5% level.)

As shown in Table 2 the mortality was significantly increased in the severely mentally retarded when compared with the general Danish population. The risk was increased in both males and females. When looking at the specific cause of mortality, the males had an increased mortality from cerebrovascular disorders, lung diseases, disorders of the digestive tract, the urogenital tract, from congenital malformations and from accidents. The mortality from cardiovascular diseases and cancer did not differ from that of the males in the general Danish population. In the

Table 2. Cause-specific mortality in the severely mentally retarded 1976–1984

Cause of death	Males			Females		
	No. of deaths	SMR	95% confidence limits	No. of deaths	SMR	95% confidence limits
Total	567	2.07	(1.90–2.25)	482	2.59	(2.36–2.83)
Cardiovascular	110	1.11	(0.92–1.34)	72	1.38	(1.10–1.75)
Cerebrovascular	33	2.68	(1.89–3.81)	30	1.92	(1.34–2.75)
Lung diseases	79	4.41	(3.53–5.52)	82	7.07	(5.69–8.81)
Cancer	58	0.84	(0.65–1.08)	79	1.35	(1.08–1.68)
Digestive tract	38	3.90	(2.80–5.42)	24	3.40	(2.22–5.20)
Urogenital	20	6.60	(4.21–10.34)	17	6.24	(3.84–10.15)
Congenital malformations	65	52.42	(38.34–71.68)	64	95.12	(68.07–132.93)
Accidents	68	3.73	(2.92–4.78)	18	1.98	(1.24–3.16)
"Avoidable mortality"	26	3.66	(2.46–5.43)	23	3.77	(2.48–5.71)

Table 3. Mortality from accidents in the severely mentally retarded

| | | Males | | | | Females | |
| | | | 95% confidence | | | | 95% confidence |
	N	SMR	limits	N	SMR	limits
All patients vs. the general Danish population	68	3.74	(2.92–4.78)	18	1.98	(1.24–3.16)
Non-institutionalized vs. institutionalized severely mentally retarded	68	0.25	(0.12–0.52)	18	0.74	(0.26–2.16)

females, mortality from all the listed causes of death was increased. As in the males, the excess mortality was especially marked in the group congenital malformations, urogenital and digestive tract and lung diseases. The excess mortality from accidents was not as marked as in the males. This is noteworthy, as the mortality rate from accidents in the general Danish population is much higher in males than in females in the relevant age groups. As regards mortality from potentially avoidable causes, there was a marked increase in both males and females.

The mortality caused by accidents was further analysed as shown in Table 3. As will be seen, the mortality from accidents was significantly increased in the institutionalized male patients when compared with those living outside the institutions. There was a slight trend in the same direction in the female patients, but this was not statistically significant. No special pattern could be identified in the types of accidents in the female patients. As shown in Table 4, some special types of accidents contributed heavily to the excess mortality from accidents in the male institutionalized patients. These causes were choking in food, which occurred with an incidence almost 100 times greater than in the general Danish population, drowning, and falls.

DISCUSSION

The finding of the excess mortality in the severely mentally retarded confirms the findings of Forsman and Åkesson (1970). One of the questions this study raises is why the cardiovascular mortality and mortality from cancer is increased in the female patients, but not in the males. A possible explanation could be that to some extent the mortality rates from these causes in the general Danish population is a product of the tobacco smoking habits, and the proportions of death from cardiovascular disorders and cancer that can be attributed to especially cigarette smoking is probably larger in the males than in the females. This

Table 4. Fatal accidents among institutionalized male severely mentally retarded

	N	SMR	95% confidence limits
Choking in food	15	97.20	(45.46–207.82)
Drowning	9	29.10	(13.53–62.59)
Falls	10	6.40	(3.40–12.04)

means that the low consumption of tobacco of the severely mentally retarded especially must be expected to have an impact on the mortality in the males, when compared with the general Danish population. The very high mortality from congenital malformations comes as no surprise. More disturbing is the high mortality from accidents and from potentially avoidable causes that here has been demonstrated. Even though the term "avoidable mortality" may not be fair when one considers the considerable difficulties in diagnosing physical disorders in this special patient group, it is noteworthy that 22% of the excess mortality in the males and 9% of the excess mortality in the females can be ascribed to excess mortality from accidents and potentially avoidable causes. When looking at the analysis of the mortality from accidents there is no obvious explanation for the differences between the male and female patients. Although the figures are small, the special pattern of fatal accidents that was noted in the male institutionalized patients with choking in food and drowning as main causes of death must raise the question of the potential preventability of these causes of death. It seems quite obvious that this mortality must be partly preventable by better staffing and training in the institutions that are responsible for the care of these patients.

REFERENCES

Breslow, N. E. (1984) Elementary Methods of Cohort Analysis. *Int. J. Epid.* **13**: 112–115.

Danmarks Statistik (1978) *Personal identification numbers and population statistics in Denmark.* Copenhagen: Danmarks Statistik.

Dupont, A. (1975) Mentally retarded in Denmark. *Dan. Med. Bull.* **22**: 243–251.

Dupont, A., Væth, M. and Videbeck, P. (1986) Mortality and life expectancy of Down's syndrome in Denmark. *J. Ment. Dif. Res.* **30**: 111–120.

Dupont, A., Væth, M. and Videbeck, P. (1987) Mortality life expectancy and causes of death of mildly mentally retarded in Denmark. Uppsala *J. Med. Sci.* Suppl. **44**: 76–82.

Forsman, H. and Åkesson, H. O. (1970) Mortality of the mentally deficient. *J. Ment. Def. Res.* **14**: 276–294.

Juul, S. (1984) *Programmer til overlevelsesberegninger*. Socialmedicinsk Institut, Aarhus Universitet, Århus.

Rutstein, D. D., Berenberg, W., Chamlers, T. C., Child, C. G., Fishman, A. P. and Perrin, E. B. (1976) Measuring the quality of medical care. *N. Engl. J. Med.* **294**: 582–588.

Sundhedsstyrelsen (1982) *Dødsårsagerne i Danmark 1980* (Causes of death in Denmark 1980). Sundhedsstyrelsen, Copenhagen.

Section II

Biomedical Aspects

Milk Cholesterol and the Developing Brain

J. Edmond, R. A. Korsak, N. Auestad and
J. W. Morrow

*Mental Retardation Research Center, UCLA School of Medicine,
Los Angeles, CA 90024-1737, USA*

Four groups of rat pups were reared: a mother reared group (MR) as controls and artificially reared groups (AR) which were fed a rat milk substitute containing low, normal or excess amounts of cholesterol. Pups were fed the milk substitute by intermittent gastric infusion in a semi-automated artificial rearing system away from their mothers from five days after birth until 17 days of age. The purpose of the study was to determine whether the amount of cholesterol in milk influenced growth and the quantity of cholesterol in brain over the period of its most rapid accumulation. We found:

(i) AR pups had growth curves similar to MR controls.
(ii) Body and brain weights were not different, irrespective of the amount of cholesterol in milk.
(iii) Excess cholesterol in milk caused a significant increase in cholesterol in plasma and livers yet the amount of cholesterol in brain was not different from the amount in brain of controls.
(iv) Feeding a milk substitute with cholesterol reduced in concentration by 75% from normal does not compromise the cholesterol content of brain in a period of dynamic growth.

INTRODUCTION

Milk is the dominant source of nutrients immediately after birth in mammalian species. During the neonatal period, sterols accumulate as part of the maturation of the central nervous system to meet the needs for growth and myelination. Natural milk contains significant amounts of cholesterol; human milk contains 20 to 30 mg/100 ml [Foman and Bartels (1960); Freedman and Goldberg (1975)] and by contrast, many milk substitutes for human infants contain minimal amounts of cholesterol, 1 to 2 mg/100 ml, [Foman and Bartels (1960); Freedman and Goldberg (1975)]. The milk of the rat, like that of the human, contains substantial amounts of cholesterol, 30 to 80 mg/100 ml [Reiser and Sidelman (1972); Kris-Etherton *et al.* (1979)]. Over the suckling period of the rat, from birth until weaning at 21 to 22 days of age, important age related events occur in brain. One such event is the onset of myelination between the 9th and 12th day when there is a substantial accumulation of sterol in brain [Cuzner and Davison (1968)]. Immediately following this event is the period, 16 to 20 days of age, when maximum myelinogenesis is evident [Cuzner and Davison (1968)]. In addition, there is the establishment of the integrity of the blood brain barrier when developmental and age related modifications in transport phenomena are evident [Cremer (1981)]. To determine whether cholesterol in milk is essential to attain normal growth and sterol content of brain in the rat during the suckling period, we have examined rat pups which have been fed rat milk substitutes containing low, normal and excess amounts of cholesterol. The milk substitutes were fed from 5 or 6 days after birth until 15 or 16 days of age to the gastrostomy reared rat pup [Sonnenberg *et al.* (1982); Smart *et al.* (1984, 1987)].

MATERIALS AND METHODS

Animals

Pregnant Sprague Dawley rats (second or third litter experience) were obtained from Bantin and Kingman (Fremont, CA) at 14 days of gestation and the time of parturition carefully noted. Pups of the same age were selected at 5 or 6 days of age and weight matched among the artificially reared groups and the mother reared group. Rat pups were reared artificially in the absence of their mothers on rat milk substitutes as described previously [Sonnenberg *et al.* (1982); Smart *et al.* (1984, 1987)]. Mother reared (MR) and artificially reared rat pups (AR) were housed in the same environment with a controlled light cycle. Animals in all groups were weighed at frequent intervals. At 15 or 16 days of age the animals were killed by decapitation. Blood and organs were taken as described previously [Sonnenberg *et al.* (1982)].

Milk Substitute

The milk substitute was formulated essentially as described previously [Smart *et al.* (1987)]. In brief, a protein-rich premilk, which contained minimal fat of mammalian origin, was constituted from a custom prepared casein-rich protein powder (Ross Laboratories, Columbus, Ohio). Soy oil, corn oil, medium chain triglyceride, palm oil, vitamins, minerals and essential amino acids were added to yield a milk substitute which closely resembled rats' milk in its gross and detailed composition.

The gross composition of the milk substitute was as follows, g/l: protein 95.4, carbohydrate 3.4, fat 122, ash 11. Vitamins were added to give a vitamin composition appropriate for rat milk [Sonnenberg *et al.* (1982)].

The mineral content of the milk substitute was, mg/ml: Ca 1.85, phosphorous 1.77, sodium 0.99, potassium 1.48, chloride 1.41, magnesium 0.18, zinc 0.023, iron 0.0073 and copper 0.0076. Taurine, glycine and arginine were included to obtain appropriate concentrations of these amino acids in plasma [Smart *et al.* (1987)]. The rat milk substitute without added cholesterol (low cholesterol) contained 8±2 mg cholesterol per 100 ml. Cholesterol was added to the normal and high cholesterol milk substitute with the other fat components, normal cholesterol at 40±5 mg per 100 ml milk and excess cholesterol at 200±15 mg cholesterol per 100 ml milk. Appropriate amounts of cholesterol were dissolved in the oil mixture with continuous stirring at 60° for 3 hours. Sufficient milk substitute was prepared with all constituents except fat, then divided into three portions; oil without added cholesterol was blended into one portion to give the low cholesterol milk whereas oil containing cholesterol was blended into the other portions to give the milks with normal and excess cholesterol, respectively. Other than for the amount of cholesterol, the milk substitutes were identical in composition.

Determination of Cholesterol and 3-Hydroxy-3-Methylglutaryl-CoA Reductase

Samples of plasma, liver, brain and lung were saponified and the non-saponifiable fraction obtained by extraction with petroleum ether as described previously [Webber and Edmond (1979)]. Cholesterol in the non-saponifiable fraction was assayed by the method of Zlatkis and Zak (1969). The amount of 3-hydroxy-4-methylglutaryl-CoA reductase activity (EC 1.1.1.34) in liver was determined as done previously [Bergstrom *et al.* (1984)].

Statistics

Analysis of variance (ANOVA) using the Bonferroni t test was done to examine differences among groups. Data are expressed as mean ± standard deviation unless indicated otherwise.

RESULTS

Growth

Rat pups in the groups fed the milk substitute from 5 or 6 days after birth with or without added cholesterol grew at the same rate as mother reared controls (Figure 1). At 15 and 16 days of age, body weights of the rat

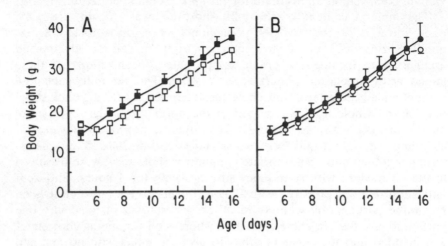

Figure 1. Growth in body weight. Mean body weights (g) from 5 or 6 to 15 or 16 days of mother reared rats (■) (n=20) panel A, and rat pups artificially reared on the milk substitute containing normal amounts of cholesterol (□) (n=10) panel A; or low amounts of cholesterol (●) (n=13) panel B; or excess amounts of cholesterol (○) (n=9) panel B. The growth curves are for rat pups whose organ and body weights at 15 or 16 days are shown in Table 1. Values given are means with standard deviations. The body weights at each point for animals in each group for experiments 1 and 2 were combined.

pups fed the milk substitutes were not significantly different (Table 1). The mean body weight of the pups in the mother reared litters were slightly greater throughout the rearing period than the mean body weight of the pups fed milk substitutes (Fig. 1). However, as shown in Table 1, the pups selected from the mother reared litters for the study at 15 or 16 days of age were weight matched with the pups in each group artificially reared on milk substitutes. Weights of brain and lung of animals in the artificially reared groups are not different (Table 1).

Cholesterol in Organs and Plasma

In a pilot experiment in which rat pups were reared from four days after birth until 17 days of age on the milk substitute containing a low concentration of cholesterol and compared to an age matched mother reared group as a control, there was no difference in body weight 40.6±1.8 g, (n=5) compared to 39.8±1.7 g, (n=5) at 17 days of age.

Table 1. Data from two experiments are presented separately. In experiment 1 rat pups were artificially reared from 5 days after birth until 15 days of age on the milk substitute low and high in its cholesterol content. In experiment 2, rat pups were artificially reared from 6 days after birth until 16 days of age on the milk substitute containing low, normal and excess cholesterol (Materials and Methods). $(n)^1$ = number of rat pups per group; nd^2 = not done. Values for the means in the same column, for each experiment, not sharing a common superscript letter are significantly different, $p \leq 0.05$, ANOVA. All values given are the means with standard deviations.

Age	Group	$(n)^1$	Body weight g	Liver weight g	Lung weight g	Brain weight g
			Body and organ weights of 15- and 16-day-old rats			
Experiment 1						
15 days	Mother Reared	(6)	35.2 ± 1.3^a	1.03 ± 0.10^a	nd^2	1.28 ± 0.04^a
	Low Cholesterol	(6)	34.8 ± 0.6^a	1.07 ± 0.09^a	nd^2	1.16 ± 0.02^b
	High Cholesterol	(6)	35.0 ± 0.6^a	1.25 ± 0.10^b	nd^2	1.16 ± 0.08^b
Experiment 2						
16 days	Mother Reared	(7)	36.3 ± 3.7^c	1.01 ± 1.14^c	0.48 ± 0.08^c	1.27 ± 0.10^c
	Low Cholesterol	(7)	36.9 ± 4.0^c	1.13 ± 0.29^c	0.43 ± 0.05^c	1.25 ± 0.03^c
	Normal Cholesterol	(10)	34.3 ± 2.7^c	1.01 ± 0.23^c	0.40 ± 0.03^c	1.22 ± 0.05^c
	High Cholesterol	(3)	34.1 ± 0.5^c	1.09 ± 0.09^c	0.47 ± 0.10^c	1.18 ± 0.02^c

However, the concentration of cholesterol in the plasma of the mother reared controls was slightly greater ($p < 0.05$) than the amount of cholesterol in plasma of the AR group, 1.28 ± 0.13 compared to 1.08 ± 0.08 mg per ml plasma. Although brain weights of the animals in the mother reared group were marginally heavier than the brain weights of the AR group 1.34 ± 0.04 g compared to 1.24 ± 0.06 g, ($P \leq 0.05$) the amount of cholesterol in brain was not different, 8.91 ± 0.20 mg/g compared to 9.21 ± 0.25 mg/g brain. These initial observations led us to complete two comprehensive experiments which involved milk substitutes containing cholesterol at three distinct concentrations (Materials and Methods).

The amount of cholesterol in plasma and organs is shown in Table 2.

Edmond et al.

Table 2. The data were obtained from animals whose body and organ weights are shown in Table 1. The experimental conditions are described under "Materials and Methods" and in Table 1. $(n)^1$ = number of animals in each group: [2]Range of values obtained from Reiser and Sidelman (1972); Kris-Etherton *et al.* (1979); nd^3 = not determined; [4] the amount of cholesterol in the milk substitutes was determined as described for plasma and organs in "Materials and Methods". Values for the means in the same column, for each experiment, not sharing a common superscript letter are significantly different, $p \leq 0.05$, ANOVA. The values given are the means with standard deviations.

	Cholesterol in milk and in plasma and organs of 15- and 16-day-old-rats					
Group	Milk		Plasma	Liver	Lung	Brain
	Cholesterol mg/100 ml	$(n)^1$	mg/ml	mg/g	mg/g	mg/g
Experiment 1						
Mother Reared	30–80[2]	(6)	1.85±0.06[a]	3.57±0.37[a]	nd[3]	7.25±0.45[a]
Low Cholesterol	8±2[4]	(6)	1.36±0.08[a]	2.74±0.33[a]	nd[3]	7.43±0.57[a]
High Cholesterol	200±15	(6)	5.96±1.84[b]	35.20±2.50[b]	nd[3]	7.34±0.47[a]
Experiment 2						
Mother Reared	30–80	(7)	1.53±0.23[c]	4.31±0.43[c]	4.86±0.46[c]	8.27±0.60[c]
Low Cholesterol	8±2	(7)	1.31±0.23[c]	3.28±0.50[c]	4.64±0.40[c]	8.53±0.39[c]
Normal Cholesterol	40±5	(10)	1.35±0.32[c]	4.00±1.13[c]	4.97±0.29[c]	8.60±0.37[c]
High Cholesterol	200±15	(3)	4.90±0.86[d]	37.90±10.00[d]	5.91±0.44[d]	8.54±0.37[c]

The data from each experiment are shown separately because the animals in experiment 2 were one day older when the experiment was completed. This is reflected in the greater amount of sterol in their brains (Table 2). A distinctive contrast is evident when the cholesterol concentrations of brain of animals are compared with the cholesterol concentrations in liver and in the plasma from blood which is available to the brain. The amount of cholesterol in brain of animals in all four groups was not different, whereas the cholesterol in plasma, liver and lung of animals fed milk containing excess cholesterol was significantly greater than the amount of cholesterol in plasma, liver and lung of all other groups. There was no significant difference in the amount of cholesterol in plasma and liver between mother reared controls and pups reared on the milk substitute containing a normal amount of cholesterol (Table 2). The activity level of 3-hydroxy-3-methylglutaryl-CoA reductase was significantly greater in

Table 3. The data shown are part of the experiments shown in Tables 1 and 2. (n)[1] = number of animals whose livers were assayed for 3-hydroxy-3-methylglutaryl-CoA reductase; each sample was assayed in duplicate as indicated in "Methods". Values for the means not sharing a common superscript letter are significantly different p ≤ 0.05, ANOVA. The values given are means with standard deviation.

Group	(n)[1]	HMG-CoA reductase in liver Activity HMG-CoA reductase pmol mevalonate formed.min⁻¹.mg protein⁻¹
Mother Reared	6	25 ± 3^a
Low Cholesterol	6	142 ± 65^b
Normal Cholesterol	6	39 ± 11^a
High Cholesterol	6	20 ± 3^a

liver of rat pups fed the milk substitute low in cholesterol than it is in liver of pups in the other three groups p ≤ 0.05, ANOVA (Table 3).

DISCUSSION

Cholesterol in Brain

It has been demonstrated in the rat by Dobbing (1963) that cholesterol can enter the brain as such and that its pattern of entry during development closely resembles the pattern of its accumulation in brain. Various estimates have been made of the contribution by exogenously derived cholesterol and by cholesterol biosynthesized *in situ* to the cholesterol pool in developing brain. Early studies suggest only about 8% of the brain's cholesterol was derived from the exogenous source [Dobbing (1963) and references cited therein]. More recently, Lopes-Cardozo and Klein (1984); Lopes-Cardozo *et al.* (1984) concluded that a considerable portion, possibly as much as 50% of the cholesterol in developing brain in the period 10 to 20 days after birth, could be derived from the exogenous source. From the study by Dobbing (1963), it is clear that cholesterol can be supplied to the brain from the blood.

Cuzner and Davison (1968) have shown that the brain of the suckling rat has a net accumulation of almost 8 mg cholesterol over the period from 4 to 16 days of age, the time frame of the feeeding study reported here. It can be calculated from the quantity of milk substitute fed (data not shown) that the pups receiving the low, normal and high cholesterol milk substitute consumed about 4, 22 and 110 mg cholesterol over the period 4 to 16 days of age.

Under the conditions of feeding of the milk substitute low in cholesterol (< 25% normal) the animals maintain a normal growth rate comparable to controls in which body and brain weight increases 2.4- and 3.3-fold respectively [Cuzner and Davison (1968)]. It has to be concluded that the demand for cholesterol to maintain adequate growth is met by increased cholesterol synthesis in the body. The activity of the rate limiting enzyme of cholesterogenesis, 3-hydroxy-3-methylglutaryl-CoA reductase, which is normally low in developing liver [McNamara *et al.* (1972)] is elevated 5-fold over the activity level in controls (Table 3). This finding suggests adaptive mechanisms are activated to compensate for the cholesterol which is omitted from the diet. When cholesterol in the milk is in excess (> 200% normal), blood concentrations of cholesterol increase 3-fold yet the concentration of cholesterol in brain is maintained at normal levels. An equivalent situation does not prevail for the liver where the concentration of cholesterol is almost 10-fold greater than in the liver of control animals. Our results demonstrate that the brain throughout the suckling period, even in the early stages of development of the blood brain barrier, has intrinsic mechanisms to maintain an optimum concentration of cholesterol. This property persists under the two distinctive dietary conditions when the milk diet administered from as early as 5 days of age either contains low amounts of cholesterol or excessive amounts of cholesterol. We conclude that mechanisms exist to protect the cholesterol status of developing rat brain in a period of dynamic growth and development. Under similar circumstances, should similar mechanisms exist to protect the cholesterol status of the human brain in early development, it can be proposed that the cholesterol content of milk substitutes will be without influence on the cholesterol content of brain.

ACKNOWLEDGEMENTS

This study was supported by USPHS grant HD11496. We thank Ross Laboratories, Columbus, Ohio, for their generous gift of custom prepared protein powder, SW8707, as a base for the preparation of rat milk substitutes.

REFERENCES

Bergstrom, J. D., Wong, G. A., Edwards, P. A. and Edmond, J. (1984) The regulation of acetoacetyl-CoA synthetase activity by modulators of cholesterol synthesis *in vivo* and the utilization of acetoacetate for cholesterogenesis. *J. Biol. Chem.* **259**: 14548–14553.

Cremer, J. E. (1981) Nutrients for the brain: Problems in supply. *Early Human Dev.* **5**: 117–132 and references cited therein.

Cuzner, M. L. and Davison, A. N. (1968) The lipid composition of rat brain myelin and subcellular fractions during development. *Biochem. J.* **106**: 29–34.

Dobbing, J. (1963) The entry of cholesterol into rat brain during development. *J. Neurochem.* **10**: 739–742.

Fomon, S. J. and Bartels, M. D. (1960) Concentrations of cholesterol in serum of infants in relation to diet. *A.M.A. J. Dis. of Child.* **99**: 27–30.

Friedman, G. and Goldberg, S. J. (1975) Concurrent and subsequent serum cholesterol of breast fed and formula-fed infants. *Am. J. Clin. Nutr.* **28**: 42–45.

Kris-Etherton, P. M., Layman, D. K., York, P. V., Frants, Jr., I. D. (1979) The influence of early nutrition on the serum cholesterol of the adult rat. *J. Nutr.* **109**: 1244–1257.

Lopez-Cardozo, M., Koper, J. W., Klein, W. and Van Golde, L. M. G. (1984) Acetoacetate is a precursor for myelinating rat brain and spinal cord. Incorporation of label from [3-^{14}C]acetoacetate, [^{14}C]glucose and ^{3}H$_2$O. *Biochim. et Biophys. Acta* **794**: 350–352.

Lopez-Cardozo, M. and Klein, W. (1984) Ketone body utilization and lipid synthesis by developing rat brain – a comparison between *in vivo* and *in vitro* experiments. *Neurochem. Int.* **6**: 459–466.

McNamara, D. J., Quackenbush, F. W., Rodwell, V. W. (1972) Regulation of hepatic 3-hydroxy-3-methylglutaryl coenzyme A reductase: developmental pattern. *J. Biol. Chem.* **247**: 5805–5810.

Reiser, R. and Sidelman, Z. (1972) Control of serum cholesterol homeostasis by cholesterol in the milk of the suckling rat. *J. Nutr.* **102**: 1009–1016.

Smart, J. L., Massey, R. F., Nash, S. C. and Tonkiss, J. (1987) Effects of early-life undernutrition in artificially reared rats: subsequent body and organ growth. *Br. J. Nutr.* **58**: 245–255.

Smart, J. L., Stephens, D. N., Tonkiss, J., Auestad, N. and Edmond, J. (1984) Growth and development of rats artificially reared on different milk substitutes. *Br. J. Nutr.* **52**: 227–237.

Sonnenberg, N., Bergstrom, J. D., Ha, Y. H. and Edmond, J. (1982) Metabolism in the artificially reared rat pup: effect of an atypical rat milk substitute. *J. Nutr.* **111**: 1506–1514.

Zlatkis, A. and Zak, B. (1969) Study of a new cholesterol reagent. *Anal. Chem.* **29**: 143–148.

Might Different Brain Information Storage Processes Operating at Different Developmental Ages Affect Compensation for Early Developmental Disabilities?

W. T. Greenough, J. E. Black, F-L. F. Chang and A. M. Sirevaag

Departments of Psychology and Cell and Structural Biology, Behavioral and Neural Biology Program and College of Medicine, University of Illinois, Champaign, IL 61820, U.S.A.

Evidence indicates that two types of brain information storage mechanisms exist. The first, termed experience-expectant, stores information in early development in networks created by stabilization of a subpopulation of previously generated synapses. Experience-expectant storage is difficult to reverse and usually limited to brief time periods for any given process. The second, termed experience-dependent, stores information throughout life by creating new synapses. In contrast to the capacity for synaptogenesis, the capacity to generate supportive metabolic structures declines with age, such that brain regions not fully developed early in life may be metabolically deprived as a result of subsequent synaptogenesis.

We present here a view of an apparent discontinuity in the way in which the developing brain acquires information from the environment – one that may have implications for the study of developmental disorders that involve or are affected by experience. An important additional point is that selective or global deficiencies may occur in brain metabolic support systems due to a developmental decline in the responsiveness of these support systems to experience. The philosophy underlying this work is that an understanding of basic mechanisms of brain development is more important to investigating deficiencies than is the development of animal models of specific aspects of deficiencies, such as morphological aberrations in the brain.

INTRODUCTION

The view to be presented here expands upon those presented by others (e.g. Gottlieb, 1983). In its simplest form, this view is that the brain acquires environmental information in two different ways, and that one of these two modes seems largely to occur only during very early postnatal (and perhaps prenatal) periods. This early form of information storage, which is involved in the shaping of sensory systems, we term experience-expectant (Black and Greenough, 1986). This term was chosen to signify that brain systems appear to be readied in advance to incorporate certain types of information, the occurrence of which is sufficiently reliable that it can be counted on as a normal part of the development process. The occurrence of visual stimulation – contrast borders, oriented patterns, and so forth – is, for example, a completely predictable aspect of the experience of a normal human, monkey, cat, or rat. Because this has remained true throughout the period over which these species have evolved, the information has become a part of the development process, and is used to assist in organizing the visual system. A failure of this process, either due to inadequate environmental stimulation or to defective neural or peripheral systems, often has devastating consequences.

The second way in which information is acquired includes what is referred to as learning, but is not restricted to what is meant by most strict definitions of that term. We refer to this form of information storage as experience-dependent to indicate that the brain system that will store this information is not readied in advance for a particular piece of information but is prepared in general to generate circuitry that incorporates information. This process is geared to the storage of information that is unique to the individual, both in terms of the sequence in which it occurs and in terms of its character – e.g. specific details of one's physical and social environment.

There are several reasons, from the perspective of behaviour, for positing that these two different forms of environmental information storage exist. The foremost is that the first process appears to be age-limited, that is, to involve what are termed critical or sensitive periods, whereas the ability to learn continues throughout life. The development of visual or auditory ability will be guided by whatever experience is available during postnatal periods of sensitivity of these systems in mammals, and later experience is very much less effective in altering the organization that has been put into place (see, e.g., Boothe et al., 1985). Information acquired later is more readily alterable; in fact, in at least some cases, highly practised habits are the most easily reversed (e.g., Hall, 1974).

Potentially the most compelling reason for positing that these two different forms of environmental information storage exist arises from neurobiological studies of the early development of central nervous system sensory information processing structures and the adult brain response to learning. These studies indicate that:

1. the development of sensory systems involves the overproduction of synaptic connections between neurons (as if in expectation of extrinsic guidance) and subsequent selective preservation of a subset of those connections, the pattern of which is determined by the sensory input that the organism has experienced;
2. when adults learn new tasks, new synaptic connections are generated as a component of learning in regions that are involved in performance of those tasks.

EXPERIENCE EXPECTANT DEVELOPMENT

Evidence for the first of these points has arisen from studies of sensory development. In the visual cortex, synapses, including those of lateral geniculate neurons carrying input from the eyes, are initially formed rather nonsystematically; guided by activity in the visual pathway, inappropriate synapses are withdrawn and appropriate ones are stabilized in the generation of a mature pattern (LeVay *et al.* 1980; Tieman, 1984). Similarly, on the dendritic receiving side, both overproduction of postsynaptic spines and initial outgrowth of inappropriately oriented dendrites that are later lost has been reported at several levels in the central nervous system, ranging from first-order sensory nuclei at all levels in the brain, from the telecephalon to the brainstem (Falls and Goebel, 1979; Brunjes *et al.*, 1982) to sensory regions of the cerebral cortex (Boothe *et al.*, 1979). The production of supernumerary or incorrectly positioned synaptic connections is so widespread during both central and peripheral nervous system development that one almost feels, when this is not evident, that it may have been masked by other processes. A very common feature is the involvement of neuronal activity in the governance of loss and stabilization. The term "experience-expectant" reflects our proposal that an excess of comparatively nonsystematically patterned connections is generated in the expectation that subsequent highly reliable development events will carve out a functionally appropriate subset of them. Figure 1 depicts this process.

EXPERIENCE DEPENDENT DEVELOPMENT

Evidence for the second process, involving the generation of new connections in response to experience, has arisen from studies of juvenile and adult animals given the opportunity to learn about a complex,

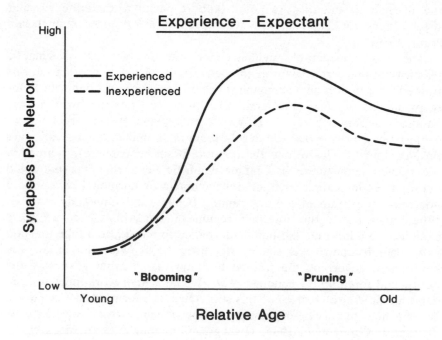

Figure 1. Schematic diagram of synapse overproduction ("blooming") and deletion ("pruning") during an experience-expectant process. (From Black and Greenough, 1986. Copyright 1986, Lawrence Earlbaum Assoc. Used by permission.)

changing environment and from adult animals that have been trained on various learning tasks. A key early observation was that the weight of some regions of the cerebral cortex was increased as a consequence of exposure to a complex environment (containing toys and a group of rats) in both juvenile and adult rats (Rosenzweig *et al.*, 1962). Following up on this finding, we and others showed that this weight increase reflected increases in dendritic field size and the associated number of synapses per neuron (Greenough and Volkmar, 1973; Turner and Greenough, 1985), and in a variety of support components including glial cells, blood vessels, and neuronal nuclear size (Black *et al.*, 1987; Diamond *et al.*, 1964; Sirevaag & Greenough, 1985, 1987). Moreover, we found that many of the effects of a complex environment seen in the juvenile brain also occured when young adult and middle-aged rats were exposed to complex environments (Juraska *et al.*, 1980; Green *et al.*, 1983; Hwang and Greenough, 1986; Black *et al.*, 1986; Black *et al.*, in press). Thus a significant capacity to construct new synapses persists throughout much of the lifespan of the rat. As noted later, capacity to generate vascular support does not keep pace with synaptogenesis as rats grow older (Isaacs *et al.*, 1986).

There is considerable evidence for the involvement of synaptic plasticity of this sort in learning in adults. In the visual cortex of adult rats trained for a month on a changing series of maze patterns, dendritic fields of pyramidal neurons were larger than in control rats that were merely handled (Greenough *et al.*, 1979). When unilateral maze training was achieved by covering one eye in split-brain rats (unlike humans, rat's eyes project almost exclusively to the opposite brain hemisphere), neurons in the trained hemisphere had larger dendritic fields than the untrained hemisphere, indicating that general metabolic or hormonal changes did not cause the brain effects of training (Chang and Greenough, 1982). When neurons in the forelimb region of sensorimotor cortex were examined in adult rats that had been trained to reach into a tube for food with one forepaw exclusively, dendritic fields were larger in the hemisphere governing the trained forelimb than in that governing the nontrained forelimb (Greenough *et al.*, 1985a). Other work indicates that dendritic field size changes of this sort reflect the formation of synapses, accompanied to varying degrees by changes in supportive tissue elements (Turner & Greenough, 1985; Hwang & Greenough, 1986; Black *et al.*, 1987; Black *et al.*, in press).

Further evidence that these synaptic changes arise as a consequence of learning rather than merely from increased nerve cell activity comes from comparison of rats learning acrobatic skills with minimal motor output with rats engaging in high levels of physical activity with minimal learning (Anderson *et al.*, in press). The acrobatic condition required rats to traverse an elevated pathway between a start and goal box. The spans, consisting initially of comparatively wide strips of wood, became increasingly intricate and difficult to negotiate as training progressed, such that the animals acquired extensive fine motor coordination. Physical activity groups were either allowed voluntary exercise in a running wheel attached to their cages or were subjected to forced exercise in a treadmill. These groups traversed substantially more distance than the acrobats. A final group received neither exercise nor training. Examination of the paramedian lobule of the cerebellum indicated little or no synaptogenesis above the untreated animals in the two exercise groups, for which nerve cell activity should have been the greatest, and considerable increase in synapses in the acrobatic learning group. Thus, in this case, learning appears to be the important aspect of the effect of experience upon synaptic connections.

SOURCE OF EXPERIENCE-DEPENDENT SYNAPSES

An important factor differentiating this lifespan type of synaptic plasticity from that of early development is the evidence that new synapses are specifically created in response to experience. An alternative view (Cotman and Nieto-Sampedro, 1984) suggests that synapse turnover may be a chronic process in the brain and that learning merely stamps in otherwise transient synapses that are the adult counterpart of the overproduced synapses of early development. While the issue is not yet settled, several results argue that synapse formation is triggered by some aspect of learning, or, as previously described, synapses form on demand (Greenough, 1985):

1. Chang and Greenough (1984) followed up the Lee *et al.* (1980) finding of synapse formation in association with long-term potentiation (LTP), an induced change in the strength of a neural pathway. Chang and Greenough found that synapses formed within 10 to 15 minutes after the electrical stimuli used to induce LTP. While the role of these synapses in LTP is not certain, the fact that synapses can form this rapidly argues that they are likely to do so under other circumstances, as in learning.

2. Increased dendritic branching in response to juvenile exposure to a complex environment is evident after only 4 days, suggesting a rapid response to experience (Kilman *et al.*, in press). Substantial increases in numbers of synapses per neuron are evident in adult rats after just 10 days of exposure (Hwang and Greenough, 1986). While no specific prediction can be made regarding the rate of appearance of increased synapse numbers under the on demand and turnover conditions, it seems intuitive that increases occur about more rapidly if their formation were driven by experience.

3. Polyribosomal aggregates (PRAs) in postsynaptic spines, which have been proposed to indicate newly forming synapses (e.g. Steward and Falk, 1986), are more common in visual cortex of rats in a complex environment than in rats in simpler housing conditions (Greenough *et al.*, 1985b). If turnover were chronic in all animals, then the same number of newly forming synapses (and hence of PRAs in spines) should be present in all groups. This finding is complicated, however, by our subsequent finding that the difference between such groups persists even after the animals have been removed from the environments for a month (Hwang & Greenough, 1986).

Thus, a growing body of evidence argues that synapses form in response to the demands of learning or information storage. If this is so, there is the question of whether all synapses so generated survive or, as in the experience-expectant condition, synapses are locally overproduced and a

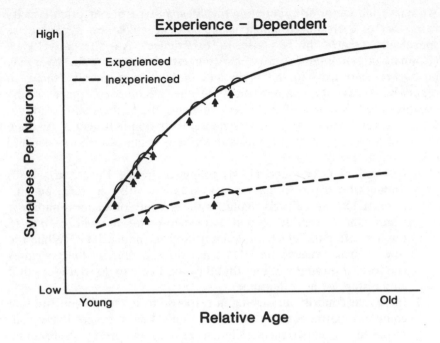

Figure 2.   Schematic diagram of synapse formation and selective retention during an experience-dependent process. The arrowheads mark salient experiences that generate local synaptic overproduction and deletion (small curves). The cumulative effect of such synaptic blooms and prunes is a smooth increase in synapses per neuron, which is greater for the animals with more experience. (From Black and Greenough, 1986. Copyright, 1986, Lawrence Earlbaum Assoc. Used by permission.)

subset is stabilized later. One possible view appears in Fig. 2, which shows that many small, localized "blooms" of synapses could build the sizeable numbers of synapses seen in animals from complex environments.

METABOLIC SUPPORT OF SYNAPTIC PLASTICITY – MORE AGE DEPENDENT THAN SYNAPTOGENESIS

There is a final aspect of these studies that may have profound implications for mental dysfunction. In weanling EC rats, metabolic support for new synapses accompanies the synapses in abundance:

Increases in the volume fraction of capillaries (through new branching), supportive astrocyte membrane surface, and energy-providing mito-chondria are all greater than the increases in the corresponding volume fraction of synaptic tissue (Black *et al.*, 1987; Diamond *et al.*, 1964; Sirevaag & Greenough, 1985, 1987). In older rats, there is a progressive decline in the response of support systems that is much more rapid and profound than the very gradual reductions in synaptogenic capacity, which is not seriously limited (in cerebral cortex) until old age (Isaacs *et al.*, 1986; Black *et al.*, 1987; Black *et al.*, in press). Thus early restriction in experience could lead to global or regional retardation in CNS metabolic support, such that the ability to use later-acquired information might be impaired. As the technology to assess such deficiencies non-invasively in humans becomes available, we would be remiss in not investigating this more directly.

This perspective on neural plasticity has some general implications for mental deficiency. Although investigators have examined genetic defects that may interfere directly with synapse production, the control of synaptogenesis has been relatively neglected. We would expect adverse consequences from synapse overproduction as well as underproduction, and from failure of both stabilization and elimination processes, and we emphasize that the *pattern* of connections is generally more important than their number. Furthermore, the timing of experience is crucial to experience-expectant processes and important to the full development of metabolic support components of brain, and forms of mental deficiency may well result from a temporal mismatch between experience and the brain's sensitivity to it. In addition, disrupted early development may put later experience-dependent systems at risk. Developmentally disabled individuals may have problems with generating rich and stimulating environments for themselves, and cognitive impairments may lower the quality of experience even further. The results of our animal are not directly applicable to humans, but we suspect that some aspects of brain pathology in the developmentally disabled may reflect their relatively impoverished experience. The availability and quality of experience is of even greater concern in that large group of individuals who suffer from concurrent mental deficiency and handicaps of perception or movement.

ACKNOWLEDGEMENT

Supported by NIMH 35321, 40631, and 43830, NIH RR 07030, T-32HD0733, PHS 5 T-32GM7143, ONR N00014-85-K-0587, the Retirement Research Foundation, and the Epilepsy Foundation of America.

54 Greenough *et al.*

REFERENCES

Anderson, B. J., Isaacs, K. R., Black, J. E., Vinci, L., Alcantara, A. A. and Greenough, W. T. In Press. Synaptogenesis in cerebellar cortex of adult rats after less than 15 hours of visuomotor training over 30 days. *Soc. Neurosci Abst.*

Black, J. E., and Greenough, W. T. (1986) Induction of pattern in neural structure by experience: Implications for cognitive development. In: M. E. Lamb, A. L. Brown and B. Rogoff (eds), *Advances in Developmental Psychology. Vol. 4*, pp. 1–50. Lawrence Earlbaum Assoc., Hillsdale, NJ.

Black, J. E., Parnisari, R., Eichbaum, E. and Greenough, W. T. (1986) Morphological effects of housing environment and voluntary exercise on cerebral cortex and cerebellum of old rats. *Soc. Neurosci. Abst.* 12: 1579.

Black, J. E., Sirevaag, A. M. and Greenough, W. T. (1987) Complex experience promotes capillary formation in young rat visual cortex. *Neurosci. Lett.* 83: 351–355.

Black,. J. E., Zelazny, A. M. and Greenough, W. T. In Press. Complex experience induces capillaries in visual cortex of adult rats. *Soc. Neurosci. Abst.* 14.

Boothe, R. G., Dobson, V. and Teller, D. Y. (1985) Postnatal development of vision in human and nonhuman primates. *Ann. Rev. Neurosci.* 8: 495–545.

Boothe, R. G., Greenough, W. T., Lund, J. S. and Wrege, K. S. (1979) A quantitative investigation of spine and dendrite development of neurons in the visual cortex (area 17) of *Macaca nemestrina* monkeys. *J. Comp. Neurol.* 186: 473–490.

Brunjes, P. C., Schwark, H. D. and Greenough, W. T. (1982) Olfactory granule cell development in normal and hyperthyroid rats. *Develop. Brain Res.* 5: 149–159.

Chang, F.-L. and Greenough, W. T. (1982) Lateralized effects of monocular training on dendritic branching in adult split-brain rats. *Brain Res.* 232: 283–292.

Chang, F.-L. F. and Greenough, W. T. (1984) Transient and enduring morphological correlates of synaptic activity and efficacy change in the rat hippocampal slice. *Brain Res.* 309: 35–46.

Chang, F.-L., Isaacs, K. R., Treacy, D. and Greenough, W. T. (1987) Synaptogenesis in aged rats associated with long term potentiation. *Soc. Neurosci. Abst.* 13: 719.

Cotman, C. W. and Nieto-Sampedro, M. (1984) Cell biology of synaptic plasticity. *Science* 225: 1287–1294.

Diamond, M. C., Krech, D and Rosenzweig, M. R. (1964) The effects of an enriched environment on the histology of the rat cerebral cortex. *J. Comp. Neurol.* 123: 111–120.

Falls, W. and Goebel, S. (1979) Golgi and EM studies of the formation of dendritic and axonal arbors: The interneurons of the substantia gelatinosa of Rolando in newborn kittens. *J. Comp. Neurol.* 187: 1–18.

Gottlieb, G. (1983) The psychobiological approach to developmental issues. In: M. M. Haith & J. J. Campos (eds), *Handbook of child psychology: vol. 2 Infancy and developmental psychobiology*, pp. 1–26. Wiley, New York.

Green, E. J., Greenough, W. T. and Schlumpf, B. E. (1983) Effects of complex or isolated environments on cortical dendrites of middle-aged rats. *Brain Res.* **264**: 233–240.

Greenough, W. T. (1985) The possible role of experience-dependent synaptogensis, or synapses on demand, in the memory process. In: N. M. Weinberger, J. L. McGaugh, and G. Lynch (eds), *Memory Systems of the Brain: Animal and Human Cognitive Processes*, pp. 77–103. Guilford Press, New York.

Greenough, W. T., Hwang, H.-M. and Gorman, C. (1985b) Evidence for active synapse formation, or altered postsynaptic metabolism, in visual cortex of rats reared in complex environments. *Proc. Natl. Acad. Sci. U.S.A.* **82**: 4549–4552.

Greenough, W. T., Juraska, J. M. and Volkmar, F. R. (1979) The training effects on dendritic branching in occipital cortex of adult rats. *Behav. Neur. Biol.* **26**: 287–297.

Greenough, W. T., Larson, J. R. and Withers, G. S. (1985a) Effects of unilateral and bilateral training in a reaching task on dendritic branching of neurons in the rat motor-sensory forelimb cortex. *Behav. Neur. Biol.* **44**: 301–314.

Greenough, W. T. and Volkmar, F. R. (1973) Pattern of dendritic branching in rat occipital cortex after rearing in complex environments. *Exp. Neurol.* **40**: 491–504.

Hall, G. (1974) Transfer effects produced by overtaining in the rat. *J. Comp. Pysiol. Psychol.* **87**: 938–944.

Hwang, H.-M. and Greenough, W. T. (1986) Synaptic plasticity in adult rat occipital cortex following short-term, long-term, and reversal of differential housing environment complexity. *Soc. Neurosci. Abstr.* **12**: 1248.

Isaacs, K. R., Black, J. E., Polinsky, M. and Greenough, W. T. (1986) Capillary morphology in visual cortex of middle-aged, but not old, rats is altered by housing environment. *Soc. Neurosci. Abst.* **12**: 1579.

Juraska, J. M., Greenough, W. T., Elliott, C., Mack, K. J. and Berkowitz, R. (1980) Plasticity in adult rat visual cortex: An examination of several cell populations after differential rearing. *Behav. Neur. Biol.* **29**: 157–167.

Kilman, V. L., Wallace, C. S., Withers, G. S. and Greenough, W. T. In Press. Four days of differential housing alters dendritic morphology of weanling rats. *Soc. Neurosci. Abst.* **14**.

Lee, K. S., Schottler, F., Oliver, M. and Lynch, G. (1980) Brief bursts of high-frequency stimulation produce two types of structural change in rat hippocampus. *J. Neurophysiol.* **44**: 247–258.

LeVay, S., Wiesel, T. N. and Hubel, D. H. (1980) The development of occular dominance columns in normal and visually deprived monkeys. *J. Comp. Neurol.* **191**: 1–51.

Rosenzweig, M. R., Krech, D., Bennett, E. L., and Diamond, M. C. (1962) Effects of environmental complexity and training on brain chemistry and anatomy: A replication and extension. *J. Comp. Physiol. Psychol.* **55**: 429–437.

Sirevaag, A. M. and Greenough, W. T. (1985) Differential rearing effects on rat visual cortex synapses. II. Synaptic morphometry. *Develop. Brain Res.* **19**: 215–226.

Sirevaag, A. M. and Greenough, W. T. (1987) Differential rearing effects on rat visual cortex synapses. III. Neuronal and glial nuclei, boutons, dendrites, and capillaries. *Brain Res.* **424**: 320–332.

Steward, O. and Falk, P. M. (1986) Protein-synthetic machinery at postsynaptic sites during synaptogenesis: A quantitative study of the association between polyribosomes and developing synapses. *J. Neurosci.* **6**: 412–423.

Tieman, S. B. (1984) Effects of monocular deprivation on geniculocortical synapses in the cat. *J. Comp. Neurol.* **222**: 166–176.

Turner, A. M. and Greenough, W. T. (1985) Differential rearing effects on rat visual cortex synapses. I. Synaptic and neuronal density and synapses per neuron. *Brain Res.* **329**: 195–203.

Correlation of Cytogenetic and DNA findings in Prader Willi Syndrome

A. Smith,[1] F. Volpato[2] & R. J. Trent[2]

[1]Cytogenetics Unit, Oliver Latham Laboratory, Department of Health,
NSW., Australia
[2]Molecular Biology Laboratory, Clinical Immunology Research Centre,
University of Sydney, NSW., Australia

Twenty four patients with Prader Willi Syndrome were investigated with high resolution cytogenetic studies and DNA. The DNA studies were performed with 2 chromosome 15q11-13 specific probes after digestion with 4 restriction enzymes.

A novel band was seen in 2 PWS individuals with BamH1 digest and p3-21 probe which was not present in 100 normal chromosomes. These 2 patients were cytogenetically non-deleted. Possible mechanisms for these findings are discussed.

INTRODUCTION

Clinical heterogeneity in the Prader Willi Syndrome (PWS) has been in evidence for some time (Mikkelsen et al., 1973; Townes and White, 1975; Fuhrmann-Reiger et al., 1984) but cytogenetic heterogeneity has only recently become apparent. Cytogenetic heterogeneity is now seen to be quite marked for the region of chromosome 15 from q11-13. There are cases of cytogenetic abnormality of chromosome 15 involving other breakpoint regions (Kucerova et al., 1979; Kawashima, 1979; Fraccaro et al., 1983) but 15q11-13 has been most frequently involved and this may represent the "critical region" (Smith, 1986). Cases have been reported with abnormality of this region present in monosomy, disomy (or normal), trisomy and tetrasomy (Table 1). The frequency of these types varies in different series but monosomy due to interstitial deletion detected on high resolution banding presently constitutes 50% of cases, other structural rearrangements of 15q11-13 up to 5% of cases and the rest have apparently normal chromosomes.

Clearly cytogenetic studies, even utilising high resolution banding (Yunis, 1976) are an insensitive tool for estimating rearrangements at the

Table 1.   Cytogenetic heterogeneity in Prader Willi Syndrome

Dosage of 15q11-13	Mechanism of origin	Reference
Monosomy	– interstitial deletion – tertiary monsomy (from reciprocal translocation)	Butler and Palmer, 1983 Mattei et al., 1984
Disomy	– normal – robertsonian translocation	Smith, 1986 Hawkey and Smithies, 1976
Trisomy	– mar – duplication	Smith et al. 1988 Pettigrew et al., 1987
Tetrasomy	– isochromosome formation	Matteri et al., 1984

DNA level. Molecular studies in PWS have to date been reported in two patients (Donlon et al., 1986) and a further five patients (Latt et al., 1987). We describe 24 patients who were studied by both high resolution cytogenetics and two chromosome 15q11-13 specific DNA probes.

METHODS

Clinical evaluation of the patients was made by both the referring doctors and one of us (AS). Classical PWS individuals were those with the first phase of the syndrome (hypotonia and failure to thrive in infancy) followed by the second phase (hyperphagia and onset of obesity) with also the characteristic facies and other phenotypic features of the syndrome (Smith and Noel, 1980). Patients who did not comply with all of these criteria were classified as atypical. We do not present the full clinical evaluation of the patients in this paper.

Cytogenetic studies were performed in each case by high resolution GTG banding by the method of Yunis, 1976, with a final resolution to the 800-band stage. On this basis, patients with 46 chromosomes were classified as deletional or non-deletional (for 15q11-13). CBG, NOR and distamycin/DAPI banding techniques were used as necessary to define structural abnormality.

DNA studies were performed by standard Southern blotting techniques (Southern, 1975). The two probes used were p3-21 and pML-34 (Donlon et al., 1986) which were kindly supplied by Professor S. A. Latt, Boston, USA. DNA from the 24 PWS patients was digested with four restriction enzymes – BglII, EcoRI, HindIII and BamHI. DNA from 100 normal chromosomes was digested with BamHI.

Table 2.   Cytogenetics of the patient group

Non-PWS n = 2	
45,XY,t(10;15) (q26;q13)	1
47,XX,+i(15) (q13)	1
PWS n = 22	
3 atypical	
46,XY	2
46,XX	1
19 classical	
47,XY,+del(15)(pter → q13)	1
45,XX,t(14;15)(p11;q11)	1
47,XXY. -non deletional	1
46,XX, del(15)(q11-13)	1
46,XX.	3
46,XY,del(15)(q11-13)	7
46,XY.	5

RESULTS

Of the 24 patients studied, 17 were males and 7 were females. The ages ranged from 3 years to 54 years. The cytogenetics of the patient group is shown in Table 2. The clinical features of the non-PWS patient with 45,XY,t(10;15) (q26;q13) have been reported (Smith and den Dulk, 1982) as have also the classical PWS patients with karyotype 45,XX,t (14;15) (p11;q11) (Smith and Noel, 1980) and 47,XY, + del(15) (pter → q13) (Smith *et al.*, 1988). The distribution of the different karyotypes in this group of patients is similar to that expected.

No abnormal DNA bands were detected in 22 of the 24 PWS patients who were studied with two DNA probes and four restriction enzymes. Two patients demonstrated a novel BamHI fragment of approximately 20 kb (normal = 25 kb) with the probe p3-21. This band was not found in 100 normal chromosomes but was present in the mother of one patient (the second family study is presently in progress (Figures 1, 2). These two PWS patients had classical clinical features and there were no deletions detectable cytogenetically.

DISCUSSION

Cytogenetic heterogeneity in the PWS is difficult to understand. The same syndrome occurring in cases of loss or excess of a chromosome region is not in keeping with current theories of either excess of a region producing a characteristic phenotype, e.g. Down's Syndrome or loss of a

Figure 1. DNA band patterns obtained with the restriction enzyme BamHI and DNA probe p3.21. N = normal pattern, P = pattern in the PWS proband. Sizes of restriction fragments (in kilobases) are shown on the left.

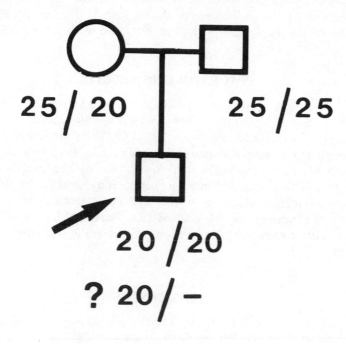

25 / 20   25 / 25

20 / 20

? 20 / –

Figure 2. DNA band patterns in a patient with PWS and his parents.

region, e.g. monosomy 13q. Indeed, in classical studies of patients with syndromes de Grouchy suggested "type" and "counter type" syndromes for excess and deficiency of the 4p, 9p and 21q regions (de Grouchy and Turleau, 1984). The cytogenetic heterogeneity in the PWS may be due to a nonspecific effect of alteration of total chromosome 15 content or a position effect. Before such theories can be accepted, true deletion or rearrangement of chromosome 15 at the DNA level must be excluded.

Several mechanisms could account for our DNA findings. One obvious explanation for the ~20 kb band is a DNA polymorphism. This would seem unlikely since it was not present in 100 random chromosomes but only the two PWS patients and one of the parents tested. Therefore, the ~20 kb band most likely represents a deletion or rearrangement which has been detected by probe p3-21. This rearrangement has been inherited from the mother in one patient. Loss of the normal 25 kb allele in this patient indicates non-paternity or a second rearrangement involving chromosome 15 which either deletes the entire region detected by probe p3-21 or fortuitously is ~20 kb in size. Non-paternity remains to be formally excluded but would seem unlikely because the ~20 kb band was not present in the 100 random chromosomes. Further studies are in progress to clarify the DNA changes obtained in the two PWS patients.

ACKNOWLEDGEMENTS

We thank Robin Murray, Margaret Cohen and Gesina den Dulk of the Oliver Latham Laboratory for excellent cytogenetic preparations; Dr Garry Warne, Endocrinologist, Royal Children's Hospital, Melbourne for cooperation with the patients in Victoria; Professor S. A. Latt, Harvard Medical School, Boston, for providing the probes; Dr Brian Learoyd and sisters Gail Honeman, Liz Jennings and Kathy Boss who so willingly collected blood from the Sydney patients; Mr and Mrs D. Robertson (Sydney) and Mr and Mrs D. Barber (Melbourne) from the Prader-Willi Syndrome Association of Australia for their continued support.

REFERENCES

Butler, M. G. and Palmer, C. G. (1983) Parental origin of chromosome 15 deletion in Prader-Willi Syndrome. *Lancet* i. 1285–6.

de Grouchy, J. and Turleau, C. (1984) *Clinical Atlas of Human Chromosomes*. Second Edition. John Wiley and Sons, New York, p. 355. p. 56. p. 155.

Donlon, T. A., Lalande, M., Wyman, A., Bruns, G., Latt, S. A. (1986) Isolation of Molecular Probes associated with the chromosome 15 instability in the Prader-Willi Syndrome. *Proc. Natl. Acad. Sci.* **83**: 4408–4412.

Fraccaro, M. Zuffardi, O., Buhler, E. *et al.* (1983) Deficiency, transposition and duplication of one 15q region may be alternatively associated with Prader-Willi (or a similar) syndrome. *Hum. Genet.* **64**: 388–394.

Furhmann-Reiger, A., Kohler, A. and Fuhrmann, W. (1984) Duplication or insertion in 15q11-13 associated with mental retardation – short stature and obesity – Prader-Willi or Cohen Syndrome? *Clin. Genet.* **25**: 347–352.

Kawashima, H. (1979) Cited by Fujita as personal communication in Fujita, H., Sakamoto, Y. and Hamamoto, Y. (1980). An extra idic (15p) (q11) chromosome in Prader-Willi Syndrome. *Hum. Genet.* **55**: 409–411.

Kucerova, M., Strakova, M. and Polivkova, Z. (1979) The Prader-Willi Syndrome with a 15/3 translocation. *J. Med. Genet.* **16**: 234–5.

Latt, S. A., Trantravahi, U., Neve, R., Nicholls, R., Ringer, S., Stroh, H., Fuller, R., Donlon, T., Kaplan, L., Wharton, R. (1987) New and better molecular probes for characterising and ultimately understanding the consequences of #15 deletions in the Prader-Willi syndrome. *Am. J. Med. Genet.* **28**: 88 Abstract.

Mattei, M. G., Souiah, N. and Mattei, J. F. (1984) Chromosome 15 anomalies and the Prader-Willi Syndrome: cytogenetic analysis. *Hum. Genet.* **66**: 313–334.

Mikkelsen, M., Dyggve, H. and Poulsen, H. (1973) (6;15) Translocation with loss of chromosome material in the patient and various chromosome aberrations in family members. *Humangenetik* **18**: 195–202.

Pettigrew, A.L., Gollin, S.M., Greenberg, F., Riccardi, V. M., Ledbetter, D. H. (1987) Duplication of proximal 15q as a cause of Prader Willi Syndrome. *Am. J. Med. Genet.* **28**: 791–802.

Smith, A. (1986) Chromosome Findings in the Prader Willi Syndrome. *ANZ J. Develop. Disab.* **12**: 13–28.

Smith, A., den Dulk, G. (1982) A severely retarded male with deletion of chromosomes 15 (pter → q13) and 10(q26 → qter). *J. Med. Genet.* **19**: 77–78.

Smith, A., den Dulk, G., Suter, M. and Lipson, A. (1988) Prader Willi Syndrome and trisomy 15q11-13. *Hum. Genet. Soc. of A'asia Annual Scientific Meeting*. Abstract.

Smith, A., Noel, M. (1980) A girl with the Prader Willi Syndrome and Robertsonian translocation 45,XX,t(14;15)(p11;q11) which was present in three Normal Family Members. *Hum. Gen.* **55**: 271–273.

Southern E. M. (1975) Detection of specific sequences among DNA fragments separated by electrophoresis. *J. Mol. Biol.* **98**: 503–517.

Townes, P. L. and White, M. R. (1975) Further identification of a D/E translocation. *Amer. J. Dis. Child.* **129**: 959–961.

Yunis, J. J. (1976) High resolution of human chromosomes. *Science* **191**: 1268–1270.

The Improved Prognosis in Cri-du-Chat (5P-) Syndrome

M. E. Carlin

Department of Pediatrics/Division of Genetics
University of Miami/Mailman Center for Child Development
P.O. Box 016820 (D-820) Miami FL. 33101 U.S.A.

Data from 62 individuals with cri-du-chat (5p-) syndrome demonstrate an improved prognosis for many parameters of health, development and longevity compared with the dismal predictions in the literature. Most have de-novo deletions and have been reared at home. The majority show similar phenotypes; 100% demonstrate significant cognitive, language and behavioral deficits. However, mortality and the incidence of major anomalies and medical complications are low. Speech has developed in 50% while 75% use signing and other communication methods. One-half of those above 10 years of age are in vocational settings. Home-rearing and early, consistent intervention are the keys to this improved outlook.

INTRODUCTION

Cri-du-chat (cat-cry) syndrome, which is caused by a loss of chromosomal material from the distal portion of 5p, presents a recognizable phenotype with a characteristic cry, certain dysmorphic craniofacial features, a slowed rate of growth and significant psychomotor retardation. Many individuals also show some orthopedic malalignments and some have anomalies in one or more major organ systems. Described in 1963 by Lejeune *et al.* most individuals born prior to 1970 were institutionalized, and many died at relatively early ages of respiratory, cardiac and/or gastrointestinal malformations and feeding complications. Standard reference sources and most of the available literature all list severe to profound retardation, absence of speech, lack of ambulation and a reduced life span as almost inevitable for these individuals. But with the inception of early interventional programs and federally mandated public education for all handicapped individuals (U.S.A. Public Law 94-142), most of these individuals now remain in a home setting, at least during

64

their childhood years. The newly emerging data gleaned from studying these individuals fail to support the very bleak outlook that has been reported previously (Carlin, 1988).

The only comparable data comes from a cross-sectional study by Wilkins *et al.* (1981, 1982a) of 86 home-reared individuals with 5p-. Notably, an unbalanced translocation was detected in 20%, and major craniofacial, cardiac, gastrointestinal and bony malformations were not infrequent. At the mean population age of 6.5 years, the average social and mental ages were 2.6 and 2.5 years respectively, with social quotients inversely proportional to the age at which early intervention began. Tables 1, 2 and 4 show comparisons between that study and data presented here on 62 individuals selected from over 100 patients with 5p monosomy who have been personally evaluated by the author.

STUDY POPULATION

The study population comes from two distinct settings. Group I is comprised of 31 patients who have been seen longitudinally; 15 of them have been followed for 10 years or more. There are 17 females and 13 males ranging in age from newborn to 34 years. Twenty-one are Caucasian, 4 Black, 5 Hispanic and 1 Israeli. Cytogenetically they include: 24 terminal deletions, 3 interstitial deletions, 2 translocations and 2 with mosaicism, one of whom has a ring 5 chromosome. No translocations have been detected in those parents available for studying. Seven members have lived in an institutionalized residential setting for an extended period of time.

The cross-sectional data on the 31 patients in Group II have been obtained through a parent questionnaire and physical examination at an annual meeting of the 5p- Society a national (USA) support group for families. These 19 females and 12 males are all Caucasian and range from 2 months to 23 years of age. Chromosome studies were not available for review on all, but 2 are known to have resulted from parental translocations. All of these individuals have been reared in a home setting. Figure 1 shows the distribution of the complete patient population by age. (See Figure 1.)

RESULTS

As has been noted previously by Wilkins (1981, 82a/82b) and others, despite the wide variations in the size and location of the deletions in these patients, remarkable phenotypic consistency exists with growth parameters and the degree of retardation being the only variables that typically worsen with increasing deletion size. Interestingly, the microcephaly, hypertelorism, micrognathia, simian creases and clinodactyly

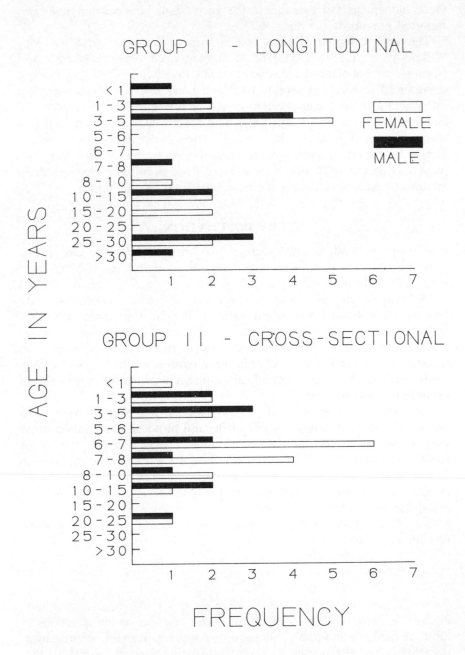

Figure 1. Distribution of cri-du-chat syndrome study population by age. Only the 28 survivors in group I are included.

Table 1.   Major anomalies in cri-du-chat syndrome

Anomalies	Group I (N = 31)	Group II (N = 31)	Wilkins (1982) (N = 86)
Congenital heart disease	4	3	30
Breakdown: (ASD)	–	2	common
(VSD)	2	1	
(PDA)	1	1[a]	common
(Tetralogy)	2	–	some
Heart murmurs	10	7	
Bradycardia	–	1	
Cleft Palate	1	1	7
Congenital hip dislocation	2	2	few
Club foot deformity	7	3	25%
Metatarsus abnormality	4	2	few
Other extremity defects	–	4	
Craniostenosis	1	–	
Scoliosis	2	2	20% >8 yrs
Gastrointestinal malformations	–	1	not rare
Undescended testicle(s)	–	2	

[a] Suspected, but unproven; has resolved spontaneously.

were already visible by 19 weeks of gestation in the 3 second trimester fetuses we have examined (Carlin and Carver 1984).

In both groups the characteristic features of a monochromatic cry, early growth failure, microcephaly and significant pyschomotor retardation have been noted in all individuals, while hypertelorism, epicanthal folds, fifth finger clinodactyly, strabismus dental malocclusion and various orthopedic deformities are present in greater than 80%. Feeding problems, often with regurgitation, as well as frequent respiratory and ear infections have occurred in 100%. Surprisingly though, fewer than one-third have major organ anomalies. Although 40% have had heart murmurs reported, only 7 have a demonstrable cardiac anomaly, and only 4 of those have been symptomatic. Fifty percent have persistent constipation; the incidence increases with age. Tables 1 and 2 list the anomalies and other medical complications encountered.

Virtually 100% have had hypotonia, at least in the early months, but 50% later develop some degree of hypertonia and experience some limitation in their range of motion at certain joints. Coordination difficulties are also present in 100%. Attention deficits are likewise universal, but medication has ameliorated them in about one-half. Behavior management techniques are also efficacious. These have

Table 2. Other medical/neurological complications in cri-du-chat syndrome

Complications	Group I N = 31	Group II N = 31	Wilkins (1982) N = 86
Poor suck/slow feeding	31	31	most
Regurgitation	29	28	
N-G tubes	3	1	
Gastrostomy	2	1	
Inguinal/abdominal hernias	5	5	common
Constipation	17	6	>50%
Frequent infections	31	31	common
Ear drainage tubes	9	6	6
Meningitis	2	2	
Pneumonia	6	8	
Urinary tract reflux/infection	2	6	
Hepatitis	1	–	
Seizures	2	1	
Hypotonia (at least early on)	31	31	most
Hypertonia	16	6	
Poor Coordination	31	31	most
Attention deficit/Hyperkinesis	31	31	most
Self-Stimulation	30	30	>75%
Voice Hypernasality	31	31	
Dental malocclusion	17	16	most
Strabismus/myopia	19	10	>50%

likewise greatly dampened the degree of self-stimulation observed. Although these counter-productive behaviors recur, withdrawal, aggression and frank psychotic behavior are all rare. Most individuals seem friendly and happy; they appear to enjoy their interactions with others.

While all subjects have demonstrated significant cognitive, language and behavioral deficits, the effects of hypoxia and institutionalization have further adversely affected their developmental profiles. On the other hand, home-rearing with early, consistent, multi-disciplinary stimulation has significantly advanced the timetables for developmental achievements and has also improved the levels of ultimate performance. Figure 2 shows some group differences regarding various developmental milestones. It is particularly important to note that no individual totally reared in an institutional setting has developed either speech or any useful vocational skills. In contrast, the use of sign language and alternate communication techniques have encouraged language development and decreased undesirable behavioral outbursts.

The literature has noted lack of speech to be an integral part of the 5p-

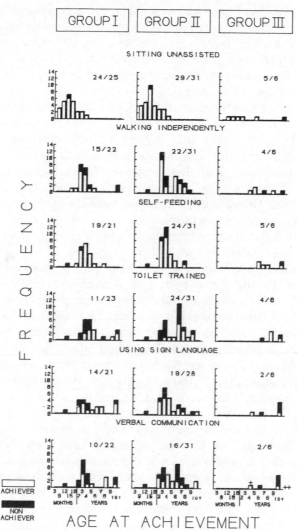

Figure 2.   Distribution by age at attainment of selected developmental skills
in cri-du-chat syndrome study population. Groups I and II are the
longitudinal and cross-sectional groups as outlined previously. Group III contains
6 of the 7 individuals from group I who are institutionalized. The achievers are
those who have mastered the task in the interval between the previous age and
that indicated for the bar. The non-achievers are those who have not yet
acquired that skill by their age at examination as indicated by the bar. The
fraction in the upper right of each graph shows the number of achievers in
comparison to the number in each group for whom the skill is appropriate and
on whom we have data.
† Used signs and words before entering a residential setting.
†† Was reared at home until age of 8 years.

syndrome and has assumed that the severe language deficits have stemmed from the broad cognitive deficits, since most individuals with cri-du-chat syndrome have IQ scores less than 35. Again, however, this current data collected from individuals reared at home, indicates that while language development significantly lags behind all other developmental milestones, early stimulation with particularly intensive language stimulation as well as the early introduction and use of sign language has resulted in the development of speech in 50% and the use of signs to communicate in 75%. Of course, signing has not been taught to everyone in this study, and the age at its acquisition and use is inversely proportional to the age at first exposure. These acquisition ages range from 2 to 20 years, but, notably, none of the children who were institutionalized before speech emerged have developed it subsequently, and even the use of signing in these settings is irregular, sparse or absent. Peak results have occurred in those who were introduced to signing between 2 and 5 years of age.

Longitudinal follow-up and analysis of the successful language development in the home-reared individuals have shown that such maturation proceeds along a predictable developmental pathway. Receptive recognition with some reciprocal behavior responses occur initially, followed rapidly by the use of various non-verbal communication methods such as pointing and pulling. These are sometimes accompanied with vocalizations. These non-verbal messages then increase in number, variety and complexity. Enthusiastic parents often report these poorly articulated phonemes as words. But, in reality, actual verbalizations and words emerge very slowly.

If signing is introduced early and used consistently most pre-school children will begin to incorporate signs into their communication repertoire. Other techniques such as the use of a communication board or a simple electronic or voice-augmented communication program have been successfully utilized by several of our school-aged children. Computer keyboard overlays utilizing these pictures and symbols then allow many of the older children and adults to use computers and various educational software packages. As verbalizations appear the alternating or concomitant use of both verbal and non-verbal methods is the rule. However, with the continued emergence of speech, there is usually a gradual decrease in signing. While speech therapy has often improved the articulation, inflection and projection, the characteristic, relatively high-pitched, monochromatic voice timbre has remained. The ultimate level of total communication skills has varied widely, but has always fallen short of exclusive verbal speech. Some form(s) of expanded communication techniques have been required by all.

Expectedly, the use of sign language and the various alternate communication techniques have encouraged language development,

Table 3. Vocational potential in cri-du-chat syndrome

Of the 10 patients above 10 years of age, 5 have been in various vocational settings.

None of the institutionalized individuals have developed vocational skills.

The various vocational settings have included:
- ○ Stuffing envelopes with promotional materials
- ○ Sorting small items for packaging
- ○ Placing dry cleaned clothes in bags
- ○ Gardening at an outdoor nursery
- ○ Making straw pictures, ornaments and wreaths

Additional skills seen:
- ○ Primer level word recognition or reading
- ○ Identify coins; count change
- ○ Read digital clocks and understand time concepts
- ○ Help with cooking, cleaning and household maintenance
- ○ Maintain personal hygiene

Vocational training should be part of each child's Individualized Educational Program (IEP)

decreased behavioral outbursts, and improved social and learning interaction. They have also facilitated the earlier introduction of vocational training and expanded the available vocational settings. In this study, one-half of the non-institutionalized individuals above 10 years of age are in vocational settings and 50% of those use some degree of verbal communication there. Table 3 highlights these vocational settings and skills.

The mortality, except for those with major anomalies or accidents, has been very low. It is summarized in Table 4. None of the remaining adolescent or adult patients in the 2 study groups have any serious health problems that currently threaten their longevity.

DISCUSSION

In recalling the devastating impact of learning about their child's diagnosis and its implications, parents of children with cri-du-chat syndrome repeatedly note that it was especially overwhelming for them to cope initially because of the dire, hopeless predictions they were given regarding their child's future. They plead for a more accurate picture coupled with specific information about intervention strategies they should employ. The recent data is quite clear. There is a direct correlation between home-rearing with the early introduction of psycho-motor and language stimulation and the ultimate level of functional

Table 4.   Mortality data in cri-du-chat syndrome

Wilkins et al. (1982)	Group I (longitudinal)	Group II (cross-sectional)
7 deaths:	3 deaths:	No deaths
2 at <6 mths – cardiac and respiratory problems	Female at 6 yrs 9 mths – pneumonia (Institutionalized)	
4 during childhood – 2 following intestinal surgery	Female at 8 yrs 9 mths – drowning (Residential school)	
2 with pneumonia	Female at 13 yrs 5 mths – congestive heart failure secondary to congenital heart disease (Institutionalized)	
1 at age 20 – cause unidentified		
Morbidity and mortality higher in those with unbalanced translocations		

achievement. Families should also be encouraged to teach and use sign language as early as the child is at all receptive and imitative, and to introduce other communication and learning techniques as the child progresses. Later educational planning should incorporate the entire communications repertoire into active vocational training as well.

It should be encouraging to these parents to know that the risks of major organ anomalies and decreased survival are low. Although the incidence of congenital anomalies and the mortality figures were higher in the previous study by Wilkins (1982a), 20% of those patients had an unbalanced translocation with either extra genetic material or other deletions in addition to the partial 5p monosomy. These individuals had most of the gastrointestinal malformations and 60% of the serious cardiac defects. Additionally, the social quotients and IQ scores were 25 and 18 points lower respectively in this group as well.

The data from this study emphasize that many of the early problems such as poor feeding, severe hypotonia, frequent infections and the very slow growth do gradually improve with age. Parents themselves report that various medical and surgical interventions for such complications as gastroesophageal reflux, orthopedic deformities, middle ear fluid, and malocclusion greatly ameliorate or even eliminate these problem(s). They further note that physical and/or occupational therapy help to counteract the effects of hypotonia and poor coordination.

In summary, the prognosis today for most parameters of health, development and longevity are much more optimistic than those that are presented in the common sources of medical information. These more realistic and hopeful expectations should now be the ones that are shared with parents to assist them in making decisions that are both well-informed and emotionally satisfying. This more favorable outlook should also be promulgated to all professionals providing services to these individuals and their families.

REFERENCES

Carlin, M. E. (1988) Longitudinal Data Shows Improved Prognosis in Cri-du-Chat Syndrome. *Am. J. Hum. Genet.* **41**: A50.

Carlin, M. E. and Carver, V. H. (1984) 19 Week Foetus with Terminal 5p Deletion Demonstrates Many Neonatal Features of Cri-du-Chat Syndrome. Program for 17th Annual Birth Defects Conference. Abs. no. 27.

Lejeune, J., Lafourcade, J., Berger, R., Violette, J., Boeswillwald, M. Serginge, P. and Turpin, R. (1963) Trois Cas de Deletion Partielle du 13ras Court d'un Chromosome 5. *C.R. Acad. Sc. (Paris)* **257**: 3098–3102.

Wilkins, L. E. (1981) The Cri-du-Chat Syndrome: Population Demographics, Prometaphase *Chromosome Analysis and Karyotype – Phenotype Correlations* (Ph.D. Dissertation). MCV Press, Richmond.

Wilkins, L. E., Brown, J. A. and Wolf, B. (1981) Psychomotor Development in 65 Home-reared Children with Cri-du-Chat Syndrome. *J. Ped.* **97**: 401–405.

Wilkins, L. E., Brown, J. A., Nance, W. E. and Wolf, B. (1982a) Clinical Heterogeneity in 86 Home-reared Children with the Cri-du-Chat Syndrome. *J. Ped.* **102**: 528–533.

Wilkins, L. E., Brown, J. A., Wolf, B., and Nance, W.E. (1982b) *The Cri-du-Chat Syndrome* (Monograph). MCV Press, Richmond.

Maternal Hyperphenylalaninemia in Israel

B. E. Cohen, M. Normand, I. Peled,
Y. Blonder, M. Tumarkin, A. Elitzur and
R. Hadar

*The Chaim Sheba Medical Center, Sackler School of Medicine,
Tel Aviv University, Israel*

Four pregnancies have been described in which dietary treatment was started prior to conception with satisfactory results for the offspring as opposed to five others where lack of dietary control produced mental retardation, microcephaly, low birth weight and congenital abnormalities. Even milder cases of hyperphenylalaninemia have to be monitored during every pregnancy to avoid dangerous levels of phenylalanine especially in the first trimester. In one of our cases a level of 12–15 mg% was thought to have produced a damaged infant. Regular checking of weekly blood phenylalanine and tyrosine levels is desirable in addition to periodic checks of trace metals, U.S. (ultra-sound) and other routine measurements.

A marked increase in phenylalanine tolerance was noted from 500 mg to 1500 mg/day so that compliance becomes easier during later stages of pregnancy. Assistance in compliance should be provided by the marital partner or other family members so that discussions prior to conception are desirable.

Since Mabry's *et al.* original description in 1963, it has been known that pregnancy in women with Classical Phenylketonuria (PKU) was associated with special risks for the fetus. The risks of untreated hyperphenylalaninemia however were brought to our attention by the classic publications of Lenke and Levy (1980) who showed that all hyperphenylalaninemic women should be carefully monitored in order to avoid damage to their fetuses. The extent of this danger has been vividly brought to light by the publications of Levy and Waisbren (1983) Drogari *et al.* (1987). Several publications have suggested that starting the diet even in the first trimester would not prevent congenital abnormalities (Murphy *et al.*, 1985; Smith *et al.*, 1979) although the mental retardation might be prevented and the only safe means of conducting these pregnancies would be pre-conceptual dietary control to reduce blood phenylalanine levels before pregnancy starts. Several reports have indicated success by these methods (Murphy *et al.*, 1985; Farquhar *et al.*, 1987; Bush and Dukes, 1985; Rohr *et al.*, 1987) but the problem of identifying these women and persuading them to start adequate dietary control and maintain it throughout the pregnancy has proved difficult.

We therefore felt it would be useful to present our experience with hyperphenylalaninemic women – both classical PKU and a typical PKU or High hyperphenylalaninemias (HPAs) in Israel. When the first publications of Lenke and Levy appeared, we tried to re-contact all our known females with PKU in order to warn them of the dangers. It then appeared that several women had already given birth to children without any dietary control so they were invited up for investigation.

Table 1 shows the details of three women with classical PKU who had given birth to 5 children without any dietary control. (Cohen *et al.*, 1986). These cases have been published previously but we now include a longer follow up. All have sub-normal I.Q.'s. Two were amenable to dietary advice if it had been offered, as was shown by later contacts with these women. In subject N.M., a subsequent effort at diet had been partly successful but was abandoned when the marriage broke up. All children were microcephalic with low birth weights and their facial appearance showed the features of the fetal alcohol syndrome as described by Lipson *et al.*, 1984, although there had been no exposure to alcohol during the pregnancy.

The two HPA women were partially controlled with blood phenyl-alanine levels and some protein restriction, but at that time we were unaware of the dangers of these lower phenylalanine levels, so that a stricter diet was not insisted on. As previously reported in the four pregnancies monitored, in only one (the second of S.N.(Z)) were blood phenylalanine levels of over 10 mg% recorded in the first trimester, and in this case a mildly affected infant was observed.

Table 2 – shows the three mothers who were carefully monitored during their four pregnancies which only commenced after the blood phenylalanine levels had been adequately controlled and who were all delivered of normal infants.

Case 1 – A.R. – identified originally by a retarded PKU sibling. She was clinically and biochemically a classical PKU with blood phenylalanine levels over 20 mg% on normal diet but although not treated dietetically in infancy, she was only border-line retarded and socially functioned well as indicated by her Vineland score of 90 (Doll, 1965). With the active assistance of her husband she was able to manage the diet excellently. During her first pregnancy she had several blood phenylalanine levels above 10 mg% in the first two months but at 6 weeks she had a

Table 1. Biochemical and clinical data on mothers and offspring with maternal hyperphenylalaninemia

Type	Name and IQ	Blood phe.	Mothers Urinary ketones	Blood tyr.	Previous abortions	No. of children
PKU Untreated	D.M.–72	25.6	+	–	–	1
	N.M.–75	30.6	+	1.4	1	1
	S.B.–55	20–30	+	–	3	3
High HPA	S.N.(Z)–65	6–14	–	1.0–3.4	–	3
	Z.N.(S)–95	8–12	–	1.2	–	2

Mother's name	Head circ.	Birth weight	Offspring Cong. heart disease	Other cong. abnorm.	Age at last visit	IQ/DQ
D.M.	31	2700	–	–	2.6	60
	28.9	2200	–	–	1.2	25
S.B.	30	2790	–	–	6.6	48
	29	2700	–	S.D.*	4.9	32
	28	2200	–	Crypt.** E.A.	1.1	25
S.N.(Z)	35.5	2980	–	–	5.0	102
	31.5	3130	–	–	3.6	76
	32.3	3580	–	–	0.7	n
Z.N.(S)	31.3	2090	–	–	2.9	110
	32.3	2280	–	–	2.9	110

spontaneous abortion – possibly related to these raised levels. She discontinued her diet for three months during which time her blood phenylalanine rose to 19.5 mg% with urine positive for phenyl-pyruvic acid etc.

She restarted her diet with 500 mg phenylalanine per day and once again became pregnant. This time her control was better and of 29 bloods only two were above 10 mg% in the first trimester (12.6 and 10.9 mg%). Her phenylalanine intake, which started at 500 mg/day was increased as the blood levels fell and reached 1000 mg/day by the second trimester and by the end of the third trimester was up to 1500 mg/day.

Tyrosine levels varied between 1.2–1.9 mg% but extra tyrosine was not available. Ultra-sound examination at 13th and 25th weeks were normal. At 41 weeks she was delivered of a normal male infant weighing 3300 g, with head circumference of 33.5 cm and length 48.5 cm, Apgar at 1″ – 9 at 5″ – 10. Physical examination and U.S. (ultrasound) of brain, chest and abdomen were normal.

At delivery the maternal blood phenylalanine was 10 mg% and tyrosine – 1.6 mg% whereas the cord blood was phenylalanine – 13.9 mg% with a tyrosine of 1.8 mg% – a ratio of 1:1.4 (phe.).

Subsequent to delivery she was kept on the identical restricted diet and her daily maternal blood phenyalalanine levels rose to 10.7–11.5–13.6 and 15.9 mg% in spite of poor appetite.

Follow-up of this boy at 3.9 yrs showed a normally developed infant with an I.Q. of 107 (Stanford-Binet-Terman & Merrill, 1973) with excellent social maturity (Vineland – 130).

After one year they decided on a further pregnancy and recommenced the restricted diet with 500 mg phenylalanine per day. Within a week her levels dropped below 10 mg% (9.4) and when subsequent weekly levels were maintained below 10 mg% contraceptive measures were discontinued. Within two months she became pregnant. Control during this pregnancy was even better and all her weekly bloods (39) were below 10 mg%. The mean and median figures are shown in the table.

Ultra-sound at the 18th, 21st and 28th weeks were normal with head and abdominal circumferences at the 50th percentile. SMAC and trace metals after 4 months on the diet during the second month of her pregnancy were normal.

After an uneventful pregnancy she was delivered of a normal boy weighing 2980 g at 41 weeks with head circumference of 33 cm and no congenital abnormalities on physical and ultra-sound examination of head, heart and abdomen. Once again her phenylalanine tolerance rose from 500 mg/day to 1000–1500 mg/day at each trimester.

At delivery the maternal phenylalanine was 6.1 mg% whereas the cord blood was 11.5 mg% with tyrosines of 1.6 and 2.1 mg% – an almost 2:1 phenylalanine ratio. Her daily phenylalanine levels were 8.7–8.9–

15.4 mg% on the identical restricted diet but her appetite was poor. After a normal meal two days later her blood phenylalanine reached 21.6 mg%. Follow up of this infant at 1.8 yrs, showed normal development with a Bayley (1969) – of 108 (Performance) and 91 (motor). His social maturity was also excellent – 100 on Vineland.

Both infants had normal phenylalanine blood levels following delivery and subsequently, and are hence heterozygotes.

Case 2 – A.C. – diagnosed as classical PKU at three months due to an affected retarded sibling and treatment started. She was one of the first cases treated by our unit and was adequately controlled for about 8 yrs when diet was discontinued. Her I.Q. then was 72! When aged 20 yrs maternal PKU was discussed and again when marriage was imminent. After their marriage an attempt at diet was unsuccessful as no family was then planned. Subsequently when they decided on a family, compliance was better and after 5 months acceptable levels were obtained. Contraceptive measures were discontinued and three months later she became pregnant. Her phenylalanine intake was 500 mg/day but in the first trimester the levels were rather higher than we had planned with four levels above 10 mg% (12.6, 13, 13.9, 15.2 mg%) and the mean was 11.1 mg% whereas the next two trimesters had means of 6.3 and 4.2 mg%.

As in the previous case her phenylalanine tolerance started at 500 mg/day rising to 1000 mg at the end of the first trimester, 1500 mg a day at the second and 1800 mg/day at term.

Trace metals, although taken several times, were only reported on once two months after the start of dietary therapy when zinc was 85 micrograms% which is the lower limit of normal for our laboratory. Tyrosine supplement was not available. Serum proteins were normal (6.8–7.4 g%). Ultra-sound was performed at 20–22–24–28–29–31–32–34 weeks. Fetal head circumference, which started at the 50th percentile decreased to the 10th percentile at the 22nd and 24th week examinations. At the 28th week it fell just below 10th percentile and hence monitored weekly thereafter even though it returned to the 10th percentile at 29 weeks and remained there until term. Abdominal circumference was on the 50th percentile throughout. The phenylalanine levels were satisfactory through the second and final trimester (see Table 2).

At 37 weeks she was delivered of a normal male infant weighing 2260 g, head circumference 30.5 cm (appropriate for gestational age) and length 46 cm. Physical and U.S. examination of chest, head and abdomen were normal. At delivery the maternal phenylalanine level was 12.7 mg% and her cord blood 25 mg% with tyrosines of 1.0 and 3.5 respectively.

Following delivery on the same restricted diet (1800 mg/day) her phenylalanine levels rose daily to 8.8–12.7–13.9–17.2–19.8–23.3 mg%.

Table 2. Biochemical and clinical data on pregnancies and offspring in maternal PKU

Mother's name	No. of bloods	Phenylalanine levels mean (mg%)	median	Pregnancies Length of diet	S.B.'s or abortions	Cord phe./yr.	Maternal phe./yr.	No. of bloods over 10 mg%
R.S.	26	9.2 4.4–3.1 5.3	4.3	23/12	1	14/1.9	7.4/1.0	1
A.C.	30	11.9 6.8–6.3 4.2	6.6	19/12	–	25/3.5	12.7/1.0	4
A.R.	29	7.8 5.0–3.4 4.3	4.2	29/12	2	13.9/1.8	10/1.6	2
	39	6.6 5.2–3.1 5.6	5.0	12/12	–	11.5/2.1	6.1/1.6	–

Mother's name and IQ	Head circum. at birth	Gestational age	Birth weight	Offspring Length	Cong. heart disease	Other cong. abnorm.	Age at last visit	DQ/IQ
R.S. – 65	32	37	2370	–	–	–	1 yr.	88/92(B)
A.C. – 75	30.5	37	2260	46	–	–[a]	1 yr.	71/57-(B)
V – 95	1 – 33.5	41	3300	48.5	–	–	3 yr.	93-(S.B.)
A.R.								
P – 75	2 – 33	41	2980	–	–	–	1 yr.	101/98-(B)

[a] Neonatal Aspergillosis at 6 weeks – Chronic Granulomatous Disease.

After return to normal diet her levels rose to 43 mg% – much higher than her usual levels not on diet possibly due to "protein guzzling" or temporary inactivation of any residual phenylalanine hydroxylase activity. During this period she appeared more confused than usual and her cognitive function, which had appeared better during pregnancy, again regressed. Unfortunately this was not measured but was our impression.

The infant's subsequent development was marked by a failure to thrive and at 6 weeks he was hospitalised. Neonatal aspergillosis was diagnosed and treated by prolonged intra-venous amphotericin. He recovered completely after six months treatment but his progress was marked by recurrent infections so that eventually chronic granulomatous disease (non sex-linked type) was diagnosed. At one year his motor development on Bayley exam was only 55 but performance was 78 – probably attributable to his prolonged hospitalisation and immobility. At 1 year 9 months his motor development was unchanged whereas his performance had deteriorated somewhat – 62. His social quotient was 76 suggesting he had not attained his maximum and the social inadequacy of his mother (Vineland – 69) suggested inadequate home stimulation. Steps have been taken to rectify this.

Case 3 – R.S. – diagnosed at 2½ yrs as classical PKU because of retardation. She was treated for the next 4 yrs but the diet was discontinued due to lack of compliance. At this time her I.Q. fluctuated between 60–70. Efforts at diet prior to marriage proved hopeless. Following her marriage, in spite of our grave doubts, she and her husband, also moderately retarded, by virtue of meticulous recording of all food intake, managed to achieve adequate compliance and after blood phenylalanine levels of below 10 mg% were achieved, contraceptive measures were discontinued. After 14 months on diet, during which time she also had a spontaneous abortion, she again became pregnant, During this pregnancy 29 weekly bloods were received with only one over 10 mg% early on. She had satisfactory mean levels during all three trimesters (9.2–3.1–5.3 mg%). She also started with a tolerance of 500 mg phenylalanine per day rising to 800 mg/day by the second trimester and 1550 mg/day by the end of the third trimester. At 37 weeks she had a spontaneous delivery of a normal female infant weighing 2370 g with head circumference of 32 cms and no abnormalities on physical and ultra-sound examination.

Maternal blood phenylalanine at delivery was 7.4 mg% with a cord blood of 14 mg% and tyrosines of 1.0 and 1.9 respectively.

In spite of her poor appetite on the identical restricted intake (1550 mg) her blood phenylalanine levels rose daily to 8.6–11.0–13.9–15.4–18.7 mg%. One month after discontinuation her level was 47.5 mg% – higher than it had ever been on normal diet.

Table 3. Psychological evaluation of PKU mothers and offspring

Name	Age yrs	Offspring IQ/DQ	Motor DQ	Social IQ (Vineland)
Y.S.	1.10	96	84	90
E.C.	1.9	62	54	76
L.R.	1.8	108	91	100
S.R.	3.9	107	–	130

Name	Age yrs	Mothers Last IQ (WISC)	Social IQ (Vineland)
R.S.	26	66	69
A.C.	26	72	69
A.R.	32	75-P -73	90
A.R.	32	95-V	90

The infant's blood phenylalanine was normal on repeated examination and follow up showed normal development (See Table 3). Performance – 96 Motor 84 and Social – 90 (Vineland).

DISCUSSION

All these women were mildly to moderately retarded as none of them had started diet soon after birth and A.C. (Case 2) the earliest to start had discontinued at 8 years. They were all known to us and we were thus able to make contact with them prior to marriage and warn them of the consequences of unplanned conception. In spite of their intellectual handicaps they were all able to follow the diet adequately and we were surprised at the ease with which they adapted to the diet and accepted the relatively unpleasant taste and smell of the low phenylalanine preparation used (Lofenalac or Phenylfree). Their motivation in wanting a family was the prime factor as well as the support of their husband in maintaining the diet. Prior efforts without these factors had been unsatisfactory. This is important in discussing maternal PKU with adolescent girls who might hesitate about informing their spouse about this disease.

In all cases phenylalanine tolerance started at 500 mg/day during the period when the dietary control was the most difficult. Subsequently, as the blood phenylalanine levels dropped, we were able to increase the phenylalanine intake to 1000 mg at the second trimester and 1500 mg daily by the third trimester or more. This means that the diet becomes progressively easier for them – a factor which should encourage them during the difficult first trimester. In our cases the infants were all heterozygotes so that much of this increased phenylalanine tolerance might be attributed to the fetal phenylalanine hydroxylase activity – a theory that gains some support from the increasing maternal phenylalanine levels immediately after delivery on the same restricted phenylalanine intake. It is unlikely the utilisation of the phenylalanine by the fetus for protein body-building could account for this increased tolerance.

Another phenomenon was the marked "overshoot" of the phenylalanine levels in the mothers after discontinuing the diet – probably due to protein "guzzling" but possibly temporary inactivation of the residual phenylalanine hydroxylase activity in the mother. The improvement in their cognitive functioning, alertness and motivation also mentioned by Murphy *et al.* (1985) was also noted but unfortunately not tested, and hence not documented.

All the infants were normal at birth and have showed normal physical and intellectual development except for Case 2 (E.C.). In this case the diet was less adequate than the others in the first trimester. The chronic granulomatous disease caused repeated infections and hospitalisations with immobility due to the infusions so that the motor delay is partly explained. The intellectual functioning was much closer to normal and the Vineland social quotient suggests that his failure to reach his potential might be related to inadequate stimulation by his mother who also shows limited capacity in this field. Steps have been taken to start an infant stimulation program to overcome this. It is doubtful whether these findings can be attributed to maternal PKU.

None of the infants showed raised phenylalanine levels after birth although their mothers still had raised phenylalanine levels. Possibly the stimulation of their phenylalanine hydroxylase activity during pregnancy helped them clear their bloods rapidly before testing. It appears that preconceptual dietary control can prevent most if not all the damage of maternal hyperphenylalaninemia especially of the severe variety. There are still however many unsolved questions. Regular monitoring of phenylalanine, tyrosine, protein, trace metals, ultra-sound, etc. are needed if we hope to prevent the serious consequences. Cord blood and maternal blood measurements are essential to estimate the danger of the maternal-fetal ratio.

The main challenge before us is to reach all the adolescent girls with hyperphenylalaninemia that might need monitoring, inform them of the dangers and see that they understand the importance of planning their pregnancies only after dietary control is adequately established. In order to achieve maximum support from their marital partners this subject should be discussed freely with them – possibly before their marriage. This has been presented by our group (Cohen *et al.*, 1988) in the form of group discussions with these adolescent girls and their mothers. It is also important to look at the psycho-social factors that make pre-conceptual dietary treatment such a problem.

REFERENCES

Bayley, N. (1969) *Manual for the Bayley scales of Infant Development*, New York, The Psychological Corp.

Bush, R. T., Dukes, P.C. (1985) Women with phenylketonuria: a successful management of pregnancy and implications – *New Zealand Med. J.* **98**, 775, 181–183.

Cohen, B. E., Szeinberg, A., Zarfin, Y., Normand, M., Peled, I., Blonder, Y., Elitzur, A., Hadar, R., and Mashiach, S. (1986) Maternal hyperphenyl-alaninemia in Israel – *J. Inher. Metab. Dis.* **9**, **Suppl. 2**, 227–230.

Cohen, B. E., Weiss, R., Hadar, R., Normand, M., Shiloh, S., and Elhanani, D. (1988) Group work with adolescent PKU girls and their mothers – *J. Inher. Metab. Dis.* **11**: 199–206.

Drogari, E., Smith, I., Beasley, M. and Lloyd, J. K. (1987) Timing of strict diet in relation to fetal damage in Maternal Phenylketonuria – *Lancet* **2**, 927–930, V.-8565.

Doll, E. A. (1965) – *The Vineland Social Maturity Scale – Manual* (Revised Ed.) – Minneapolis Educational Test Bureau.

Farquhar, D. L., Simpson, G. K., Steven, F., Munro, J. F. and Farquhar, J. W. (1987) Pre-conceptual dietary management for Maternal Phenylketonuria – *Acta Paediat. Scand.* **76**: 279–283.

Lenke, R. R. and Levy, H. L. (1980) Maternal phenylketonuria and hyper-phenylalaninemia: an international survey of the outcome of untreated and treated pregnancies – *New Engl. J. Med.* **303**, 1202–1208.

Levy, H. L. and Waisbren, S. (1983) Effects of untreated maternal phenyl-ketonuria and hyperphenylalaninemia on the fetus – *New Eng. J. Med.* **309**: 1269–1274.

Lipson, A., Beuhler, B., Barley, J., Walsh, D., Yu, J., O'Halloran, M., and Webster, W. (1984) maternal hyperphenylalaninemia fetal effects – *J. Pediat.* **104**: 216–220.

Mabry, C. C., Denniston, J. C., Nelson, T. L., Son, C. D. (1963) Maternal phenylketonuria: a cause of mental retardation in children without the metabolic defect – *New Eng. J. Med.* **269**: 1404–1408.

Murphy, D., Saul, I., and Kirby, M. (1985) Maternal phenylketonuria and phenylalanine restricted diet: studies of 7 pregnancies and offsprings produced – *Irish J. Med. Sci.* **154**: 2, 66–70.

Rohr, F. J., Dohert, L. B., Waisbren, S. E., Bailey, I. V., Amplola, M. G., Benecerraf, B. and Levy, H. L. (1987) New England Maternal PKU Project: Prospective study of untreated and treated pregnancies and their outcomes – *J. of Ped.* **110**: 391–398.

Scott, T. M., Fyfe, W. M., Hart, D. M. (1980) Maternal phenylketonuric abnormal baby despite low phenylalanine diet during pregnancy *Arch. Dis. Child.* **55**: 634–649.

Smith, I., Erdohazi, M., Macartney, F. J., Pincott, J. R., Wolff, O. H., Brenton, D. P., Biddle, S. A., Fairweather, D. V. & Dobbing, J. (1979) Fetal damage despite low phenylalanine diet after conception in a phenyl-ketonuric woman – *Lancet* **1**, 8106, 17–19.

Terman, L. M. and Merrill, M. A. (1973) *Stanford Binet Intelligence Scale-Manual*, Boston, Houghton-Mifflin Corp.

Application of Valine, Isoleucine and Leucine (VIL) to Treatment of Phenylketonuria

H. K. Berry[1], R. L. Brunner[1], M. M. Hunt[1] and P. P. White[2]

[1]*University of Cincinnati College of Medicine and Children's Hospital Medical Center, Cincinnati, Ohio 45229 USA*
[2]*Metabolic Disease Center, Children's Hospital Medical Center, Cincinnati, Ohio 45229 USA*

Investigators have observed adverse behavioural changes, impaired neuropsychological performance, impaired choice-reaction time, deficits in visual-motor integration and cognitive problem-solving, and IQ deficits in patients with PKU following termination of dietary treatment. Successful reinstatement of the low-PHE diet has been difficult or impossible to achieve.

In human trials with two adolescents, motor and cognitive functioning improved with the addition of VIL to their low-PHE diet. The improvement was not sustained during periods off VIL. In a subsequent study, measurements of PHE concentrations in serum and cerebrospinal fluid (CSF) before and after VIL administration showed reductions in CSF PHE of 15% to 40% compared to pre-VIL concentrations, although serum PHE concentrations were unaffected. Neuropsychological test performance of six patients showed improvement in abstract reasoning and motor problem-solving during VIL treatment. Recently a multi-centre, double-blind study was completed of VIL effects in adolescents and young adults with PKU. Significant improvement in timed visual-attentional processing was obtained. All these data point to significant health benefit from VIL as a supplemental treatment for individuals with PKU.

Phenylketonuria (PKU) is an inherited metabolic disorder in which the activity of phenylalanine hydroxylase, the enzyme responsible for conversion of phenylalanine to tyrosine, is absent or drastically reduced (Jervis, 1953; Kaufman and Max, 1971). Treatment for PKU consists of restriction of phenylalanine in the diet to effect reductions of phenylalanine and/or its metabolites in the brain (Bickel *et al.* (1953); Armstrong and Tyler, 1955). Untreated PKU usually results in progressive mental deterioration and measured intelligence (IQ) < 50 (Jervis 1963). Treatment must begin before three months of age and continue throughout early childhood to prevent irreversible structural and functional damage to the brain (Hudson *et al.* 1970; Smith and Wolff, 1974; Brunner *et al.* 1983). During the more than 20 years since new-born screening for PKU became effective, a considerable population of early treated adolescent and young adult patients has accumulated.

The success of low phenylalanine diets in preventing or ameliorating the deleterious effects of high plasma phenylalanine levels on individuals born with PKU had gradually given rise to new problems. After treated individuals are past the most critical stages of brain development, and the phenylalanine restricted diet is relaxed or terminated, they experience toxic reactions to their high plasma phenylalanine levels. The effects are acute in that they are directly correlated to plasma phenylalanine concentrations and are usually reversible if a phenylalanine restricted diet can be reinstated.

Brunner *et al.* (1983) showed significant deficits in IQ and achievement tests between early treated PKU patients and their unaffected siblings. Using a battery of neuropsychological measures sensitive to brain dysfunction, they found a pattern of neuropsychological deficits, the degree of which was negatively correlated to current serum phenylalanine concentration as well as to serum phenylalanine levels during one and two years prior to testing. Krause *et al.* (1985) found that plasma phenylalanine concentrations greater than 1.3 mM (21 mg%) were associated with impaired performance on tests of highly integrative neuropsychological function, particularly choice reaction time. These effects were fully reversible by lowering serum phenylalanine levels. Seashore *et al.* (1985) described decrease in mean IQ from 104 to 90 after periods off diet of 4 to 7 years. Most children showed deficits in visual-motor integration or cognitive problem solving. Holtzman *et al.* (1986), evaluating the PKU Collaborative Study population, found significant differences in IQ scores at ages 8 and 10 years between PKU subjects off diet since 6 or 8 years compared to their parents, unaffected siblings, or PKU subjects who remained on diet.

Increased serum phenylalanine concentrations may be from deliberate liberalization of the diet or failure to adhere strictly to the dietary regimen. The low phenylalanine diet is relatively easily maintained during periods of rapid growth in infancy and early childhood. During adolescence and adulthood, as somatic growth slows and the utilization of phenylalanine decreases, it becomes increasingly difficult to achieve and maintain low serum phenylalanine concentrations by dietary restriction alone (Hunt *et al.* 1985), and dietary control, once lost, is difficult or impossible to reinstate. Michals *et al.* (1985) found that of 43 PKU patients returned to diet therapy, 23 were unable to maintain dietary restrictions after a trial of 1 to 6 months. Hogan *et al.* (1986), after a trial with reinstatement of diet in adolescents with PKU, concluded that in the absence of a powerful external motivating factor, compliance with the dietary regimen was virtually impossible to maintain.

A counter-treatment to prevent the behavioral changes that frequently accompany dietary deregulation was suggested by the recognition that PHE and other large neutral amino acids (LNAA) share common receptor sites on a blood-brain barrier transport system (Oldendorf, 1973; Anderson *et al.*, 1976; Pardridge, 1983). Administration of other LNAA to patients with elevated plasma phenylalanine concentrations may reduce the amount of phenylalanine reaching the brain and prevent some of the toxic of phenylalanine on the central nervous system.

Induction of PKU in pregnant rats by combined feeding of an excess (3%) of phenylalanine and an inhibitor of phenylalanine hydroxylase (p-chlorophenylalanine) produced lower fetal brain weight, reduced fetal body weight, and maze learning deficits in the offspring (Butcher, 1970; Berry *et al.*, 1977). Fetal brain weight was a reliable indicator of intrauterine damage and was used as an index of the degree to which dietary supplements of large neutral amino acids moderated the abnormalities associated with experimentally induced PKU (Brunner *et al.*, 1978).

Fetuses from PKU animals fed a supplement of valine, isoleucine, and leucine (VIL) had brain weights in the range of pair-fed control animals, while fetuses from PKU animals fed tryptophan or methionine had lower brain weights, comparable to fetuses from mothers fed the PKU inducing diet alone. The VIL supplement resulted in approximately 30% increase in the concentrations of valine, isoleucine, and leucine in brain and plasma of PKU-VIL animals compared to PKU animals. Phenylalanine concentrations in blood were in the same range, but phenylalanine content of brain of PKU-VIL fetuses was reduced to 64% of that found in PKU fetal brain (Table 1).

In a subsequent experiment with adult rats we showed that VIL-treated hyperphenylalaninemic animals had significantly better performance in a complex water maze than PKU animals without VIL supplementation (McSwigan *et al.*, 1981).

In short-term trials with two adolescents motor and cognitive functioning improved with the addition of VIL to their low-phenylalanine diet (Berry *et al.*, 1977). Anderson and Avins (1976) had shown that increasing serum levels of amino acids which competed with phenyl-alanine for transport across the blood brain barrier lowered brain phenylalanine in hyperphenylalaninemic rats and reduced the brain-serum phenylalanine ratios. We extended the observations to children

Table 1. Effect of VIL supplement amino acid concentration in brain and plasma of fetal rats exposed to experimentally induced PKU

Amino acid	Plasma μmol/liter		Brain μmol/gram	
	PKU	PKU-VIL	PKU	PKU-VIL
Phenylalanine	2452	2408	2460	1586
Valine	229	359	172	225
Isoleucine	91	117	66	94
Leucine	184	195	183	178

Table 2. Change in phenylalanine concentration before and after administration of VIL[a]

Patient	CSF	Serum
1	69	97
2	68	98
3	85	99
4	60	83
5	75	92
6	67	95
Mean	70	94

[a] Calculated at $100 \times \dfrac{\text{post-VIL phenylalanine concentration}}{\text{pre-VIL phenylalanine concentration}}$

with PKU by administering a supplement of VIL to subjects with PKU, both with unrestricted diet of natural protein and with the low-phenylalanine diet (Berry *et al.*, 1982). The dosage of 200 mg/kg L-leucine and 150 mg/kg each of isoleucine and valine was designed to approximately double the amount of branched-chain amino acids in the diet. Phenylalanine was measured in blood and cerebrospinal fluid (CSF) before and after VIL treatment. Changes in serum phenylalanine concentrations were relatively small (Table 2) while the CSF phenylalanine decreased by approximately 30%.

A pilot study was then undertaken to assess whether VIL affected neuropsychological functioning of subjects with PKU and to examine factors that might relate to individual differences in response to VIL (Jordan *et al.*, 1985). Assessment of outcome was by a battery of neuropsychological tests which were sensitive to changes in the phenylalanine concentrations. Patients were referred because of school and

Table 3. Mean T-scores on neuropsychological
tests

Patient	Pre-VIL	Post-VIL	Change
1	5.2	20.6	+15.5
2	29.0	45.3	+16.3
3	38.4	49.9	+11.5
4	20.7	44.6	+23.9
5	59.2	65.8	+6.7
6	35.7	54.6	+18.9
Mean			+15.5

family reports of cognitive and behavioral difficulties that may have been related to PKU. The test battery was administered before and after short term trials of administration of VIL, usually 6 weeks to 3 months. All data were converted to standardized scores with a mean of 50 and standard deviation of 10 (Table 3). Mean change from pre- to post-VIL was 15.4, or 1.5 S.D. The smallest change occurred in the patient who had the highest pre-VIL score.

These results encouraged us to begin a comprehensive, randomized, double-blind, placebo-controlled study of the effects of VIL as a counter-treatment for PKU (Berry et al., 1987). The placebo consisted of a mixture of arginine and aspartic acid, substances not known to affect phenylalanine transport.

VIL or the placebo mixture was administered in a random sequence for four periods of 3 months each. No other changes were made in dietary management during the 12 months of the study. Biochemical and neuropsychological tests were carried out before and at the end of each period. The initial phase of the study, which is still on-going, had several objectives. Compliance with the strict low-phenylalanine dietary regimen decreases with time, and motivation on the part of the adolescent or adult with PKU is less than for the parents (Brunner et al. 1987). The first objective was to determine if any treatment regimen could be maintained over a long period. Non-compliance was usually apparent after introduction of the VIL or placebo mixture. More than 25% of subjects were dropped before the end of the first 6 months of a year-long trial.

A second objective was to assess safety of long term administration of valine, isoleucine, and leucine as crystalline L-amino acids. Mean serum phenylalanine concentrations during VIL and placebo periods were not significantly altered from baseline values (Table 4). Mean concentrations of valine, isoleucine, and leucine increased during administration of VIL and were within normal limits during placebo periods (Table 5). Alloisoleucine, an abnormal metabolite of isoleucine, was not detected.

Table 4. Description of subjects (n = 16)

	Mean (S.D.)	Range
Age	15.6 (4)	10–23
IQ score	95 (11)	75–116

Serum phenylalanine – μm		
Baseline	1179 (309)	660–1612
VIL	1200 (285)	624–1715
Placebo	1109 (321)	503–1733

Table 5. Serum amino acids (micromol/L)

Test	Baseline	VIL	Placebo	Normal[a]
Valine	178 ± 47	392 ± 244	210 ± 87	207 ± 80
Isoleucine	48 ± 14	116 ± 98	59 ± 34	63 ± 25
Leucine	87 ± 19	187 ± 150	105 ± 39	126 ± 46
Tyrosine	37 ± 10	39 ± 17	39 ± 14	68 ± 32

[a] Normal ranges: Metabolic Disease Center Laboratory, Children's Hospital Medical Center, Cincinnati, Ohio.

All values for blood urea nitrogen, serum creatinine and serum transaminases were within normal limits and were unchanged by administration of VIL or placebo (Table 6).

A third objective was to test the hypothesis that administration of branched chain amino acids to subjects with PKU who have behavioral or neuropsychological deficits will bring about improvement of the deficits. In this area the study design imposed stringent requirements. Study subjects must have been diagnosed in the newborn period and treated early so that IQ scores were in the normal range (> 80 by standardized tests). The majority of subjects exhibited relatively minor deficits. In earlier studies patients demonstrating the greatest improvements were those with the most significant deficits.

Results of attentional/memory tests are shown in Table 7. The Continuous Performance Test (CPT) (Anderson *et al.*, 1969) is a computer based vigilance task. In the CPT there were more omissions during baseline than during VIL or placebo periods; false alarms (responses to a non-critical signal) were also fewer during VIL than during Baseline or placebo periods; the differences did not achieve statistical significance.

The Randt Memory Test (Randt and Brown, 1983) evaluates primary

Table 6. Summary of biochemical measurement on serum constituents (mean ± S.D.)

Test	Baseline	VIL	Placebo	Normal[a]
Blood Urea Nitrogen				
Mg/dL	12 ± 4	12 ±4	12 ± 5	6–20
Serum Creatinine				
Mg/dL	0.7 ± .3	0.8 ± .2	0.7 ± .2	<1.0
Serum Transaminases				
SGOT IUaca	23 ± 5	21 ± 6	24 ± 11	8–40
SGPT IUaca	12 ± 4	12 ± 5	14 ± 5	3–36

[a] Normal ranges: Chemistry Laboratory, Children's Hospital Medical Center, Cincinnati, Ohio.

Table 7. Attentional and memory tests

Test	Baseline	VIL	Placebo
Continuous Performance Test			
Misses (median)	2.17	.46	1.05
False alarms (median)	5.50	2.33	3.00
Mean response time (msec)	389.4 ± 63.3	380.5 ± 62.2	416.6 ± 125.3
Randt Memory Test			
Total score	137.9 ± 7.1	141.8 ± 8.3	140.8 ± 9.5
Attention Diagnostic Method			
Total time (sec)	437.3 ± 165.5[B]	374.2 ± 136.7[A]	412.4 ± 8.6[B]

[A,B] $p \leq .05$. Scores bearing the same letter or no letter in the superscript were not significantly different.

rote, associative, discourse and incidental memory functions. In the Randt Memory Test there were no treatment-related effects.

The Attention Diagnostic Method (Rutten and Block, 1975) is a task requiring attention and short term memory. The mean times for completion of the ADM task were affected significantly by treatment, indicating better performance with VIL than either placebo or baseline measurements.

Higher order tests which engage more of the subjects' resources simultaneously may be more impaired by elevated phenylalanine. The more complex mental processing requirements of the ADM task may have made it more sensitive to the effects of elevated phenylalanine and thus more responsive to effects of VIL.

The results obtained here were consistent with earlier experiments which indicated improvement in specific cognitive processes on administration of VIL to PKU subjects. VIL counter treatment had a significant beneficial effect on complex visual attention performance. This is the first major effort to improve the treatment of PKU for adolescents and young adults since the introduction of low phenylalanine formulas over 30 years ago.

REFERENCES

Andersen, A. E. and Avins, L. (1976) Lowering brain phenylalanine levels by giving other large neutral amino acids. *Arch. Neurol.* **33**: 684–686.

Anderson, V. E., Siegel, F. S., Fisch, R. O. and Wirt, R. D. (1969) Responses of PKU children on a continuous performance test. *J. Abnormal Psych.* **74**: 358–362.

Armstrong, M. A. and Tyler, F. H. (1955) Studies on phenylketonuria. I. Restricted phenylalanine intake in phenylketonuria. *J. Clin. Invest.* **34**: 565–580.

Berry, H. K., Butcher, R. E., Brunner, R. L., Bray, N. W., Hunt, M. M. and Wharton, C. H. (1977) New approaches to treatment of phenylketonuria. In P. Mittler (ed), Research to Practice in *Mental Retardation*. **Vol. 3**, pp. 229–239. University Park Press, Baltimore.

Berry, H. K., Bofinger, M. K., Hunt, M. M., Phillips, P. P. and Guifoile, M. B. (1982) Reduction of cerebrospinal fluid phenylalanine after oral administration of valine, isoleucine and leucine. *Pediatr. Res.* **16**: 751–755.

Berry, H. K., Brunner, R. L., Hunt, M. M. and White, P. P. (1987) Valine, isoleucine, leucine (VIL): A new treatment for phenylketonuria. *Soc. Neuroscience Abst.* **13** (3): 1598.7.

Bickel, H., Gerrard, J. and Hickmans, E. M. (1953) Influence of phenylalanine intake on phenylketonuria. *Lancet* **2**: 812–813.

Brunner, R. L., Vorhees, C. V., McLean, M. S., Butcher, R. E. and Berry, H. K. (1978) Beneficial effect of isoleucine on fetal brain development in induced phenylketonuria. *Brain Res.* **154**: 191–195.

Brunner, R. L., Jordan, M. K., Berry, H. K. (1983) Early treated phenylketonuria: neuropsychological consequences. *J. Pediatr.* **102**: 831–835.

Brunner, R. L., Brown, E. H. and Berry, H. K. (1987) Phenylketonuria revisited: treatment of adults with behavioral manifestations. *J. Inher. Metab. Dis.* **10**: 171–173.

Butcher, E. R.: Learning impairment associated with maternal phenylketonuria in rats. (1970) *Nature* **226**: 555–556.

Hogan, S. E., Gates, R. D., MacDonald, G. W., Clarke, J. T. R. (1986) Experience with adolescents with phenylketonuria returned to phenylalanine restricted diet. *J. Am. Dietet. Assn.* **86**: 1203–1207.

Holtzman, N. A., Kronmal, R. A., van Doorninck, W., Azen, C., and Koch, R. (1986) Effect of age at loss of dietary control of intellectual performance and behavior of children with phenylketonuria. *N. Engl. J. Med.* **314**: 593–598.

Hunt, M. M., Berry, H. K., White, P. P. 1985. Phenylketonuria, adolescence and diet. *J. Am. Dietet. Assn.* **85**: 1328–1334.

Hudson, F. P., Mordaunt, V. L. and Leahy, I. (1970) Evaluation of treatment begun in first three months of life in 184 cases of phenylketonuria. *Arch. Dis. Child.* **45**: 5–12.

Jervis, G. A. (1953) Phenylpyruvic oligophrenia: deficiency of phenylalanine oxidizing system. *Proc. Soc. Exp. Biol. Med.* **82**: 514–515.

Jervis, G. A. (1963) The clinical picture. In: F. L. Lyman (ed), *Phenylketonuria*. pp. 52–61. Charles C. Thomas, Springfield.

Jordan, M. K., Brunner, R. L., Hunt, M. M. and Berry, H. K. (1985) Preliminary support for the oral administration of valine, isoleucine and leucine for phenylketonuria. *Develop. Med. Child. Neurol.* **27**: 33–39.

Kaufman, S. and Max, E. E. (1971) Studies on the phenylalanine hydroxylating system in human liver and their relationship to pathogenesis of PKU and hyperphenylalaninemia. In H. Bickel, F. P. Hudson, and L. I. Woolf (eds) *Phenylketonuria and Some Other Inborn Errors of Amino Acid Metabolism.* pp. 13–19. George Thieme Verlag, Stuttgart.

Krause, W., Halminski, M., McDonald, L., Dembure, P., Salvo, R., Friedes, D., Elsas, L. (1985). Biochemical and neuropsychological effects of elevated plasma phenylalanine in patients with treated phenylketonuria. *J. Clin. Invest.* **75**: 40–48.

McSwigan, J. D., Vorhees, C. V., Brunner, R. L., Butcher, R. E. and Berry, H. K.: Amelioration of maze deficits from induced hyperphenylalaninemia in adult rats using valine, isoleucine and leucine. *Behavior. Neur. Biol.* **33**: 378–384, 1981.

Michals, K., Dominik, M., Schuett, V., Brown, E., and Matalon, R. (1985) Return to diet therapy in patients with phenylketonuria. *J. Pediatr.* **106**: 933–936.

Oldendorf, W. H. (1973) Saturation of blood brain barrier transport of amino acids in phenylketonuria. *Arch. Neurol.* **28**: 45–48.

Pardridge, W. M. (1983) Brain metabolism: A perspective from the blood-brain barrier. *Physiol. Rev.* **63**: 1481–1535.

Randt, C. T. and Brown, E. R. (1983) *Administration Manual, RANDT Memory Test*. Life Science Associates, Bayport NY.

Rutten, J. W. and Block, J. R. (1975) *The Attention Diagnostic Method: A Test Manual*. Hofstra University, Hempstead, NY.

Seashore, M. R., Friedman, E., Novelly, R. A., Bapat, V. (1985) Loss of intellectual function in children with phenylketonuria after relaxation of dietary phenylalanine restriction. *Pediatrics* **75**: 226–232.

Smith, I. and Wolff, O. H. (1974) Natural history of phenylketonuria and influence of early treatment. *Lancet* **2**: 540–544.

The Postpubertal Fra(X) Male: A Study of the Intelligence and the Psychological Profile of 17 Fra(X) Boys

M. Borghgraef[1], J. P. Fryns[1], R. Van den Bergh[2], K. Pyck[2] and H. Van den Berghe[1]

[1]*Centre for Human Genetics and* [2]*Children's Psychiatry, University of Leuven, U.Z. Gasthuisberg, Herestraat 49, B-3000 Leuven, Belgium*

In this paper we present the results of a psychological study performed on 17 postpubertal fra(X) boys, and compare the results with the findings in a control group of 12 fra(X) negative boys of the same age and the same IQ level. An important finding is the clear shift towards a lower level of intellectual functioning in the postpubertal fra(X) positive males compared to the prepubertal group. In the analysis of the cognitive functions we found a specific decline in school achievement, short term memory and abstraction; better results were obtained for sequential thinking and visuospatial perception. In 70% of the fra(X) boys verbal IQ was higher than performance IQ, but this was also found in the control group. In addition to a global language retardation, more pronounced than in the control group, fra(X) boys presented characteristic speech disturbances like rapid speech rhythm, stuttering and echolalia.

Attention Deficit Hyperkinetic Disorder (ADHD) was twice as common in fra(X) compared to the control group. The ADHD decreases with age in contrast with the autistic behaviour which shows only a mild drop with age. The social functioning in the fra(X) boys was slightly lower than the control group, but their adaptive behaviour was better than expected from their intelligence level.

INTRODUCTION

In the past few years increasing interest was given to the psychological profile of fra(X) males, especially to their intellectual development (for review, see Veenema *et al.*, 1987). Some studies suggested specific patterns of developmental and behavioural problems i.e. autistic features and hyperkinetic behaviour also called Attention Deficit Hyperkinetic Disorder (ADHD) (for review, see Borghgraef *et al.*, 1987).

In a previous study (Borghgraef *et al.*, 1987) we investigated the intellectual level, speech and language development and the presence of ADHD and autism of 23 prepubertal fra(X) boys. This study confirmed that, in comparison to a control group of boys of the same age and of the same IQ with a non-specific type of mental retardation, a distinct pattern of cognitive and emotional dysfunctions can be demonstrated in the fra(X) syndrome. In addition, some of these behavioural patterns were found to be clearly age-dependent. The aim of the present study was to examine a group of postpubertal fra(X) boys (ages between 15 and 22 years) with the help of the same parameters and the same criteria as defined in the previous study.

MATERIAL AND METHODS

Subjects

17 postpubertal fra(X) positive boys between the age of 15 and 22 years, were investigated. In all patients the diagnosis of fra(X) syndrome was confirmed using standard cytogenetic techniques with M199 lymphocyte cultures and screening of 100 cells for the presence of an Xq27.3 fragility (Fryns, 1984).

The results were compared to the findings in 12 fra(X) negative boys of the same age with 'nonspecific mental retardation'. The intellectual level, and the socio-economic origin of both groups of patients were as identical as possible.

Method

As a general rule we used as intelligence test the Wechsler scales (WPPSI, WISC, WAIS) and/or the Terman test (Terman & Merrill, 1973; Wechsler, 1974; Stinissen and Vander Steene, 1981; Van Haasen *et al.*, 1985). In severely mentally retarded males observation and measurement with the BOS-2-30 and the SON were done (Snijders & Snijders-Oomen, 1975; Van der Meulen and Smrkovsky, 1983). The verbal development level was tested with the Reynell scales, and the UTANT test was used for boys with better verbal functioning (Kohnstamm *et al.*, Reynell, 1977).

Diagnostic evaluation of the behavioural problems was made by clinical observation with objective scales. The Attention Deficit Hyperkinetic Disorder was evaluated with the observation list for the evaluation of children with possible Minimal Brain Defect (MBD) (Department of Children's Psychiatry, University of Leuven), and the autistiform behaviour with the Auti-scale (Van Berckelaer-Onnes *et al.*, 1981).

Finally, we used the PAC1 and 2 (Günzburg scale) (Günzburg, 1977) to evaluate the abilities in social functioning and independence.

Table 1. Personal and clinical data of the 17 fra(X) boys

Name	Age (years, months) at investigation	Age at diagnosis (years)	% fra X positive cells	Medical data	IQ level
1. St.B.	15 yrs 6m	11 yrs	18	n.s.[a]	51
2. St.P.	15 yrs 10m	13 yrs	11	epilepsy	25
3. T.A.	16 yrs	13 yrs	8	prematurity	25
4. D.S.	17 yrs 4m	13 yrs	35	n.d.[b]	35
5. S.J.	17 yrs 9m	13 yrs	26	epilepsy pre- and perinatal problems	43
6. D.K.	17 yrs 10m	12 yrs	18	epilepsy	<19
7. V.P.	18 yrs 5m	14 yrs	14	epilepsy	18
8. T.G.	18 yrs 7m	15 yrs	n.d.	n.s.	28
9. V.W.	19 yrs 1m	17 yrs	32	psychiatric syndrome	53
10. M.S.	19 yrs 1m	15 yrs	5	n.s.	35
11. S.R.	19 yrs 4m	16 yrs	20	n.d.	45
12. S.H.	20 yrs	20 yrs	18	n.s.	46
13. V.S.	20 yrs 5m	16 yrs	34	n.s.	74
14. L.E.	20 yrs 9m	17 yrs	7	epilepsy	36
15. V.P.	20 yrs 9m	16 yrs	13	perinatal problems Gilles de la Tourette	36
16. St.St.	21 yrs 7m		27		30
17. V.H.	22 yrs 7m	16 yrs	3	epilepsy	19

[a] no particularity   [b] no data

Table 2. Proportional distribution of both groups of patients in relation to the intellectual level

Intellectual level (IQ distribution)	Fra(X) boys			Control group		
	No.	%	Mean IQ	No.	%	Mean IQ
Mild (52–68)	2	11	63	2	16	52
Moderate (36–51)	5	29	43.5	4	33	46
Severe (35–20)	7	38	30	6	50	30
Profound (<19)	3	16	<19	0	–	–
Total	17		34.4	12		38.5

RESULTS

General, clinical data

In Table 1, we summarized the most important personal and clinical data of the 17 fra(X) boys.

The mean age at diagnosis was 14 years, and the mean percentage of positive fra(X) cells was 18%.

In 11 boys psychomotor retardation was noted by the parents before the age of one year. 8 parents mentioned already some hyperkinetic behaviour in their young child, and 2 others observed autistic features at the same period of age.

The mean IQ of the fra(X) boys was 34.5, and the mean mental age was about 5 years.

Intelligence

The IQ levels in the fra(X) boys were widespread, but the majority had a moderate to severe mental retardation (see Table 2). Two boys were mildly mentally retarded, 5 were moderately retarded, 7 were severely and 3 profoundly mentally retarded. The mean IQ for the group was 34.5.

As a control group we selected 12 boys with non-specific mental retardation of the same age and with the same IQ distribution as the fra(X) positive boys.

We were able to collect longitudinal follow-up data on IQ-testing of 11 fra(X) boys and 9 boys of the control group at different ages. An explicit falling line with a strong correlation between IQ and age was found in the fra(X) group. In the control group IQ levels were much more stable with age (see Fig. 1).

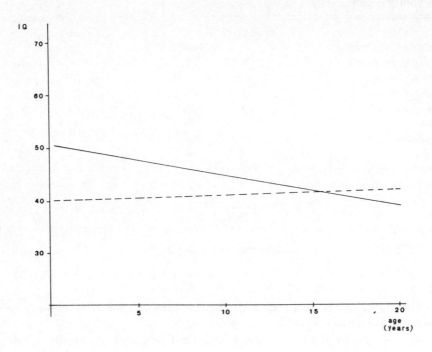

Figure 1.   The fluctuation of IQ with age in the fra(X) group (full line) and the
control group (dotted line).

Fra(X) correlation coefficient	0.84
direction coefficient	−0.56
Control group correlation coefficient	0.61
direction coefficient	0.10

In all boys (fra(X) and control group) with mild mental retardation at
young age a significant decline of IQ was noted. 50% of the fra(X) boys,
who had a moderate mental retardation at early age were severely
mentally retarded at adult age, compared to 20% of the boys of the
control group.

In both groups the IQ profile showed an obvious dysharmony: 70% of
the boys of both groups have a better verbal IQ than performance IQ.

Subtest analysis of the results of Wechsler and Terman scale testings
shows a specific decline for the subtests (artithmetic, digit span,
similarities and object assembly) which evaluate respectively school
achievement, memory and abstraction faculty. Better results were

Table 3. Distribution of the Attention Deficit Hyperkinetic Disorder (ADHD) in both groups in relation to the intellectual level

Intellectual level	Fra(X) boys with ADHD		Control group with ADHD	
	No.	%	No.	%
Mild	0	0	0	0
Moderate	1	16	0	0
Severe	2	28	2	33
Profound	2	66	–	–
Total	5	29	2	16
Fisher's exact probability test		Prob.: 0.1903		

obtained for the subtests "block design" and "picture-arrangement" evaluating sequential thinking and visuospatial perception.

Speech and language development

Speech and language development were delayed in all boys. The language developmental level of the fra(X) boys was 5 years, compared to 6 years in the control group. In general the language performances were found to be strongly dependent of the IQ-level. The language-age level of the severely retarded fra(X) boys was 3yrs 7m, and the age-level of the moderately and mildly retarded fra(X) boys was 5yrs 11m.

The results on the Reynell test showed a difference of one year between the level of understanding (receptive language) and the level of expressive language in both groups. The results on the UTANT test showed a good performance on vocabulary and description-ability, and very poor results on analogies/opposition subtest and grammar, compared to the control group.

Characteristic disturbances in the fra(X) group were echolalia and stereotyped speech as well as a more rapid speech rhythm and stuttering.

Hyperkinesis (Attention Deficit Hyperkinetic Disorder (ADHD))

Analysis of all collected data on behaviour, obtained from individual observations, indicated that the ADHD was twice as common in fra(X) syndrome, compared to the control group. A hyperkinetic behaviour was present in 29% of fra(X) versus 16% of the control group (see Table 3).

Moreover, this ADHD was found to be related to the intellectual level in both groups: the most severe hyperkinetic behaviour was seen in the severely to profoundly retarded. The different symptom categories of the

Table 4. The association of fra(X)/non-specific mental retardation – autistiform behaviour in relation to the intellectual level

Intellectual level	Fra(X) boys with autistic behaviour		Control group with autistic behaviour	
	No.	%	No.	%
Mild	0	–	0	–
Moderate	0	–	1	25
Severe	3	50	0	–
Profound	1	33	0	–
Total	4	23	1	8
Fisher's exact probability test	Prob.: 0.2495			

ADHD were separately evaluated: poor attention and concentration, extreme hyperactivity and impulsivity were the most evident in the fra(X) group.

Autistiform behaviour

The association "mental retardation-autistic behaviour" was present in 23% of the fra(X) boys, compared to 8% of the control group.

As in the hyperkinetic syndrome, the autistic behaviour fluctuated with the intelligence level and was most pronounced in the severely and profoundly retarded (see Table 4).

Analysing the different symptom categories, the fra(X) boys presented distinct motor and sensitive troubles like fluttering, stereotypies of movements and hypersensitivity to noises. Relational problems and echolalia were also more frequent in fra(X).

Social functions

Social performance of the fra(X) patients was lower than of the boys of the control group. The level of social functioning was 42% for the fra(X) group and 55% for the control group and was not age dependent but strongly correlated with the intelligence level.

In the analysis of the different categories of the PAC (Günzburg, 1977) we observed a specific decline for "socialization" (play function and daily domestic affairs) in the severely and profoundly retarded, and a decline for "communication" (school achievement) in the moderate and mildly retarded.

DISCUSSION

Previous studies on fra(X) males have suggested a distinct pattern of characteristic and universal developmental and behavioural disturbances (for review see Veenema and Geraedts, 1987). The aim of the present study was to better delineate and describe the psychological profile and development of patients with fra(X) syndrome.

In a previous study, we performed extensive psychodiagnostic examinations in 23 pre-pubertal fra(X) boys, aged between 2 years and 12 years and observed a distinct and typical pattern of developmental and behavioural problems in fra(X) boys. We also found strong evidence for age-dependence of IQ level and behaviour characteristics (Borghgraef et al., 1987).

After these findings we decided to study a group of 17 pubertal and young adult fra(X) patients with the same parameters and criteria and with special attention for the fluctuation of the intellectual level over age and with a detailed outline of social functioning. The results were also compared to a group of 12 males of the same age and IQ with "nonspecific" mental retardation.

Reviewing the literature data on intelligence in the fra(X) syndrome, we found a strong agreement in the different studies: most of them indicate that the majority of fra(X) patients, mostly adults, are moderately to severely mentally retarded (Theobald et al., 1987; Bregman et al., 1987; Rochi et al., 1987). In the present study of 17 pubertal fra(X) patients, 29% were moderately mentally retarded and 38% severely retarded. A smaller number was found in the profoundly retarded (16%) and in the mildly retarded (11%) group.

Another important finding in most studies is the negative correlation between age and level of intellectual functioning. Jenssen-Hagerman et al. (1983) and Paul and Leckman (1984) noted a progress in intellectual performances in childhood, followed by a plateau and finally a drop during puberty. Lachiewicz et al. (1987) examined retrospective data and observed a negative correlation between IQ and age with a decline during middle childhood years. Partington et al. (1984) and Theobald et al. (1987) did not find a significant decline of intelligence level with age and asserted that the majority of fra(X) boys present a non-progressive moderate to severe mental retardation from birth on.

Comparing the results of the present study with the data on the prepubertal fra(X) boys of the previous studies, a clear shifting towards a lower level of intellectual functioning is noted. 47% of the young fra(X) boys were mildly mentally retarded compared to only 11% of the postpubertal group.

The present data seem to confirm the hypothesis of a decline in intelligence performance with age. We attempted to confirm this finding by a longitudinal, longterm follow-up of 11 fra(X) boys, and compared these data with follow-up findings in 9 boys of the control group. In both groups a strong correlation was found between IQ and age, with a distinct drop of the intellectual performance with age in the fra(X) boys: all mildly mentally retarded fra(X) males dropped to the level of moderate retardation and 50% of the moderately mentally retarded became severely retarded. As Lackiewicz et al., (1987) we have no arguments to explain this intellectual decline by a deterioration or loss of acquired abilities. Their cognitive functioning is improving with age. A more evident explanation is that fra(X) boys learn at a slower rate than expected from their initial IQ level. This decline might be induced by the behavioural problems with poor attention and social disability and a poor stimulating environment.

In the analysis of the cognitive profile by subtest examination of the Wechsler scale testings, the fra(X) boys of this study showed a specific decline in arithmetics, digit span, object assembly and similarities, which evaluate school achievement, short term memory and abstraction faculty. Compared to the control group, better results were obtained for block design, and picture arrangement which evaluate sequential thinking and visuospatial perception.

In 70% of the fra(X) boys of the present study verbal IQ is higher than performance IQ. This dysharmonic profile was also observed in several other studies (for review see Rochi et al., 1987).

We noted the same difference with higher verbal IQ than performance IQ also in the control group, indicating that this finding is not a specific feature of the fra(X) syndrome.

Further evaluation of the speech and language development showed in general a lower developmental level in fra(X) boys: they scored at a 5 year age level, compared to a 6 year age level in the control group. In both groups the language performances were strongly dependent of IQ level. In addition to the global language retardation, fra(X) boys presented some very characteristic speech disturbances like rapid speech rhythm and stuttering. The most distinct findings were the presence of echolalia and stereotyped speech, and those were noted by Rhea et al. (1987), Levitas et al. (1983a) and Newell et al. (1983), Jenssen-Hagerman et al. (1985).

Echolalia and stuttering were not so frequently observed in the prepubertal fra(X) boys (Borghgraef et al., 1987) and seemed to be a characteristic finding at postpubertal age.

The Attention Deficit Hyperkinetic Disorder was twice as common in fra(X) boys (29%) compared to the control group (16%). In our experience, poor attention and concentration, extreme hyperactivity and impulsivity are the most obvious symptoms in the fra(X) syndrome.

Furthermore this behavioural disorder seems to be strongly age-dependent. In previous studies we concluded already that behaviour problems decrease with age (Borghgraef *et al.*, 1987). This is confirmed in this study for the ADHD: 67% of the prepubertal boys present hyperkinesis, compared to 29% of the older boys. This age-dependence is not so evident for the autistic behavioural characteristics, which show a smaller drop with age. 23% of the postpubertal fra(X) boys still present autistic features, versus 39% in the prepubertal group. The most distinct symptoms were fluttering, stereotypy of movements and visual/auditory hypersensitivity. On the other hand, the relational disturbance was less pronounced.

In the literature different reports have present data on the incidence of the fra(X) syndrome in autistic children, ranging from 0% to 16% (see Wahlström *et al.*, 1986).

Few data are available on the frequency of autistic characteristics in fra(X) patients. It is now estimated that 25% of fra(X) positive males demonstrate austistic behavioural characteristics (see Brown *et al.*, 1986).

With regard to the social functioning, fra(X) boys in the present study performed slightly lower than the control group with a specific decline for "socialisation" and "communication" abilities. We agree with the findings in other studies: Bregman *et al.* (1987) stated that the adaptive behaviour of fra(X) patients is better than expected from their intelligence level, Loesch *et al.* (1987) estimated that their good verbal and social performances are masking poor intelligence performances and Dykens *et al.* (1987) concluded that fra(X) boys are certainly applicants for early intervention programs, as they have optimal learning possibilities at pre-school age.

REFERENCES

Borghgraef, M., Fryns, J. P., Dielkens, A., Pyck, K. and Van den Berghe, H. (1987) Fragile (X) syndrome: a study of the psychological profile in 23 prepubertal patients. *Clin. Genet.* **32**: 179–186.

Bregman, J. D., Dykens, E., Watson, M., Ort, S. I. and Leckman, J. F. (1987) *J. Am. Ac. Child Psych.* **26**: 463–471.

Brown, W. T., Jenkins, E. C., Cohen, I. L., Fish, G. S., Wolf-Schein, E. G., Cross, A., Waterhouse, L., Fein, D., Mason-Brothers, A., Ritvo, E., Ruttenberg, B. A., Bentley, W. and Castells, S. (1986) Fragile X and autism: a multicenter survey. *Am. J. Med. Genet.* **23**: 341–352.

Dykens, E. M., Hodapp, R. M. and Leckman, J. F. (1987) Strengths and weaknesses in the intellectual functioning of males with fra X syndrome. *Am. J. Ment. Def.* **92**: 234–236.

Fryns, J. P. (1984) The fragile X syndrome. A study of 83 families. *Clin. Genet.* **26**: 497–528.

Fryns, J. P., Kleczkowska, A., Kubien, E., and Van den Berghe, H. (1984)

Cytogenetic findings in moderate and severe mental retardation. A study of an institutionalized population of 1991 patients. *Acta Paed. Scand.* Supplement 313.

Gunzberg, H. C. (1977) *Progress Assessment Chart of Social and Personal Development Manual (2 vols.).* SESA Publications Ltd. Stratford-upon-Avon.

Jenssen-Hagerman, R. and McKenzie-McBogg, P. (eds) (1983) *The Fragile X Syndrome. Diagnosis, Biochemistry and Intervention.* Spectra Publishing, Dillon-Colorado.

Kohnstamm, G. A., Messer, A. P. and De Vries, A. K. (1971) *De Utrechtse taalniveau Test voor 4-7 jarigen.* p. 5 Swets & Zeitlinger,, Amsterdam.

Lachiewicz, A. M., Gullion, C. M., Spiridigliozzi, C. A. and Aylsworth, A. S. (1987) Decline in IQ's of young males with the fra(X) syndrome. *Am. J. Mental Retardation.* **92**, 272–278.

Largo, R. H. and Schinzel, A. (1985) Developmental and behavioral disturbances in 13 boys with fragile X syndrome. *Eur. J. Pediatr.* **143**: 269–275.

Levitas, A., McBogg, P. and Hagerman, R. (1983) Behavioral dysfunction in the fragile X syndrome. In: Jenssen-Hagerman, R. and McKenzie-McBogg, P. (eds), *The Fragile X Syndrome. Diagnosis, Biochemistry and Intervention.* pp. 153–173. Spectra Publishing, Dillon-Colorado.

Loesch, D., Hay, D. A., Sutherland, G. R., Halliday, J., Judge, C. and Web, G. C. (1987) Phenotypic variation in male-transmitted fra(X): genetic inferences. *Am. J. Med. Genet.* **27**: 401–417.

Newell, K., Sanborn, B. and Hagerman, R. (1983) Speech and language dysfunction in the fragile X syndrome. In: Jenssen-Hagerman, R. and McKenzie-McBogg, P. (eds). *The Fragile X Syndrome. Diagnosis, Biochemistry and Intervention.* pp.175–200. Spectra Publishing, Dillon-Colorado.

Partington, M. W. (1984) The fragile X syndrome II: preliminary data on growth and development in males. *Am. J. Med. Genet.* **17**: 175–194.

Paul, R. and Leckman, J. F. (1984) Behavioral phenotype. In: J. M. Opitz and G. R. Sutherland (eds). Conference Report. *Am. J. Med. Genet.* **17**: 50–52.

Reynell, J. (1977) *Reynell Developmental Language Scales (revised).* N.F.E.R., Windsor, Berks.

Rhea, P., Dykens, E., Leckman, J. F., Watson, M., Breg, W. R. and Cohen, D. J. (1987) A comparison of language characteristics of mentally retarded adults with fra X syndrome and those with nonspecific mental retardation and autism. *J. of Autism and Developmental Disorders*, **17**.

Rocchi, M., Archidiacono, N. and Filippi, G. (1987) X-linked mental retardation: Martin-Bell syndrom. *J. Génét. Hum.* **35**, 351–379.

Stinissen, J. and Vander Steene, G. (1981) *W.P.P.S.I.: Wechsler Preschool and Primary Scale of Intelligence. Handleiding bij de Vlaamse aanpassing.* p. 158. Swets & Zeitlinger, Amsterdam, Lisse.

Terman, L. M. and Merril, M. A. (1973) *Stanford-Binet Intelligence scale, Form L-M: Manual for the third revision.* Haughton-Mifflin, Boston.

Theobald, T. M. and Hay, D. A. (1982) Behavioural correlates of the fragile X syndrome. *Behaviour Genetics* **12**: 599.

Theolbald, T. M., Hay, D. A. and Judge, C. (1987) Individual variation and specific cognitive deficits in the fra(X) syndrome. *Am. J. Med. Genet.* **28**: 1–11.

Van Berckelaer-Onnes, I. A., Harinck, F. J. H. and Smit, M. (1981) *Auti-schaal. Ten behoeve van de onderkenning vam vroegkinderlijk autisme.* p. 24. Swets & Zeitlinger, Amsterdam, Lisse.

Van der Meulen, B. F. and Smrkovsky, M. (1983) *Baylen Ontwikkelingsschalen. BOS 2-30. Handleiding.* p. 183. Swets & Zeitlinger, Amsterdam, Lisse.

Van Haasen, P. *et al.* (1985) *Wechsler Intelligence Scale for Children. Revised*: Nederlandstalige Uitgave. Handleiding voor Instucties en Scoring. Swets & Zeitlinger, Amsterdam, Lisse.

Veenema, H. and Geraedts, J. P. M. (1987) The fra(X) syndrome in a large family. II. Psychological investigations. *J. Med. Genet.* **24**: 32–38.

Venter, P. A., Op't Hof and Coetzee, D. J. (1986) The Martin-Bell syndrome in South-Africa. *Am. J. Med. Genet.* **23**: 597–610.

Wahlström, J., Gillberg, C., Gustavson, K. H. and Holmgren, G. (1986) Infantile autism and the fra(X). A Swedish multicenter study. *Am. J. Med. Genet.* **23**: 403–408.

Section III

Clinical Practice

Behaviour in Children with Fetal Alcohol Syndrome

J. L. Nanson

Psychology Department, Alvin Buckwold Centre,
University Hospital, Saskatoon, Canada

Twenty children with FAS/FAE were assessed in terms of intelligence and behaviour and were compared to normal children and to ADD (Attention Deficit Disorder) children. Although the FAS children were significantly more retarded, their problems with inattention and behaviour were similar to those of ADD children. This suggests that treatment techniques currently used with ADD may be helpful for FAS children. In addition, the data suggest that FAS children may experience a decline in intellectual skills beginning in middle childhood.

Fetal alcohol syndrome (FAS) and fetal alcohol effects (FAE) are now recognized as one of the leading causes of mental retardation and birth defects. The incidence of FAS/FAE is estimated to anywhere from 1:57 live births to 1:900 births depending on the population studied (Clarren & Smith, 1978; May *et al.*, 1980). In a recent study of children with physical, developmental or learning problems in northern Canada (Asante, 1985) 30% of the 586 children referred met the criteria for FAS/FAE. In a Saskatchewan study (Habbick & Zalesk, 1980; Nanson *et al.*, 1981) 114 children of 176 referred with suspected FAS/FAE met the criteria for the diagnosis.

Intellectual problems including mental retardation and learning disabilities are the most common finding in FAS/FAE (Clarren & Smith, 1978; Cooper, 1987). The average IQ reported in FAS/FAE is 65 (Little & Streissguth, 1981) but the range of functioning in children with FAS/FAE is wide (Nanson *et al.*, 1981; Majewski, 1981). The level of intellectual functioning is thought to be relatively stable and not amenable to effort to stimulate the child's intellectual development (Streissguth *et al.*, 1985).

The behavioural manifestations of FAS/FAE vary with age. Infants with FAS/FAE are described as irritable, jittery, tremulous and difficult to feed (Pierog *et al.*, 1979). Hyperactivity, attention deficits, a short attention span and fine motor dysfunction have been noted in a number of follow up studies of older children with FAS/FAE (Aronson *et al.*, 1985; Streissguth *et al.*, 1985).

In addition to the full blown syndrome of FAS/FAE, it is now recognized that consumption of lesser amounts of alcohol during pregnancy may compromise the later development of the child even in the absence of the classical features of FAS-FAE (Gusella & Fried, 1985; Landesman-Dwyer *et al.*, 1978; Landesman-Dwyer *et al.*, 1981; O'Connor *et al.*, 1986; Shaywitz *et al.*, 1980; Streissguth *et al.*, 1985; Streissguth *et al.*, 1984). Taken together, the results of these studies suggest that consumption of small amounts of alcohol during pregnancy is not associated with FAS/FAE but is associated with lower birth weights; abnormal behaviour during the neonatal period; lower scores on infant developmental tests; growth retardation; increased restless and short attention span; and fine motor dysfunction. These abnormalities are all similar but milder than those seen in classical FAS/FAE. They suggest that physical growth and the development of the CNS is much more sensitive to the effects of maternal alcohol intake than are the craniofacial features and can be adversely affected by the consumption of smaller amounts of alcohol. Since physical growth and the development of the CNS occur during the entire pregnancy whereas the craniofacial features are present by the end of the first trimester of pregnancy, the teratogenic effects of alcohol can affect these systems throughout the entire pregnancy. Thus it is not surprising that lower dosages of alcohol during pregnancy have real but more subtle effects on growth and the CNS.

Children with FAS/FAE are frequently described as hyperactive, distractible, impulsive, and having short attention spans (Aronson *et al.*, 1985; Kyllerman *et al.*, 1985; Streissguth *et al.*, 1985). In addition, maternal alcohol consumption during pregnancy, in "social" amounts, is associated with inattention (Streissguth *et al.*, 1984), fidgety, and restless behaviour (Landesman-Dwyer *et al.*, 1981). Thus children with FAS/FAE appear similar to the classical descriptions of hyperactive children (Loney, 1980; Levine & Oberklaid, 1980) although perhaps more intellectually impaired. In addition, preschool children of social drinkers appear to display behaviour similar to preschoolers who go on to be diagnosed as ADD or ADD-H.

The present study is an attempt to bridge the gap between studies of the attention in the offspring of social drinkers and the clinical observations that children with FAS are "hyperactive". In this study the behaviour of children with FAS/FAE diagnosed by the usual criteria were assessed using three questionnaires. Their performance was compared to that of other hyperactive children who were not FAS and to normal children. It was hypothesized that if prenatal exposure to alcohol is one of possibly many final common pathways by which hyperactivity is caused then children with FAS/FAE should show similar but more severe deficits in attention and behaviour.

METHOD

Sixty children aged 5 to 12 years participated in the study, 20 children in each group; normal, FAS/FAE and hyperactive (ADD). FAS subjects were recruited from a pool of children diagnosed as FAS or FAE following the criteria set forth by Rosett and Weiner (1980) who are followed by the Department of Pediatrics, University Hospital Saskatoon (Habbick & Zaleski, 1980; Nanson *et al.*, 1981). Children within the age range (5–12 years) wth FAS/FAE were selected for possible inclusion if they met the following additional criteria: previous intellectual assessment had resulted in an IQ of 75 or more (on either a Wechsler or the Stanford Binet Scale); secondly, the referring physician judged the child to be free from neurological impairments caused by conditions other than prenatal exposure to alcohol and finally, the child had to be living in a stable, English speaking home.

A total of 35 children from the total pool of FAS patients met all of these criteria. Consent was given for 20 children to be seen. One subject was currently being treated with methylphenidate (Ritalin) and was seen after he had been off medication for 24 hours, as is common in studies of hyperactive children receiving stimulant medication (Cunningham & Barkley, 1979; Grenell *et al.*, 1987).

The majority of the children with FAS had been diagnosed early in life and all but two were living in adoptive homes or stable, long term foster placements. The remaining two were being cared for by parents who had recovered from their alcoholism. All the children spoke English as a first language although the majority were of North American Indian ancestry.

Hyperactive subjects were recruited from a pool of children diagnosed as ADD/ADD-H following the criteria set forth in the DSM III (1980) who are followed by the Department of Psychiatry, University Hospital Saskatoon. Children within the age range (5–12 years) with ADD were selected for possible inclusion if they met the same criteria as those with FAS/FAE and were also free of any signs of FAS/FAE.

A total of 45 children from the total pool of ADD patients met all of these criteria. Consent was obtained for 21 children to be seen. One subject was later dropped from the analyses as she was later found to function currently within the mentally retarded range. The majority of the ADD subjects were currently being treated with stimulant medication and were seen after they had been seen off medication for at least 24 hours.

Normal subjects were recruited in two ways. Firstly, sibling controls of the FAS/FAE and ADD/ADD-H subjects were used when available and in addition normal children of hospital staff were also used to increase the sample size. All normal children met the same criteria as the other two groups. A total of 20 normal children were recruited via the two methods. None were currently receiving stimulants or other psychotropic medications.

The measures chosen for this study were Connors Abbreviated Parent Teacher Questionnaire (APTQ, Connors, 1973); SNAP (Swanson *et al.*, 1981) and the Child Behavior Checklist (CBC,. Achenbach & Edelbrock, 1978). The APTQ was chosen because it is the most commonly used method of assessing hyperactive behaviour and of monitoring the child's response to treatment, particularly drug treatments. The SNAP is an extension of the DSM III criteria for ADD and was included to assess the extent to which children with FAS also met the criteria for ADD. In addition, the CBC was included to assess a wider range of behaviour problems.

It was predicted that the normal children would have lower scores on the Connors Scale, SNAP and Achenbach than either of the clinical groups; that there would be no differences between the FAS/FAE and ADD/ADD-H children on the three scales; and that the Connors Scale and the SNAP would show substantial correlations in each of the three groups.

Intelligence was assessed using the Wechsler Intelligence Scale for Children – Revised (WISC-R) or Wechsler Preschool and Primary Scale of Intelligence (WPPSI).

IQ and age were analyzed in a 3 × 2 ANOVA using diagnostic groups and age (younger vs older) as blocking variables. The data from the three parent questionnaires were analyzed using a 3 × 2 ANOVA. Two scores were derived from the CBC; a hyperactivity score based on the hyperactivity scale and an overall score which is based on all of the internalizing and externalizing scales and is a general index of psychopathology (Achenbach & Edelbrock, 1978).

RESULTS

Table 1 gives the ages, IQ's and sex ratios for each group.

The ADD children referred were more homogeneous in terms of age than were the normal or FAS children however, these differences did not reach statistical significance. As expected, the children with FAS were significantly more intellectually impaired than were the normal or ADD children (F[2,54] 23.337, p <0.001). A series of planned comparisons indicated that the FAS children had a significantly lower IQ than either of the other two groups (Normal vs FAS F[1,54]=33.22, p <.0001; FAS vs. ADD F[1,54]=36.7091, p <0.001) and that there were no differences in

Table 1.

	Normal		FAS		ADD	
	Younger	Older	Younger	Older	Younger	Older
Age	7.3	11.2	7.4	10.3	8.6	10.5
S.D.	1.5	0.8	1.0	1.1	0.6	0.8
Range (lower limit)	5.5	10.4	5.5	8.8	7.5	9.4
(upper limit)	9.7	12.0	8,2	11.6	9.3	11.3
IQ	108	103	78	78	110	104
S.D.	14.7	8.7	9.8	20.6	18.5	13.6
Range (lower limit)	83	88	73	50	80	88
(upper limit)	123	115	94	112	129	117
* of males/10	7	5	2	4	10	8

Table 2.

	Normal		FAS		ADD	
	Younger	Older	Younger	Older	Younger	Older
Connors	5	2	14	14.1	16	16
S.D.	4	2.2	8.1	5.6	3.2	5.9
Range (lower limit)	0	0	3	4	11	5
(upper limit)	12	7	27	25	21	23
SNAP (total)	15	7	30	33	32	32
S.D.	9	4	17	32	7	10
Range (lower limit)	1	0	8	10	22	11
(upper limit)	26	15	50	56	43	48
CBC hyperactivity	60	51	76	72	70	70
S.D.	2	2.7	8.7	8.3	6.3	8.7
Range (lower limit)	55	51	63	60	66	63
(upper limit)	63	68	87	83	75	80
CBC total	51	49	67	66	69	66
S.D.	6	7.2	13.1	9.7	5.4	10.9
Range (lower limit)	42	36	48	47	58	45
(upper limit)	82	62	59	82	74	80

IQ between the normal and ADD subjects ($F[1,54]$ 8.73, $p > 0.25$).

The results of the parent questionnaires; the Connors, SNAP and the CBC hyperactivity and CBC total scores are given in Table 2. A total of three sets of parental data were eliminated due to errors made in completing the questionnaires, leaving data from nine younger and nine older FS children, nine older ADD children and ten from each of the other groups. The ADD children were rated on a week during which the children received stimulant medication for all but the 24 hour period in

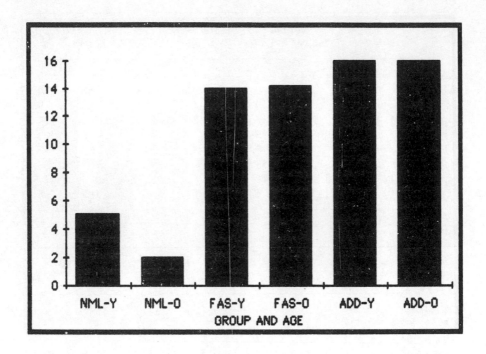

Figure 1.   Connors scores.

which they were seen for the assessment. All of the normal children and all but one child with FAS were not receiving any psychoactive medication so that their scores on the same measures reflect their unmedicated state.

On the Connors, there were significant main effects for diagnosis but not for age or for the interactions (F[32,54]=30.0854, p <0.001). A series of planned comparisons indicated that there were no differences between the ADD and FAS children (FAS vs ADD F[1,50)=1.2309, p >.25) but that the normal children had significantly lower Connors scores (FAS vs Normal F[1,54]=35.8101, p <.001, Normal vs ADD F[1,54]=51.8805, p <.001. This is shown graphically in Figure 1.

On the SNAP there were significant main effects for diagnosis but not for age or for the interactions (F[2,54]=22.1225, p <0.001). A series of planned comparisons indicated that there were no differences between the ADD and FAS children (FAS vs ADD F[1,50]=.0002, p >.25) but that the normal children had significantly lower SNAP scores (FAS vs Normal F[1,54]=32.8990, p <.001, Normal vs ADD F[1,50]=33.6697,

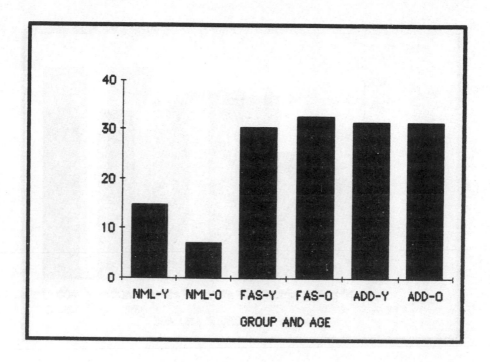

Figure 2. Snap scores.

p >.001). This is shown graphically in Figure 2.

On the Achenbach Hyperactivity Scale there were significant main effects for diagnosis but not for age or for the interactions (F[2,54]= 22.0212, p <0.001). A series of planned comparisons indicated that there was a trend towards a significance difference between the ADD and FAS children (FAS vs ADD F[1,54]=3.9662, p=.05) but that the normal children had significantly lower scores (FAS vs Normal F[1,54]=40.4671 p <.001, Normal vs ADD F[1,50]=21.6717, p <.0001. This is shown graphically in Figure 3.

On the CBC total score, there were significant main effects for diagnosis but not for age or for the interactions (F[2,54]=15.8172, p <0.001). A series of planned comparisons indicated that there were no differences between the ADD and FAS children (FAS vs ADD F[1,50]=.1170, p >.25) but that the normal children had significantly lower Connors scores (FAS vs Normal F[1,50]=19.0983, p <.001, Normal vs ADD F[1,50]=26.1929, p <.001. This is shown graphically in Figure 4.

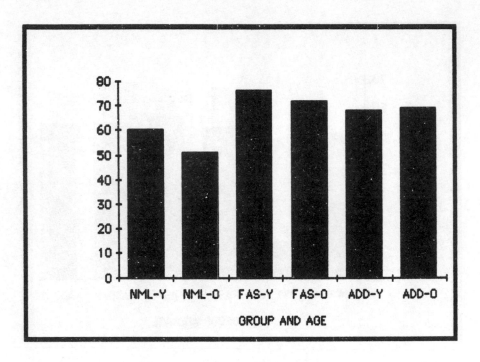

Figure 3.   CBC hyperactivity.

DISCUSSION

None of the normal children met the usual criteria for hyperactivity on their Connors or SNAP scores. Seven of the younger and nine older FAS children did meet the usual criteria for ADD based on their SNAP scores. Only one had been previously diagnosed as having concurrent ADD. Interestingly, this child was also the brightest child with FAE referred to the study (IQ 112) which suggests that for the more intellectually impaired children their attention deficits were assumed to be included within the diagnosis of FAS.

All but one older subject with ADD continued to meet the criteria for ADD even though they were receiving therapeutic dosages of stimulant medication. This suggests that these children may have had a more severe attention deficit disorder than did the children with FAS who were rated on the basis of an unmedicated state. Alternatively, because the children with FAS were more intellectually impaired, they may have had fewer demands placed on them for sustained attention and independent work so

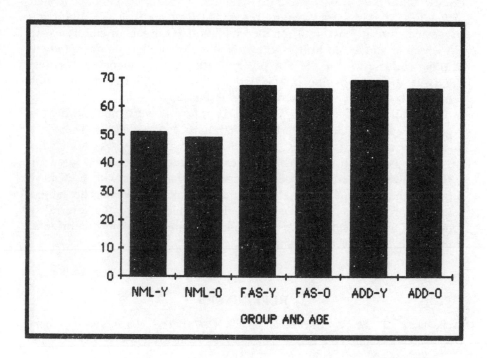

Figure 4. CBC total scores.

that they were not perceived as being as attention-disordered as were the children with ADD. The data from the three parent scales suggests that children with FAS have problems with attention and hyperactivity that are similar to those of other children with ADD.

The mean IQ levels of the children with FAS were at the upper end of the borderline range. This mean is above the mean reported in the literature for children with FAS (Little & Streissguth, 1981; Majewski, 1981). However, this reflects the selection criteria used as only children with IQ scores of 75 or greater were referred. This may have tended to bias the sample in favour of children with FAE as the severity of the intellectual impairment is generally related to the severity of the physical anomalies (Streissguth *et al.*, 1985). Nevertheless a number of the children with FAS tested below 75. This suggests that children with FAS experience a decline in measured IQ, beginning in middle childhood. Children with Down syndrome experience such a decline at these ages (Putman & Rynders, 1984) which is generally thought to be related to difficulties with abstract thinking, a skill which generally develops in middle childhood. It is possible that children with FAS experience similar difficulties at this age. Previous research (Streissguth et al., 1985) has suggested that at least until middle childhood IQ levels of children with FAS remain stable but little is known about the intellectual development of older children with FAS. The present data are not adequate to address the issue of any possible intellectual decline in FAS but the question remains one which is worthy of future research.

The majority of children with ADD referred were males which is typical in studies of ADD (Barkley, 1980; Ross & Ross, 1982). There was a bias in favour of females in the FAS groups. This was somewhat surprising as sex ratios in FAS have generally reported equal (Majewski, 1981). However there has been a suggestion that males with FAS have more anomalies than do females (Qazi & Masakawa, 1976). The subject selection procedure may have biased the sample toward the referral of females, if females suffer fewer anomalies and are also somewhat brighter on average than are males with FAS.

REFERENCES

Achenbach, T. M. & Edelbrock, C. S. (1978) The classification of child psychopathology: A review and analysis of empirical efforts. *Psychological Bulletin*, **85**, 1275–1301.

American Psychiatric Association (1980) *Diagnostic and Statistical Manual of Mental Disorders* (3rd ed.). Washington, D.C.: Author.

Aronson, M., Kyllerman, M., Sabel, K.-G., Sandin, B. & Olegard, R. Children of alcoholic mothers: Developmental, perceptual and behavioural characteristics. *Acta Paediactria Scandinavia*, **74**, 27–35.

Asante, K. O. (1985) *Report on the survey of children with chronic handicaps and fetal syndrome in the Yukon and Northwestern British Columbia*. Terrace, British Columbia.

Barkley, R. A. (1980) *Hyperactive Children: A Handbook for Diagnosis and Treatment*. New York: Guilford.

Clarren, S. K. & Smith, D. W. (1978) The fetal alcohol syndrome. *The New England Journal of Medicine*. **298**, 1063–1067.

Connor, C. K. (1973) Rating scales for use in drug studies with children. Pharmacotherapy of Children [Special issue] *Psychopharmacology Bulletin*, 24–28.

Cooper, S. The fetal alcohol syndrome. *Journal of Child Psychiatry and Psychology*, **28**, 223–227.

Cunningham, C. E. & Barkley, R. A. (1979) The interactions of normal and hyperactive children with their mothers in free play and structured tasks. *Child Development*, **50**, 217–224.

Ferguson, H. B., & Rapoport, J. L. (1983) Nosological issues and biological validation. In M. Rutter (Ed.) *Developmental Neuropsychiatry*. New York: Guilford.

Grenell, M. M., Glass, C. R. & Katz, K. S. (1987) Hyperactive children and peer interaction: Knowledge and performance of social skills. *Journal of Abnormal Child Psychology*, **15**, 1–13.

Gusella, J. P. & Fried, P. A. (1985) *Effects of maternal social drinking and smoking on offspring*. Paper presented at the Society for Research in Child Development meeting, Toronto, Ontario.

Habbick, B. F. & Zaleski, W. A. (1980) Fetal alcohol syndrome. *Continuing Medical Education Newsletter*, p. 14.

Kyllerman, M., Aronson, M., Sabel, K.-G., Sandin, B. & Olegard, R. Children of alcoholic mothers: Growth and motor performance compared to matched controls. *Acta Paediactria Scandinavia*, **74**, 20–26.

Landesman-Dwyer, S., Keller, S., & Streissguth, A. P. (1978) Naturalistic observations of newborns: Effects of maternal alcohol intake. *Alcoholism: Clinical and Experimental Research*, 171–177.

Landesman-Dwyer, S., Rogozin, & Little, R. E. (1981) Behaviour correlates of prenatal alcohol exposure: A four-year follow up study. *Neurobehavioral toxicology and Teratology*, **3**, 187–193.

Levine, M. D. & Oberklaid, F. (1980) Hyperactivity: Symptom complex or complex symptom? *American Journal of Diseases in Childhood*, **34**, 409–414.

Little, R. E., & Streissguth, A.P. (1981) Effects of alcohol on the fetus: Impact and prevention. *Canadian Medical Association Journal*, **125**, 159–164.

Loney, J. (1980) Hyperkinesis comes of age: What do we know and where should we go? *American Journal of Orthopsychiatry*, **50**, 28–42.

Majewski, F. (1981) Alcohol embryopathy: Some facts and speculations about pathogensis. *Neurobehavioral Toxicology and Tetralogy*, **3**, 129–144.

May, P. A., Hymbaugh, K. J., Aase. J. M. & Samet, J. M. (1983) Epidemiology of Fetal Alcohol Syndrome Among American Indians of the southwest. *Social Biology*, **30**, 374–387.

Nanson, J. L., Zaleski, B. F., Habbick, B. F., & Casey, R. E. Fetal alcohol syndrome in Saskatchewan. *Perinatal Bulletin*, **12**, 14–16.

O'Connor, M. J., Brill, N. J. & Sigman, M. Alcohol use in primiparous women older than 30 years of age: Relation to infant development. *Pediatrics*, **78**, 44–450.

Pierog, S., Chandavasu, O., Wexler, I. (1979) Withdrawal symptoms in infants with fetal alcohol syndrome. *Journal of Pediatrics*, **90**, 630–633.

Putman, J. W. & Rynders, J. E. (1984) Advancing the development of intelligence in adults with Down syndrome. In S. Pueschel & J. E. Rynders (eds.) *Down syndrome: Advances in biomedicine and the behavioural sciences*. Cambridge Mass: Ware Press.

Quay, H. C. & Peterson, D. R. 1983) *Manual for the Revised Behavior Problem Checklist*. Coral Gables Florida: University of Miami.

Quinn, P. O. & Rapoport, J. L. (1974) Minor physical anomalies and neurologic status in hyperactive boys. *Pediatrics*, **53**, 742–747.

Rosett, H. L. & Weiner, L. (1985) Alcohol and pregnancy: A clinical perspective. *Annual Review of Medicine*, **36**, 73–80.

Ross, D. M. & Ross, S. A. (1982) *Hyperactivity: Current Issues, Research and Theories*. (2nd ed.) New York: Wiley.

Shaywitz, S. E., Cohen, D. J. & Shaywitz, B. A. (1980) Behavior and learning difficulties in children of normal intelligence born to alcoholic mothers. *Journal of Pediatrics*, 978–982.

Streissguth, A. P., Barr, H. M., Darby, B. L., & Martin, D. C. (1985) Prenatal alcohol exposure and offspring performance on the Wisconsin Fine Motor Performance Battery. Paper presented at the Society for Research in Child Development meeting, Toronto, Ontario.

Streissguth, A. P., Clarren, S. K., & Jones, K. L. (1985) Natural history of the Fetal Alcohol Syndrome: A 10-year follow-up of eleven patients. *Lancet*, **10**, 85–92.

Streissguth, A. P., Martin, D. C., Barr, H. M., Sandman, B. M., Kirchner, G. L., & Darby, B. L. (1984) Intrauterine alcohol and nicotine exposure: Attention and reaction time in 4 year old children. *Developmental Psychology*, **20**, 533–541.

Swanson, J. M., Nolan, W., & Pelham, W. E. (1982) The SNAP rating scale. *Resources in Education*.

Waldrop, M. & Halverson, G. E. (1971) Minor physical anomalies and hyperactive behaviour in young children. In J. Hellmuth (ed.) *Exceptional Infant*. New York: Bruner/Mazel.

Waldrop, M., Peterson, F., & Bell, R. Q. (1968) Minor physical anomalies and behaviour in preschool children. *Child Development*, **39**, 391–400.

The Effect of Lithium on the Periodicity of Aggressive Episodes

S. P. Tyrer and Y. Shakoor

Prudhoe Hospital, Prudhoe, Northumberland NE42 5NT, England and Department of Statistics, University of Newcastle upon Tyne, England

The effect of lithium on the periodicity of aggressive behaviour in 17 mentally handicapped adults was assessed by periodogram analysis. In six patients lithium rendered a pre-existing cycle unobtainable; in a further six there was a reduction in cycle frequency. In the two patients that showed a lengthening of the periodicity of their aggressive cycle there was no effect of lithium on their aggressive behaviour. The results are surprising and contrary to work in manic-depressive patients showing that lithium lengthens cycle frequency. It is possible that the mode of action of lithium in reducing aggressive behaviour is through different mechanisms than are involved in the treatment of affective disturbance.

INTRODUCTION

Lithium has been used for three decades in the treatment of mania and in the prophylaxis of recurrent affective illness. It has more recently been found to be effective in impulsive aggressive outbursts (Sheard *et al.*, 1976). In mentally handicapped individuals with affective disorder lithium has been used successfully in the prophylaxis of manic depressive disease (Reid, 1985) and has also been found to reduce aggressive episodes in mentally handicapped individuals with persistent violence towards others (Tyrer *et al.*, 1984; Craft *et al.*, 1987).

It is not known precisely how lithium exerts its action. Lithium has a large number of effects on physiological processes of which probably the most important in the elucidation of its therapeutic action are its inhibitory effect on second messenger systems, in particular cyclic adenosine monophosphate (cyclic AMP), its action on inorganic channel fluxes, especially sodium and calcium, and the effect of the drug in sensitizing post-synaptic serotonin receptors. These effects of lithium are at the cellular level but it is likely that the actions of the drug may affect other physiological processes, including circadian rhythms. The control of

121

periodic variations in the majority of functions in living organisms probably depends upon some form of endogenous oscillator, but environmental factors determine the influence of this. All animals, including human beings, have a number of physiological rhythms concerned with light, temperature, sound and other environmental cues and if these rhythms are disrupted changes in mood can result. The effect of jet lag in promoting psychiatric disturbances clearly shows this (Jauhar and Weller 1982). Wehr and Goodwin (1980) showed that nine out of ten manic-depressive patients they studied had their resting-activity cycle uncoupled from other circadian rhythms. Any manoeuvre that resynchronises these rhythms may stabilise affective disorder (Halberg, 1968).

These physiological cycles are persistent and continue even in the absence of environmental cues. Rats are usually active at night and sleep during the day. Under normal circumstances, their behaviour is influenced by external light. However, if kept in total darkness or blinded, rats will still retain regular, approximately equal, cycles of activity and sleep. When lithium is added to the food of such rats there is a lengthening of the resting-activity cycle (Kripke and Wyborney, 1980).

In manic depressive patients there is evidence that the circadian rhythms are faster than normal (Atkinson et al., 1975). Most circadian rhythms have periodicities of about twenty-four hours but in some manic-depressive subjects many rhythms, i.e. those concerned with body temperature, pulse rate, blood pressure and other physiological functions oscillate at a frequency of less than 24 hours. In such patients lithium treatment slows down these abnormally fast free-running rhythms and there is a concomitant improvement in the patient's mood state (Pflug et al., 1976; Kripke et al., 1978).

The periodicity of aggressive behaviour in humans has not been widely studied. In the course of an investigation to determine the effect of lithium on the frequency of aggressive episodes in mentally handicapped patients in a large hospital, an opportunity arose to investigate the influence of lithium on the frequency of aggressive behaviour.

PATIENTS AND METHODS

Twenty-six mentally handicapped patients at two hospitals in Northumberland, with at least four episodes of aggressive behaviour recorded each month over the previous six months, entered a trial to compare the effect of adding lithium or placebo medication to their existing neuroleptic and/or anti-convulsant treatment. All pre-existing medication was kept constant during the period of the study. Patients received lithium and placebo in a cross-over design for a period of two months each. All patients were given placebo for one month at the beginning of the investigation so as to provide a baseline of behaviour. The study

Table 1. Study design

| | Phase | | |
	1	2	3
Group A	Placebo	Lithium	Placebo
Group B	Placebo	Placebo	Lithium
Time period	1 month	2 months	2 months

design is illustrated in Table 1. The nature of the medication was blind to patients, investigators and nurse raters although the investigators were aware that the first month's treatment was with inactive medication. No patients with mood disturbance were included. Blood was taken at 2-weekly intervals and 12-hourly lithium levels were maintained beween 0.5–0.8 mmol/l. These results were kept blind to the investigators by a previously described procedure (Tyrer *et al.*, 1984).

Behaviour was rated according to a scale designed for the rating of disturbed behaviour in mentally handicapped patients (El Kaisi and McGuire, 1974) that was modified by the substitution of two items that were felt to be more relevant to the population under study. This scale rates four aspects of behaviour under the headings of aggression, hyperactivity anti-social behaviour and destructiveness. Five behaviours are described in each section. Two of the items involved in the aggression section are concerned with self-assault. Each item of behaviour is marked on a four point scale according to whether it is marked, moderate, slight or absent. Three points were given for every item recorded as 'marked', two for 'moderate' and one for 'slight' and the total score for the four behaviours included were summed to obtain a total score. Nine of the patients had incomplete nurse records and their results are not included in the analysis. The scores for aggressive and self-assaultive behaviour were given three times the weighting compared with the scores on other items as this behaviour is qualitatively distinct from the other items, and it was with this aspect of the patient's behaviour that we were primarily concerned.

Where missing values occurred in the data, which occurred rarely, these were substituted by the overall mean score within the placebo/lithium period in which they occurred, and if there were several missing values together, these were replaced by random numbers, taking care that these would not introduce any other periodic effect. The first two weeks of each new phase of the study were excluded from the analysis to combat any carry-over effect from the previous phase.

The observations recorded are part of a time series, i.e. a collection of observations made sequentially in time. Since we are interested in the

Table 2.   Peak periodicity of disturbed behaviour

No.	Sex	Age	Placebo	Lithium	Response to lithium
	Patient details		Peak frequency of periodogram (days) Phase		
1	F	21	27	No cycle	Very good
2	F	28	3	No per[a]	Very good
3	F	20	No per	10	Very good
4	F	29	22	No per	Good
5	M	22	16	5	Very good
6	M	24	72	44	Very good
7	M	50	12	No per	Very good
8	F	29	27	4	Fair
9	F	25	28	No per	Fair
10	F	29	7	No per	Fair
11	M	18	29	24	Fair
12	M	27	No per	No per	Fair
13	F	19	20	No per	No effect
14	F	33	34	14	No effect
15	M	15	9	12	No effect
16	M	21	36	44	No effect
17	M	24	28	21	No effect

2 months or 60 days – 2 weeks carry over c. 46/47 days
[a] No per = no significant periodicity obtained.

frequency element of the data, we adopted a technique known as Spectral analysis, which is akin to Fourier analysis, and is concerned with approximating a function by a sum of sine and cosine terms. The aim is to discover periodicities in a series that, on visual inspection, does not appear to show any cyclical change, because of the presence of random variation, or noise. Periodograms were plotted for each patient, and the degree of significance of the frequency peaks was determined, allowing for the presence of white noise (random variation). Details of the analysis can be found in Chatfield (1984).

RESULTS

The results of the periodogram analysis are illustrated in Table 2.

The details of the patients are listed primarily according to clinical response to lithium, which was made before the nature of the drug in each phase of the trial was known. In patient number 1 lithium reduced the disturbed behaviour so effectively that it was not possible to carry out a periodogram analysis for the lithium phase of the trial. In all other cases there was sufficient recorded behaviour to enable analysis of this nature. In the Table 'No per' indicates that the behaviour did not follow any clear pattern and no significant periodicity was obtained.

It can be seen that lithium shortens the cycle frequency in six patients and lengthens it in two. In a further six patients no periodicity could be established; five of these patients were female. In only one patient was the reverse true, a cycle being established on lithium when none was previously apparent. In one patient there was no periodicity during either the placebo or lithium phase.

The design of the study involved half the patients receiving lithium after a period of three months placebo treatment whereas half received placebo after lithium. In the patients that received inactive medication after the lithium phase and in whom the periodicity was abolished by lithium, three out of four patients again demonstrated periodicities of their disturbed behaviour.

DISCUSSION

A time series analysis of this nature is fraught with difficulties. Establishing cycles of behaviour on the basis of six months recordings, using two different types of medication, means that it is difficult to accurately determine persistent cycle frequencies. The significance of the measures of periodicity is not easy to determine because of the large numbers of variables that must enter into periodic behaviour disturbance. One has only to look at profound effects of changes of staff, alteration of rota systems, changes in recreational activity, alterations in the weather, with compounding effects on whether ward-based or environmental activities are preferred, to see that many different factors affect the periodicities of disturbed behaviour in a hospital setting. Furthermore, although the nurses were well trained in the rating scale, many different individuals were involved in the ratings, and these are bound to be reflected in the accuracy of the results obtained.

Despite these sources contributing to high variance the results suggest that lithium has a predominant effect on the periodicities of aggressive behaviour. In twelve of the sixteen patients where a cycle was obtained in both the placebo and lithium phases, no cycle could be established when lithium was given or the existing cycle was reduced in frequency. In only two patients did lithium increase the periodicity of the cycle and in both these patients there was a poor response to the drug. It could reasonably be argued that as lithium is reducing the frequency of aggressive behaviour in over two-thirds of the patients that it is not surprising the cycles of aggressive behaviour are abolished. However, the periodogram analysis is involved in determining frequencies of behaviour, not with the severity of this. Of the six patients who responded well to lithium and where there was sufficient data to analyse differences between the placebo and the lithium phases, half of these had definite cycles in the placebo phase. Furthermore, in three of the six patients where no cycle could be obtained during the lithium phase of treatment, there was only a poor or fair response to the drug. This being said, where the effect of the drug dramatically reduces a target behaviour, there are difficulties in showing any changes of frequency of this behaviour and this is demonstrated in patient number 1.

The results tentatively suggest that there may be a difference in the response of male and female patients to lithium in terms of the effect of the drug on aggression cycle frequency. In five of the eight female patients no cycle could be established when on lithium and in two of the remaining three patients lithium reduced the frequency of the cycle. Only in one of the eight male patients could no cycle be found during the lithium phase of the study. Although female patients receiving lithium had a slightly better response to the drug than male patients (Tyrer *et al.*, 1984), this is unlikely to be the whole explanation for this finding. This needs to be substantiated in a larger population.

These results are disparate from work in manic-depressive patients and in normal subjects showing that lithium lengthens physiological cycles (Pflug *et al.*, 1976; Kripke *et al.*, 1978). These authors have shown that lithium lengthens pathologically short resting-activity cycles occurring in manic-depressive patients and improvement in mood is associated with this. If there is a disturbance in the circadian rhythms of the aggressive patients in this study which is being altered by lithium and the drug is producing an associated benefit because of this, the work of these authors would suggest that patients with fast-running cycles would be more likely to respond to lithium than those with slow cycles. Five of the seven patients who had cycles of twenty-seven days or less had a fair or good response to lithium whereas only one of six patients who had a cycle of twenty-eight days or longer had a good response to lithium.

It is possible that the fundamental cycle in many of our patients is faster than is indicated in the Table and the most significant cycle obtained by periodogram analysis is actually a harmonic of a faster cycle. This is suggested in patient number 1 who has significant cycling at an interval of three days but in whom the most significant cycle frequency obtained when all frequencies were analysed was twenty-seven days. Four out of the five patients who showed a very good response to lithium and who had a significant cycle during the placebo phase, had baseline periodicities that were multiples of three viz. three, twelve, twenty-seven and seventy-two. Only three of the remaining patients had a cycle during the placebo phase that was also divisible by three. This could well be a chance finding.

Lieber (1978) has shown that murders and aggravated assaults were significantly increased in Florida around the time of the full moon. Patients, with cycles around 28 days were equally represented in the good and poor responders to lithium.

CONCLUSION

This is a preliminary study with a relatively small number of patients and any conclusions of this work can only be very provisional. The results suggest that lithium reduces the cycle length of patients with aggressive behaviour or renders existing cycles unobtainable. As lithium normally lengthens biological rhythms this effect is difficult to explain and may reflect a different mode of action of the drug in aggressive behaviour. There was a tendency for patients with shorter cycles to have a better response to lithium treatment than those with cycles of 28 days or more. The periodicity of cycles of aggressive behaviour may affect response to lithium although this needs to be determined by a larger study.

REFERENCES

Atkinson, M., Kripke, D. F. and Wolf, S. R. (1975) Autorhythmometry in manic-depressives. *Chronobiologia*, **2**, 325–335.

Chatfield, C. (1984) *The Analysis of Time Series: An Introduction*. 3rd ed., pp. 127–168. Chapman and Hall, London.

Craft, M., Ismail, I. A., Krishnamurti, D., Matthews, J., Regan, A., Seth, R. V., North, P. M., (1987) Lithium in the Treatment of Aggression in Mentally Handicapped Patients: A Double Blind Trial. *Brit. J. Psychiat.*, **150**, 685–689.

El Kaisi, A. H., and McGuire, R. J. (1974) The effect of sulthiame on disturbed behaviour in mentally sub-normal patients. *Brit. J. Psychiat.*, **124**: 45–49.

Halberg, F. (1968) Physiologic considerations underlying rhythmometry with special reference to emotional illness. In: de Auriaguerra, J. (Ed.) *Cycles Biologiques et Psychiatrie*, Masson et Cie, Paris, pp. 73–126.

Jauhar, P. and Weller, M. P. (1982) Psychiatric Morbidity and Time Zone Changes: A Study of Patients from Heathrow Airport. *Brit. J. Psychiat.* **140**: 231–235.

Kripke, D. F., Mullaney, D. J., Atkinson, M. and Wolf, S. (1978) Circadian rhythm disorders in manic-depressives. *Biological Psychiatry*, **13**: 335–351.

Kripke, D. F. and Wyborney, V. G. (1980) Lithium slows rat circadian activity rhythms. *Life Sciences*, **26**: 1319–1321

Lieber, A. L. (1978) Human Aggression and the Lunar Synodic Cycle. *J. Clin. Psychiatry*, **39**, 385–392.

Pflug, B., Erikson, R. and Johnsson, A. (1976) Depression and daily temperature. *Acta Psychiatrica Scandinavica*, **54**: 254–266.

Reid, A. H. (1985) Psychiatry and Mental Handicap. In: (Eds. Craft, M.,

Bicknell, J. and Hollins, S.) *Mental Handicap*, pp. 317-332. Bailliere Tindall, London.

Sheard, M. H., Marini, J. L., Bridges, C. I. and Wagner, E. (1976) The effect of lithium on impulsive aggressive behaviour in man. *Am. J. Psychiatry* **133**: 1409-1413.

Tyrer, S. P., Walsh, Angela, Edwards, D. E., Berney, T. P., and Stephens, D. A. (1984) Factors associated with a good response to lithium in aggressive mentally handicapped subjects. *Prog. Neuro-Psychopharmacol. & Biol. Psychiat.* **8**: 751-755.

Wehr, T. A. and Goodwin, F. K. (1980) Desynchronization of circadian rhythms as a possible source of manic-depressive cycles. *Psychopharmacology Bulletin* **16**, 19-20.

Quality of Life as an Issue in Providing Medical Treatment for Handicapped Children

D. R. Mitchell

University of Waikato, Hamilton, New Zealand

This paper reports on the results of a study of parents' views on the relative importance of various grounds for withholding medical treatment from seriously ill handicapped children. Of the seven grounds ranked by the respondents, futility of treatment received the highest weighting and cost to society the lowest, with quality of life being ranked third. These rankings were broadly similar for parents of disabled and non-disabled children living in New Zealand and in Canada.

INTRODUCTION

Nowhere does the question of quality of life loom so large than on those occasions when a decision has to be made whether a handicapped person with a life-threatening illness should receive medical treatment. In making this decision, arguments frequently centre around the issue of whether the present or projected quality of life of a particular handicapped person is so low as to be not worth sustaining. Classic cases in the British and Canadian courts, for example, have hinged on the legitimacy of giving consideration to quality of life as a ground for withholding treatment (Mitchell, 1985). Similarly, in addressing the ethical issues involved in this area, many writers have presented arguments as to what constitutes the minimal criteria for "humanness". These criteria frequently centre on attempts to define quality of life in terms such as being able to envisage a future and to have desires about that future (Tooley, 1973), being capable of meaningful relationships (Singer, 1983), having a life purpose and being able to enjoy a loving relationship (Young, 1979), and being able or potentially able to exercise choice (McCloskey, 1980).

Quality of life also figures prominently in paediatricians' views as to whether handicapped infants suffering from life-threatening illnesses should be given medical treatment. In a recent study of 18 New Zealand hospitals, for example, the writer found that most respondents said that they took quality of life into account, some rating it as the most important factor (Mitchell, 1986). Similarly, Shaw *et al.* (1977), found that US physicians gave high priority to quality of life when they made decisions not to treat.

Apart from a study by Shepperdson (1983), who surveyed the attitudes of 78 parents of children with Down's syndrome towards providing life-supporting treatment to disabled children, little is known of how parents feel about the issue of withholding treatment and the importance they accord to quality of life in making decisions in this area. In Shepperdson's study, 37 of the 77 parents accepted the idea of foregoing treatment of severely disabled children, but only one-third considered that children with Down's syndrome fell into this category.

The purpose of the research reported in this paper, then, was to obtain information from parents on the importance of various factors in providing medical treatment for severely ill disabled infants. Data will be reported from samples of parents of disabled and non-disabled children living in British Columbia, Canada and in New Zealand.

SUBJECTS

The subjects for this study comprised 77 parents of developmentally disabled children and 15 parents of non-disabled children living across the province of British Columbia, together with 15 parents of develop-mentally disabled children and 17 parents of non-disabled children located in two urban areas in New Zealand (Avery, 1986). Both groups of disabled children were made up predominantly of those with intellectual disabilities (47% in BC and 36% in NZ) or with multiple disabilities (30% in BC and 35% in NZ), with smaller proportions having physical disabilities (19% and 24%, respectively).

PROCEDURES

In both locations, parents were interviewed in their own homes by researchers who were experienced in working with families of disabled children. In the case of the BC sample, the interviewers were generally working in a professional relationship with the parents.

After being asked their views on whether treatment should be provided for a series of five cases portrayed in brief vignettes (not reported here), the parents were then asked to consider, if treatment were not to be given, what grounds would best justify such a decision. They were asked to rank the following seven grounds in order of priority:

1. Child's probable level of functioning or intelligence.

Table 1.   Priorities accorded to various grounds for withholding treatment

Grounds for withholding treatment	Median scores			
	BC Normal N=15	BC Disabled N=77	NZ Normal N=17	NZ Disabled N=15
Futility of treatment	1.33	1.36	1.18	1.21
Type of treatment	2.50	2.03	2.06	2.13
Potential quality of life	3.00	3.26	3.75	3.21
Probable functional level of child	3.83	4.03	4.00	4.40
Possible adverse effects on family	4.50	4.98	4.50	4.80
Willingness to raise child at home	5.50	5.39	5.50	5.56
Cost to society	6.60	6.66	7.04	6.96

2. Potential quality of life (ie, degree of dependence on others, ability to communicate with others, possibility of marriage or employment).
3. Cost to society (ie, expense of hospital care, residential care, specialised education, and training).
4. Possible adverse effects on the family (ie, increased demands on the family's time and finances, changes in lifestyle, possible lack of understanding from others).
5. Parents' willingness to raise the child at home.
6. Type of treatment necessary (ie, whether the treatment is intensive or non-intensive, painful or painless, long-term or short-term, complicated or straight-forward).
7. Futility of treatment (ie, the child will not live long, whether treated or not). For the purpose of analysis, these rankings were then allocated weightings from 1 to 7. The highest ranking of 1 was categorised as "extremely important", 2 and 3 as "important", 4 and 5 as "little importance" and 6 and 7 as "no importance". The distribution of the four groups of parents across these four categories on four of the grounds for withholding treatment is shown in a series of graphs in the next section. As well, median rankings were calculated for each of the seven grounds and these are portrayed in Table 1.

RESULTS

From Table 1 it can be seen that the four groups of parents rated the seven grounds for withholding treatment in an identical order. Futility of treatment was considered to be the most important ground, followed by

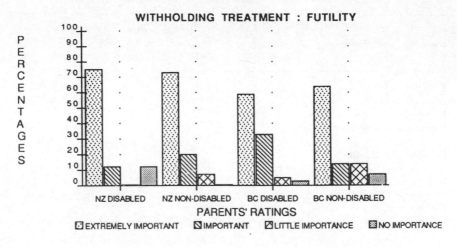

Figure 1.   Withholding treatment: futility.

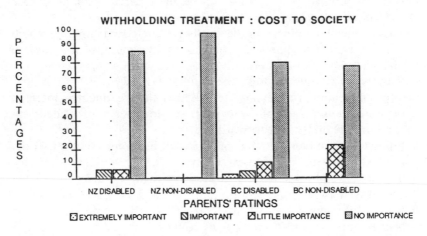

Figure 2.   Withholding treatment: cost to society.

the type of treatment, with cost to society being rated as the least important.

The actual distribution of the ratings for the highest and lowest ranked grounds, along with those for the variable of particular interest in this paper – quality of life – are portrayed in Figures 1, 2, and 3, respectively.

Figure 1 shows that futility of treatment received high ratings as a ground for withholding treatment by all four groups of respondents.

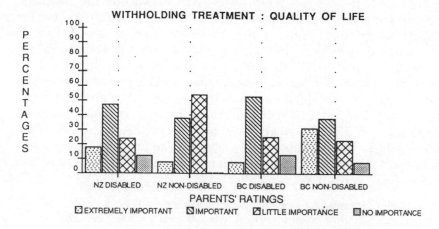

Figure 3. Withholding treatment: quality of life.

Those who rated it as being extremely important ranged from 59% of the BC parents of disabled children to 73% of the NZ parents of disabled children. Their views were encapsulated in the comments of one parent who said, "If the child is not going to live, then it may go through painful treatment for nothing". In contrast, cost to society was uniformly rated as of no importance. It was so rated by between 80% (BC parents of non-disabled children) and 100% (NZ parents of non-disabled children) of the subjects. Respondents offered a range of reasons for rejecting this as a ground for withholding treatment: "The state provides services for normal people who 'cost' society, like alcohol abusers, so they can provide it for others." "You can't set a price on a child."

Quality of life, ranked third out of the seven grounds for withholding treatment, received ratings across the whole spectrum of importance. For example, the BC parents of disabled children included 8% who considered quality of life to be extremely important, 53% who gave it moderately high ratings, 25% who considered it to be of little importance and 10% who gave it the lowest ratings.

DISCUSSION

This study shows that parents of developmentally disabled and non-disabled children in both British Columbia and New Zealand have similar views as to the degree of importance that should be accorded to various grounds for withholding treatment from seriously ill disabled children. While, in general, these parents generally favoured providing such treatment, when asked to consider what grounds would justify withholding treatment, the highest priority was given to whether the treatment would actually prolong the child's life, followed by a concern for the character of the treatment. At the other end of the scale, the parents were in broad agreement that factors relating to cost to society and the impact of the child with a disability on his or her family were the least justifiable grounds for withholding treatment. The presumed potential quality of life of the child with a disability received intermediate-level ratings, with parents expressing a broad spectrum of views as to its significance for deciding whether or not to provide treatment. These findings suggest that parents broadly reflect the ethical position argued by Mr Justice McKenzie in his judgement in the case of Stephen Dawson in the Supreme Court of British Columbia:

> It is not appropriate for an external decision-maker to apply his standards of what constitutes a livable life and exercise the right to impose death if that standard is not met in his estimation. The decision can only be made in the context of the disabled person viewing the worthwhileness or otherwise of his life in its own context as a disabled person. . . (Supreme Court of British Columbia, 1983).

ACKNOWLEDGEMENT

The writer should like to acknowledge the contributions made by Julie Avery in the development of many of the ideas expressed in this paper.

REFERENCES

Avery, J. (1986) *Parents' views on the witholding of life-supporting medical treatment from seriously ill disabled children*. Master of Social Science thesis, University of Waikato, Hamilton, New Zealand.

McClosky, H. J. (1980) Handicapped persons and the rights they possess. In: R. S. Laura (ed), *Problems of Handicap*. Macmillan, Melbourne.

Mitchell, D. R. (1985) Ethical and legal issues in providing medical treatment for seriously ill handicapped persons. *Aust. NZ. J. Dev. Dis.* **10**: 245–256.

Mitchell, D. R. (1986) Medical treatment of severely impaired infants in New Zealand hospitals. *NZ. Med. J.* **99**: 364–368.

Shepperdson, B. (1983) Abortion and euthanasia of Down's syndrome children – the parents' view. *J. Med. Eth.* **9**: 152–157.

Shaw, A., Randolph, J. G., and Manard, B. (1977) Ethical issues in pediatric surgery: a national survey of pediatricians and pediatric surgeons. *Pediatr.* **60**: 588–599.

Singer, P. (1983) Non-intervention in children with major disabilities. *Aust. Ped. J.* **19**: 215–216.

Supreme Court of British Columbia (1983) In the matter of Stephen Dawson and
     in the matter of a judicial review of a decision of Her Honour Judge Byrne.
     Vancouver Registry.
Tooley, M. A. (1973) A defence of abortion and infanticide. In: J. Feinberg (ed),
     The Problem of Abortion. Wadsworth, Belmont, California.
Young, R. (1979) What is wrong with killing people? *Philos.* **54**: 51–528.

Varieties (Classification) of Behavioural and Emotional Disorders in Retarded Children

A. Gath

The Maudsley Hospital and Hilda Lewis House, Bethlem Royal Hospital, London, England

In a paper published in 1986 (Gath and Gumley 1986) 38% of children with Down's syndrome and 48% of children with a similar degree of retardation were judged to have significant behaviour disorder, which was sufficiently severe and sufficiently prolonged to cause additional handicap or suffering to the child and the immediate family.

An attempt was made to classify these disorders using the currently available criteria of ICD 9 and DSM III.

The present paper discusses further the advantages and disadvantages of diagnostic classification for this range of disorders. Specific issues advanced begin with modifications now proposed in ICD 10 and DSM III R particularly in relation to pervasive developmental disorders.

Secondly, it is considered whether similar diagnoses have the same associations in Down's Syndrome, in children with demonstrable brain damage and in those for whom no medical aetiology has been demonstrated.

Thirdly, from those children who have siblings close in age, a comparison is made between the types of reaction seen in retarded and normal children exposed to the same environmental stress.

Finally, brief vignettes are presented of cases falling within the criteria of the main diagnostic groups.

Classification is a tool by which meaning may be attached to diagnostic findings in clinical and research reports, (Rutter and Gould, 1985). It provides a reliable framework whereby comparison may be made between groups of children in order to plan appropriate services or to search for common factors to improve the understanding of particular problems. The advantages are in better communication between clinicians, research workers and service managers. There are disadvantages of such diagnostic classification as they are open to abuse, particularly in the field of mental retardation where there is a long history of less than helpful labelling, which can often degenerate into becoming perjorative and prejudiced. However, abuse is minimised by adherence to good clinical practice. Thus any professional report should describe the findings and the implication in that particular child and not merely consist of a list of unexplained diagnostic jargon. Such reports should include the positive factors in each case. Strengths as well as needs should be noted.

Clinical work with mentally retarded children endorses the usefulness of a multiaxial framework of classification. Multiple problems are more often the rule than the exception. Some estimate of the degree of cognitive retardation is necessary as well as noting specific delays out of phase with the overall level of development. Any additional medical problem, such as epilepsy, or underlying condition such as mucopoly-saccharidosis, must be coded as well as pertinent family factors relevant to the management of the problems under consideration. These considerations can be coded under four of the codes of ICD 9. The remaining code, the first concerned with psychiatric diagnosis, is to be considered in this paper.

The use of a psychiatric diagnostic classification that is applicable for all children enables the research worker to look at the manifestation of behavioural disturbance and emotional distress across the whole intellectual range and, by comparison with children of normal intelligence, begin to distinguish between problems that arise from mental retardation or the common underlying cause and those that can possibly be attributed to family or other environmental factors, with important implications for treatment. A major problem in the ICD 9 version of classification lay in the limited categories available for the most severely disturbed children. In an earlier paper (Gath and Gumley, 1986), 38% of children with Down's syndrome and 48% of a group of children with similar retardation of other or unknown aetiology had emotional or behavioural problems that were of "sufficient severity and sufficiently prolonged to cause suffering and additional handicap to the child and the family", thus fulfilling the definition of psychiatric disorder. Dissatisfaction was expressed with the category of "Psychosis with origin specific to childhood". Not only did this category appear inappropriate to the children whose behaviour some attempt was being made to understand, but the old problem of perjorative labelling was there. Similar problems are seen in a second epidemiological paper published at the same time, (Gillberg et al., 1986). The difficulties have been tackled in the newer versions currently available, in DSM IIIR, or in preparation in ICD 10. The inclusion of the "Pervasive Developmental Disorders" is helpful and seems appropriate for the group of children in the comparative study of Down's syndrome children and others with a similar degree of retardation. The diagnostic categories for the two groups are amended as in Tables 1 and 2.

Table 1. Psychiatric diagnoses of Down's syndrome children with deviant behaviour

Diagnosis (ICD 10)	Boys	Girls	Total
Autism	2	0	2
Pervasive developmental disorder	9	8	17
Unsocialized conduct or mixed disorder	13	8	21
Mixed disorder	6	3	9
Emotional disorder	3	3	6
Hyperkinetic disorder (with developmental delay)	2	2	4
Hyperkinetic conduct disorder	9	5	14
Undiagnosed	0	1	1
Total	44	30	74

Table 2. Psychiatric diagnoses of non-Down's retarded children with deviant behaviour

	Boys	Girls	Total
Autism	2	1	3
Pervasive developmental disorder	14	10	24
Unsocialized conduct disorder	4	12	16
Mixed disorder	7	4	11
Emotional disorder	2	2	4
Hyperkinetic disorder (with developmental delay)	6	3	9
Hyperkinetic conduct disorder	1	1	2
Undiagnosed	3	2	5
Total	39	35	74

The allocation of reliable diagnoses within these categories of developmental disorder is not easy. Although for planning of services, the useful concept of social impairment (Wing and Gould, 1979) may be sufficient, a more rigorous approach is required in research, if further understanding of the aetiology of the disorders is to be achieved. Recently attention has once again been drawn to possible behavioural phenotypes of disorders, because of recent advances made in genetics. The highly specific problem of hyperphagia in Prader-Willi syndrome and the common occurence of autistic-like behaviours in the Fragile-X syndrome are examples of behaviours which might have genetic bases. Autistic-like disorders are also found in Tuberose Sclerosis, which is now

Table 3. Psychiatric diagnosis in non-Down's retarded children with deviant behaviour by presence of established brain damage

	Brain damage	No medical cause
Autism	1	2
Pervasive developmental disorder	9	11
		(3 specific syndromes, 2 no information)
Unsocialized conduct disorder	1	9
Emotional disorder	4	1
Hyperkinetic disorder (with developmental delay)	5	4
Hyperkinetic conduct disorder	2	3

known to be due to a gene malfunction on chromosome 9 (Hunt and Dennis, 1987).

As can be seen in Tables 1 and 2, there is little evidence for a specific disorder to be connected with the trisomy 21. Although not common, disorders with characteristics satisfying criteria for autism are found in children with Down's syndrome and at a not markedly dissimilar rate as in children of similar intellectual disability.

The comparison group of retarded children could be further sub-divided according to the medical diagnosis of an underlying aetiology. Table 3 compares the diagnostic grouping in those where actual brain damage is apparent from neurological examination or from clear evidence from the history and those in whom no medical abnormalities or aetiological factors have been found. The small group of children with a specific syndrome, such as San Fillippo disease, have been excluded. The one striking difference is in the conduct disorder group which is almost entirely confined to those without a medical diagnosis.

Only a few of the children with hyperkinetic disorder or hyperkinetic conduct disorder showed stereotypies, which were more likely to occur in children who showed social impairment and were diagnosed as pervasive developmental disorder. Extremely hyperactive behaviour was most common in brain damaged children who were diagnosed as having a pervasive developmental disorder. Hyperkinetic disorder, uncomplicated by severe impairment in social relationships, occurred in similar numbers in Down's syndrome, brain damaged children and in children with no medical diagnosis. Hyperkinetic conduct disorder was most common in Down's syndrome.

Family size tended to be larger (mean – 4.7) in the Down's syndrome children with unsocialized conduct disorder. Otherwise, there were few

Table 4. Deviancy in sibling and behavioural status of index retarded child

Behaviour of index
(The behavioural category 1 represents no disorder. Category 2 is the borderline
group and category 3 means definite psychiatric disorder present.)

	1		2		3		Total
Whole group		(%)		(%)		(%)	
Deviant sibs	14	(24)	11	(23)	28	(37)	53
OK sibs	45		37		48		130
Total	59		48		76		183
Down's							
Deviant sibs	5	(15)	5	(18.5)	12	(35)	22
OK sibs	29		22		22		73
Total	34		27		34		95
Non-Down's							
Deviant sibs	9	(36)	6	(29)	16	(38)	31
OK sibs	16		15		26		57
Total	25		21		42		88

indications that psycho-social factors were particularly important in conduct disorders, in contrast with what is usually associated with conduct disorder in the general population. The numbers, however, are not large.

Where there was a sibling close in age, a comparison could be made between the types of reaction seen in retarded, index child and the disorders found in their siblings of normal intelligence but exposed to some of the same environmental stresses, particularly those operating in the family. Table 4 shows the percentage of siblings with emotional or behavioural deviancy, as rated by parents and teachers using Rutter scales according to the psychiatric status of the index retarded child (Gath and Gumley, 1987). The behavioural category 1 represents no disorder. Category 2 is the borderline group and category 3 means definite psychiatric disorder present.

In the Down's syndrome group, deviancy in the siblings of normal intelligence tends to be more common in those families where the retarded children have definite disorders, but this is not the case in the Non-Down's group as a whole.

Reading problems in siblings had been found to be more common and associated with behavioural deviance in the brothers and sisters of children with no medical diagnosis.

There are 12 pairs of index child and normal sibling in the Down's syndrome group and 16 pairs in the Non-Down's group where both have

Table 5.   Psychiatric diagnoses in index retarded children and their siblings

N	Index (Down's and non-Down's)	Sibling		% of siblings with disorder
10	Emotional disorder	5	Emotional	
		5	No disorder	50
29	Hyperkinetic	4	Hyperkinetic	
		2	Conduct/mixed	
		2	Emotional	
		21	No disorder	28
57	Conduct/mixed	4	Conduct/mixed	
		2	Hyperkinetic	
		2	Emotional	
		49	No disorder	14
41	Pervasive developmental	3	Emotional	
		1	Hyperkinetic	
		1	Conduct/mixed	
		36	No disorder	12
5	Autism	5	No disorder	0

a disorder to which a diagnosis has been allocated (Table 5). 9 of the 16 index children in the Non-Down's group were suffering from brain damage or a specific syndrome thought to be the causative factor underlying the retardation.

Emotional disorders in the retarded children tend to be associated with both emotional disorders in the siblings next in age and in psychiatric illness in parents. Conduct disorder in both retarded and normal sibling occured in two families with no medical diagnosis and in one Down's syndrome family where a mother was coping alone, both children had a hyperkinetic conduct disorder. If there were hyperkinetic symptoms in the retarded child, there was a tendency for the siblings to show similar traits. Pervasive developmental disorder tended to be associated with emotional disturbance in the sibling, if both children were considered to have behaviour or emotional problems.

CONCLUSIONS

The use of a psychiatric diagnostic classification in the study of retarded children with behavioural problems is helpful in understanding the nature and possible treatment strategies. Emotional disorders are likely to be a manifestation of a predisposition to anxiety and depression that the retarded child may share with other members of the family. Similarly, there is a tendency for hyperkinetic behaviour in siblings to affect retarded child and normal sibling alike. Other disorders are more associated with the underlying pathology and require a different approach.

REFERENCES

American Psychiatric Association (1980) *Diagnostic and Statistical Manual of Mental Disorders* (3rd Edition, DSM-III). Washington, D.C. American Psychiatric Association.

American Psychiatric Association (1987) *Diagnostic and Statistical Manual of Mental Disorders* (3rd Edition – Revised, DSM-III-R. Washington, D.C. American Psychiatric Association.

Hunt, A. and Dennis, J. (1987) Psychiatric disorder among children with tuberose sclerosis. *Developmental Medicine and Child Neurology.* **29** 190–198.

Gath, A. and Gumley, D. (1986) Behaviour problems in retarded children with special reference to Down's Syndrome. *British Journal of Psychiatry* **149** 156–161.

Gath, A. and Gumley, D. (1987) Retarded children and their siblings. *Journal of Child Psychology and Psychiatry* **28** 715–730.

Gillberg, C., Persson, E., Grufman, M. and Themner, U. (1986) Psychiatric disorders in mildly and severely mentally retarded urban children and adolescents: epidemiological aspects. *British Journal of Psychiatry* **149** 68–74.

Rutter, M. and Gould, M. (1985) Classification. In Rutter, M. and Hersov, L. (eds) *Child and Adolescent Psychiatry: Modern Approaches*. 2nd Edition. Blackwell.

Rutter, M., Schaffer, D. and Shepherd, M. (1975) *A Multi-Axial Classification of Child Psychiatric Disorders* World Health Organization.

Wing, L. and Gould, J. (1979) Severe impairments of social interaction and associated abnormalities in children: epidemiology and classification. *Journal of Autism and Developmental Disorders* **9** 11–30.

The Management of Down's Syndrome Children and their Families in General Practice

J. C. Murdoch and V. E. Anderson
*Department of General Practice, Otago Medical School,
P.O. Box 913, Dunedin, New Zealand*

The mothers of 35 children with Down's syndrome (D.S.) and their general practitioners (G.P.) resident in the South Island of New Zealand were interviewed to explore parent and doctor perceptions of the importance of the G.P. assuming responsibility for various aspects of care and satisfaction of both with the care received and provided. The results show that the G.P.'s had considerable insight into the family situation but had a tendency to underestimate the problems parents face in obtaining services and in their interactions with professionals while overestimating the prevalence of negative attitudes which parents experience in the community. A general sense of agreement was found concerning the G.P.'s perceived role, the treatment of episodic illness and the ongoing supervision of general health care being seen as the G.P.'s prime responsibility. Parents surprisingly felt that G.P.'s should also be involved in giving information on the cause of D.S. and genetic counselling. Significant dissatisfaction was recorded by parents in the G.P.'s role in coordinating the care of the child and in referral for visual and hearing assessment. The information revealed by this study can be applied to the vocational training of the G.P. so that their role in the care of D.S. people can be further enhanced.

INTRODUCTION

Down's syndrome comprises the largest single easily identifiable group of intellectually handicapped persons, and in those who live in the community, responsibility for medical care lies in the hands of the general practitioner. In New Zealand there are approximately 2000 general practitioners who provide care to individuals and families on a fee-for-service basis. In previous studies in Scotland, Murdoch (1984a, 1984b, 1984c) has emphasised the key role of the general practitioner in assisting

143

the optimal medical advice and care for the Down's infant and child. These papers looked separately at the view of care obtained by the general practitioner, the mother and the so-called expert. This study was designed to look at the care given by the general practitioner from the point of view of the practitioner and the parents simultaneously, with a view to identifying areas of significant agreement and disagreement between the two.

METHODOLOGY

Forty-eight Down's syndrome children aged between 18 months and 12 years were identified through a survey of local general practitioners and from the records of the Society for the Intellectually Handicapped (IHC). The final sample comprised 45 families, 22 of whom lived in Otago/ Southland and 23 in metropolitan Christchurch. The parents were contacted and after the purpose of the study was explained to them, all but one agreed to take part. The children's general practitioners were then mailed questionnaires with a covering letter explaining the study and 28 general practitioners of 35 children agreed to take part (78%) of whom 14 lived in Otago/Southland and 14 in Christchurch.

The mothers were interviewed using a structured questionnaire, designed to obtain data on parents' perceptions of the role of the general practitioner in management, a history of their consultations with the doctor, and an indication of the services which might be offered in a general practitioner's practice. For each item mothers were asked to rate on a 1–9 scale ("extremely important" to "unimportant") the extent to which they perceived this to be a service the general practitioner should be able to provide; indicate whether or not they had required this service from their doctor, (yes/no) and finally to evaluate the care they had received by means of their agreement or disagreement with a series of statements about the care given (Likert Scale format). Questions investigating the parents' perceptions of the problems they faced in the care of their child and the effects on the family were also asked. These included (1) the attitude of others and community acceptance, (2) problems of obtaining services, (3) problems of obtaining information, (4) intellectual and emotional adjustment, (5) demands on time, health and finance, (6) effect on family relationships and functioning and (7) restrictions on the employment, leisure and social activities of the parents. Mothers were asked to rank these in the order of the severity of the problems each had presented. They were then asked to rate each problem on a scale of 1–9 ("very severe problems" to "no problem").

The questions put to the general practitioners were 90 in number and all but six items corresponded closely with the questions asked of the parents. The remainder addressed the respondents' demographic data and detail from practice notes. They were asked to indicate on a scale of 1–9 (ranging from "extremely important" to "unimportant") the extent to which they perceived the services to be those which a G.P. should offer; and secondly to rate on a Likert scale (ranging from "strongly agree" to "strongly disagree") the extent to which a general practitioner feels at ease or competent in providing each service. Questions focusing on the impact of a Down's syndrome child on the family, and on the problems that have arisen relating to the child's management – comparable to those asked of the parents – were asked in order to detect differences that may exist between how mothers describe their problems and how professionals perceive mothers' problems.

The association between parent and general practitioner response was examined by the Wilcoxon matched pairs test described by Seigel (1956).

RESULTS

For the purposes of this paper we will concentrate on the differences in perception between the mothers and the general practitioners. Essential background will first be given, however, to the experience which the family and the general practitioners had of each other.

Twenty-five of the childen had been born in the care of that doctor and had remained with his practice and, of these families, thirteen had been attending the same doctor for 10 years or more. The general practitioners were attending to all the family members in 30 of the families. While 16 of the 45 families had had a change of doctor since the Down's child's birth, only 3 of the families had changed doctors because of dissatisfaction with his/her management, one family having changed twice. The reasons given were refusal of home visits, incorrect prescribing, poor medical care and a pessimistic attitude on the part of the doctor. All but one of the children had seen the doctor over the previous year, mainly for respiratory infections. Eight of the 28 doctors had had no previous experience of a Down's child in their practice and only seven had had a non-professional contact with persons with the syndrome.

The mean ratings of the importance of various general practitioner services as perceived by mothers and doctors are seen in Table 1. Both mothers and doctors saw such services as having an important contribution to make to all the aspects of care examined, and the mean ratings for both groups are all above the mid-point on the scale. There is significant disagreement over the importance of the general practitioner's role in the provision of information about the cause of the syndrome (p < 0.001) and in genetic counselling (p < 0.001) and in both cases the mothers rate the importance of the service higher.

The responses tend to suggest that the doctors are generally willing to assume a wider role for themselves than parents are willing to grant,

Table 1. Mean ratings of the importance of various G.P. services as perceived by parents and G.P.s and a measure of disagreement between them

Questionnaire item	Parents (N = 35) mean[1]	sd	G.P.s (N = 35) mean	sd	p	z
Information on cause	1.6	1.1	2.7	1.2	***	3.3
Information on prognosis	2.7	1.4	2.8	1.1		0.5
Referral to services	2.5	1.4	3.0	1.7		1.7
Co-ordination	3.7	1.8	3.1	2.1		0.3
Medical care	1.5	0.9	1.5	0.8		0.3
Vision/hearing assessment	2.0	1.2	2.6	1.5		1.6
Child-care advice	3.8	1.8	3.2	1.3		1.8
Developmental advice	5.0	1.8	4.0	1.3		1.8
Long-term planning	4.1	1.8	3.9	1.3		0.1
Genetic counselling	1.8	1.2	3.2	1.9	**	3.2
Parent counselling	2.9	1.7	2.3	1.2		1.9
Contact availability	2.2	1.4	2.3	1.5		0.1
Availability of appointments	2.6	1.5	2.3	1.3		1.3
Family orientation	2.6	1.8	2.3	1.4		1.5
Care for all family members	2.5	1.5	2.3	1.2		1.2
Continuity of care	2.4	1.2	3.0	1.4		1.5
Information on treatment and progress	2.1	1.1	2.5	1.2		1.4

[1] A scale of 1–9 was used. A score of 1 indicates the service is extremely important; 5 indicates the service is of moderate importance; 9 indicates the service is unimportant.
** $p < 0.01$
***$p < 0.001$

particularly with respect to "parent counselling", "advice on developmental aspects of child care", and "advice on child rearing practices", but these differences are not statistically significant. Not surprisingly, "medical care" receives the most consistent rating from both mothers and doctors.

The mothers were asked if they had consulted their doctor about various service areas and then asked whether they had received some form of assistance. Figure 1 shows the reports of all 45 families in this respect. Again this shows that the general practitioners are performing adequately in the provision of medical services but there are potentially serious trends in the areas of vision and hearing testing. It may be

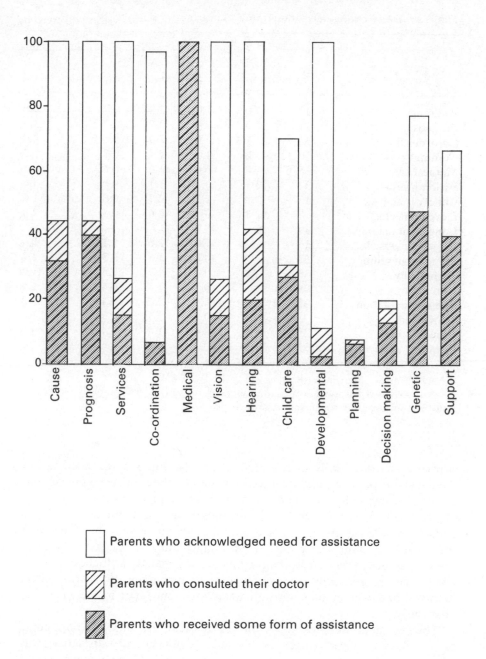

Figure 1. Parents' reports of various services by their G.P.s (N=45).

Table 2. Satisfaction scale – descriptive statistics

Service Area	N^2	Parent (N = 35) mean^3	sd	G.P. (N = 35) mean	sd	p	z
Aetiology	12	2.0	1.0	2.2	0.7		0.8
Prognosis	14	2.3	0.9	2.7	0.7		1.1
Co-ordination	32	3.1	0.6	2.0	0.5	***	4.0
Community services	10	3.0	1.1	2.4	0.8		1.2
Medical care	35	1.7	0.6	1.6	0.5		0.5
Vision/hearing	34	3.1	0.9	2.1	0.6	***	3.6
Child care advice	15	2.9	1.2	2.7	0.8		1.1
Developmental advice	7	2.1	0.8	2.6	0.5	*	2.0
Long term planning	19	2.8	0.7	–	–		–
Genetic counselling	16	2.2	1.0	2.6	1.1		1.0
Parent counselling	33	2.2	0.8	1.8	0.3	*	2.1
Availability	35	1.9	0.4	1.7	0.4		1.9
Continuity	35	1.9	0.5	1.7	0.4		1.6
Family orientation	35	2.0	0.5	1.7	0.4	*	2.2
Information	35	2.4	0.7	2.1	0.7		1.4
Conduct	35	2.0	0.6	1.8	0.4		0.6
General satisfaction	35	1.9	0.7	2.2	0.6		1.2

[2] N = number of parents responding
[3] A scale of 1–5 was used. A score of 1 indicates the respondent is strongly satisfied. A score of 5 indicates the respondent is strongly dissatisfied
  * p<0.05
  *** p<0.001

surprising to the family doctor that so few parents see the need to ask advice about planning and decision-making. At the same time the parents were asked who else they consulted about these problems. A wide range of professionals and services were consulted. It would appear that the 20 children attending the early intervention programme were provided with the most consistent safety net. A worrying feature is the fact that 24 of the 45 families answered in the negative to the question "Is there anyone who oversees your child's care, who is in communication with others involved and who makes sure all areas are being met in the best way possible?"

The satisfaction expressed by the parents with the various components of the doctors' care is seen in Table 2. Significant dissatisfaction was expressed in the areas of overall coordination and referral for vision and hearing testing. Because of these factors, the mothers seem to be less satisfied than the doctors in the care given but in terms of the key issues of medical care, availability, continuity and general satisfaction, the parents seem to be well pleased with the service on the whole.

Mothers and general practitioners were asked to respond to a number of items on a scale designed to assess their perception of the impact of a Down's child on the family and the responses are seen in Table 3. The doctors over-estimated the negative impact of the child on the family particularly with regard to neighbourhood acceptance, restricted holidays (both p < 0.001), restricted outings and social contacts and the ability to treat the Down's child as a normal child (p < 0.01) and restricted employment (p < 0.05).

DISCUSSION

Murdoch (1982, 1984a, 1984b, 1984c, 1984d) in a series of studies in Scotland, has described the prevalence of Down's syndrome people under general practitioner care, the relative morbidity of parents and children, the experience of general practitioner care when the mother returned from hospital after birth, and the special difficulties for the general practitioner in the care of the family with a Down's syndrome member. This is the first study which has looked at the views of the mothers and the general practitioner simultaneously and it again underlines themes apparent in the previous studies.

The first concerns the very positive aspects of the general practitioner's role. Twenty of the 28 doctors had known the families for 5 years or more and in most cases the same person was providing care for the whole family. Although there had been 19 changes of doctor, only 4 of these were due to dissatisfaction with the doctor's performance. Gray (1979) has described the tendency to change general practitioner as being more common in the families with handicapped children but there seems little evidence of that in this group. Both the parents and the general practitioners saw general practice as having a significant contribution to make to all the various aspects of care examined. This was particularly so in the areas usually associated with the delivery of good primary health care, i.e. the provision of medical care, availability of the service, continuity of doctor, where there was concordance between the mothers and the doctors in their perception of the services given. The responses indicated the importance of the moral support given by the doctor in the course of the consultations and this underlines the necessity of the use of a patient-centred model for the conduct of the consultation, so that the visit for the intercurrent respiratory infection can be used to promote health in other ways. It is interesting, however, that the mothers seem to feel that this role should go further and that they rate "information on cause" and "genetic counselling" almost as highly in both importance and satisfaction. Murdoch (1984c) has described the necessity of a contract between mother and doctor in these families and it seems that heed

Table 3. Impact-on-family scale descriptive statistics

Questionnaire item[4]	Item statistics						Subscale statistics						
	Parents		G.P.s				Parents		G.P.s				
	mean[5]	sd	mean	sd	p	z	mean	sd	mean	sd	p	z	
Restricted (1) employment	3.1	1.3	3.5	1.1	*	2.0			Financial				
Extra expenses (20)	3.2	1.1	3.3	0.7		0.9	3.2	0.9	3.6	0.7		1.7
Relationship with (2) other children	2.3	1.2	2.6	1.1		1.0							
Neighbourhood (3) acceptance	1.8	0.8	2.6	0.8	***	3.3							
Restricted outings (5)	1.5	0.7	2.1	0.7	**	2.6							
Family gives things (8)	2.4	1.1	2.5	0.9		0.9			Familial/social				
D.S. child/sibling (10) relationships	1.7	0.7	1.9	0.7		0.4	1.9	0.5	2.4	0.5	***	3.9
Consider no further (13) pregnancies	2.3	1.0	2.9	1.1		1.7							
Less time for other (15) family members	1.9	0.8	2.2	0.8		1.3							
See family and (16) friends less	1.7	0.5	2.3	0.8	**	3.0							
Restricted holidays (17)	1.6	0.5	2.2	0.7	***	3.4							

Table 3. continued

| | Item statistics | | | | | | Subscale statistics | | | | | |
| | Parents | | G.P.s | | | | Parents | | G.P.s | | | |
Questionnaire item[4]	mean[5]	sd	mean	sd	p	z		mean	sd	mean	sd	p	z
Parent fatigue (4)	2.6	1.0	2.9	1.1		1.3							
Living day to day (7)	2.1	0.8	2.0	0.7		1.9							
Burden not understood (11)	2.3	0.9	2.3	0.7		0.3	Personal strain	2.3	0.6	2.4	0.5		0.4
Travelling to G.P. (18)	2.0	0.7	2.2	0.8		1.0							
Finding reliable child care (21)	2.7	1.2	2.7	0.9		0.9							
Relatives understanding (6)	1.7	1.0	2.1	0.9		1.8							
Treat child as a normal child (9)	1.5	0.5	2.2	0.8	**	2.6	Mastery	2.0	0.5	2.2	0.5		1.7
Closer family (12)	2.7	1.1	2.4	0.8		0.9							
Discuss child with partner (14)	2.0	0.9	2.2	0.6		0.7							
Parents feel better about selves (19)	2.3	0.8	2.5	0.6		1.4							

[4] Brackets indicate questionnaire numbering
[5] A scale of 1–5 was used. A score of 1 indicates no negative impact. A score of 5 indicates a large degree of negative impact
* p<0.05   ** p<0.01   *** p<0.001
Parents mean total scale score was 2.1 (sd 0.4); G.P.s was 2.5 (sd 0.4). A z score of 2.9 was calculated (p<0.01).

should be taken of the ratings given to the topics in Table 1 for the purposes of drawing this up.

The second theme concerns the deficiencies in the care provided by these doctors which illustrates a general problem when generically trained professionals have to care for a comparatively rare syndrome. In spite of a wealth of studies indicating the need for hearing and vision testing in Down's syndrome individuals, the professionals seem to be behind mothers in their awareness of this issue. The relatively low priority accorded to these issues by the general practitioners suggests that there is still a considerable risk that optimal development might not be achieved through "authoritative ignorance". The results also reveal a problem for these families in terms of overall coordination. It is not perhaps surprising that the general practitioners were not providing a coordinating role but the sad fact was that many of them thought they were and that in more than half of the cases the mothers were aware of no one having a coordinating role. While this study refers only to the situation in New Zealand in 1986, my opinion is that it reflects a universal problem and it is sobering to reflect how much damage in outcome for the family and the child is being suffered as a result.

The final theme concerns the relatively pessimistic view which these professionals had of these families' plight in contrast to that of the mothers. Although it is possible to exaggerate this finding it probably relates to the lack of experience which the doctors had of Down's syndrome at a social level. This defect might easily be corrected by the doctors spending some time with these families in purely social interactions but this seems to be too high a price for most professionals to pay. Less threatening might be the organising of educational sessions for students and established practitioners in which they gain some insight into the realities of having a Down's syndrome child as previously described by Murdoch (1979). The problem with this approach is that teachers tend to ask "model" families to provide the cast for such productions and the practical help given is therefore minimised. The attitudes revealed in this study are bound to affect the doctor's performance in delivering appropriate health care to such families.

In conclusion we live in an age when patient-centredness is in vogue in Family Medicine/General Practice (Levenstein *et al.* 1986) and when every self-respecting undergraduate and postgraduate programme will have as its objectives seeing childhood chronic illness from the family's point of view. It is therefore enlightening to discover that, at least in New Zealand in 1986, these objectives were not being translated into performance for the 35 families involved. The hopeful fact is that the results of this study show that progress might be made if the mothers and doctors could discuss the issues involved and use them to draw up a contract for their future relationship with each other.

REFERENCES

Gray, D. J. P. (1979) The handicapped child in general practice. *Hunterian Soc. Trans.* **28**: 121–175.

Levenstein, J. H., McCracken, E. C., McWhinney, I. R., Stewart, M. C., and Brown, J. B. (1986) The patient-centred clinical method. 1. A model for the doctor-patient interaction in family medicine. *Family Practice* **3**: 24–30.

Murdoch, J. C. (1979) Paediatric teaching in general practice. *Allgemeinmedizin International* **4**: 178–179.

Murdoch, J. C. (1982) A survey of Down's syndrome under general practitioner care in Scotland. *J. Roy. Coll. Gen. Practit.* **32**: 410–418.

Murdoch, J. C. (1984a) Comparative morbidity of Down's syndrome children and their parents. In J. M. Berg (ed.) *Perspectives and Progress in Mental Retardation*. Vol. 11 pp. 47–53. University Park Press, Baltimore.

Murdoch, J. C. (1984b) Experience of mothers of Down's syndrome and spina bifida children on going home from hospital in Scotland. 1971–1981. *J. Ment. Defic. Res.* **28**: 123–127.

Murdoch, J. C. (1984c) The family care of the Down's syndrome child. *J. Mat. Child Health* **9**: 69–72.

Murdoch, J. C. and Ogston, S. A. (1984d) Down's syndrome and parental psychological upset. *J. Roy. Coll. Gen. Practit.* **34**: 87–90.

Seigel, S. (1956) *Non parametric statistics for the behavioural sciences*. McGraw-Hill Book Company, Tokyo.

Health Care for the Developmentally Disabled. Is It Necessary?

H. Beange and A. Bauman

Health Promotion Unit for the Developmentally Disabled,
Royal North Shore Hospital, Pacific Highway, St. Leonards,
N.S.W. 2065 Australia and
Department of Public Health, University of Sydney, N.S.W. 2006,
Australia

251 patients who attended a Health Promotion Clinic for the Developmentally Disabled are described. They were predominantly young adults, the majority of whom lived in the community and obtained their health care from general practitioners. Modifiable health risk factors were found including obesity, hypertension, inactivity and polypharmacy. There was a high prevalence of chronic medical disorders, especially sensory and neurological problems. The average number of impairments in addition to cognitive disability was two per person. Two thirds of these conditions were previously undiagnosed. It is concluded that regular comprehensive accessible health care is needed by disabled people wherever they live.

The aim of this study was to determine the frequency of medical problems in a case series of developmentally disabled people and to examine their needs for health care. They were found to have many disorders which gave opportunities for primary, secondary and tertiary prevention.

Policies of de-institutionalisation have thrown a spotlight on individuals with disability. Placement in community houses has raised general public awareness and increased optimism about possibilities for improvement. Health and fitness are important under these circumstances. However there has been a tendency to deny that special health problems exist, and to hope that all disabled people living in the community could be cared for by existing services. Reality suggests that such is not the case. Medical care was easily available in institutions. There are now geographical, financial, and organizational barriers to overcome including the need for the majority of clients to be escorted to medical care.

154

Health is obviously a problem because mortality is high among developmentally disabled persons. (Forssman and Akesson, 1970; Fryers, 1984). It is often taken for granted that this increased death rate is caused by the intrinsic factors of associated disabilities. Life expectancy can also be decreased by modifiable extrinsic factors such as the living environment and personal lifestyle. Both these factors deserve scrutiny.

Many published surveys have shown the greater prevalence of associated disorders in disabled people. The results of nine studies are summarised in Table 2. These surveys suggest that the group possesses many complex chronic medical needs requiring a wide range of specialist services. Medical reasons are a frequent cause of return to institutional care from community placement (Keys *et al.*, 1973) and families can be opposed to community care because of the medical needs of their disabled relatives (Conroy, 1985). Thus medical needs play a central role in determining placement (Seltzer and Krauss, 1984).

The frequency of medical disorders in the intellectually disabled has been studied mainly in institutions and in children. There is a dearth of published information about the health of adults and those who live in the community (Rubin, 1987).

METHODS

This study is an analysis of the health problems and the health needs of a case series. It describes persons who have attended a Health Promotion Clinic for the Developmentally Disabled at Royal North Shore Area Health Service since August 1986. The patients attended for a general check-up and advice about diet and exercise, so the bias may have been to the motivated well rather than the worried sick. This large case series is probably representative of the total population of disabled people living in the catchment area of the health service. A further community based prevalence study in the entire area will test this assumption. The disabled population ostensibly have access to a wide range of health services in this middle class area which is well provided with health resources.

Only 17% of the patients had symptoms, the majority (49%) wanted a check-up, 37% had a desire to improve weight or fitness, 4% had other reasons.

The total number seen was 251. There were 129 females, 122 males. The majority (60%) were young adults between 20 and 30 years, but 17% were below 20 years and 25% were over thirty. The youngest patient was 18 months and the oldest patient was 62. The mean age was 28 years.

A clinical judgment of degree of intellectual disability was assisted by educational history and sometimes by results of formal psychometric testing. 40% were judged to be of mild or borderline degree of handicap, 34% moderate, 13% severe, 13% profound. Thus about 40% appeared to

Table 1.   Diagnostic Categories

	No.	%
Down's syndrome	74	29
Other genetic disorders	19	7.5
Cerebral palsy	17	7
Identified syndromes	41	17
Multiple congenital anomalies (unclassifiable)	19	7.5
Undiagnosed	81	32
Total	251	100.0

have I.Q. above 50, 60% below 50, which is similar to the distribution found in the recent population surveys of Fishbach and Hull (1982); and Mulcahy *et al.* (1983)

The majority of these individuals lived in the community. 46% were in their own homes, 39% lived in group homes, 8% in a hostel, 7% in institutions.

Table 1 illustrates the diagnostic features of the sample.

RESULTS

Risk Factors

Risk factors for disease were examined and results compared with those of the Risk Factor Prevalance Study by the National Heart Foundation (1983) in a survey of 7,500 Australians. This was a representative random population survey of cardiovascular risk factors.

The frequency of hypertension was basically the same as the general population but fewer of our subjects were under treatment. It was noted that none of the Down's Syndrome subjects were hypertensive. The age adjusted prevalence of hypertension in those disabled persons who did not have Down's Syndrome was 15%, slightly greater than the prevalence of 10% in the general population of the same age.

Nutritional disorders were increased in the study group. The measurement used was the Body Mass Index, described by Bray, 1978, and expressed as kilograms per metre squared (kg/m^2). An index less than 20 represents underweight, 21–25 is normal weight, 26–30 overweight, more than 30 is obesity. In this sample the age adjusted prevalance of both underweight and obesity was significantly higher than in the general population.

Obesity is a well known risk factor for hypertension, heart disease, diabetes and osteo-arthritis. Undernutrition is also associated with increased mortality, according to Belloc (1973). The most underweight individual died a few months later and some of the other undernourished subjects were subject to frequent illness.

Cholesterol levels were similar to those of the general population, 30% having levels higher than 5.5 mmol/litre. However public health education on risk factors and "healthy lifestyle" was not reaching our clients.

Only two of these subjects had ever been married, both of them female: this is a frequency of less than 1%, contrasting with the seventy per cent of the National Heart Foundation 1983 population who were "ever married" at the time of the survey. Marital status is a major demographic difference between the disabled and the non disabled. As Lee *et al.* (1987) have shown in Australia, never being married is associated with an increased mortality rate. As single people have a higher death rate than married people, the single state of disabled clients could be considered a health risk.

Analysis of our first 100 patients showed some interesting variations in other health practices. This sample smokes and drinks less than average Australians, which should be beneficial. However the disabled subjects take less exercise and sleep a great deal more than the general population (National Heart Foundaton, 1983). Belloc and Breslow (1972) showed that sleeping more than 9 hours is associated with poor health, and that exercise is associated with good health.

The last risk factor is polypharmacy. 38% of our sample were on daily prescribed medication (excluding the oral contraceptive), most commonly anti-psychotics and anticonvulsants. One man was taking 8 medications, one woman was taking 9. Polypharmacy is of questionable value and causes iatrogenic disease (Aman, 1987; Tu, 1979). There were three cases of drug induced Parkinsonism, one of macrocytic anaemia due to years of unnecessary nitrofurantoin, two cases of leucopenia associated with the use of carbamazepine.

Frequency of Medical Problems

There were many associated chronic conditions and these were present almost as frequently in the mildly as in the severely disabled. These frequencies have been observed in other surveys and our figures are in the middle range as shown in Table 2. Considering that the majority of our subjects lived in the community, the prevalence of medical disorders is high.

Ocular Disease was present in 38% and was the commonest problem. Conical corneas and cataracts were the most serious with potential for loss of sight. Refractive errors and astigmatism were prevalent, and many individuals needed spectacles. Squints had often been untreated with poor functional and cosmetic results.

E.N.T. conditions occurred in 28%, 20% of which was deafness. Because hearing tests in school had been normal it was often assumed that no further testing was necessary. Many with bilateral deafness had lost their speech. Prescribed hearing aids were not always worn.

Gross dental disease was present in 29%. This ranged from complete loss of teeth to widespread caries, and severe periodontal disease. Oral hygiene was deficient and the majority of these patients were unable to clean their own teeth, or to manage dentures successfully. As good nutrition partly depends on dentition, this is another remediable health problem.

16% had active epilepsy, 19% other forms of obvious neurological disease. The epilepsy was usually treated by a general practitioner and drug reviews and blood counts were needed. There were 8 cases of Alzheimer's Disease, all of them with Down's Syndrome.

Subjects were reckoned to have behavioural disturbance if this contributed significant additional handicap. 24% had behavioural problems. A few were in active therapeutic programmes but the usual treatment was by a major tranquillizer.

Active psychosis undergoing psychiatric treatment was present in 4%.

Hypertension was present in 13%. No cases of hypertension were associated with Down's Syndrome. Other cardiovascular disease, mainly congenital heart disease, was seen in 6%. There was one case of stroke due to carotid artery disease.

Skin disease was present in 25%. Many of these conditions were severe and needed referral to a dermatologist. Poor hygiene and obesity were contributing factors.

Genito-urinary conditions occurred in 16%, commonly urinary tract infections and menstrual disorders.

Gastro-intestinal disorders were seen in 9%. This includes two active carriers of Hepatitis B. Both of these had Down's Syndrome and lived at home with younger siblings.

Musculo-skeletal conditions were frequent at a rate of 28%. Typical examples weree scoliosis, Perthe's Disease, osteo-arthritis, contractures and congenital hip disease. Two women were referred for hip replacements.

Endocrine disease occurred in 9.5%. The commonest was thyroid disease especially in those with Down's Syndrome, where it was seen in 22%.

Respiratory disease was relatively rare at 5% and asthma was seen in only 6 persons or 2%. This is less frequent than in the Australian community. Each case of asthma occurred in a mildly retarded person.

Table 2. Prevalence of medical problems reported in developmentally disabled persons

Disorder	Frequency Range in other surveys[a] %	Present survey n	Present survey %
Eye conditions	23–57	95	38
Hearing loss	3–24	50	20
Other E.N.T. conditions	15–27	21	8
Dental disease	11–27	72	29
Epilepsy	21–34	41	16
Other neurological disease	12–55	48	19
Psychiatric	10–14	11	4
Behavioural problems	17–56	61	24
Obesity	10–22	52[b]	22
Hypertension		30[b]	13
Other cardiovascular	5–23	15	6
Daily prescribed medication	30–58	95	38
High cholesterol > 5.5		69[b]	30
Genito-urinary	5–11	40	16
Gastro-intestinal	1–22	23	9
Musculo-skeletal	13–54	71	28
Endocrine disease	3–11	24	9.5
Dermatological	4–35	64	25
Asthma		6	2
Other respiratory disease	7–13	8	3
Other		18	7
Total n	From 48–800	251	100

[a] Decker *et al.*, 1968, Eaton & Menolascino, 1982, Fox *et al.*, 1985, Larson & Lapointe, 1986, Minihan, 1986, Nelson & Crocker, 1978, Schor *et al.*, 1981, Smith *et al.*, 1969, and Tuppurainen, 1983.
[b] Total n 233.

No person with Down's Syndrome complained of asthma.

Other occasional disease encountered included microcytic anaemia, inguinal hernias and prostatic hypertrophy.

An estimate was made of the average number of chronic additional disabilities. Health problems were only counted if they were considered to be significant enough to impair function and warrant treatment. The average number of extra disorders was two. Some persons, had as many as 4 or 5. In many cases the physical difficulties were more limiting than intellectual disability. New diagnoses of previously undetected conditions were made in 66% of the subjects.

DISCUSSION

These results indicate a significant burden of chronic ill-health. If these conditions had been identified and treatment given it may be concluded that medical care was satisfactory. However more than half the conditions were unrecognised and untreated. Neglect of periodic physical examinations leads to false optimism about the health of disabled people.

The majority of these individuals were looked after by general practitioners, and presented themselves only for intercurrent illness. It was exceptional for any specialist to be involved. The commonest referrals from the clinic were to the ophthalmologist, the audiology/E.N.T. clinic, and the dental clinic. Neurologists, dermatologists, orthopaedic surgeons, psychiatrists, gynaecologists, endocrinologists, cardiologists, geneticists, were also frequently consulted. The children had sometimes seen pediatricians, but adults were rarely in contact with specialist physicians.

Preventive health care is a contentious issue in Australia where practitioners reimbursed on a fee for service system are discouraged from screening patients. However this special population cannot be expected to arrange their own preventive care. Renewal of tetanus and diptheria immunization, mammograms for women over 40 years, Papanicolaou smears of sexually active females, Hepatitis B profiles, and checks of the skin and testes for neoplastic disease had been neglected in the great majority. There needs to be a fail-safe mechanism for keeping preventive measures up to date.

Our obese patients were encouraged to diet and all those who were stiff, inactive, lacking in muscular strength urged to take more exercise. The results have been encouraging and suggest that primary prevention of disease is possible in the disabled population.

Medical diagnosis still depends on adequate history taking. Most of our clients had communication problems, and did not present symptoms until disease was advanced. The medical record is therefore vital and should follow the patient from one residence to another and from one doctor to another. The medical records of our clients were often unavailable.

In summary, the patients who have attended our clinic have increased health risks for disease, namely obesity, hypertension, inactivity and overmedication. In addition to intellectual disability they have an average two chronic physical disorders per person. Our patients obtained their health care mainly from general practitioners, and two thirds of their medical conditions were previously undiagnosed. They had difficulties in access to medical care and were not communicating successfully with their doctors. Preventive health care was neglected.

The conclusion drawn is that developmentally disabled people wherever they may live need easy access to comprehensive regular health care, which is specific to their needs. Periodic health examinations are required and preventive health care must be scheduled into their programmes. There is a case for a specialised health service for disabled persons similar to that provided by geriatricians for the elderly population.

To avoid the selection bias which is possible in a hospital case series, a population based survey of medical disorders in intellectually disabled persons is planned and will be reported when completed.

Health care may be as important for disabled persons as special education. Katherine Mansfield defined health as "the power to live a full adult, breathing life in close contact with what I love – the earth and the wonders thereof. . . I want to be all I am capable of becoming". A disabled person deserves to be what he or she is capable of becoming.

REFERENCES

Aman, M. G. (1987) Overview of Pharmacotherapy: Current status and future directions. *J. Ment. Def. Res.* **31**: 121–130.

Belloc, N. B. and Breslow, L. (1972) Relationship of Physical Health Status and Health Practices. *Prev. Med.* **1**: 409–421.

Belloc, N. B. (1973) Relationship of Health Practices and Mortality. *Prev. Med.* **2**: 67–81.

Bray, G. A. (1978) Definition, measurement, and classification of the symptoms of obesity. *Int. J. Obes.* **2**: 99–112.

Conroy, J. W. (1985) Medical Needs of Institutionalised Mentally Retarded Persons: Perceptions of Families and Staff Members. *Am. J. of Ment. Defic.* **89**: 510–514.

Decker, H. A., Herberg, E. N., Haythornthwaite, M. S., Rupke, L. K. & Smith, D. C. (1968) Provision of Health Care for Institutionalised Retarded Children. *Am. J. of Ment. Defic.* **73**: 283–293.

Eaton, L. F. and Menolascino, F. J. (1982) Psychiatric Disorders in the Mentally Retarded: Types Problems and Challenges. *Am. J. Psychiatry* **139**: 1297–1303.

Fishbach, M. and Hull, J. T. (1982) Mental Retardation in the Province of Manitoba. *Canada's Mental Health* **30**: 16–29.

Forssman, H. F. and Akesson, H.O. (1970) Mortality of the Mentally Deficient: A Study of 12,903 Institutionalised Subjects. *J. Ment. Defic. Res.* **14**: 276–294.

Fox, R. A., Hartney, C. W., Rotatori, A. F. and Kurpiers, E. M. (1985) Incidence of Obesity Among Retarded Children. *Education & Training of the Mentally Retarded*, September: 175–181.

Fryers, T. (1984) Mortality and Cause of Death. In: *The Epidemiology of Severe Intellectual Impairment. The Dynamics of Prevalence.* pp. 139–141. Academic Press, London.

Keys, V., Boroskin, A. and Ross, R. (1973) The Revolving Door in an MR Hospital: A Study of Returns from Leave. *Mental Retardation*, **11(1)**: 55–56.

Larson, C. P. and Lapointe, Y. (1986) The Health Status of Mild to Moderate Intellectually Handicapped Adolescents. *J. Ment. Def. Res.* **30**: 121–128.

Lee, S. H., Smith, L., d'Espaignet, E. and Thomson, N. (1987) Marital Status Differentials. In: *Health Differentials for Working Age Australians.* pp. 24–27. Pub. Australian Institute of Health, Canberra.

Minihan, P. M. (1986) Planning for Community Physician Services Prior to Deinstitutionalisation of Mentally Retarded Persons. *Am. J. Pub. Health* **76**: 1202–1206.

Mulcahy, M., O'Connor, S., Reynolds, A. (1983) Census of the Mentally Handicapped in the Republic of Ireland, 1981. *Irish Medical Journal* **76**: 71–75.

National Heart Foundation of Australia, *Risk Factor Prevalence Study No. 3* (1983), Canberra (Australia).

Nelson, R. P. and Crocker, A. C. (1978) The Medical Care of Mentally Retarded Persons in Public Residential Facilities. *N. Eng. J. Med.* **299**: 1039–1044.

Rubin, I. L. (1987) Health Care Needs of Adults with Mental Retardation. *Mental Retardation* **25(4)**: 201–206.

Schor, E. L., Smalky, K. A. and Neff, J. M. (1981) Primary Care of Previously Institutionalised Retarded Children. *Pediatrics* **67**: 536–540.

Seltzer, M. M. and Krauss, M. W. (1984) Family, Community Residence, and Institutional Placements of a Sample of Mentally Retarded Children. *Am. J. of Ment. Defic.* **89**: 257–266.

Smith, D. C., Decker, H. A., Herberg, E. N. & Rupke, L. K. (1969) Medical Needs of Children in Institutions for the Mentally Retarded. *Am. J. of Pub. Health* **59**: 1376–1384.

Tu, Jun-bi. (1979) A Survey of Psychotropic Medication in Mental Retardation Facilities. *J. Clin. Psychiatry,* **40**: 125–128.

Tuppurainen, K. (1983) Ocular findings Among Mentally Retarded Children in Finland. *Acta Ophthalmologica* **61**: 634–644.

A Study of Expressed Emotion of the Primary Caregiver of Adolescents with Developmental Retardation: Preliminary Findings

D. R. Dossetor, D. D. Stretch and A. R. Nicol

*Department of Psychiatry, Leicester Royal Infirmary,
Leicester LE2 7LX, England*

Expressed emotion (EE) was measured in the parental primary caregiver (PCG) of 92 adolescents with developmental retardation to examine its associated characteristics. High EE was found in 35% and in 27% this was due to high levels of emotional overinvolvement. The low frequency of high EE critical comments and hostility indicates the acceptance and tolerance of these PCGs. High EE was significantly related to the psychological well-being of the PCG, the quality of the PCG's marital relationship, the expressed dissatisfaction with services, the difficulty of looking after the adolescent, and psychiatric disorder in the adolescent. Further study may prove EE to be a useful indicator of risk in families with an adolescent with developmental retardation living at home and provided for by community services.

INTRODUCTION

The last 20 years has seen a concerted move in the United Kingdom to provide for people with developmental retardation in the community. For children and adolescents this has largely meant care by their family. Although the declared motive for the development of this "community care" was to move away from the harmful environmental effects of institutional care there has been limited study of this alternative.

Expressed emotion (EE) is an empirically derived construct of the emotional qualities a relative shows towards a dependent patient. EE, which measures qualities of warmth, emotional overinvolvement, hostility, positive and critical comments of the relative toward the patient is assessed in the Camberwell Family Interview, a semi-structured interview which evaluates these qualities by both content and quality of expression

163

(Leff & Vaughn, 1985). The concept of EE has proved a useful one in the community care of a wide range of psychiatric conditions such as schizophrenia, depression (Hooley *et al.*, 1986), obesity (Fischmann-Havstad & Marston, 1984) and anorexia nervosa (Szmukler *et al.*, 1985) in which it is highly predictive of outcome. More recently EE has been studied and found valuable in a number of chronic medical conditions such as Parkinson's disease, inflammatory bowel disease, stroke (Weddel, 1987) and dementia (Orford *et al.*, 1987). Family functioning is difficult to assess objectively, however EE has proved a reliable independent measure of change in the quality of a relationship in families attending child guidance clinics with a range of problems (Leff, J. *et al.*, Personal communication).

Greedharry (1987) reported high EE in 2 of the parents or next of kin of 10 retarded people aged 16–50 receiving short term care in a large hospital. This is an interesting but limited study. The group is small, presumably heterogenous, and there is no information on abilities or psychiatric disorder.

Adolescence is the most stressful period of life for many with developmental retardation as these individuals and their families become more dissimilar from their non-retarded neighbours. For this group there are limited alternatives to living at home and the day time facilities available after school leaving are not as enriching as those in schools for severe learning difficulties. Epidemiological statistics provide evidence to these pressures. The National Development Group (1977) reported that for those aged 15–20 longterm admissions to hospital are at a rate twice that at any other age (25 versus 11/100,000) and there is a similar age peak for referral to outpatient, day patient and short term in-patient care. Richardson *et al.* (1979) in their Aberdeen study of those born with developmental retardation between 1952–54 found that breakdown of family care with residential placement in the under fifteens was for reasons of excessive burden of care, whereas for those over 15 it was because of difficulties of management. Of these, 80% had behavioural disturbances and 70% had threatened or broken homes. Such data illustrates the psychological pressures faced by both adolescents with developmental retardation and their families.

AIMS

This study sought to examine the value of EE as measure of the quality of the relationship between the parental primary care giver (PCG) and an adolescent family member with developmental retardation. The aim was to examine the relationship between EE and the qualities of well-being of the adolescent and the PCG, and the PCG's support system. It is part of a wider study of the dependency needs of adolescents with developmental retardation.

METHODS

All 233 adolescents aged 14–19 attending schools for severe learning difficulties in a large health district (total population of 900,000) were categorised by their form teacher and head teacher according to the WHO ICD9 descriptions of profound, severe, moderate and mild developmental retardation (see table). For the purpose of the study we excluded 43 adolescents comprising the 32 who were in long term care, 4 in recent foster family placement, 2 whose parents spoke no English, and 5 families who did not wish to participate. The 92 cases studied consisted of 52 adolescents who used short term care in the last year and these were matched by ICD9 category of retardation, age, sex and school with 40 others who did not use short term care. This is therefore a stratified sample selection in which all those with profound or severe retardation were studied. Of those with moderate retardation subsequent statistical checks have confirmed that the test sample is representative of those not selected. The number with mild retardation is small and is not representative.

All the retarded adolescents selected were living at home and although the number of hours they spent in face to face contact with the PCG was evidently greater than 35 per week this was not formally measured.

The PCG was interviewed at home by the same investigator (DRD) partly on their own and partly with the retarded adolescent. The extensive two and a half hour interview included: information on service usage, a modified Camberwell Family Interview, a Rutter Marriage Rating (Quinton, Rutter & Rowlands, 1976) and the Handicaps Behaviours Skills Questionnaire (Wing, 1981) from which the presence of psychiatric disorder was assertained. The General Health Questionnaire (60 item) was also completed by the PCG to provide data on their psychiatric well-being (Goldberg, 1972). The investigator was trained and clinically checked in the recognition of EE, which was rated from tape recordings of the interview. The reliability of the EE ratings were independently assessed (by ARN) and will be the subject of a further report. The criteria for high EE using the established scales was 5 or more critical comments, any rating of hostility, or an emotional overinvolvement rating of 3 or more.

Differences between groups were determined using the Mann Whitney-U Test or Chi Square Test as appropriate.

Table 1. Breakdown of population of 233 adolescents 14–19 years attending schools of severe learning difficulty

ICD 9 ability level	Profound	Severe	Moderate	Mild	Totals
Breakdown of sample by ability	30	54	97	52	233
Exclusions	8	16	19	0	43
Total included in study	22	38	26	6	92
Not included in test sample	0	0	52	46	98

RESULTS

Of the total group if 92 PCGs interviewed, 32 showed high EE (35%). Remarkably few PCGs showed high EE due to critical comments (7) towards their retarded adolescent. One of these showed hostility. However a significant minority did show emotional overinvolvement (25). Despite this indication of their acceptance and tolerance of their adolescent, the PCGs, as a group, showed only moderate amounts of warmth (mean score of 2.82 on a scale 0–5) and positive comments.

High EE was significantly related to: (a) the quality of the marriage (p<0.0001); (b) the general psychiatric health of the PCG (p=0.0113); (c) the presence of psychiatric disorder in the retarded adolescent (p=0.036); (d) an interviewer global rating (0–4) of dissatisfaction expressed towards services (p=0.0024); (e) the PCG's declared rating of the degree of overall difficulty in bringing up the retarded individual (p=0.013) and of recent difficulties (p=0.0002).

Other variables that were not significantly related to the presence of expressed emotion included: (a) the use of short term care; (b) the ICD9 category of retardation or mental age of the adolescent; (c) the presence of hyperactivity, unhappy mood, autistic features or physical ill health in the adolescent; (d) the number of professional services in contact in the last 6 months or the adequacy of available services in the PCG's view.

DISCUSSION

A significant minority of PCGs (35%) showed high EE for their adolescent with severe developmental retardation. However the low frequency of high EE hostility (1%) and critical comments (8%) in conjunction with the relatively high frequency of emotional over-involvement (27%) in our study is notable. EE studies of schizophrenia have found high EE from emotional overinvolvement in 15–20% of relatives, but in neurotic and chronic medical conditions the frequency is much less. Our results may reflect the youth of the study sample or the need for a high level of care extending from infancy. Greedharry's study of a retarded group similarly showed that high EE was due to the presence of high emotional overinvolvement. However the lower frequency of high EE in his study in may reflect the older age of the retarded people and a more stable stage of the life cycle.

The association of high EE with psychological well being and the quality of the marriage of the PCG, and psychiatric disorder in the adolescent suggests that it may be a useful indicator of psychological need in the family. However these are the results of the initial analysis of our study data. Further examination will provide information on the sensitivity of EE for picking up psychiatric morbidity. Follow up studies will be required to test the predictive validity of high EE, particularly emotional overinvolvement, in this population.

These findings emphasise the importance of considering the emotional quality of the relationship with the primary care giver when assessing the problems faced by adolescents with developmental retardation. Awareness of EE may help to identify adolescents with retardation and their families who need help in the network of community care and to focus intervention to avoid unwanted family breakdown during this difficult transitional stage.

REFERENCES

Fischmann-Havstad, L. and Marston, A. (1984) Weight loss maintenance as an aspect of family emotion and process. *Br. J. Clin. Psychol.* **23**: 265–271.

Goldberg, D. (1972) Detection of psychiatric illness by questionnaire. *Maudsley Monographs.* **21**. Oxford University Press: Oxford.

Greedharry, D. (1987) Expressed emotion in families of the mentally handicapped: a pilot study. *Br. J. Psych.* **150**: 400–402.

Hooley, J., Orley, J. and Teasdale, J. (1986) Levels of expressed emotion and relapse in depressed patients. *Br. J. Psych.* **148**: 642–647.

Leff, J. and Vaughn, C. (1985) *Expressed emotion in families. Its significance for mental illness.* Guildford Press: London.

National development group for the mentally handicapped. (1977) *Helping mentally handicapped school leavers.* Pamphlet 3. DHSS: London.

Orford, J., O'Reilly, P. and Goonatilleke, A. (1987) Expressed emotion and perceived family interaction in the key relatives of elderly patients with dementia. *Psychol. Med.* **17**: 963–970.

Quinton, D., Rutter, M. and Rowlands, O. (1976) An evaluation of an interview assessment of marriage. *Psychol. Med.* **6**: 577–586.

Richardson, S., Katz, M. and Koller, H. (1979) Some characteristics of mentally retarded young adults in a British city. A basis for estimating some service needs. *J. Ment. Def. Res.* **23**: 275–286.

Szmukler, G., Eisler, I., Russell, G. and Dare, C. (1985) Anorexia nervosa, parental "expressed emotion" and dropping out of treatment. *Br. J. Psych.* **147**: 265–71.

Weddel, R. (1987) Social, functional, and neuropsychological determinants of the psychiatric symptoms of stroke patients receiving rehabilitation and living at home. *Scand. J. Rehabil. Med.* **19(3)**: 93–98.

Wing, L. (1981) A schedule for deriving profiles of handicaps in mentally retarded children. In: Cooper, B. (Ed.) *Assessing the needs of the mentally handicapped.* Academic Press: London.

Section IV

Families, Consumers and Caregivers

Living with Disabled Intellectually Handicapped Persons

**P. Pagliano, P. Gannon, W. Patching, J. Parker,
D. Ainge, and P. Berry**
*Division of Special Education and Clinical Services
Department of Pedagogics and Scientific Studies in Education
James Cook University of North Queensland, Australia*

This paper presents findings of a study designed to elicit parents' perceptions of how they cope with dependants who have an intellectual disability.

The study has a theoretical orientation based on personal construct psychology, and, as a methodology, employs the specific use of repertory grids constructed from a sample of elements (potential stressors) and constructs (self-perceived feelings) provided by parents.

Results are reported in the form of individual and group profiles obtained from grid output analysis. Group profiles are presented in combined parents/mothers/fathers formats. In addition, general and specific factors relating to coping will be extracted from the profiles.

The continued success of deinstitutionalization will depend on the ability of the family to cope with the burden of caring for the disabled member (Fadden, Bebbington and Kuipers, 1987). A consequence of the adoption of the normalization principle has therefore been an increase in research in families of people with intellectual disabilities (Wikler, 1986). This has been accompanied by a similar increase in the quest of the researcher for greater conceptual sophistication. Schaffer (1986) predicted that future research in child psychology will be more collaborative, and concerned with a wider set of problems which require multiple research skills and techniques drawn from both pure and applied research. These observations are especially relevant for future research in the area of living with a person with an intellectual disability. Already several major reviewers of the literature have called for the design of a research model which can encompass a wide spectrum of urgently required, yet interrelated outcomes.

Seven parameters of an adequate research model have been distilled from the review literature. First, the authors of three papers, Byrne and Cunningham (1985), Crnic, Friedrich and Greenberg (1983) and Gallagher, Beckman and Cross (1983) have stated that a research model must retain an individual level, clinical interactional analysis component, which can be used to consider the individual family unit as having individual needs requiring individual solutions. Second, the model must also simultaneously include a method for group investigation of general trends, which is neither based upon the assumption of homogeneity among families nor on the assumption that a pathological response is inevitable (Byrne *et al.*, 1985). Third, such a model would need to embrace transactional features in which all elements of the system, both human and ecological, can be assumed to interact with and influence all other elements (Byrne *et al.*, 1985). Fourth, some bipolar construct mechanism is required which could enable the investigators to describe the possible range of family adaptations, including self evaluations of how well parents perceive their environment. This aspect of the model could have valuable applied research implications, especially in the area of defining coping strategies (Cunningham, 1985) and in research as praxis, stressing a democratized process of emancipatory inquiry characterized by negotiation, reciprocity and empowerment (Lather, 1986). Five, sufficient flexibility in design is necessary to facilitate an interdisciplinary approach, with input from such disciplines as special education, sociology, social work, stress theory psychology and family therapy (Wikler, 1986). Six, a high tensile structure is needed so that researchers can move towards eliminating further methodological inadequacies such as investigator bias. Finally, the model would need the cohesion necessary to maintain all six attributes within a longitudinal paradigm.

With the view to developing a more adequate research model, the research described here employed repertory grid techniques (Kelly, 1955; Bannister and Mair, 1968; Salmon, 1976). This approach, which affords a large measure of client delimitation as to what will be investigated rather than that determined by the investigator, includes a built-in attempt to overcome the potential invalidating effects of investigator bias, unbalanced research focus, and restrictive samples (e.g. mother only). Grids provide a very clear attitudinal structure, a pattern of the affective relationship between a person and the environment. In essence, they comprise potential stressors (elements) and self perceived feelings (constructs). Since the elements define the parents' environment and the constructs provide a definite overview of the bipolar range of important feelings parents may experience, the relationship between the elements and constructs (the grid) should provide information regarding the way people feel towards their environment. Completed grids provide an account of a particular parental personal construct system at a particular point in time. As such they present an indication of stress levels associated with selected aspects of the environment. The grid ratings can be complemented by data from demographic surveys, case histories, and other measures of performance (ability and personality). The data can also be analysed at an individual or group level.

This paper describes the development and administration of repertory grids specifically constructed in an attempt to build the adequate research model described above. The aim of this study was to develop a set of grids to analyse how a set of parents of people with intellectual disabilities tended to perceive negative or positive aspects of their lives.

METHOD

Instrument Development

The constructs and elements used to create the bank of repertory grids was elicited from the mothers and fathers of the handicapped persons through a series of semi-structured interviews. These interviews, undertaken over a period of six months focused on positive as well as negative aspects of family life with a handicapped person.

The results of these interviews provided the data base for the development of the grids used in the main study. A total of 22 grids was produced. Each grid comprised between four and nine elements, and between four and eight bipolar constructs logically selected from a total of thirty-two. Each construct consisted of five descriptive statements that could be used to rate each element across a five point scale (positive (1) through neutral (3) to negative (5)). Thus a very substantial number of parent responses was collected.

Administration of the Repertory Grids

Each family in the study was visited on a regular basis for approximately one year by a member of the research team. The grids were administered in random order and the researcher and parent could communicate to each other when necessary for purposes of clarification.

FAMILIES

Fifty-two families are participating in the study. They reside in Townsville, a tropical city in Northern Australia with a population of approximately 105,000. Parents range in age from 27 to 73 years (mean 47 years) and, as a group, the families include 53 offspring (21 females, 32 males; age range of one to 34 with a mean of 18 years) who were assessed as having intellectual disabilities (either mild, moderate, severe or profound). Grid data is still in the process of being collected. Hence the data on which the results reported in this paper are based are, at the present time, incomplete. To date, thirty-two mothers and 13 fathers have completed all grids, an additional 11 mothers and 3 fathers have responded to some of them.

RESULTS

Taking the most global measure possible, both mothers and fathers indicated that they were able to cope with the upbringing of a disabled progeny. The mean response for all mothers on all grids being 2.75 and for fathers 2.82 indicates a high level of congruence between the two parents. Table 1 indicates mean ratings for mothers and fathers over the 22 grids, thus suggesting some general trends. The results of grids 6 and 7 are of interest in that mothers tend to rate themselves higher in terms of domestic organization and care than fathers' self ratings. This is reflected in grid 7 in which fathers rate their partners more highly than themselves in this respect ($X^2 = 85.5$, df = 2, p <.001). Mothers tend to rate fathers as less involved. In other words, fathers tend to think of their partners as more involved and competent in the upbringing of their handicapped child, and this is consistent with the mothers' own opinions. For both mothers and fathers, grids 5, 8, 9, 14, 15, 16 and 19 indicate factors of discontent. Grid 5 refers to adaptive functional behavior such as 'money handling', 'attending school', and 'finding one's way about'; grid 14 is the effect on the parent of the disabled person's acceptance of own limitations, aggression, and ability to cooperate with others; grid 15 refers to the ways parents cope with their offspring's needs in such areas as supervision, attention seeking and problems in accepting change; grid 16 reflects the effects of the disabled individual's behaviours on the parents, including factors such as destructiveness, self injurious behaviours, unusual mannerisms and sexual behaviours. Grid 8 shows a tendency towards the negative on the parents' decision to keep the family member with a disability at home, their expectations for their disabled offspring and 'the future'; grid 9 indicates that parents tend to feel the disabled person has had a negative effect upon their career, leisure time, physical and emotional health; grid 10 indicates that both parents tend to feel the same way about these factors.

In addition, fathers tend to be slightly more negative than mothers. Fathers differ significantly from their partners on grid 13 ($X^2 = 16.8$, p <.001), 12 ($X^2 = 9.6$, p <.01). They also tend to be more negative on grids 21 and 22 although differences between partners on these grids do not reach statistical significance. Fathers are more negative (grid 13) in their conception of the effect on them of the level of mobility, emotional development, sexuality and state of health of the disabled person. Grid 20 refers to the disabled child's effect on the parent in terms of social,

Table 1. Grid mean rating, all mothers and fathers

Grid	Rating mean (mothers)	St.dev. (mothers)	N of (mothers)	Rating mean (fathers)	St.dev. (fathers)	N of (fathers)
1 Communication	2.606	.742	43	2.559	.682	15
2 Social skills	2.881	.745	43	2.810	.604	16
3 Daily living skills	2.583	.829	43	2.734	.788	16
4 Domestic skills	2.580	.696	43	2.934	.695	16
5 Community skills	3.003	.650	43	3.256	.370	16
6 Parent-self-organisation	1.798	.355	34	2.215	.659	13
7 Parent-partner-organisation	2.490	.697	36	1.403	.212	13
8 Parent-self-expectations	3.275	.686	36	3.290	.725	13
9 Parent-self-leisure	3.161	.598	36	3.215	.388	13
10 Parent-partner-leisure	3.076	.477	36	3.358	.508	13
11 Parent-medical services (1)	2.711	1.052	36	2.362	1.068	13
12 Parent medical services (2)	2.056	1.030	36	2.192	.882	13
13 Parent-self-personal	2.808	.695	36	3.197	.561	13
14 Parent-self-child behaviour (1)	3.031	.552	36	3.185	.372	13
15 Parent-self-child behaviour (2)	3.056	.629	36	3.382	.383	13
16 Parent-self-child behaviour (3)	3.131	.461	34	3.355	.298	13
17 Effect of others on parent (1)	2.529	.453	34	2.480	.438	13
18 Effect of others on parent (2)	2.358	.413	34	2.376	.389	13
19 Effect of others on child	2.414	.393	33	2.343	.279	13
20 Effect on family relationships	2.845	.646	33	3.148	.668	13
21 Effect on partner's life	2.926	.638	32	3.034	.477	13
22 Effect on parent of local conditions	2.990	.484	32	3.075	.594	13

Table 2. Element mean ratings, father, case 38

GRID01F	1.0	1.0	1.0	1.0	1.0	1.0	1.0	1.0	1.0
GRID02F	3.0	1.7	1.0	1.0	1.0	1.0	4.0		
GRID03F	1.1	1.0	1.0	1.1	1.1	1.1			
GRID04F	1.1	3.5	1.1	1.1	1.1				
GRID05F	2.0	4.3	3.1	3.3	4.9				
GRID06F	2.8	1.6	2.2	1.6	2.8				
GRID07F	1.2	1.2	2.5	1.8	1.3				
GRID08F	1.8	1.8	1.8	2.6	1.2	4.8			
GRID09F	2.5	2.8	1.5	3.3	3.0				
GRID10F	3.3	2.3	1.0	4.0	4.0				
GRID11F	3.2	3.4	2.8	4.8					
GRID12F	3.7	3.8	3.5	3.8					
GRID13F	1.9	1.8	1.4	1.9	3.3	1.5			
GRID14F	2.1	2.0	3.9	2.7	1.4	1.3			
GRID15F	3.2	1.3	3.3	3.7	3.5				
GRID16F	3.0	3.2	3.3	3.2	3.0	3.3			
GRID17F	1.2	3.0	3.0	3.0	3.0	2.7	2.2		
GRID18F	2.0	3.0	2.8	3.0	3.0	2.4	2.0		
GRID19F	1.0	3.0	2.8	3.0	3.0	2.8	1.2		
GRID20F	2.8	1.8	3.0	1.8	1.8				
GRID21F	2.6	2.4	3.0	1.8	1.4				
GRID22F	3.8	3.7	3.5	1.7	3.8	4.0			

sexual relationships with partner and relationships with others. Fathers tend to believe these factors have a negative effect upon their partners (although this is not wholly shared by the mothers). Finally, fathers tend to be more negative than mothers on the effect of the locality in relation to services and support for their disabled offspring and family.

FAMILY CASE STUDY

The clinical significance of the grid procedure in identifying individual family needs is illustrated in the following example. The mother and father of a 21 year old Down syndrome male completed all the grids. The results are shown in Tables 2 and 3. The major problems identified by the father are:

1. inability of his son to handle money
2. difficulties in going out alone
3. the deleterious effect of his son on the physical and emotional health of his wife
4. the inadequate knowledge of the medical profession in relation to his son's health needs

Table 3. Element mean ratings, mother, case 38

GRID01M	2.0	2.2	1.8	1.2	2.2	2.8	2.0	1.0	1.0
GRID02M	2.0	2.0	2.2	2.2	1.7	1.7	5.0		
GRID03M	2.7	2.4	2.4	2.6	2.6	2.6			
GRID04M	2.1	3.6	2.4	2.6	2.5				
GRID05M	3.0	4.8	4.4	4.9	5.0				
GRID06M	2.4	2.0	2.2	1.6	2.0				
GRID07M	2.8	2.5	2.2	1.2	2.0				
GRID08M	1.2	2.6	2.6	4.0	3.0	5.0			
GRID09M	3.3	3.3	3.3	3.3	3.3				
GRID10M	3.0	3.5	3.3	4.0	4.0				
GRID11M	4.8	4.4	3.4	4.8					
GRID12M	4.0	4.2	4.3	4.2					
GRID13M	2.5	2.9	2.8	2.3	3.9	2.6			
GRID14M	3.9	3.0	3.1	2.7	3.0	2.3			
GRID15M	3.8	3.0	4.0	4.0	3.0				
GRID16M	3.0	3.0	4.0	4.0	4.0	3.0			
GRID17M	1.8	3.0	1.8	3.0	3.0	3.3	3.3		
GRID18M	1.8	3.0	2.0	3.0	3.0	4.0	3.8		
GRID19M	1.4	3.0	1.4	3.0	3.0	2.2	2.2		
GRID20M	2.2	2.0	1.0	1.0	4.0				
GRID21M	2.2	1.0	1.0	1.0	3.0				
GRID22M	3.3	3.5	3.3	1.3	2.7	3.7			

5. the difficulty of accessibility appropriate to medical facilities.

Major issues affecting the mother are reported as being:

1. the effect on the mother of coping with her son's demands
2. inadequate skills of her son in coping with money, finding his way about, going out alone and telephone usage
3. conflicts between provision of "care" as opposed to independence and the "future" provision of services
4. the deleterious effect upon the physical and emotional health of her husband
5. many problems relating to the medical profession including inadequate advice, poor feedback and poor attitude to herself and her husband
6. the need for supervisor for her "rather demanding" son
7. the problems associated with her son's unusual mannerisms, sexual behavior and preoccupations
8. the inadequate help, in general, provided by "professionals"
9. the effect of their son on the family's relationship with neighbours.

The implications of the present study for both the parents and son can be seen to be very substantial. None of the problems however, is insurmountable. A reasonable inter-disciplinary case approach by a "mental handicap" team of professionals could manage the problems identified by the mother and father for their own benefit and that of their son. Such an approach reiterates the clinical usefulness of the repertory grid procedures developed in this project; highlights the message from the literature of the importance of the heterogeneous nature of the problems of the families in the study; and finally the relationship between services and family needs as a whole must be malleable and carefully structured. The repertory grid research methodology appears to meet the seven parameters of an adequate research model outlined in the introduction.

DISCUSSION

Repertory grid data enable the researcher to consider the individual family as having individual needs requiring individual solutions. Furthermore through individual grid analysis the data can be used by professionals for counselling and advisement. As Rutter (1985) has pointed out coping mechanisms – namely what a person does about a stressful situation – need to have two features. First, coping with a situation demands basic problem solving skills to alleviate the nature of the problem. Secondly, coping strategies must regulate emotional distress. Adaptation, as an epigenic process, should therefore reflect both kinds of mechanisms. The repertory grids do allow for this process to occur.

Through the compilation of group data, general trends can be identified. Compared to parents of non-handicapped children, parents of children with an early identified and severe intellectual disability are presented with a lifelong situation involving extraordinary human effort. Parents must provide or arrange provision of health welfare and educational services often in a context of harsh economic and social circumstances. The results of this study show a tendency, on some very important factors, that these parents do not have an easy passage. On 7 of the 22 grids, both parents tend to rate themselves and each other as being negatively affected by their handicapped offspring. Fathers are more negative than mothers and tend towards the negative distribution on 11 of the 22 grids. It is most interesting to note however, that the most positive aspect of their ratings relate to each other. While fathers think their partners are better at the daily living arrangements, a finding agreed to by the mothers, they also rate themselves as positive in this connection.

Perhaps the main finding is that the resilience in the family of coping with the demanding needs of an intellectually disabled person is reflected in the dynamics of the family itself. Further studies using similar techniques are to be undertaken to investigate the role of extended family members, siblings and professionals in the coping processes of parents with mentally handicapped offspring. Future exploration of the developing repertory grid research model will be in the areas of increased interdisciplinary input, attention to eliminating methodological inadequacies and discovering ways to include a longitudinal dimension.

ACKNOWLEDGEMENT

This research project is funded by a three-year grant from the Australian National Health and Medical Research council. The James Cook University Research team comprises Professor Paul Berry (Head of the School of Education and the Department of Pedagogics and Scientific Studies in Education), Associate Professor Jim Parker, Dr Bill Patching (Chairman of the Division of Special Education and Clinical Services), Dr Paul Gannon, Paul Pagliano and David Ainge (Research Officer).

REFERENCES

Bannister, D. and Mair, J. M. M. (1968) *The Evaluation of Personal Constructs*. London and New York, Academic Press.

Byrne, E. A. and Cunningham, C. C. (1985) The effects of mentally handicapped children on families – A conceptual review. *Journal of Child Psychology and Psychiatry*, **26**, 6, 847–864.

Crnic, K. A., Friedrich, W. N., and Greenberg, M. T. (1983) Adaptation of families with mentally retarded children: A model of stress, coping and family ecology. *American Journal of Mental Deficiency*, **82**, 2, 125–138.

Cunningham, C. (1985) Training and education approaches for parents of children with special needs. *British Journal of Medical Psychology*, **58**, 285–305.

Fadden, G., Bebbington, P., and Kuipers, L. (1987) The burden of care: The impact of functional psychiatric illness on the patient's family. *British Journal of Psychiatry*, **150**, 285–292.

Gallagher, J. J., Beckman, P., and Cross, A. H. (1983) Families of handicapped children: Sources of stress and its amelioration. *Exceptional children*, **50**, 1, 10–19.

Kelly, G. (1955) *The Psychology of Personal Constructs* (2 vols). New York: Norton.

Lather, P. (1986) Research as praxis. *Harvard Educational Review*, **56**, 3, 257–277.

Rutter, M. (1985) Family and school influences: Meanings, mechanisms and implications. In A. R. Nicol (ed.). *Longitudinal Studies in Child Psychology and Psychiatry*. Chichester: John Wiley & Sons.

Salmon, P. (1976) Vocational guidance. In Mittler, P. (ed.). *The Psychological Assessment of Mental and Physical Handicaps*. Norwich: Fletcher.

Schaffer, H. R. (1986) Child psychology: The future. *Journal of Child Psychology and Psychiatry*, **27**, 6, 761–779.

Wikler, L. M. (1986) Families stress theory and research on families of children with mental retardation. In J. J. Gallagher and P. M. Veitze (eds.). *Families of Handicapped Persons: Research, Programs, and Policy Issues*. Baltimore: Brookes.

Financial Costs for Home-Reared Children with Down Syndrome: an Australian Perspective

P. Gunn and P. Berry

*Schonell Special Education Research Centre, University of Queensland
St. Lucia, 4067 Australia*

Over a 4 week period, 37 families with a child with Down syndrome and 30 comparison families recorded the expenses involved in rearing their children. In addition, holiday expenses and other major expenses were recorded at the end of the year. It was found that there were additional expenses for the families with the Down syndrome child and they participated less in activities such as dance, music, gymnastics and sports.

Little is known about the financial burden on families with a handicapped child, although it is generally acknowledged that there is an emotional burden. It is also implicitly acknowledged that there is a financial burden as in many countries, monetary assistance is provided to the families. In Australia, a Handicapped Child's Allowance which is not means tested has been provided for 'severely handicapped children' requiring 'constant care and attention' living at home. For 'substantially handicapped children' (needing only marginally less 'care and attention' than severely handicapped children) the allowance has been means tested.

There have been a few investigations into the financial costs of rearing a handicapped child. All have recognized the limitations in assessing social costs through a list of financial expenditures. One Australian study (Rees and Emerson, 1983) investigated the costs of caring for 51 disabled children living at home in New South Wales and whose families had indicated the need for Health Commission residential care. The children came from a wide range of social groups; the majority were selected at random from waiting lists for residential care and their handicaps included intellectual as well as physical and sensory problems. The authors reported that monthly expenditure per child on 11 items, using minimal cost estimates, amounted to approximately $230 per month. The

11 items of expenditure were medication, special equipment and aids, medical insurance, transport, day care or school fees, domestic help, temporary care, special food, extra items and extra clothing. The figures need to be adjusted to account for changes in medical insurance introduced in 1984 as well as for inflation.

Another study by Chetwynd (1985) in New Zealand has also shown that raising an intellectually handicapped child at home incurs an extra financial burden on families. This study involved 91 families with an intellectually handicapped child and showed that these families spent an average of NZ$17 extra per week on household items (such as food, electricity and household supplies) and a further NZ$27 a week on items specific to the child's handicap such as special toys, equipment and health care. In addition, the families reported substantial major expenses on house alterations, improvements to heating and major items of special equipment. Of note in these latter figures is the high variation of cost for families and the extreme burden at the upper limits.

The present study was devised to investigate the extent to which Australian families with Down syndrome child incurred financial expenses. By focussing on one specific handicap, the study avoided some of the difficulties of interpreting the costs reported by Rees and Emerson for children with a great variety of handicapping conditions. In addition, the data was collected from families who were not waiting for residential care for the handicapped child so that the costs reported may be seen as part of each family's normal ongoing expenses.

METHOD

Subjects

The families in this study were recruited during 1984 in a variety of ways. Thirty-seven families with a child with Down syndrome (Ds) had been involved in a longitudinal study of the development of their child. When the present study commenced, these children (23 boys, 14 girls) ranged in age from 1 year 9 months to 8 years 9 months. Those siblings who were in the same age range as these children with Ds were studied as a sibling comparison group. There were no more than two children from any one family in this sibling group and 25 families provided information on both a child with Ds and either one or two siblings. There were 14 boys and 18 girls in this sibling group. In addition to this comparative data, further information was collected for all siblings of the children with Ds who were of school age or younger. This provided data for 9 siblings (6 boys, 3 girls) below 1 year 9 months of age and for 24 siblings (15 boys, 9 girls) who were more than 8 years 9 months of age.

Another group of 20 families with 30 children (17 boys, 13 girls)

Table 1. Occupation of fathers

Occupation	Down syndrome group		Comparison group	
Upper professional	10	(27.0%)	7	(35.0%)
Lower professional	2	(5.4%)	3	(15.0%)
Managerial/proprietors	4	(10.8%)	1	(5.0%)
Clerical and related workers	6	(16.2%)	6	(30.0%)
Craftsmen	9	(24.3%)	2	(10.0%)
Operators, process workers, drivers	4	(10.8%)	0	(0.0%)
Service workers/labourers	2	(5.4%)	1	(5.0%)

between 1 year 9 months and 8 years 9 months provided further information. These children showed no developmental delay and most had been involved in previous comparison groups for various studies concerned with the development of the children with Ds.

All the families were intact and no father was unemployed during the year of the study. The fathers worked in a range of occupations from semi-skilled to professional but they were predominantly white collar or skilled workers. Table 1 shows the distribution according to the hierarchical groups of Australian occupations described by Broom and Jones (1976).

Two mothers of the children with Ds and two mothers in the comparison group were employed in full-time occupations outside the home and two other mothers in the comparison group were employed part-time. Both the families with children with Ds and the comparison families lived in a range of Brisbane suburbs which were distributed from the inner city to the outer suburbs to the north, west and south. Neither group of families was clustered in any one socio-economic area.

In summary, there were three groups.

Group 1: 37 children with Ds, chronological age range 1 year 9 months to 8 years 9 months (Mean = 5 years, SD = 19 months)

Group 2: 32 siblings of children with Ds, chronological age range 1 year 9 months to 8 years 9 months. (Mean = 5 years, SD = 27 months)

Group 3: 30 comparison children, chronological age range 1 year 9 months to 8 years 9 months. (Mean = 5 years 4 months, SD = 24 months)

At the time of the study, the Handicapped Child's Allowance was $85 per month.

Procedure

The families of children in Groups 1, 2 and 3 were asked to complete a series of questionnaires. The first questionnaire was concerned with the weekly expenses involved in raising the children which were *additional* to the basic costs for food, shelter and clothing. It included items such as regular medication, special foods, transport, extra lessons, specialist (e.g. therapeutic) costs and baby sitting. Four copies of this questionnaire were delivered to each family over a four week period so that the ongoing expenses could be recorded each week. In categories such as transport and special foods where siblings share expenses, mothers were asked to allocate the total costs between the individual children. A second questionnaire was devised to try to estimate holiday costs for each family. The information required here was concerned with holiday accommodation, travel and entertainment.

A final questionnaire at the end of the year gathered information on the major costs involved in rearing the children in Groups 1 and 3 which were additional to those costs covered by either the holiday or weekly expenses questionnaires. These costs included medical insurance premium, additional medical costs not covered by insurance or Medicare, school fees, special programs, special toys and equipment. Twenty-one of the families with a child with Ds were later interviewed to confirm the details of these major expenses.

RESULTS

Weekly expenses

The information from the weekly expenses questionnaires provided an estimate of the extra mean weekly expenses per child for the three age-matched groups (see Table 2). In all categories, there was wide variation with a standard deviation at least equal to the mean. Table 3 illustrates the number of families experiencing different levels of these expenses.

The cost of medication, special foods, transport and specialists are higher for the group with Ds while the expenses for activities (music, ballet, swimming, guides, etc.) is lower. The costs for siblings is much lower than for the comparison children in the special foods, transport, and activities categories. The food and transport costs are probably lower for both the children with Ds and their siblings as these are shared costs. Only 20 of the 30 comparison children shared these costs with another sibling. The activities costs are less likely to be shared and it was found that twenty-three (77%) of the comparison children but only 16 (50%) siblings and 13 (35%) children with Ds were involved in at least one such activity.

Table 2. Mean weekly expenses for each group

Category of expense	Ds group n = 37 Mean	Ds siblings n = 32 Mean	Comparison group n = 30 Mean
Medication	$3.67	$1.59	$1.14
Special Foods	$0.90	$0.01	$0.14
Transport[a]	$7.32	$2.11	$3.32
Activities	$1.91	$2.14	$4.18
Specialists	$1.40	$0.13	$0.22

[a] Covers petrol and oil costs, not depreciation, registration, insurance of car.

Note: (1) Age range 1 year 9 months to 8 years 9 months.

(2) Weekly expenses for 4-week questionnaire period.

Table 3. Number of families for each level of expense

Weekly expense	Less than $1.00		$1.00 to $4.99		$5.00 to $9.99		$10 or more	
Medication								
Ds group	10	(27%)	14	(38%)	9	(24%)	4	(11%)
Ds siblings	18	(56%)	12	(38%)	2	(6%)	0	(0%)
Comparison group	17	(57%)	13	(43%)	0	(0%)	0	(0%)
Special Foods								
Ds group	34	(92%)	2	(5%)	1	(3%)	0	(0%)
Ds siblings	30	(94%)	1	(3%)	1	(3%)	0	(0%)
Comparison group	29	(97%)	1	(3%)	0	(0%)	0	(0%)
Transport								
Ds group	10	(27%)	5	(14%)	7	(19%)	15	(41%)
Ds siblings	19	(59%)	6	(19%)	6	(19%)	1	(3%)
Comparison group	13	(43%)	9	(30%)	5	(17%)	3	(10%)
Activities								
Ds group	24	(65%)	8	(22%)	4	(11%)	1	(3%)
Ds siblings	16	(50%)	11	(34%)	4	(13%)	1	(3%)
Comparison group	9	(30%)	11	(37%)	6	(20%)	4	(13%)
Specialists								
Ds group	32	(86%)	2	(5%)	1	(3%)	2	(5%)
Ds siblings	31	(99%)	1	(3%)	0	(0%)	0	(0%)
Comparison group	28	(93%)	1	(3%)	1	(3%)	0	(0%)

Gunn and Berry

Table 4. Maximum expense for one child in each group per week

Category of expense	Ds child	Siblings	Comparison child
Medication	$12.00	$5.68	$4.72
Special Foods	$6.50	$0.25	$4.29
Transport	$33.00	$13.75	$15.00
Activities	$9.30	$15.00	$17.00
Specialists	$24.00	$3.75	$5.25

Note: Weekly expenses for 4-week questionnaire period.

In addition to these costs, the questionnaire showed that families with children with Ds spent more on baby sitting fees ($3.09 per week) than the comparison families ($1.40 per week).

The maximum expense for one child is also of interest and the comparative costs for each category per week are shown in Table 4.

For medication, transport, and specialist categories the range of costs extends considerably higher for the children with Ds than for the other children.

For those siblings who were younger than the age-matched groups, the weekly expenses were zero or minimal for transport, activities, and specialists. For the older siblings, there were no expenses for special foods and only one visit to a specialist by one child. A comparison with the sibling expenses in the age-matched group suggests that apart from special foods at younger ages and activities at older ages, the expenses are higher for the middle age period.

Holiday expenses (Groups 1 to 3)

The main differences between families for holiday expenses were in connection with transport costs and child care. The families with children with Ds did not travel as much as other families and they spent more on child care during this period. Interviews with the parents revealed that one family had bought a caravan and another a camper/trailer as they believed this was the best way of holidaying with their children with Ds. The sleeping/eating facilities would be constant and cause less stress than new accommodation.

Major expenses (Groups 1 and 3)

Three in four families paid private medical insurance premiums in addition to the Medicare levy. This proportion was the same for families with a child with Ds and for the comparison families whose children were not Ds. Except for one mother who gave pregnancy costs as the reason for the extra insurance, all the families paid the private insurance because of their children. Only four families, however, stated that they had been influenced by the specific needs of the child with Ds in making the decision to pay the private insurance premium. The children with Ds with severe health problems were usually treated within the (free) public hospital health system. The extra insurance cover appeared to be directed at covering unexpected rather than chronic childhood complaints. The mean insurance cover for 1984 was $734 for the families with a child with Ds and $705 for the comparison families.

Interviews

Interviews showed that many parents had been involved in a variety of extensive programs during the child's early years. In addition, costly equipment such as trampolines, play gyms and even swimming pools had been purchased for the benefit of the child with Ds. The capital cost of this equipment is not well reflected in the present study since many of the items had been purchased before the study began.

It was also found that although the State government provided part-time special preschool education free of charge, most families also enrolled their child with Ds at local kindergardens, child care centres or preschools. Since this child usually attended one of those centres for at least one year more than the comparison children, the fees for this period were an extra financial commitment for these families.

Other costs mentioned during an interview included extra clothing because the younger children dribbled so much, wasted food because the child was difficult to feed, nappies and training pants for an extended toilet training period, special boots, and more expensive clothes to help the child 'to look nice'.

DISCUSSION

This study has been concerned only with a group of intact families with no unemployment. It has also been demonstrated that raising a child with Down syndrome incurs additional financial costs for a family beyond those needed for a non-handicapped child. Compared to the other two main reports, Chetwynd (1985) and Rees and Emerson (1983), the present study affirms two main points. First, in almost all cases, children with Down syndrome require services and attention which cost more than their siblings or other non-handicapped children. Second, some handicapped children, compared to both their siblings and other children, present a very serious financial burden for their families. The actual amounts in this connection vary considerably, due not only to the specific needs of the child but also to the wishes of the parents.

It is noteworthy that the emphasis on costs for *essential* items for the handicapped, as opposed to the non-handicapped child, is significant. On items such as 'activities', the average amount that the non-handicapped comparison group had at their disposal was about twice that for either the children with Down syndrome or their siblings. It may be thought that the smaller amount spent for the child with Down syndrome reflects a lack of appropriate community activities for handicapped children. This does not seem to be the complete explanation, however, as the amount is also low for siblings. It seems rather that the extra financial costs involved in rearing a child with Down syndrome result in a 'double disadvantage' – not only does it, in general, cost more to rear them, but it also results in less participation in valued activities such as dance, music, riding, gymnastics, sports, and so on. The cost of essential items may preclude the ability of a family to provide those 'extras' which might be available in many families without a handicapped child.

The implications, therefore, of this study are in the area of policy development. Realistic levels of financial support are required for families with a disabled child. Such support should not only provide essential medical services for that child, but it should also be sufficient to cover special school fees, protheses, special diets, travel costs, holiday relief and baby sitting needs. Disabled children should also be helped to take part in community valued leisure and recreational activities, such as sport, travel, dance, riding and holidays.

The contemporary philosophy of service delivery for parents of handicapped children is both community and family based. The cost of full-time residential care provided by Australian government bodies has been estimated to be at least as high as $160 a day and provides a further economic argument for extra financial aid to the families since their commitment to their handicapped child presents such great financial savings to the community at large.

ACKNOWLEDGEMENT

The authors thank the Reserve Bank of Australia for financial support, Leslie Goodman and Jamie Melcher for help with the data collection and analysis, Sannie Pritchard for her secretarial contribution, The Honourable Mr Justice Davies and his associate Graeme Johnson for advice regarding decisions of the Administrative Appeals Tribunal, and most of all, the families who contributed information so patiently to the study.

REFERENCES

Administrative Appeals Tribunal (1984) Decision Handicapped Child's Allowance, applicant J. P. Seager.

Broom, L. and Jones, F. L. (1976) *Opportunity and attainment in Australia.* Canberra: A.N.U. Press.

Chetwynd, S. (1985) Some costs of caring at home for an intellectually handicapped child. *Australia and New Zealand Journal of Developmental Disabilities*, *11*, 35–40.

Rees, S. and Emerson, A. (1983) The costs of caring for disabled children at home. *Australian Rehabilitation Review*, *7*, 26–31.

The Long Term Influence of the Family of Upbringing on Young Adults with Mild Mental Retardation

**S. A. Richardson, K. J. Goulden, H. Koller
and M. Katz**
*Albert Einstein College of Medicine, 1300 Morris Park Avenue,
Bronx, New York 10461, USA*

Two measures of the family, stability and social class, were examined alone and in combination with measures of the child, to predict the adult functioning of young people who had been identified as mildly mentally retarded in childhood. Examination of all the measures in conjunction with one another best approximates an ecological model, in which the child's intrinsic and developmental characteristics interact over time with environmental experiences to determine the life course of the individual. Family stability was an important predictor of adult functioning for males, especially in combination with the child's characteristic of brain dysfunction. These factors predicted less well for females.

Research dealing with the families of persons who are mentally retarded has focused predominately on families in which there is a severely mentally retarded child. This paper will focus on families with a mildly mentally retarded (MMR) child and explore the question of whether the kind of family with which the MMR child lives has a continuing influence into adulthood. This question is part of the broader question we are pursuing of why some MMR adults function better than do others. To our knowledge there is no research dealing with this issue. Studies that have followed children with MMR into adulthood have not related their childhood to their adult lives. Without the benefit of previous research we have had few guidelines to help our enquiry.

To provide a conceptual map of the territory we wished to explore, we adapted the approach used by Bronfenbrenner (1979) in *The Ecology of Human Development*. This is shown in schematic form in Figure 1. It resembles a time clock with birth at 12 o'clock and the life course of the individual proceeding through childhood and adulthood in a clockwise

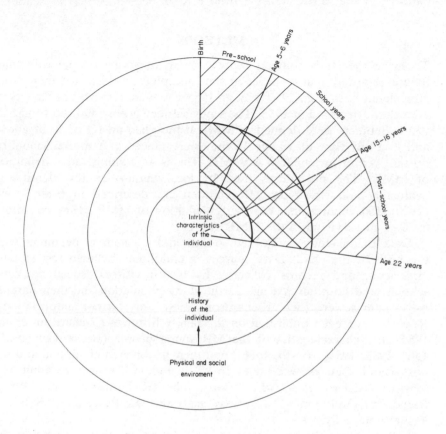

Figure 1.

direction. The face of the clock is divided into concentric circles. The inner circle represents the intrinsic characteristics of the individual, for example, the sex of the person and whether or not the person has any brain dysfunction. The outer circle represents the social and physical environment that the person experiences. The intermediate circle depicts the history of the individual, determined by the intrinsic characteristics of the person in interaction over time with the environment. The history up to any point in time in some ways influences the history after that point in time. Because our longitudinal study has followed young people with MMR up to age 22, we will focus on these years, examining the impact of the characteristics of the MMR children and the environmental factors relating to their families on the MMR when they become adults. The majority of the MMR adults had no MR services since leaving school.

METHODS

To make the study subjects representative of young people with mild mental retardation at a particular time and place, we selected them from all children born from 1951 through 1955 who were residents of the city of Aberdeen, Scotland in 1962. The study subjects were followed to age 22 years. Subjects were defined as MMR if they had an IQ of 50 or above and if at any time up to age 15 they were placed in a special school or training center for children with MR. This is an administrative definition of MMR. The procedures used by local authorities for identifying, evaluating and classifying MR children are described in Birch *et al.* (1970). 154 children met our study definition of MMR. They constitute 89% of all survivors in the MMR range.

Data for the study were obtained from multiple sources beginning with the birth of the child. Data sources in childhood included test results, interviews, and records collected by health visitors, social workers, schools, and hospitals. At age 22 the study population and their parents were interviewed (See Richardson, 1981 for further information). Reports have been published on the family histories (Richardson *et al.*, 1985), the characteristics of the MR young people (Richardson *et al.*, 1981, 1983, 1984a, 1985b, 1986), and their histories in childhood and the post-school years between ages 16–22, including a history of adult MR services (Richardson *et al.*, 1984b), jobs (Richardson *et al.*, 1988), friendships (Koller *et al.*, in press), marriage (Koller *et al.*, 1988), and leisure time activities.

Following are the variables and their definitions that are used in the present analysis.

ENVIRONMENT (OUTER CIRCLE ON FIGURE 1)

Social class

The measure was developed by the British Registrar General's Office to arrange census data into five social classes and constituted a socio-economic ranking of occupations of the head of the household. Persons of similar occupation tend to share a common experience and mode of life so the occupations grouped within a social class category provide a general indicator of the family life style. The scale ranges from Social Class I, Professional, which includes doctors, lawyers, and company directors, to Social Class V, unskilled, which includes laborers, railway porters and road sweepers. This family measure has had widespread use in epidemiological research. For some children it was not possible to assign a social class on the scale of I–V because there had been no consistent head of the household in the child's history. This includes children brought up in a series of foster homes and/or residential placements or where the head of the household was chronically unemployed. The social class measure of the family was obtained at the time the child was aged 8–10.

Family Stability

The scale is made up of two components. One part measures the degree of continuity of the same two parents throughout the child's upbringing. The other part is the extent to which the child experienced parental abuse, neglect, marital strife and discord, and various forms of pathological psycho-social parental behavior. The stable end of the 5 point scale includes families in which the child lived throughout with the same two parents who were in at least moderately good health, father was employed with reasonable steadiness, mother may or may not have worked outside the home, aberrant or disturbed behavior was not noted in the parents, and there was no evidence that the child was not well cared for. The unstable end of the scale includes families with disorganization, disruptions and discord, and the child was abused, neglected or abandoned; parent(s) were incompetent or exhibited disturbed behavior, necessitating intervention by authorities; the child's upbringing was marked by uncertainty, including a series of different caretakers.

The measures of social class and family stability show an association, with higher social class families more often being stable.

INTRINSIC CHARACTERISTICS OF THE MMR INDIVIDUAL (INNERMOST CIRCLE ON FIGURE 1)

Gender

Brain Dysfunction

This was a composite measure using clinical judgment based on the medical history of the child and the mother's reproductive history. Evidence was ordered in terms of the probability that there were indicators of brain dysfunction. They included genetic abnormalities, cerebral malformations, postnatal injuries, cerebral palsy, microcephaly, macrocephaly, uncomplicated epilepsy, autism and being small for gestational age. The clinical judgments were made by Dr Keith Goulden, a pediatric neurologist.

THE HISTORY OF CHILDHOOD (INTERMEDIATE CIRCLE ON FIGURE 1)

The individual is the resultant of the ongoing interaction between his or her intrinsic characteristics over time with the environment.

IQ. This measure is based on intelligence tests given at 8–10 years of age. For most of the 1952–1954 births the WISC was used. For the remaining subjects the Terman Merrill test was used and these scores were than adjusted to be comparable with WISC scores.

Childhood Behavior

An overall measure of behavior disturbance was developed, which included separate measures of emotional disturbance, aggressive-conduct disorder, antisocial and hyperactive behavior. The severity of each type of behavior disturbance was based on the amount of time and degree to which the problem impaired the individual's ability to function as expected and evidence of concern about the behavior by the subject, the family or some authority. A six point scale was used ranging from 0, no disturbed behavior, to 5, severely disturbed. For this paper an overall measure combining the types of disturbance was used. The assessment was made for the entire childhood period, up to age 15 years.

HISTORY OF YOUNG ADULTHOOD (INTERMEDIATE CIRCLE ON FIGURE 1)

Three of the measures deal with the job history and one measure with behavior disturbance. The time span of the measures was the six year period from age 16 to 22.

Time Out of the Labor Force

The number of months spent neither employed nor unemployed seeking employment, divided by months between leaving school and reaching age 22 years 3 months. We excluded time as a housewife or in full time education, because the former is an unpaid job and the latter leads to more skilled job performance. The major use of time out of the labor force was to attend adult MR services. Minor uses of time out were because of injury or sickness, time spent in prison, and time spent at home, not seeking employment.

Rate of Unemployment

The number of months out of work but seeking employment divided by months in the labor force.

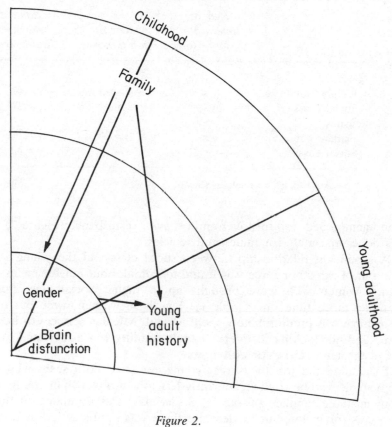

Figure 2.

Rate of Job Turnover

Number of jobs held per year in the labor force.

Behavior Disturbance

The same measure used in childhood was also developed for the adult years.

RESULTS

To explore whether the family's influence continues into young adulthood, we first examined the correlations between the family measures and the young adult's history measured by time out of the labor force,

Table 1. Correlations between measures of the family in childhood and adult functioning[a]

	Rate of time out of the labor force	Rate of job turnover	Adult behavior disturbance
Males			
Family Stability	n.s.	r=.22	r=.47
Social Class	n.s.	n.s.	r=.27
Females			
Family Stability	n.s.	r=.30	r=.31
Social Class	r=−.21	r=.23	r=.32

[a] p < 0.05 for all correlations shown.

time unemployed, job turnover and behavior disturbance (Figure 2). This was done separately for males and females.

A significant relationship between social class and the young adult's time out of the labor force was found for females but not for males, with young women who were brought up in higher social class families spending more time out (Table 1). For these women, time out of the labor force was predominately spent in adult MR day services or being at home and not looking for work. Family stability was not related to time out of the labor force for either sex.

Examining the job measures, young adults of both sexes who came from stable families had significantly less job turnover than young adults from unstable families (Table 1). Social class was unrelated to the job measures for males, but for females there was significantly less turnover for young women who were raised in higher social class families. Thus, job turnover was related to family environment for both sexes, but family stability was a better predictor for males, whereas social class was a better predictor for females.

In a previous paper we reported that adult behavior disturbance occurred significantly more often in unstable families in an analysis done for both sexes combined (Richardson *et al.*, 1985a).

Thus far, the later effects of the family on their children's lives has been examined without regard to the effects of the child's characteristics. Now, measures both of the family and the child will be considered as a set of independent variables to determine their combined influence on the dependent variables of their later adult histories. To do this we used stepwise multiple regressions. The R^2's shown in Table 2 were all statistically significant. They indicate the size of the variance provided by the independent variables of the child and the family in predicting the

Table 2. Stepwise multiple regressions using family and child characteristics to predict adult functioning

Childhood factors *(independent variables)*	*Adult outcomes* *(dependent variabes)*		
	Time out of labor force	*Job turnover*	*Adult behavior*
Males			
Family			
Family stability	B=.27	B=.33	B=.26
Social class	–	–	–
Child			
IQ	–	–	–
Brain dysfunction	B=.65	B=.33	–
Childhood behavior	–	–	B=.49
Overall prediction	R^2=.37	R^2=.15	R^2=.40
Females			
Family			
Family stability	–	B=.30	–
Social class	–	–	B=.32
Child			
IQ	B=−.46	–	–
Brain dysfunction	–	–	–
Childhood behavior	–	–	B=.37
Overall prediction	R^2=.21	R^2=.09	R^2=.26

various measures of adult history. The models approximate the ecological model more adequately than the results so far given and are represented in Figure 3.

For both sexes the multiple regressions predicted adult behavior disturbance, with the prediction being stronger for males ($R^2 = .40$) than females ($R^2 = .26$). The factor in the childhood period that contributed most to the prediction for both sexes was childhood behavior disturbance. The prediction was increased by family stability for males only and social class for females only. The size of the contributing factors is shown by the relative size of the beta weights.

The multiple regressions also predicted time out of the labor force. The model was stronger for males ($R^2 = .37$) than for females ($R^2 = .21$). The independent childhood variables that contributed to the outcome differed by sex. For males, brain dysfunction was the major contributor to time out of the labor force, with family stability also contributing; for females the only variable that contributed was IQ, with women with lower IQs spending more time out of the labor force.

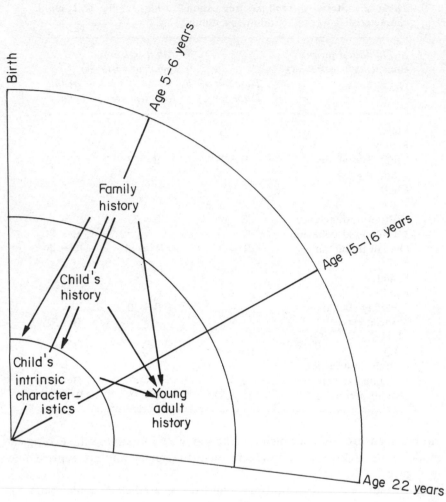

Figure 3.

The predictive models were weak for job turnover and non-significant for unemployment.

DISCUSSION

We have used two measures to determine the role of the family in predicting the functioning of MMR adults. The results suggest that different aspects of the family affect males and females differently. In predicting both job turnover and adult behavior disturbance, family stability was important for males and social class was important for females. Further sex differences emerged in the analysis. For the males, family stability and brain dysfunction, in a linear combination of equal weights, predicted rate of job turnover, whereas family stability was the sole predictor of rate of job turnover for the females. Also, for the females, social class and childhood behavior combined with equal weights to predict adult behavior.

The importance of using multivariate analyses, in which the family measures are examined in conjunction with the characteristics of the individual, can be seen from the results. Time out of the job market was best predicted for males by the combination of brain dysfunction and family stability, even though the simple relationship between family stability and time out of the job market was not significant. For females, family stabililty was the only independent variable to predict job turnover, and social class was the lone predictor of adult behavior disturbance when all factors were taken into account, despite the simple relationships that were found. This indicates an overlap of information between family stability and social class.

Gender is an intrinsic characteristic of the individual that was used in the ecological model. As such, it might have been entered into the statistical analyses as another independent variable. For these analyses, we chose to use gender as a control variable, in order to more fully understand how childhood factors may differ in their influence on the later lives of males and females.

The results have been used to illustrate some of the initial steps we have taken to examine the long term influence of the family on their MMR children, or the more general question, "Why do some young adults who are MMR function more effectively than others?" Following are some of the issues that need to be examined as the exploration is continued.

1. Are there other characteristics of the family that are salient influences in the lives of their children that are not tapped by the concepts of social class and family stability?

2. Family environment was selected because of the known importance of its role in the socialization of children. What other environmental factors in childhood have salient influences?

3. What other characteristics of the child, intrinsic or developmental, may be important influences on the child's life course?

4. We have only looked at the combined effects of the environment and the individual during childhood. Yet from an ecological perspective it is important to also include environmental – individual interactions on a continuing time base in the adolescent and adult years. For example, none of the independent variables we used in the childhood years predicted rate of unemployment. It may be that unemployment is influenced by the kind of work a person does. For example, a person

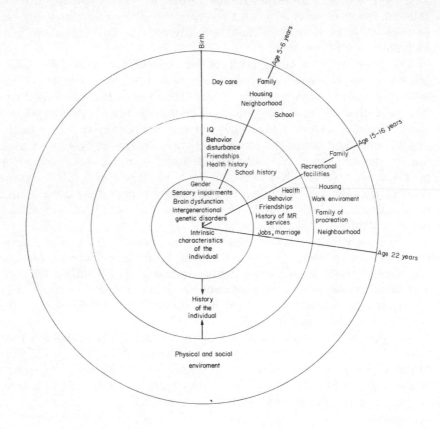

Figure 4.

working in seasonal industries, such as construction, may be periodically laid off and wait for similar employment, in order to benefit from seniority and experience.

The need for a more comprehensive set of variables from various parts of the ecological model is apparent, because none of the results accounted for as much as half the variance in the predictions and the simple correlations, although significant, were generally low. Figure 4 gives some examples of additional variables that may strengthen the ecological model. It is hoped that this paper illustrates the value of an ecological conceptualization of socialization.

ACKNOWLEDGEMENT

This study was supported by the Foundation for Child Development, the William T. Grant Foundation, the National Institute of Child Health and Human Development Grant No. HD07907, the G. Harold and Leila Y. Mathers Charitable Foundation, the Charitable Trust of Mrs Abby R. Mauze, the Scottish Home and Health Department, and the Social Science Research Council of the United Kingdom. The authors wish to thank R. Illsley, J. McLaren, and the late G. Horobin of the British Medical Research Council for their help and support.

REFERENCES

Birch, H., Richardson, S. A., Baird, D., Horobin, G., and Illsley, R. (1970) *Mental Subnormality in the Community: A Clinical and Epidemiological Study*, Baltimore: the Williams & Wilkins Co.

Bronfenbrenner, U. (1979) *The Ecology of Human Development*. Cambridge: Harvard University Press.

Koller, H., Richardson, S. A., and Katz, M. (1988) Marriage in a Young Adult Mentally Retarded Population. *J. Ment. Defic. Res.*, **32**, 93–102.

Koller, H., Richardson, S. A., and Katz, M. (In press) Peer Relationships of Mildly Retarded Young Adults Living in the Community. *J. Ment. Defic. Res.*

Koller, H., Richardson, S. A., Katz, M., and McLaren, J. (1983) Behavior disturbance since childhood in a five-year birth cohort of all mentally retarded young adults in a city. *Am. J. Ment. Defic.*, **87**, 4: 386–395.

Richardson, S. A. (1981) Growing up as a mentally subnormal young person. A follow-up study. In: S. A. Mednick and A. E. Baert (eds.), *Empirical Basis for Primary Prevention: A Prospective Longitudinal Research in Europe*. London: Oxford University Press.

Richardson, S. A., Katz, M., and Koller, H. (1986) Sex differences in the numbers of children administratively classified as mildly mentally retarded: An epidemiological review. *Am. J. Ment. Defic.*, **91**, 3: 250–256.

Richardson, S. A., Koller, H., and Katz, M. (1985a) Relationship of upbringing to later behavior disturbance of mildly retarded young people. *Am. J. Ment. Defic.*, **90**, 1: 1–8.

Richardson, S. A., Koller, H., and Katz, M. (1985b) Appearance and mental retardation. Some first steps in the development and application of a measure. *Am. J. Ment. Defic.*, **89**, 5: 475–484.

Richardson, S. A., Koller, H., and Katz, M. (1988) Job Histories in Open Employment of a Population of Young Adults with Mental Retardation: I. *American Journal of Mental Retardation*, **92**, 6: 483–491.

Richardson, S. A., Koller, H., Katz, M., and McLaren, J. (1981) A functional classification of seizures and its distribution in a mentally retarded population. *Am. J. Ment. Defic.*, **85**, 5: 457–466.

Richardson, S. A., Koller, H., Katz, M., and McLaren, J. (1984a) Patterns of disability in a mentally retarded population between ages 16 and 22 years. In: J. Berg (ed.), *Perspectives and Progress in Mental Retardation. Volume II: Biomedical Aspects*, Baltimore: University Park Press.

Richardson, S. A., Koller, H., Katz, M., and McLaren, J. (1984b) Career paths through mental retardation services: An epidemiological perspective. *Applied Research in Mental Retardation*, **5**: 53–67.

Consumers' View of a Community Care Program

A. Takahashi and M. Ooshima

Kisen Center for Developmental Disabilities,
Kodomono Seikatu Kenkyu-jo, Japan and
Department of Social Welfare, Aichi Prefectural Colony Institute of
Developmental Research, Kasugai, Aichi 480–03, Japan

The purpose of this study was to find out the accessibility and feasibility of formal care programs in Japan from the point of view of parents as the consumers. Two survey studies of similar kind were conducted in 1981 and 1988 respectively, subjects of which were parents of handicapped children of under eight years of age. The result shows that parents as consumers are not fully satisfied by services provided by governmental programs. Parents need services to be much closer to them and to act as "key-person" in the framework of a total community care program.

PURPOSE AND METHOD OF THE RESEARCH

During the past two decades, Japan has enacted much legisation on supportive systems for people with handicaps. Some of these systems are well planned and organised. For example, mass screening test for inborn metabolic errors is administered to more than 90% of new-born babies in Japan today, and health examination for infants and pre-school age is reported to reach an effective rate of higher than 80%. It is officially said that, through the health examination and diagnostic and therapeutic services, theoretically all cases of handicapping conditions can be identified and treated effectively. Most of these statements are made by governmental or professional persons in the role of service provider.

Through our clinical experience with parents of handicapped children, the following questions came to mind: are parents and families of handicapped children, being consumers of services provided by government, really satisfied by such services, and do they consider their services to be really effective and helpful for their children? We conducted survey studies of parents of handicapped children of under 8 years of age in both

1981 and 1988. The number of subjects in each survey was 477 in 1981 and 368 in 1988, respectively. A part of the 1981 survey was reported at the Toronto Congress of IASSMD in 1982. Most of the subjects were members of parents associations of retarded citizens in the area where the subjects lived. We used a questionnaire method. The main categories of questionnaire are time and person of first suspicion, time and place of diagnosis, time lag between first suspicion and diagnosis, satisfaction of explanation, reliability of health examination, expenses in medical care and reliability of official facilities.

RESULTS

1) The time of first suspicion of abnormal development in the child, and the person who mentioned it first were almost the same for two surveys as shown in the Tables 1 and 2. Table 1 shows that family and medical clinics are the biggest source of suspicion of a child's disorder even though the governmental health examination system is supposed to be the first place to identify abnormal development of infants. As seen in Table 2, some 60% of children were first mentioned as having their developmental abnormality before the age of one year. But, governmental health examination for the first year of infancy is not effective in its operation because examination for this period is entrusted to general practitioners who are not necessarily paediatricians or psychiatrists specialising in developmental disorders. Eighteen months examination is considered to be much better in its functioning level since psychologists and welfare workers as well as paediatricians are involved in the 18 month and 3 year examinations. However, our survey revealed that more than half of handicapped children had their abnormality suspected before the age of 18 months. It means that 18 months examination is too late for those whose abnormality was suspected earlier than that age, and parents cannot wait until 18 months without a precise diagnosis and prognosis for the condition of the child.

2) Those parents who may be experiencing unease and anxiety are inclined to seek someone outside the governmental care system who could give seemingly hopeful advice and help to the parents. In relation to this matter, our survey revealed that 57.9% of parents with some suspicion of their child's abnormality had someone to consult for advice and help, but 25.3% of parents failed to find a person in a nearby area to consult, regarding their child. For those parents, it can be said that today's supportive services are not sufficient to meet their needs.

3) Regarding the facility where definite diagnosis was given, most cases

Table 1. Facilities/Person of first suspicion

	1981	1988
Family	53.2%	44.6%
Medical Doctor	30.2	37.5
Health Examination	10.1	12.0
Others	2.1	3.8
N.A.	4.4	2.2

Table 2. Time of first suspicion

	1981	1988
before 3 M.	23.3%	33.4%
before 1 Y.	22.0	29.6
1 – 2 Y.	29.8	22.0
2 – 3 Y.	21.8	12.0
3 Y. –	2.3	1.9
N.A.	0.8	1.1

were given diagnosis at medical clinics and hospitals. In Japan there are two kinds of medical facilities: one is general clinics and hospitals; and the other is so-called 'centres' for handicapped persons. Comparison of the ratio of those two types of facilities shows that the latter was slightly higher in 1981 but, in 1988, the ratio was reversed. It is thought that, during the past seven years, general medical facilities improved their level of diagnosis of developmental disorders in the early stages of life.

4) The time lag between the first suspicion of the condition and the definite diagnosis was investigated. This time lag is defined as the period of time during which parents were experiencing uncertainty and anxiety of the child's condition. Needless to say, the shorter this time lag, the better for parents and children. On this point, the results of both surveys showed almost the same tendency; i.e. about 40% of subjects had to wait less than three months until a definite diagnosis was given, 50% less than six months, and 70% less than one year. The problem is how to shorten this time lag, and also how to deal with parents during these hard times.

5) The next question related to when parents were told about the diagnosis of their child: did they think the doctor's explanation of the condition and treatment was satisfactory? Both surveys on this

question show almost the same figures. Among all parents under survey, 47–48% thought that the doctor's explanation was enough; 42–43% felt it insufficient and 6–7% thought no explanation was given at all. The fact that almost half of subjects were not satisfied by the explanation at the time of diagnosis indicated critical defects within our service. The unsatisfied half of parents might seek a person who could give them some hope for the future of their child, but sometimes the advice received was neither scientific nor realistic. This could result in a loss of time for the child to receive an appropriate intervention program.

6) As for the utility and effectiveness of the health examination system for infants and pre-school children which is provided by the government to be the key measure in the official care program for developmental disorders in Japan, official statistics reported that, among all children under the prescribed age, about 80% of them underwent health examination. However, according to our study, only 66.3% (18 months) and 45.1% (3 years) underwent the examination (Table 4). In addition, out of total subjects, 33.5% in 1981 and 32.6% in 1988 of parents answered that they thought the health examination to be helpful in rearing their handicapped children but on the other hand 32.9% in 1981 and 39.9% in 1988 took it to be of no help. This result showed a big discrepancy between the central intention of the official measure and the real response of parents as the consumers.

7) A similar attitude of parents was seen in the answers to the question on the person whom parents consulted with and relied upon in dealing with difficulties in rearing their handicapped children. In the present care system of Japan, Welfare Offices, Public Health Centers, Municipal Offices as well as Child Guidance Centers are expected to play key functions and they are supposed to be the essential resources in the community. However, as shown in Table 3, parents considered the day care center, parents with a handicapped child other than officers of parents association, the Child Guidance Center and the hospital to be helpful in the past and chose the same four to be the resources to contact in the future.

8) Moreover, to the question on which facilities or persons gave parents displeasure or dissatisfaction when consulted, the worst five by parents' choice were, as shown in Table 3, hospital, Welfare Office and Municipal Office, Child Guidance Center and Public Health Center. Considering the results given in the above two questions, it has been evident that, while governmental plan puts the first responsibility in the service network for handicapped people on Welfare Office and Municipal Offices, Child Guidance Centers and

Table 3. Parents' evaluation of resources: effectiveness in the past, present choice, and displeasure, 3 choices per subject (1988)

Resources	Past	Present	Displeasure
1. Day care center	67.4%	56.5%	5.2%
2. Parents with handicapped child	38.6	44.8	0.3
3. Family	33.4	32.6	1.6
4. Hospital	20.4	17.1	16.3
5. Child guidance center	20.4	16.6	12.0
6. Public health center	16.0	6.0	11.1
7. Special hospital for handicapped persons	15.2	16.6	6.5
8. Center for handicapped	14.1	9.2	3.3
9. Relatives	12.0	6.0	2.2
10. School teacher	7.3	13.9	1.6
11. Kindergarden	7.1	0.8	5.7
12. Neighbors	6.3	1.6	1.4
13. Welfare office	6.0	6.0	12.5
14. Friends	5.7	7.6	0.0
15. Officer of parents' association	4.1	3.5	0.8
16. Volunteer	3.5	0.5	0.3
17. General practitioner	3.3	2.4	4.1
18. Adviser for handicapped person	3.0	1.9	0.5
19. Home helper	0.8	0.0	0.0
20. Welfare commissioner	0.3	0.8	0.8

Public Health Centers, parents as the consumers do not believe in their effectiveness; also, the governmental program does not coincide with the preferences of parents as consumers. This discrepancy should be urgently studied regarding its cause and ways to overcome it.

9) In relation to the category of medical care, two problems became evident. One is the shortage of dental clinics which can be consulted easily by parents with handicapped children, whereas the Japanese Ministry of Health and Welfare disclosed their concern about a possible surplus of dentists in the near future. The second is the burden on parents to bring their child to hospital or clinic to get a diagnosis and treatment. Today, direct medical expenses for handicappd people is borne by the government. But, more than 20% of parents complained of financial difficulty for transportation and of difficulty in getting help to take care of the child on their way to and from hospital or the clinic. There is no way to subsidise or provide manpower for these problems yet.

CONCLUSION

Japan has developed a well-planned supportive care system for the handicapped citizen from the legislative point of view. We examined some parts of the system from the consumer's point of view, and found that there exists several discrepancies between expected effect of the planned system and the actual effect evaluated by consumers, some of which concerned very fundamental problems in the developing care system for handicapped people. In order to bridge such discrepancies and to make care systems more effective for and closer to the person who needs support, consumers' views should be taken into consideration in the process of planning of programs and also in monitoring procedures. For this purpose, the authors put emphasis on the importance of establishing primary care centers in each community. The center should be the initial contact point for families with suspicion, worry or difficulty regarding a child's development. The center can also act as the liaison between the consumer and the service provider. The center should be well known in the community and be easy to reach geographically as well as psychologically for the person who needs help and support. The fundamental function of the center is to act in the front line of service and to be integrated into the total care system. Therefore, the center need not have an impressive building or specialised staff; rather, it should utilise already existing resources in the area. The important functions of the primary center are i) to stimulate potential resources in the community, ii) to coordinate those resources, iii) to connect the community with secondary or tertiary centers of higher level of specialty, and iv) to monitor the operation of service systems. Parents and families should be encouraged to take part in the operation of the primary center in order to ensure the consumers' view of its activity.

REFERENCE

Takahashi, A. (1982) Parents' views of community care programs. Paper given at 6th Congress of International Association for the Scientific Study of Mental Deficiency. Toronto.

Building a Family Classification System: Families with Mentally Retarded Children

I. T. Mink

Neuropsychiatric Institute, University of California,
760 Westwood Plaza, Los Angeles, CA 90024-175919, U.S.A.

This paper is a synthesis of research from five separate samples: U.S. families with slow learning, TMR, and SMR children and Japanese families with EMR and SMR children. Cluster analysis of psychosocial measures of the home environment for each sample yielded distinctive family types. Comparison of the profiles of the types from all of the samples revealed ten essentially different family types. Of these, eight family types appeared in more than one sample: control-oriented, responsive-to-child, cohesive, expression-oriented, moral-religious-oriented, conflictual, achievement-oriented, and low disclosure. Two of these general family types are discussed in depth as is the possibility of building a classification system of families.

Observers of scientific endeavor (Cattell, Coulter, & Tsujioka, 1966; Hempel, 1961, 1967; Quay, 1979) have noted that an increase in understanding often accompanies the ability of investigators to classify the individuals, entities, or events in their field of study. This comes about because classification is considered the first step *away from* adequate description of events *toward* theoretical formulation about the relationships between these particular events and other entities. Knowledge expands once theories or laws are established in a field and investigators are able to explain, predict, and ultimately understand the nature of the events.

In order for a classification system to be useful though, it must meet certain criteria. First, the characteristics that define a category must be clearly described and this cluster of characteristics must be observable in one or more situations. Second, there must be reliability. The assignment of an individual or entity to a category must be consistent or stable over a reasonable period of time. Third, there must be validity. The cluster of characteristics should be different from other clusters and should demonstrate relationships with variables that are different from the ones used to determine the cluster. Fourth, the classification system must have utility. The clusters should "have differential relationships to etiology, treatment, and prognosis" (Quay, 1979, p. 3).

Since the advent of family studies in the United States, various family classification systems have been reported (see Fisher, 1977; Mink, 1986). Some classifications have been heuristic (Burgess & Locke, 1945; Farber, 1960; Miller, 1964), while others have been empirical (Mink, Blacher, & Nihira, in press; Mink, Meyers, & Nihira, 1984; Mink, Nihira, & Meyers, 1983; Moos & Moos, 1976; Riskin & Faunce, 1970a, 1970b, 1970c; Tax, 1979).

In addition, many classification systems have evolved from the observation of patients in treatment (Ackerman & Behrens, 1956; Kantor & Lehr, 1975; Minuchin, Montalvo, Guerney, Rosman, & Schumer, 1967; Tseng & McDermott, 1979; Voilland, 1962). These systems have good clinical utility, however, some lack operational definitions of variables and reported reliability and validity. Such deficiencies do not allow other investigators to replicate classification categories.

This paper is concerned with an important aspect of the first criterion of a classification system: the demonstration of identified categories in more than one sample. It is a synthesis of three previously reported typologies (Mink *et al.*, 1983, 1984, in press) and two new typologies (Mink & Nihira, 1988).

METHOD

Subjects

There were five separate samples of families, three in the United States and two in Japan. In the U.S. samples, there were 218 families with slow learning children (SL) enrolled in classes for the educably mentally retarded (EMR) or educationally handicapped, 115 families with trainably mentally retarded children (TMR), and 97 families with severely mentally retarded children (SMR). In the Japanese samples, there were 90 families with EMR children and 103 families with TMR children.

Table 1 presents descriptions of the families. Overall, in comparison to the Japanese samples, the U.S. samples have a much lower percentage of two parent families and a much higher percentage of parents with post-secondary school education. The Japanese families are at about the same socioeconomic level as the U.S. SL and TMR families. U.S. TMR families, though, have the highest parental educational attainment and socioeconomic level of the five samples.

With respect to the children, the occurrence of Down Syndrome is

Table 1. Description of families with developmentally disabled children

Variable	American			Japanese	
	Slow learner	TMR	SMR	EMR	TMR
Family:					
% Father-figures present	75.7	83.5	88.7	96.7	97.1
% Parents married	70.2	81.7	85.0	97.8	95.2
% Father-figures >					
high school education	43.0	61.5	67.6	33.3	23.0
% Mother-figures >					
high school education	39.5	47.4	65.1	0.0	8.7
Mean family SES (Duncan)	38.0	48.0	58.7	49.3	40.6
Mean N of children in home	3.0	2.5	2.3	1.6	1.3
Child:					
% Down Syndrome	N.A.	47.8	9.3	7.8	3.9
% Male	58.7	56.5	66.0	54.4	49.5
% White	66.5	79.1	73.2	N.A.	N.A.
Mean age	12.4	12.7	5.8	10.7	9.8
Mean I.Q.	69.8	41.5	N.A.	65.6	39.4
Number of families)	(218)	(115)	(97)	(90)	(103)

quite different in U.S. and Japanese TMR families. There are more boys in U.S. SMR families. U.S. SL and TMR children are older than Japanese children. Mean IQs for U.S. and Japanese TMR children are about the same, but are higher for U.S. SL children than for Japanese EMR children.

Interviews and Instruments

Home visits were made to participants in all samples. Questionnaires and instruments pertaining to charactcristics, attitudes, and behaviors of the child and family were usually answered by the mother. Interviewers rated the family on child-rearing practices and selected aspects of the home environment. Instruments were separated into two categories for the purposes of analysis: those providing variables for the cluster analyses and those providing variables for the validity phase of the studies, the criterion analyses.

Cluster analyses

Instruments were selected to provide a comprehensive picture of the psychosocial environment of the home (for further explication see Mink *et al.*, 1983, 1984, in press). The Home Observation for Measurement of the Environment Inventory (*HOME*, Bradley & Caldwell, 1979) provided variables related to the reinforcement aspects of home with TMR and SMR children, while the Henderson Environmental Learning Process Scale (*HELPS*, Henderson, Bergan, & Hurt, 1972) provided these measures for homes with SL and EMR children. The Family Environment Scale (*FES*, Moos & Moos, 1986) provided measures of the social-environmental climate of the home for all samples. The Home Quality Rating Scale (*HQRS*, Meyers, Mink, & Nihira, 1977) supplied variables concerned with child-rearing practices and other aspects of the family environment for all samples.

Measures from these instruments provided the variables that were used in the five cluster analyses.

Home Observation for Measurement of the Environment

Stimulation through toys, games, and reading materials (MATSTIM)
Pride, affection, and warmth (PAW)
Stimulation of academic behavior (ACASTIM)
Modeling and encouraging of social maturity (SOCMAT)
Language stimulation or verbal responsivity (LANGSTIM)
Physical environment organized and clean (PHYSENV)
Variety of stimulation (VARIETY)
Avoidance of restriction and punishment (ACCEPT)

Henderson Environmental Learning Process Scale

Extended interests and community involvement (COMINV)
Provision of a supportive environment for school learning
    (SCHLEARN)
Educational expectations and aspirations (EDEXPECT)

Family Environment Scale

Expressiveness (EXPRESS)
Achievement orientation (ACHIEVE)
Moral-religious emphasis (MORREL)
Control (CONTROL)
Cohesion, independence, and organization vs. conflict (COHCNF)
Intellectual-cultural and active-recreational orientation (INTREC)

Home Quality Rating Scale

Harmony of the home and quality of parenting (HARMONY)
Concordance in parenting and marriage (CONCORD)
Openness and awareness of the respondent (OPEN)
Quality of the residential environment (RESENV)
Quality of the residential area (RESAREA)

Criterion analyses

Variables that described family and child characteristics and behaviors, and that were not used in the cluster analyses, were employed in this phase of the studies. Besides basic demographic data and indices of child and family adjustment from questionnaires, there were measures of adaptive behavior (Nihira, Foster, Shellhaas, & Leland, 1974), and for the U.S. samples, measures of stressful life events (Holmes & Rahe, 1967) and self-concept (Coopersmith, 1975).

Statistical Procedures

All five analyses employed the K-means clustering procedure with covariance standardization (Engelmann, 1979). This is an iterative partitioning method that sorts cases into clusters depending on the Euclidean distance between the cases and the centers of the clusters. For each sample, several solutions with different numbers of clusters were produced and examined. The optimal solution was selected on the basis of cluster stability, the distance matrix, and investigator judgment. Profiles were then plotted for each family type discovered. Once the cluster analyses were completed, differences between the clusters on the criterion variables were examined using chi-square or F and t tests.

RESULTS & DISCUSSION

The cluster analyses reveals seven distinct family types in the U.S. SL sample, five in the U.S. TMR sample, five in the U.S. SMR sample, seven in the Japanese EMR sample, and six in the Japanese TMR sample – altogether 30 different family types. However, inspection and comparison of the profiles of these family types reveals that there are essentially ten different family types (see Table 2). Of these, the following eight types appear in more than one sample: control-oriented, responsive-to-child, cohesive, expression-oriented, moral-religious-oriented, conflictual, achievement-oriented, and low disclosure.

It is assumed that these eight types represent general family types. It is not claimed that all of the sample family types subsumed under a general family type are identical; there are minor variations throughout on certain psychosocial variables. In addition, some sample types are variant with respect to overall profile elevation and others with respect to portions of the profile.

In the validity phase of the studies, inspection of the criterion variables for the sample family types subsumed under a general type reveal similarity in parent and child characteristics on some variables irrespective of culture; other variables are markedly different in the two cultures.

Consideration will be given to two of these general family types

Table 2. Presence of types in families with developmentally disabled children

| | | American | | Japanese | |
Family type	Slow learner	TMR	SMR	EMR	TMR
Control-oriented		X	X	X	X
Responsive-to-child		X	X		X
Cohesive	X	X	V	X	
Expression-oriented	X			X	X
Moral-religious-oriented	X		V	V	X
Conflictual	X	X		V	
Achievement-oriented	X		V	X	X
Low disclosure	X	X		X	
Learning-oriented	X				
Growth-promoting					X

(figures presented will show only those psychosocial variables which are common to all of the sample family types). Variables are coded with a designation which can be found in the above description of variables.

Control-oriented families

This general family type occurs in U.S. TMR (N=34), U.S. SMR (N=27), Japanese EMR (N=21), and Japanese TMR (N=9) samples. It does not occur in the U.S. SL sample (see Figure 1). Overall, this type is characterized by elevated scores on control (the family is run by a set of rules and procedures), low scores on harmony (family adjustment is low, as is acceptance of and coping with the retarded child), and somewhat lower scores on cohesion vs. conflict (family members display anger and aggression).

In terms of the criterion analyses (see Mink *et al.*, 1983, 1984, in press; Mink & Nihira, 1988), all of these types (in comparison with other types in their respective samples) have among the highest percentage of father-figures present, the highest percentage of retarded sons, the lowest percentage of children with Down Syndrome, and the lowest child adaptive behavior scores. U.S. types have among the highest socio-economic levels and the most highly educated father-figures, while Japanese types have among the lowest socioeconomic levels and the least educated father-figures.

Certain questions occur about the control-oriented family type. First, why does the type not appear in the U.S. slow learner sample? Perhaps it is not an appropriate pattern for families with higher functioning children. This only can be determined by examining a sample of normally functioning children. Second, why are there more boys than girls in this type? There are probably differences in child-rearing practices for the two

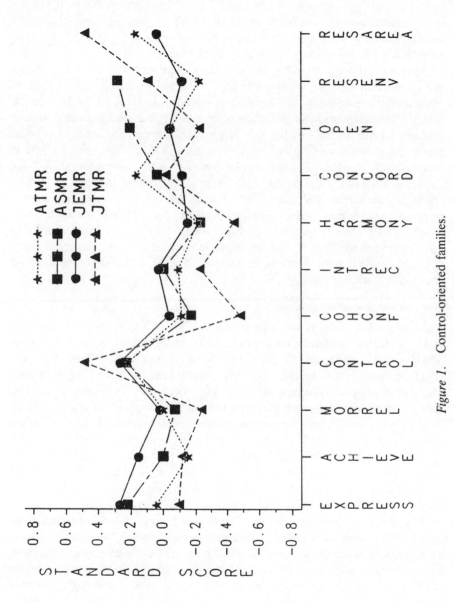

Figure 1. Control-oriented families.

sexes. In their pioneering study, Sears, Maccoby, and Levin (1957) found sex-linked differences in child-rearing on issues concerning control of behavior. Third, why does the U.S. SMR type have an elevated score on openness and awareness of the child's disability? From birth, there are clear indications of disability in SMR children; parents are, therefore, well acquainted with their children's condition. In addition, both mothers and fathers in this group are highly educated.

Finally, while the profiles of the Japanese groups and the U.S. groups are reasonably similar, what accounts for the major differences in fathers' educational attainment and family socioeconomic level? That is, why do the U.S. control-oriented families have highly educated fathers and high socioeconomic status, while the same family types in Japan have less educated parents and lower socioeconomic status? The answer lies in cultural differences. Earlier studies of the same samples show that Japanese parents, in general, score lower on control than U.S. parents (Nihira, Tomiyasu, & Oshio, 1987; Nihira, Webster, Tomiyasu & Oshio, in press). In addition, overt "control" within the family is not considered desirable by the Japanese middle class; "a mother who took an authoritarian attitude would be regarded as lacking in human feeling" (Hendry, 1986). Adherence to this standard may not be as strong in lower socio-economic families.

Responsive-to-child families

This general family type appears in the U.S. TMR (N=27; formerly termed child-oriented, expressive), U.S. SMR (N=11), and Japanese TMR (N=11) samples. It does not occur in the U.S. SL or Japanese EMR samples (see Figure 2). This type is characterized by relatively elevated scores on language stimulation, acceptance, cohesion vs. conflict (family members demonstrate commitment and support of one another), intellectual-cultural and active recreational orientation (family members are interested in and pursue extra-family activities), and openness (parental forthrightness and awareness of the child's disability). Low scores are on moral-religious emphasis and control for all groups, on concordance for the U.S. TMR and SMR groups, and on variety of stimulation for U.S. SMR and Japanese TMR groups.

The criterion analysis reveals a lower percentage of intact homes in the two U.S. groups; in contrast, all Japanese families are two-parent. Fewer U.S. fathers have progressed beyond high school, while more Japanese fathers have, and also have attained a relatively high socioeconomic status. U.S. TMR children tend to be white and have high adaptive behavior; many are Down Syndrome. Japanese TMR children have low IQ scores, high adaptive behavior, and low maladaptive behavior.

Several questions arise with this family type. First, since the type appears only in samples with lower functioning TMR and SMR children,

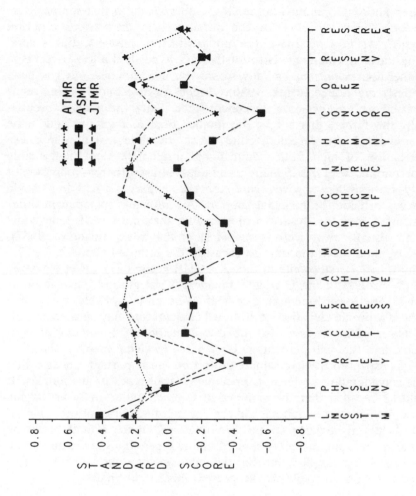

Figure 2. Responsive-to-child families.

is it disability-specific? It may be, but it also may be measurement-specific. The *HOME* is used in all three of the samples where this type appears, but it is not used in the U.S. SL and the Japanese EMR samples. Unfortunately, an adequate answer to this question only may be obtained by using the HOME with families having higher functioning children and determining whether this type appears in that sample.

Second, what accounts for the differences in the various criterion analyses? At present, there are no satisfactory answers, but several findings deserve comment. Both of the U.S. types had a low percentage of father-figures present and low scores on concordance. As has been previously mentioned (Mink, 1986), absence of a secondary caregiver is associated with a low score on concordance. Since the person absent is usually the father, this allows the mother time to focus on and to be responsive to her retarded child. Also of note, is the Japanese constellation of high father educational attainment, and high family socioeconomic level. As in many traditional cultures, there is a division of family responsibility, wives care for the home and children while husbands provide the financial support. Additionally, in Japan in order for salaried men to advance professionally, they must work long hours and are usually away from home most of the week (Imamura, 1987). Mothers, then, have the time to focus on the retarded child.

Third, the overall profile of the U.S. SMR group has a lower elevation than the profiles of the U.S. and Japanese TMR groups, what accounts for this? The lower functioning of SMR children is probably responsible for the low profile elevation. Additional contributors may be the very low percentage of intact families, the low educational attainment of both parents, and the high percentage of families receiving financial aid.

With respect to the five samples reviewed, an important question that needs consideration is the nonappearance of all types in all samples. It should be recalled that the samples of families under study are highly diverse with respect to culture and the degree of handicap of the retarded child. While it remains to be demonstrated, there actually may be cultural-specific and disability-specific family types. It also may be that all types exist in all samples, but that the incidence of a particular type is so low as to be undetectable by the present method of analysis.

CONCLUSION

Time does not allow for a review of all eight of the general family types. Of the two reviewed, it seems reasonable to conclude that the sample profiles of the control-oriented and the responsive-to-child general family types display a good resemblance to each other.

Of the six types which are not reviewed, the profiles in the expression-oriented general type display good resemblance, those in the cohesive and moral-religious-oriented general types display reasonable similarity, and those in the conflictual, achievement-oriented, and low disclosure general types display some resemblance to each other.

Although eight of the distinct family types appear in both the Japanese and the U.S. samples, in any consideration of a family type it is important to remember the culture in which it occurs. Examination of the control-oriented type demontrates this – the variable of control has different saliency and is endorsed in different social strata in the U.S. and Japan.

The results of this paper represent another essential building block in the construction of a classification system. Other remaining essentials are: the determination of reliability in the assignment of families to types over time and the demonstration of the clinical utility of the family types.

REFERENCES

Ackerman, N. W., & Behrens, M. D. (1965) A study of family diagnosis. *American Journal of Orthopsychiatry*, **26**, 66–78.

Bradley, R. H., & Caldwell, B. M. (1979) Home observation for measurement of the environment: A revision of the preschool scale. *American Journal of Mental Deficiency*, **84**, 235–244.

Burgess, E. W., & Locke, H. J. (1945) *The family: From institution to companionship*. New York: American Book Co.

Cattell, R. B., Coulter, M. A., & Tsujioka, B. (1966) The taxonomic recognition of types and functional emergents. In R. B. Cattel (Ed.), *Handbook of multivariate experimental psychology*, Chicago, IL: Rand McNally.

Coopersmith, S. (1975) *Coopersmith self-esteem behaviors*. San Francisco: Self Esteem Institute.

Engleman, L. (1979) K-means clustering. In W. J. Dixon & M. B. Brown (Eds), *BMDP Biomedical Computer Program P-Series* (pp. 648.1–652.1). Berkeley: University of California Press.

Farber, B. (1970) Family organization and crisis: Maintenance of integration in families with a severely mentally retarded child. *Monographs of the Society for Research in Child Development*. **25**(1).

Fisher, L. (1977) On the classification of families: A progress report. *Archives of General Psychiatry*, **34**, 424–433.

Hempel, C. G. (1961) Introduction to problems of taxonomy. In J. Zubin (Ed.), *Field studies in the mental disorders* (pp. 3–22). New York: Grune & Stratton.

Hempel, C. G. (1969) Ideal types in social science comply with covering law requirements: Typological methods in the social sciences. In L. I. Krimerman (Ed.), *The nature and scope of social science: A critical anthology* (pp. 445–456). New York: Appleton-Century-Crofts.

Henderson, R. W., Bergan, J. R., & Hurt, J., Jr. (1972) Development and validation of the Henderson environmental learning process scale. *Journal of Social Psychology*, **88**, 185–196.

220 Mink

Hendry, J. (1986) *Becoming Japanese: The world of the preschool child.* Honolulu: University of Hawaii Press.

Holmes, T. H., & Rahe, R. H. (1967). The social readjustment rating scale. *Journal of Psychosomatic Research*, **11**, 213–218.

Imamura, A. E. (1987) Urban Japanese housewives: At home and in the community. Honolulu: University of Hawaii Press.

Kantor, D., & Lehr, M. (1975) *Inside the family.* San Francisco: Jossey-Bass.

Meyers, C. E., Mink, I. T., & Nihira, K. (1977) *Home quality rating scale.* Pomona, CA: UCLA/Neuropsychiatric Institute-Lanterman State Hospital Research Group.

Miller, S. M. (1964) The American lower classes: A typological approach. In F. Reissman, J. Cohen, & A. Pearl (Eds.), *Mental health of the poor* (pp. 139–154). New York: The Free Press.

Mink, I. T. (1986) Classification of families with mentally retarded children. In J. J. Gallagher & P. M. Vietze (Eds.), *Families of Handicapped Persons: Research, Programs, and Policy Issues* (pp. 25–43). Balitmore: Brookes Publishing Co.

Mink, I. T., Blacher, J., & Nihira, K. (in press) Taxonomy of family life styles: III. Replication with families with severely retarded children. *American Journal of Mental Retardation.*

Mink, I. T., Meyers, C. E., & Nihira, K. (1984) Taxonomy of life styles: II. Homes with slow-learning children. *American Journal of Mental Deficiency*, **89**, 111–123.

Mink, I. T., & Nihira, K. (1988) [A comparison of Japanese and American family types]. Unpublished raw data, manuscript in preparation.

Mink, I. T., Nihira, K., & Meyers, C. E. (1983) Taxonomy of family life styles: I. Homes with TMR children. *American Journal of Mental Deficiency*, **87**, 484–497.

Minuchin, S., Montalvo, B., Guerney, B. G., Rosman, B. L., & Schumer, F. (1967) *Families of the slums: An exploration of their structure and treatment.* New York: Basic Books.

Moos, R. H., Insel, P. M., & Humphrey, B. (1974) *Family, work and group environment scales manual.* Palo Alto, CA: Consulting Psychologists Press.

Moos, R. H., & Moos, B. S. (1976) A typology of family social environments, *Family Process*, **15**, 357–371.

Moos, R. H., & Moos, B. S. (1986) *Family environment scale manual.* Palo Alto, CA: Consulting Psychologists Press.

Nihira, K., Foster, R., Shellhaas, M., & Leland, H. (1974) *AAMD Adaptive Behavior Scale.* Washington, DC: American Association on Mental Deficiency.

Nihira, K., Tomiyasu, Y., & Oshio, C. (1987). Homes of TMR Children: Comparison between American and Japanese Families. *American Journal of Mental Deficiency*, **91**(5), 486–495.

Nihira, K., Webster, R., Tomiyasu, Y., & Oshio, C. (in press) Child-environment relationships: A cross-cultural study of educable mentally retarded children and their families. *Journal of Autism and Developmental Disorders.*

Quay, H. C. (1979) Classification. In H. C. Quay & J. S. Werry (Eds.), *Psychopathological disorders of childhood* (pp. 1–42) (2nd ed.). New York: Wiley.

Riskin, J., & Faunce, E. E. (1970a) Family interaction scales: I. Theoretical framework and method. *Archives of General Psychiatry*, **22**, 504–512.

Riskin, J., & Faunce, E. E. (1970b) Family interaction scales: II. Data analysis and findings. *Archives of General Psychiatry*, **22**, 513–526.

Riskin, J., Faunce, E. E. (1970c) Family interaction scales: III. Discussion of methodology and substantive findings. *Archives of General Psychiatry*, **22**, 527–537.

Sears, R., Maccoby, E., & Levin, H. (1957) *Patterns of child-rearing*. Evanston, IL: Row & Peterson.

Tax, B. (1979) Sociocultural milieus: A cluster-analytic approach to the identification of social classes. In B. Prahl-Anderson, C. J. Kowalski, & P. H. J. M. Heyendael (Eds.), *A mixed longitudinal interdisciplinary study of growth and development* (pp. 193–213). New York: Academic Press.

Tseng, W. S., McDermott, J. F., Jr. (1979) Triaxial family classification. *American academy of child psychiatry*, **18**, 22–43.

Voilland, A. L. (1962) *Family casework diagnosis*. New York: Columbia University Press.

Factors Influencing and Factors Preventing Placement of Severely Handicapped Children: Perspectives from Mothers and Fathers

J. Blacher and B. Bromley

Families Project, School of Education, University of California, Riverside, California 92521, U.S.A.

This paper reports perspectives on out-of-home placement of severely handicapped children, drawn from a longitudinal program of research. To explore factors influencing and factors preventing placement, 26 couples who had recently placed their child were interviewed. Results revealed that mothers and fathers had very similar perceptions of influences in the placement process. On Factors Influencing Placement, each parent viewed the other spouse's attitude toward placement as the primary influence, although both acknowledged the strong influence of day to day stress and pessimism about the child's future functioning. On Factors Preventing Placement, both parents ranked attachment to the child way ahead of other influences. Findings are incorporated into a conceptual model developed for studying the placement process.

Public policy, education, and professional opinion in the United States continue to promote normalization and deinstitutionalization, the belief being that the best place to live for most handicapped children and youth is in their natural homes. However, out-of-home placement of handicapped children and young adults continues to occur, and severely handicapped individuals are considered at highest risk for such placement. In the U.S. institutional populations have dropped annually since the 1960s (Lakin, Hill, Hauber, Bruininks, & Heal, 1983), but the availability of non-institutional placements has increased, offering handicapped persons a variety of living settings and alternative careprovider arrangements.

A MODEL OF PLACEMENT

Our program of research explores factors influencing parents to keep their severely handicapped child at home versus place their child out of the natural home. It is a longitudinal project entitled "Out-of-Home Placement of Severely Handicapped Children: Correlates and Consequences" funded by the National Institute of Child Health and Human Development (HD21234; Blacher, 1986). The project actually began in 1982 as a study of 100 families with a severely handicapped young child living at home. The research aim included a variety of issues related to family adjustment to a severely handicapped child. This Project is unique in the United States because it is the only one we know of that studies placement prospectively as well as retrospectively.

The conceptual model guiding this study is portrayed in Figure 1. It is an attempt to understand the impact of the severely handicapped child on the family and the dynamics of the placement decision-making process. We are also interested in how this process is related to outcome – whether to place the child or not (Cole, 1986). The boxes represent the following constructs:

Child Characteristics

Previous studies of correlates of placement have identified maladaptive behavior or behavior problems (e.g., Borthwick-Duffy, Eyman, & White, 1987; Downey, 1965; Eyman & Call, 1977; Seltzer & Krauss, 1984; Sherman, 1988; Tausig, 1985), low IQ or more severe retardation (Downey, 1965; Eyman & Call, 1977; Eyman et al., 1972; Meyers et al., 1985; Saenger, 1960), and age (Borthwick-Duffy et al., 1987; Eyman & Call, 1977; Meyers et al., 1985; Sherman, 1988). In our study, however, the children included were relatively homogeneous with respect to these variables at the beginning of the Project.

Family Characteristics

Previous findings on family characteristics related to placement are equivocal. Variables such as marital status (Germain & Maisto, 1982; Hobbs, 1964; Saenger, 1960), socioeconomic status (Appell & Tisdall, 1968; Farber, et al., 1960; Shellhaas & Nihira, 1969; Stone, 1967) and family size (Appell & Tisdall, 1968; Farber et al., 1960; Sherman 1988; Tausig, 1985) have related in some studies but not in others.

We are exploring relationships among family adjustment, coping, impact of the child, aspects of the family environment and quality of the home. In one previous, comparative study (Blacher et al., 1987) we found that families with severely retarded children scored significantly lower on

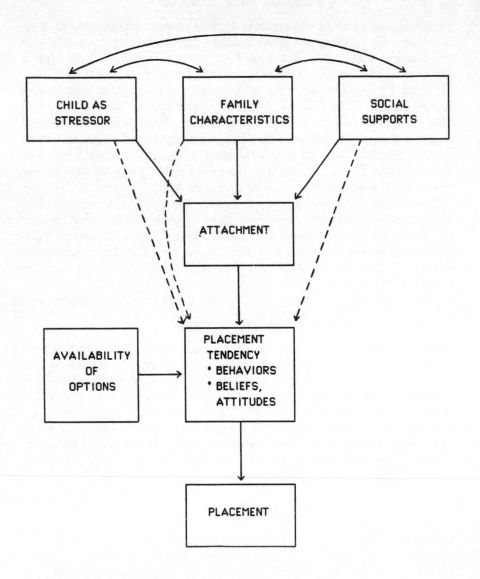

Figure 1.   A model of placement.

family adjustment measures and significantly higher on daily life impact than families with mildly and moderately retarded children. While the mildly retarded child's impact on the family gradually decreased as the child grew older, the severely retarded child's impact appeared great and relatively constant through childhood.

Social Support

Forms of social support believed to influence the placement decision include respite care, services offered by the public schools, and spousal support (Blacher & Prado, 1986; Cohen & Warren, 1985). We have found, for example, that while public schooling may not serve to prevent placement for these families, it certainly brings them relief and satisfaction and appears to delay placement to some extent (Meyers & Blacher, 1987). Other influences on the placement decision may include advice from professionals (especially physicians), advice from friends, and the availability of training in how to access community and support services (Andrew et al., 1965; Downey, 1965; German & Maisto, 1982; Suelzle & Keenan, 1981). It is not always clear, though, whether these social support influences serve to prevent placement or actually promote it.

Attachment

We have hypothesized elsewhere (Blacher, 1984a, 1984b; Blacher, 1986) that attachment between parents and a severely handicapped child may moderate the family's decision to place the child out of the home. We have also shown elsewhere (Blacher & Rousey, 1988) that higher levels of child-demonstrated attachment behaviors are significantly associated with a tendency to keep, versus place, the child.

Placement Tendency

We have hypothesized that placement can be conceptualized as a process, rather than as a single act. Tendency to place may begin with occasional thoughts and progress through stages of more concentrated consideration, to active searching for a placement, to actual placement. In one study (Blacher, 1986) we measured placement tendency annually over a three-year period. We learned that once parents take active steps to explore the possibility of placement (e.g., ask around, visit placements), placement was inevitable. However, it was a process that, for our sample, took about two-and-a-half years to complete. Another component of placement tendency includes parents' beliefs and attitudes toward placement.

Availability of Placement Options

We also hypothesize that placement is affected by the availability, and perhaps variety, of placement facilities.

Placement

This is the main outcome variable of the Families Project. For purposes of this study, placement is defined as any residential environment other than the home of the natural family. Foster homes, group homes, intermediate care facilities, and larger state-operated facilities are types of out-of-home placements (Baker *et al.*, 1977). A handicapped child is considered placed if he or she lives in one of these residential environments and if the parents have no definite plans to return the child home.

FACTORS INFLUENCING PLACEMENT

Little is known about the factors influencing out-of-home placement of severely handicapped children today. Research conducted in the 1960s and 1970s does not provide accurate information on the correlates and processes of placement in the 1980s. Furthermore, much of this earlier research failed to control for the length of time between the placement and the time of data collection (Caldwell & Guze, 1960; Wynne & Rogers, 1985). Moreover, most studies of placement focused on maternal feelings and attitudes, disregarding fathers' impressions of the placement experience, their role in placement, and their own reasons for placing their children. Also, samples often contained families of children with mild to profound retardation, with different levels or types of handicaps, and of all ages. Typically, researchers have not taken into account the role of extenuating or moderating circumstances in the parents' decision. Thus, this literature tells us little about which severely handicapped children will be placed and about the decision-making process involved in the placement.

One question of interest was whether parents' responses to placement would vary according to the age of the child at placement or the time since the child was placed. In a recent study of 56 parents (who were practically all mothers), we found surprisingly little relationship between the age of the child when placed (2–6 years, 7–11 yrs., 12–16 yrs.), the sex of the child, and the time since placement (1–6 months, 7–14 months, 15–23 months) (Bromley, 1988). This interview was also designed to explore the relationship of other moderator variables (e.g., the parents feelings of attachment or guilt) to the placement decision. There was a significant age effect for the dimension of guilt, with parents of children who were older at placement (ages 12 to 16) scoring higher than parents of younger children (ages 7 to 11 years: F (2,50) = 6.25, p < 0.01). In the present analysis we wanted to look further at a sub-group of these families, to determine the fathers' role in assessing factors influencing their placement decision.

Mothers' and Fathers' Views of Factors Influencing Placement

This study was designed as a clinical interview of parents who have recently placed their severely handicapped child. The primary purpose was to describe parents' reasons for placing their child and to explore reasons why they did not make the placement earlier.

SUBJECTS

Subjects were 26 families that met the following criteria: 1) they had a child between the ages of 2 and 16 years at the time of placement; 2) the child was considered "severely handicapped" according to school or Regional Center criteria (Regional Centers are part of a state-wide service delivery network in which all identified handicapped children in California are registered); 3) both parents would complete the interview; 4) the child's parents spoke fluent English and had a telephone; and 5) the child had been placed out of the home no longer than 24 months. We learned that during a one-year period (1983–84), only 91 severely handicapped children were placed out-of-home in all of California. That is why we extended our sampling criteria to include children placed within the last two years.

Families included in this study represented a subsample of about half of the subjects in the Bromley (1988) study. Demographics from the larger sample indicated that: children ranged in age from 2.8 to 17.5 years and 64% were male. The large majority were Caucasian (73%); others were Black (11%), Hispanic (4%), mixed ethnicity or other (13%). All were considered "severely handicapped" by virtue of their level of retardation and accompanying disorders (e.g., autism, cerebral palsy). Comparisons between sex and ethnicity of the children in this sample and the population of severely handicapped children in the state of California, taken from state records available to us, attests to the general representativeness of the sample (Bromley, 1988).

Primary parents from this broader sample (mainly mothers) ranged in age from 19 to 68 years ($\overline{X}$ = 38); secondary parents (mainly fathers) from 23 to 60 years ($\overline{X}$ = 41). Educational levels of parents ranged from tenth grade through advanced degrees, with about half of the mothers and half of the fathers having some college degree (A.A., B.A., M.A., Ph.D., or J.D.). Socio-economic status, measured according to the Duncan scale (Duncan, 1961), indicated a primarily middle class group of parents.

MATERIALS AND PROCEDURES

Families who qualified for this study were interviewed in their own home, often for two hours or more. Most parents appeared open and honest concerning their feelings about their handicapped child and how they made the decision to place. Scales and interview protocols, developed for the purposes of this study, were completed independently by mothers and fathers.

Factors Influencing Placement (FIP)

This 20-item scale lists possible reasons for placement of a severely handicapped child, such as: child characteristics (medical problems, child's size, level of retardation), family characteristics (parental health, financial considerations, marital status), and social support (babysitting, schooling, therapy programs). Parents were asked to indicate on a scale of 1 (no influence) to 5 (large influence) the impact of each reason on their decision to place.

Factors Preventing Placement (FPP)

This 20-item scale lists factors perceived by parents as delaying the placement decision, such as: child characteristics (low levels of maladaptive behavior, potential to learn new skills), family characteristics (close sibling relationships, parental attachment to child, feelings of guilt), and social support (advice from friends or relatives to raise the child at home). Scoring followed the above format, from 1 (no influence preventing placement) to 5 (strong influence preventing placement).

Here we provide descriptive information regarding the placement decision. Specifically: (1) What reasons do mothers and fathers perceive as most important in the decision to place their child, and to what extent do they agree? (2) What reasons do parents perceive as most important in delaying placement, and to what extent do they agree?

RESULTS

Factors influencing placement

Frequency distributions for the both scales were generally bimodal, with parents either indicating no or little influence (1,2) or strong or very strong (4,5). In Table 1 items are ranked based on the percentage of mothers endorsing each item as a strong or very strong influence.

Overall, mothers and fathers perceived the influence of items influencing placement in highly similar ways. A Spearman rank order

Table 1. Factors influencing placement

Item	Mothers % Indicating strong influence[a]	Rank	Fathers % Indicating strong influence[a]	Rank
1. My spouse's attitude toward placement	69	1.5	77	15.
2. Day-to-day stress	69	1.5	69	3.0
3. My child's level of functioning and potential for future learning	61	3.0	77	1.5
4. Medical or physical problems of my handicapped child	50	4.5	61	4.5
5. My child's behaviors	50	4.5	61	4.5
6. Feelings of my nonhandicapped children	46	6.5	44	6.0
7. Availability of respite care	46	6.5	31	10.5
8. Availability of babysitters	42	8.0	31	10.5
9. Advice from professionals	35	9.5	35	8.5
10. Financial considerations	35	9.5	23	12.5
11. Arguments with my spouse	32	11.0	19	14.5
12. My child's physical size	27	12.5	19	14.5
13. Advice from friends or relatives (other than spouse)	27	12.5	8	18.5
14. Job opportunities for myself or my spouse	23	14.5	23	12.5
15. My social life and support from friends	23	14.5	15	16.5
16. No appropriate schooling or therapy available	20	16.0	38	7.0
17. Others who have recently placed	19	18.0	8	18.5
18. Arguments and conflicts with my handicapped child	19	18.0	15	16.5
19. My health or my spouse's health	19	18.0	35	8.5
20. Being a single parent	8	20.0	4	20.0

[a] as denoted by a score of 4 or 5 on a Likert scale 1–5

correlation between mothers' and fathers' ratings was a highly significant $r_s = 0.79$ ($p < 0.001$). Moreover, no differences between the percent of mothers and fathers endorsing any individual item were significant by Chi Square analyses.

The strongest perceived influence on placement for each parent was, interestingly, the perceived attitude of the spouse. Other strong influences were day to day stress, the child's lack of future potential, and medical and behavioral problems. Items receiving fewest endorsements as strong influences were lack of services, influences of other parents who had placed, arguments and conflicts with the handicapped child, and parents' health. (Being a single parent was not relevant for this subsample of intact families.)

Factors preventing placement

Mothers and fathers also perceive the influence of items preventing placement in similar ways (Table 2). The strongest item influencing parents to keep their child at home was attachment to child. Thoughts that someone else would be raising the child, availability of schooling, and guilt about breaking up the family (reflected in several items) were also ranked highly. Factors receiving fewest endorsements were advice from friends or doctors to raise the child at home, lack of know-how in finding a placement, and religious beliefs. The similarity of mothers' and fathers' rankings were not quite as striking. While the Spearman rank order correlation was $r_s = 0.66$, ($p < 0.01$), there were significant differences (determined by Chi Square analyses) on two items in the percentage of parents endorsing these as strong influences on *preventing* placement. More fathers strongly endorsed item #16, "My spouse's attitude toward placement" as an important influence ($X^2 = 4.16$, $p < .05$). More mothers endorsed the item #14, "Raising this child was no more difficult than raising any of my other children" ($X^2 = 3.88$, $p < .05$).

DISCUSSION

Mothers and fathers appear to be in some communication regarding placement, as their endorsement of items was highly similar. Overall, both groups were most influenced by their spouse's attitude, day-to-day stress, and awareness of their child's future potential. These children were quite handicapped, and while they were living at home they undoubtedly created some burden for their families. Furthermore, placement may not have occurred unless, or until, both parents were in agreement on the issue. Some fathers, initially unwilling to place, were influenced to place by their wife's attitude. One father said, "I didn't understand, at the time, what my wife was going through."

When we examined the perceived factors preventing placements, several differences between mothers' and fathers' views did emerge. Fathers indicated that they were more strongly influenced by their wives' attitudes; our intensive interviews revealed that some fathers were often willing to place, but felt their wives' preference to keep the child at home strongly prevented the family from initiating placement. Some denial on mothers' part may also have been operating to prevent placement. Despite their child's severe retardation, often accompanied by additional handicaps, a significant proportion of mothers indicated that their handicapped child was no more difficult to raise than their non-handicapped children.

On the other hand, mothers and fathers agreed on the major item by far preventing placement – attachment to child. The strength of this finding was unexpected; it has often been an unspoken assumption that parents who place their handicapped child must not be emotionally attached. These data suggest that throughout the placement process strong attachment to the child is most salient. One parent remarked that, when she placed her child, "Part of me went with her." Many parents might have placed sooner if they had not felt deeply attached to the child and subsequently guilty about relinquishing their responsibility.

From a conceptual standpoint, this study contributes to our model of placement (Blacher, 1986) by further developing the construct of "placement tendency". Thus, the tendency to place the child out of the home appears to be related to parental perceptions of burden of care, child's future potential, availability of schooling or supports, and spouse's attitudes. Furthermore, this study has elaborated factors preventing placement, highlighting the role of parent-child attachment and the subsequent feelings of guilt and concern about the child once placed. It suggests that, while not preventing placement, attachment may delay the decision.

ACKNOWLEDGEMENT

Preparation of the manuscript was supported by Grant No. HD21324 from the National Institute of Child Health and Human Development to the first author.

REFERENCES

Andrew, G., Kime, W. L., Stehman, V. A., & Jaslow, R. I. (1965). Parental contacts along the route to institutional commitment of retarded children. *American Journal of Mental Deficiency*, **70**, 399–407.

Appell, M. J., & Tisdall, W. J. (1968). Factors differentiating institutionalized

Table 2. Factors preventing placement

Item	Mothers % Indicating strong influence[a]	Mothers Rank	Fathers % Indicating strong influence[a]	Fathers Rank
1. I was very attached to my child	85	1.0	72	1.0
2. Thoughts that someone else would be raising my child	58	2.5	46	6.5
3. Free, appropriate schooling was available for my child	58	2.5	42	8.0
4. Thoughts of placement made me feel guilty or that I was a bad parent	50	5.0	50	3.5
5. My nonhandicapped children enjoyed/got along with their handicapped sibling	50	5.0	48	5.0
6. I felt my child would never understand why he was no longer living at home or that he would think he was unloved	50	5.0	46	6.5
7. My child learned skills at school that made him easier to have at home	46	7.0	8	17.0
8. Availability of respite care	42	8.5	23	13.0
9. My spouse helped me a lot with our handicapped child at home	42	8.5	54	12.0
10. My child doesn't present any particular problems	38	10.5	36	11.0

(continued)

Table 2 – continued

Item	Mothers		Fathers	
	% Indicating strong influence[a]	Rank	% Indicating strong influence[a]	Rank
11. Availability of babysitters	38	10.5	15	14.0
12. I knew I wouldn't get a chance to see my child very often	36	12.0	38	9.5
13. I couldn't find a placement that was nice enough for my child	35	13.5	38	9.5
14. Raising this child was no more difficult than raising any of my other children	35	13.5	8	17.0
15. No placements were available	27	15.0	31	12.0
16. My spouse's attitude toward placement	19	16.0	50	3.5
17. Advice from doctors or other professionals	15	17.5	8	17.0
18. Advice from friends to raise my child at home	15	17.5	4	19.5
19. I didn't know how to go about getting a placement	8	19.0	12	15.0
20. My religious beliefs made placement difficult	4	20.0	4	19.5

[a] as denoted by a score of 4 or 5 on a Likert scale, 1–5.

from non-institutionalized referred retardates. *American Journal of Mental Deficiency*, **73**, 424–432.

Baker, B. L., Seltzer, G. B., & Seltzer, M. M. (1977) *As close as possible: Community residences for retarded adults*. Boston: Little, Brown and Company.

Blacher, J. (1984b) Attachment and severely handicapped children: Implications for intervention. *Developmental and Behavioral Pediatrics*, **5**, 178–183.

Blacher, J. (1986). *Placement of severely handicapped children: Correlates and consequences*. (Grant No. HD21324). Washington, DC: National Institute of Child Health and Human Development.

Blacher, J., Nihira, K., & Meyers, C. E. (1987) Characteristics of home environment of families with mentally retarded children: comparison across levels of retardation. *American Journal of Mental Deficiency*, **91**, 313–320.

Blacher, J. (1986, March). *Assessing placement tendency in families with children who have severe handicaps*. Paper presented at the Annual Gatlinburg Conference on Research and Theory in MR/DD, Gatlinburg, TN.

Blacher, J., & Rousey, A. M. (1988, March). *Families who place their severely handicapped child: Differentiating characteristics and influences*. Paper presented at the Annual Gatlinburg Conference on Research and Theory in MR/DD, Gatlingburg, TN.

Blacher, J., & Prado, P. (1986) The school as respite for parents of children with severe handicaps. In C. L. Salisbury & J. Intagliata (Eds.) *Respite care: Support for persons with developmental disabilities and their families* (pp. 217–234). Baltimore: Paul H. Brookes.

Borthwick-Duffy, S., Eyman, R. K., & White, J. F. (1987). Client Characteristics and residential placement patterns. *American Journal of Mental Deficiency*, **92**, 24–30.

Bromley, B. E. (1988) *Out-of-Home Placement of Severely Handicapped Children: Factors Influencing Parental Decisions*. Unpublished doctoral dissertation. University of California, Riverside.

Caldwell, B. M., & Guze, S. B. (1960) A study of the adjustment of parents and siblings of institutionalized and non-institutionalized retarded children. *American Journal of Mental Deficiency*, **64**, 845–861.

Cohen, S., & Warren, R. D. (1985) *Respite care: Principles, programs, and policies*. Austin, TX: Pro-Ed.

Cole, D. A. (1986) Out-of-home placement and family adaptation: A theoretical framework. *American Journal of Mental Deficiency*, **91**, 226–236.

Downey, K. J. (1965) Parents' reasons for institutionalizing severely mentally retarded children. *Journal of Health and Human Behavior*, **6**, 147–155.

Duncan, O. D. (1961) A socioeconomic index for all occupations. In A. J. Reiss (Ed.), *Occupations and social status* (pp. 109–161). NY: MacMillan.

Eyman, R. K., & Call, T. (1977). Maladaptive behavior and community placement of mentally retarded persons. *American Journal of Mental Deficiency*, **82**, 137–144.

Eyman, R. K., O'Connor, G., Tarjan, G., & Justice, R. S. (1972) Factors determining residential placement of mentally retarded children. *American Journal of Mental Deficiency*, **76**, 692–698.

Farber, B., Jenne, W. C., & Toigo, R. (1960) Family crisis and the decision to institutionalize the retarded child. *Council for Exceptional Children Research Monograph*, **1** (Series A).

German, M. L., & Maisto, A. A. (1982) The relationship of perceived family support system to the institutional placement of mentally retarded children. *Education and Training of the Mentally Retarded*, **17**, 17–23.

Hobbs, M. (1964). A comparison of institutionalized and non-institutionalized mentally retarded. *American Journal of Mental Deficiency*, **69**, 206–210.

Lakin, K. C., Hill, B. K., Hauber, F. A., Bruininks, R. H., & Heal, L. W. (1983) New admissions and readmissions to a national sample of public residential facilities. *American Journal of Mental Deficiency*, **88**, 13–20.

Meyers, C. E., & Blacher, J. (1987) Parents' perception of schooling for severely handicapped children: Home and family variables. *Exceptional Children*, **53**, 441–449.

Meyers, C. E., Brothwick, S. A., & Eyman, R. K. (1985) Place of residency by age, ethnicity, and level of retardation of the mentally retarded/ developmentally disabled population of California. *American Journal of Mental Deficiency*, **90**, 226–270.

Saenger, G. (1960) *Factors influencing institutionalization of mentally retarded individuals in New York City: A study of the effects of services, personnel characteristics, and family background on the decision to institutionalize.* Albany: New York State Department of Health Resources Board.

Seltzer, M. M., & Krauss, M. W. (1984) Family, community residence, and institutional placements of a sample of mentally retarded children. *American Journal of Mental Deficiency*, **89**, 257–266.

Shellhaas, M. D., & Nihira, K. (1969). Factor analysis of reasons retardates are referred to an institution. *American Journal of Mental Deficiency*, **74**, 171–179.

Sherman, B. R. (1988) Predictors of the decision to place developmentally disabled family members in residential care. *American Journal of Mental Retardation*, **92**, 344–351.

Stone, N. D. (1967) Family factors in willingness to place the mongoloid child. *American Journal of Mental Deficiency*, **72**, 16–20.

Suelzle, M., & Keenan, V. (1981) Changes in family support networks over the life cycle of mentally retarded persons. *American Journal of Mental Deficiency*, **86**, 267–274.

Tausig, M. (1985) Factors in family decision-making about placement for developmentally disabled individuals. *American Journal of Mental Deficiency*, **89**, 352–361.

Wynne, M. E., & Rogers, J. J. (1985) Variables discriminating residential placement of severely handicapped children. *American Journal of Mental Deficiency*, **89**, 515–523.

Video-Directed Parent Training: Effectiveness and Dissemination

B. L. Baker

Department of Psychology, UCLA, Los Angeles, CA. 90024, USA

Parent training is an effective but often unavailable intervention for families with developmentally disabled children. This paper reports on the development, evaluation, and dissemination of a video-directed group parent training program that is easy and cost-effective to implement. We developed and pilot tested a self-help skills teaching program that includes four video tapes and a manual. In a formal evaluation, video-directed training produced gains generally equivalent to live-led group training and superior to a delayed training control. We disseminated the program by orienting interested community agency staff to it. Although only 23% of them implemented the program, participating families showed significant benefits.

"Videotape recording represents a technological breakthrough with the kind of significance for psychiatry that the microscope has had for biology." (Bailey & Sowder, 1970, p. 1).

"Psychologists generally are not well educated in video technology, nor are professional video producers generally well educated in psychology. Thus, few quality video-based psychological interventions have been made available to the professional community." (Hosford & Mills, 1983, p. 143).

While the earlier quote speaks to the promise of video for service delivery, the more recent quote notes how that promise remains to be fulfilled. This paper reports on video-directed packages to provide cost-effective training for parents of developmentally disabled children.

BACKGROUND

The philosophy that would keep retarded children in the community and fill their lives with needed services often runs headlong into budgetary restrictions. More than ever it is important to develop and evaluate cost-effective approaches to service delivery.

From among the many needs faced by a family with a developmentally disabled child, we will focus on just one – the need to learn better teaching and behavior management methods. It is generally recognized that early skill training is especially important if retarded children are to become as independent as possible in adulthood. It is also increasingly accepted that parents are integral to that learning, and can be trained as more effective teachers (Baker, 1984). But how should that training be done, for maximal benefit with minimum cost, not only in staff time but in parent time as well?

There is considerable evidence that behavioral parent groups are effective relative to non-behavioral groups (Tavormina, 1975) and individual training (Brightman et al., 1982). Surprisingly, however, most agencies do not offer such programs, relying instead on individual consultation, often relatively unstructured and responding to, rather than anticipating, family crises. In contrast to the considerable investment in evaluating mental health program effectiveness, there has been scant attention to program dissemination, and what we do know is generally discouraging. Our experience with extensive inservice staff training (Berlin and Baker, 1983) has been that high turnover rates, limited behavioral competency of staff, and perceived role discrepancy between most staff persons' jobs and the many tasks involved in conducting parent training resulted in even the best intentioned staff doing little implementation.

Training packages using video have much promise as illustrated by the highly successful language training program reported by McConkey & McEvoy (1984). Staff need not be highly familiar with behavioral methods to implement such a program. With a brief orientation a mental health professional could be prepared to implement a program. Moreover, a video program may have advantages in its own right, as parents can be exposed to a variety of instructive examples. We could envision a time when agencies have available a library of parent training programs, in areas as diverse as self-help skills, language, social skills, or self-advocacy. Parents could routinely go through such programs, in small groups or individually at home, thereby raising their expertise to a level where individual staff counseling could be more effectively used.

This paper concerns a video program aimed to instruct parents about teaching developmentally disabled children self-help skills. We will look at three efforts that follow naturally: (1) development of the training package; (2) evaluation of its effectiveness relative to traditional training; and (3) dissemination to other agencies.

DEVELOPMENT OF THE TRAINING PACKAGE

This program was modified from the longer Parents as Teachers training curriculum that we have developed and studied at UCLA (Baker et al.,

1984; Baker, 1986). The self-help module involved a pretraining assessment, four weekly group meetings, four subsequent weeks of teaching at home with no meetings, and an individual posttraining assessment session. The four group meetings covered: (1) assessing self-help skills and identifying one skill to teach; (2) using behavioral teaching techniques and developing individualized programs; (3) using reinforcers, and (4) troubleshooting problems.

The training package consists of a self-instruction manual and 4 video tapes, each tape lasting about 35 minutes and taking a group of parents through a 2 hour session. The self-help skill manual presents behavior modification principles and programs in an easily read and parent-oriented fashion; it was an earlier version of our book *Steps to Independence* (Baker & Brightman, 1988).

Each of the four video tapes features a moderator who introduces the main topics, highlights important points, describes group exercises, and closes the meeting with a summary and homework assignment. Video-tapes also show an ongoing parent training group listening to mini lectures by a leader, discussing topics, and watching examples of parent teaching. Each videotape contains four or five interspersed instructions for the viewers to "stop the tape" and carry out a group exercise or discussion of their own. The principal roles of the facilitator are to present the videoprogram, monitor time, and stimulate group exercises and discussion.

We pilot-tested the initial version of the video-program with two groups of 4 and 5 parents, respectively. We were pleased to discover that parents became involved in the program – they didn't switch the TV station to watch a favorite program! – and all but one of them completed the program. They improved in their knowledge of teaching principles and evaluated the program highly. However, the parents and our staff facilitators did have a number of suggestions for improving the tapes, especially for giving each meeting more structure. We then did some further filming, added more titles and summaries, and reedited the video program. At this point we were ready for a larger, more formal, evaluation.

EVALUATION OF EFFECTIVENESS: VIDEO VS LIVE VS NO TRAINING

We have described this study in more detail elsewhere (Kashima, Baker & Landen, in press). Sixty-one families were recruited through state agencies responsible for assessment and referral of developmentally disabled individuals in Los Angeles County, California. Within each agency families were assigned at random (with several unavoidable exceptions) to one of three groups: video-directed training, live-led training, or waiting list – delayed training. Subsequently, the three delayed training groups were randomly assigned to training format, with two video and one live. Content of the two training formats was the same, except for the way in which information was presented – by an experienced leader or by video. The three groups in the live-led condition were led by staff of our program who had each led numerous parent training groups utilizing the Parents as Teachers curriculum. The three groups in the media-based condition were facilitated by individuals who had comparable experience to live leaders in working with families of developmentally disabled children but who had not conducted parent training groups.

Table 1a summarizes demographic characteristics of these families. For data analysis, one parent in each family was designated the "primary parent." This was the mother except in two cases where there was clear apriori evidence that the father would take primary responsibility for attending meetings, teaching, and completing measures. The three conditions did not differ significantly on any demographic variable. The average parent was in her mid 30s with two years of college education. Most families were intact and incomes were above average. The ethnic composition was generally representative of the areas of Los Angeles from which the sample was drawn. The target children were between 2 and 11 years old, with a mean age of 6 years. The most frequent child diagnoses were mental retardation (etiology unknown), Down syndrome, and autism.

We first looked at families' participation in and satisfaction with the video program. For these analyses, we also included results of the two video and one live groups subsequently conducted with delayed training families. We first examined completion rates. A family was classified as having completed training when the primary parent attended at least 3 of 4 meetings and the pre and post assessments. In the video-led groups, 28 of 33 (85%) completed training; this was a good rate, and comparable to the 20 of 22 (91%) for live-led groups.

Consumer satisfaction responses from primary parents who completed initial or delayed training are shown in Table 2a. The evaluations were very positive, with 98% of parents indicating that they would recommend the program to other parents much or very much. On the self evaluation, parents gave themselves high scores for completing readings, understanding the material, and teaching at home, but lower scores for keeping records and confidence in teaching. Evaluations by parents trained in the video condition did not differ from those in live-led training.

We assessed knowledge of teaching principles with the Behavioral Vignettes Test (Baker & Heifetz, 1976). Twenty items describe situations that reflect a range of common problems encountered in teaching and behavior problem management with a developmentally disabled child.

Table 1. Parent and child demographics for format comparison and dissemination studies

| | Media study A Format study | | | | Dissemination study B |
	Video	Live	Control	Total	Video
Variable					
	Parent demographics by condition[a]				
	$n=22$	$n=19$	$n=20$	$N=61$	$N=19$
Age (in years): mean primary parent	36.2	36.8	35.0	36.0	38.9
Education (in years): mean primary parent	13.2	15.0	13.9	14.0	13.5
Marital status % single	22.7	15.8	10.0	16.4	26.3
Employment full-time % primary parent	40.9	36.8	35.0	37.7	15.8
Ethnicity (prim. par.) %					
Caucasian	50.0	63.2	55.0	55.7	–
Hispanic	27.3	21.1	30.0	26.2	–
Asian	22.7	10.5	5.0	13.1	–
Black	0.0	5.3	10.0	4.9	–

(continued)

Table 1 – continued

	Media study				B
	A				Dissemination study
	Format study				
Variable	Video	Live	Control	Total	Video
Family income %					
less than $24,999 (US)	31.8	10.5	33.3	25.4	23.5
25,000–34,999	18.2	10.5	33.3	20.3	17.6
35,000–49,999	13.6	42.1	22.2	25.4	47.0
more than $50,000	36.4	36.8	11.1	28.8	11.8
Child demographics by condition[a]					
Age: mean years (range 2.0–14.4)	5.5	6.5	6.2	6.0	5.3
Child diagnosis: %					
MR, cause unknown	36.4	10.5	30.0	26.2	36.8
Down syndrome	22.7	26.3	15.0	21.3	21.1
autism	9.1	31.6	15.0	18.0	26.3
cerebral palsy	4.5	10.5	30.0	14.8	10.6
other	27.3	21.1	10.0	19.7	5.3

[a] Adapted from Kashima, Baker, & Landen (1988).

Table 2. Parent evaluation questionnaire, post-training for format comparison and dissemination studies

	A Format study		B Dissemination study
	Percentage of parents in each condition who reported Much (6) or Very Much (7) on a 7-point scale		Percentage of parents in each condition who reported Much (4) or Very Much (5) on a 5-point scale
	Video[a]	Live[a]	Video
	n=27	n=18	N=19
A. Program evaluation			
1. Appropriateness of the approach	93	100	95
2. Helpfulness of group	93	89	100
3. Helpfulness of leader	89	94	100
4. Competence of leader[b]	100	90	100
5. Recommend program	96	100	100
6. Overall feeling (positive)	74	89	95
	Percentage of parents in each condition who reported Most (3) or All (4) on a 4-point scale		Percentage of parents in each condition who reported Most(3) or All (4) on a 4-point scale
B. Self evaluation			
1. Attending meetings	100	100	100
2. Completing readings	88	83	100
3. Teaching	84	72	94
4. Keeping records	32	28	47
5. Understanding material	100	100	100
6. Confidence in teaching (6 or 7 on a 7 point scale)	56	56	89

[a] Missing: Live=2, Video=1
[b] Obtained from subsample N=10 (Live) & N=14 (Video).

For each, parents select the one of four alternative responses that they think would be most effective. By an analysis of variance, the three conditions changed differentially over time (F (2,44) = 6.45, $p < 0.01$). Video-led and live-led families increased significantly and differed significantly from the control families, who did not change. Parents in live training, however, showed significantly greater gains than those in video (t (31) = 2.03, $p = 0.05$).

We assessed child self-help skills with the Mini-PI, an individualized subset of skills from the Performance Inventory which contains 38 self-help skills each broken down to a hierarchical scale of component steps (Brightman *et al.*, 1982). Parents check the step that most accurately describes their child's performance level. Gains in targeted skills were statistically significant for both video and live conditions. However, change scores for the two training conditions did not differ. Finally we examined the extent of teaching at home, post-training and at a one year follow-up. We were encouraged to see much useful teaching and, again, the two training conditions did not differ.

At this point, we had established to our satisfaction that the video program was a reasonable alternative to the more costly live-led format. Parents had completed the media program, evaluated it highly, gained in knowledge of teaching principles, and increased their children's self-help skills. The obvious next step was to disseminate the program more widely, and study whether other service providers would implement it and whether their parents would benefit as ours had.

DISSEMINATION

Participation

We sent a brochure describing the program to schools, clinics, parent associations and other agencies in Los Angeles County that serve mentally retarded children. We screened interested participants on the phone, making clear that our aim was to have participants facilitate at least one small parent group using our video package in the ensuing six months. Forty three potential facilitators each attended a 3-hour orientation meeting in groups of 6 to 10. Five had come as observers or to accompany a facilitator and did not plan to implement, and 3 participants were parents. Our present discussion is based on the 35 participants who were professionals and who, at the end of the orientation meeting, indicated that they would facilitate at least one group. They completed measures of demographics and their current job responsibilities, knowledge of behavioral principles, and expectations about problems in implementing parent training.

These facilitators were predominantly female (71%), and well educated; 74% had a masters or doctoral degree. Their average age was 40 years and they had been on the job for an average of 8 years. Positions included special education teachers (43%), other service providers (e.g. counselors) (29%), administrators (20%) and psychologists (9%). Half (49%) worked in public schools and the other half were distributed among private schools (14%), state Regional Centers (23%) and other agenices (14%).

Implementation

Three months following the orientation workshop a staff member not involved in the workshops conducted follow-up interviews by phone. At that time, 8 (23%) of participants had implemented at least one parent training group with our media package. Of the remaining 27, 6 had taken some steps to implement, 12 still professed plans to, and 9 reported that they had decided not to implement.

The 9 who indicated a clear decision not to implement at the 3 months follow-up were given a list of reasons and asked which applied. The most frequent response was that "I find that implementing the program does not really fit with my job responsibilities." Most of these participants indicated that there had been changes in their position, or duties, or the population they worked with.

Six months following orientation, an additional follow-up found several more taking steps to implement but no evidence of any additional participants completing a training group. It is possible that some of these participants later facilitated a group, but this seems unlikely as they had to obtain the tapes from us. Hence, we conclude that only 23% of participants facilitated a group, and that if a potential facilitator did not begin almost immediately, he or she did not begin at all.

The 8 implementers were contrasted with the 27 non-implementers, in a search distinguishing characteristics. The groups did not differ by demographic characteristics, such as age, sex, education, position, or years on the job, although with this small a sample a difference needs to be quite striking to reach statistical significance. We did find that implementers were generally better prepared to conduct behavioral parent training. Their pre score on a 10 item form of the Behavioral Vignettes Test was 8.4, compared with 6.3 for non-implementers (t (33) = 2.78, $p < 0.01$) and fully 88% of implementers reported that they personally used behavioral principles extensively in their work, compared with 33% of non-implementers (Chi Square (1) = 5.28, p < 0.05).

Impact on families

The next question of interest was whether the results for parents trained by the media package facilitated by agency professionals were comparable to those found in our own controlled study. Facilitators were given an evaluation packet for each participating family. Before training the primary parent completed a Demographic questionnaire and the 10 item Behavioral Vignettes Test; after training, the same parent repeated the BVT and completed a slightly simplified version of the Consumer Satisfaction Questionnaire.

We report here on results obtained from the first 19 families (trained in 5 groups) on which we received complete data. The parent and child demographics are shown in Table 1b. They were quite similar to those reported for parents trained directly by us, except that somewhat fewer primary parents were working and there were correspondingly fewer families in the highest income group.

The 10 item Behavioral Vignettes Test scores increased modestly, although significantly, from a mean of 4.9 to 6.1 (t (18) = 3.45, $p < 0.01$). Parents responses to the Consumer Satisfaction measure were, as in the UCLA sample, highly positive, as shown in Table 2b. Once again, though most parents truthfully admitted that they had not done much record keeping.

These measures indicate comparability in the sample and the results between UCLA sponsored groups and those conducted by agency facilitators. While this is encouraging, the gains in knowledge were only modest; moreover, in this study we were not able to examine the extent to which parents actually implemented programming and how well they followed through over time.

We are left with several conclusions and, typically, even more uncertainties. We can conclude that parents enjoy video-directed training and evaluate it highly. We can conclude that training groups extensively based on video can produce effects comparable to groups with highly experienced live leaders. We can conclude that with brief orientation, some agency personnel can be effective facilitators, and that the parents they train benefit. On a more pessimistic note, though, we can conclude that the majority of professionals who went through orientation did not implement the program. We do not know whether this is particular to our program – perhaps with another type of program more would have implemented. Despite our efforts to draw out this response, however, the non-implementers consistently spoke highly of the program. We need to know much more about what types of video programs can be most readily disseminated, which service providers to enlist as facilitators, and how to best help facilitators carry out the program.

ACKNOWLEDGEMENT

This research was supported by Grant DE GOO 84-35061 from the U.S. Department of Education to the author. I gratefully acknowledge the collaboration of Dr Patrice Yasuda during the pilot phase, and Drs Kathleen J. Kashima, Sandra J. Landen, and Richard Wenzlaff throughout the project. We appreciate the efforts of the group facilitators and are indebted to our research assistants, especially Mary Kripner, Lisa Lieurance, Anne Maxwell, Erik Oranchak, and Moi Wong.

REFERENCES

Bailey, K. & Sowder, A. (1970) Audiotape and videotape in self-confrontation in psychotherapy, *Psychological Bulletin*, **74**, 127–137.

Baker, B. L. (1984) Intervention with families with severely retarded children. In J. Blacher (Ed.). *Young severely handicapped children and their families: Research in review*, pp. 319–375. New York: Academic Press.

Baker, B. L. (1986) Parents as teachers: A programme of applied research. In D. Milne (Ed.). *Training behaviour therapists: Methods, evaluation and implementation with parents, nurses and teachers*, pp. 92–116. London: Croom Helm.

Baker, B. L. & Brightman, A. J. (1988) *Steps to Independence: A guide for parents and teachers of children with special needs*. Baltimore: Paul Brookes.

Baker, B. L., & Heifetz, L. J. (1976) The READ Project: Teaching manuals for parents of retarded children. in T. D. Tjossem (Ed.), *Intervention strategies for high risk infants and young children*. Baltimore, MD: University Park Press.

Baker, B. L., Prieto-Bayard, M., & McCurry, M. (1984). Lower socioeconomic status families and programs for training parents of retarded children. In J. M. Berg (Ed.), *Perspectives and progress in mental retardation, Vol. I – Social, psychological, and educational aspects*. Baltimore: University Park Press.

Berlin, P. H., & Baker, B. L. (1983). *Role conflict and organizational climate as predictors to implementation of a parent training program*. Unpublished manuscript, UCLA.

Brightman, R. P., Baker, B. L., Clark, D. B., & Ambrose, S. A. (1982) Effectiveness of alternative parent training formats. *Journal of Behavior Therapy and Experimental Psychiatry*, **13**, 113–117.

Hosford, R. E. & Mills, E. E. (1983) Video in social skills training. In P. W. Dowrick and S. J. Biggs (Eds.). *Using video*, pp. 125–150. New York: Wiley.

McConkey, R. & McEvoy, J. (1984) Parental involvement courses: contrasts between mothers who enroll and those who don't. In J. M. Berg (Ed.). *Perspectives and progress in mental retardation, Vol. I – Social, psychological and educational aspects*. Baltimore: University Park Press.

Tavormina, J. B. (1975) Relative effectiveness of behavioral and reflective group counselling with parents of mentally retarded children. *Journal of Consulting and Clinical Psychology*, **43**, 22–31.

Section V

Developmental and Psycholinguistic Considerations

Learning to Learn: The Difficulties faced by Infants and Young Children with Down's Syndrome

J. G. Wishart

Edinburgh Centre for Research in Child Development,
Department of Psychology, University of Edinburgh,
7 George Square, Edinburgh EH8 9JZ, Scotland

This paper reports results from a series of interlinked, longitudinal studies of early learning in Down's Syndrome (DS). The first set of studies monitored the development of a concept of objects, a fundamental step in early cognitive development. The second used operant learning techniques to examine learning styles used at different stages in development. Results suggest strongly that the course of early learning in infants and young children with DS differs fundamentally from that seen in non-handicapped children. Although early ability was found to be greater than would have been expected given ability levels at later ages, this early potential was put to poor use: difficult learning situations were avoided, performance was poorly motivated, and newly-acquired cognitive skills were inadequately consolidated.

Down's Syndrome (DS), the most common form of mental handicap, is the best known but probably the most misunderstood of all of the mentally handicapping conditions. Although recent research in genetics and the neurosciences has led to huge advances in our understanding of DS (see Patterson, 1987, for an overview), many professionals working in the community still hold outdated conceptions of the nature of DS and of its developmental implications. More importantly, many hold unnecessarily pessimistic views on the level of ability attainable by children with DS. These views are frequently passed on to parents, often insensitively and with little consideration of the adverse effects this may have on the way parents will then respond to and interact with their DS child.

Although it is important to be realistic about the limits imposed on development by the genetic imbalance present in DS, there would nonetheless still seem to be cause to be optimistic about the prospects of improving developmental outcome in DS. Recent years have seen numerous examples of children and young adults with DS achieving skills previously thought to be outwith their limited capacities to learn. These achievements have ranged from the practical, passing a driving test, to the more "academic", successfully learning to read at 3 years of age (Buckley, 1985). Such achievements must lead us to question our previous estimates of the ceiling imposed on development by the genetic component in DS. How far previous estimates of potential are inaccurate remains to be seen (Rynders *et al.*, 1978), but sufficient evidence has already accumulated to suggest that with the appropriate support and input, children with DS in future generations will undoubtedly fare better than previously.

A major focus of psychological research into DS should be to define that appropriate support and input. The majority of early intervention programmes being used at present are largely based on teaching principles already known to be successful with non-handicapped children. Despite their wide-scale adoption and their undoubted popularity with parents of handicapped children, these programmes have been shown to have disappointingly little effect on subsequent levels of cognitive achievement (Gibson & Fields, 1984; Cunningham, 1986). Any gains demonstrated have tended to be insubstantial, short-term and highly specific; "untreated" DS children soon catch up (Sloper, Glenn & Cunningham, 1986). This is not to deny that overall levels of achievement have risen in the present generation of DS children. This, however, would seem more likely to be due to factors such as improved health, better educational provision, changing medical, social and parental attitudes to mental handicap, factors other than early intervention.

The failure of present intervention methods to produce lasting benefits should not lead to premature pessimism over the prospects of further facilitating developmental progress in children with DS. In the design of most intervention programmes, it has been implicitly assumed that cognitive development in the mentally handicapped is simply a sloweddown version of normal development – equivalent in structure and organisation, only progressing more slowly and to a lower ceiling. Increasingly, however, research studies are finding evidence that learning processes in children with mental handicap may differ in quite fundamental ways from those seen in normal development (Zigler & Balla, 1982; Morss, 1983, 1985; Duffy & Wishart, 1987; Wishart, 1986, 1987a).

If this *is* the case, the failure of present methods of intervention to produce lasting benefits is perhaps not surprising. To be effective, any early intervention programme will need to be tailored to the specific needs and skills of the child with DS and will have to be firmly based in an understanding of the developmental processes operating in handicap.

Our present understanding is woefully inadequate for this purpose. To date, most studies of development in handicap have concentrated on the end product rather than the dynamics of learning, providing developmental information on "milestone" achievement but giving little insight into cognitive processes. The longitudinal studies to be reported in outline here hoped to go some way towards filling that gap. Our project has focussed on cognitive development in the first five years of life: research suggests that learning experience in these early years may be even more formative for the handicapped than for the non-handicapped child (Kearsely, 1979; Seligman, 1975).

The studies fall into two main sets. The first has monitored object concept development, an important early step in cognitive development. The second has used an operant learning paradigm to investigate how the infant with DS responds to different success/failure ratios in a learning situation. These studies will provide a detailed data-base on the nature, course and parameters of early learning in children with DS. From this, we hope to describe the natural learning style of the child with DS and to investigate the relationship between early learning style and subsequent developmental progress. In particular, we hope to find some explanation for the progressive decline in developmental rate seen in DS as the children grow older.

OBJECT CONCEPT STUDIES

The term "object concept development" perhaps needs some explanation. To understand even the simplest event, an infant needs to acquire an understanding of physical reality and of the laws that determine that reality. Basic to that understanding is learning the defining properties of objects – learning, for example, that when an object is put inside something, it continues to exist, even though it cannot be seen. Developing a comprehensive, working concept of an object is a fundamental step in early cognitive development. It is normally achieved within the first two years of life, in a sequence of six well-defined, hierarchical stages (Piaget, 1937). Development is indexed by performance on a series of search tasks in which the hiding sequence increases in complexity according to the stage being tested. In all but the simplest of these tasks, the infant must choose between one of two identical occluders in order to retrieve the hidden toy; unless he or she fully comprehends the particular hiding sequence, performance can only be at chance level.

Figure 1 shows (in ascending order of difficulty) the four hiding tasks we used in our longitudinal study:

Task 1: a one-cup, Stage III–V task   (5 months)
Task 2: a two-cup, Stage IV–V AAB task   (10 months)

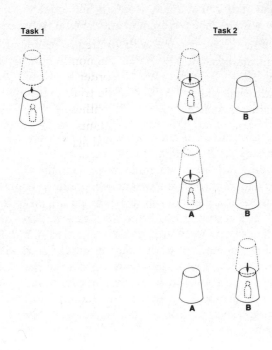

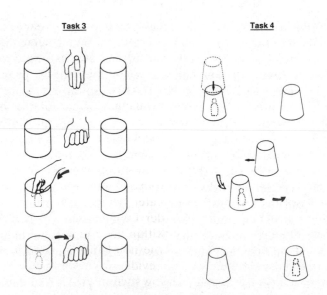

Figure 1.   The four hiding tasks used in the longitudinal study of object concept
development.

Task 3: a two-cup, Stage V–VI, inference task   (15 months)
Task 4: a two-cup, Stage V–VI, switching task.   (22+ months)

Order of difficulty of these tasks had already been ascertained in a cross-sectional normative study involving 228 non-handicapped babies (Wishart & Bower, 1984). In that study, in order to score a pass on any task, infants had to succeed on all four of the trials presented. The age at which 75% of babies passed is given in parentheses.

Both DS and non-handicapped infants were included in the study. Subjects were matched for chronological age and also, retrospectively, for developmental stage. This method of mental age matching, matching by transition points in development of the object concept, allows precise matching on specific tasks at specific points in development while leaving open the option that processes prior to and subsequent to acquisition of any stage in development might differ in the two subject groups. The original design was semi-longitudinal. Subjects would enter the study at different ages and development would then be monitored in each subject over one major stage transition, thereby providing a spread of data on all of the stages and stage transitions under investigation. By the end of the study, a total of 30 DS infants will have completed testing. Age at entry ranged from 4 months to 2 years 9 months. A smaller-scale study was also carried out with 3–5 year old DS and non-handicapped children (monitoring period = 2½ months; N = 24).

All subjects were tested fortnightly on all four tasks, with the criteria for a pass being raised to all-correct performance in two successive testing sessions. Because of the interesting developmental patterns which were emerging, particularly in post-acquisition performance, both qualitative and quantitative aspects of developmental progress on all levels of task were monitored in the younger subject groups over longer periods than was originally intended, over periods ranging from 9 months to 3 years (length of participation being determined by developmental stage on entry). It was therefore possible to collect developmental data over several stage transitions for many subjects.

Overall, as was to be expected, cognitive development in the DS group lagged behind the non-handicapped group. However, cognitive ability in the DS infants proved to be much greater than would be inferred from levels of ability generally found in older DS children. Many DS infants succeeded on some of the tasks while within the normal age ranges, a few actually passing earlier than some of the non-handicapped controls (see Table 1). Less encouraging was the evidence of important, counter-productive elements in the early learning style of the DS subjects. When records were matched for cognitive stage, important differences distinguished pre- and post-acquisition performance in the DS and non-handicapped subject groups. These differences proved to be consistent

Table 1. Interim results for younger subjects in longitudinal study of object concept development

Age (in months) of achievement of success on hiding tasks 1–4.				
DS subjects:				
	Task 1	Task 2	Task 3	Task 4
Mean age	7.75	10.50	19.25	18.0
Range	6.25–10.75	7.25–14.0	14.5–26.75	11–25.25
Non-handicapped subjects:				
	Cross-sectional normative data (Bower & Wishart, 1984)			
Age at which 75% of Ss passed	5.0	10.0	15.0	22+
	Longitudinal date (control group)			
Mean age	4.75	7.75	12.25	14.5
Range	4.0–5.75	4.75–8.5	9.25–14.25	10.25–17.0

Note: All months have been rounded up to nearest .25.

within individual DS subjects at different points in their development and across the group as a whole. Performance of DS subjects was characterised by two clear patterns:

i) low-level engagement in tasks passed to criterion in earlier testing sessions, with the eventual reappearance of errors on these tasks, and

ii) marked avoidance of tasks more than one step above the subject's current developmental status.

Both positive and negative methods were used by DS subjects to "switch out" of tasks which were either too easy or too difficult for them. Most disturbing was the evidence of an increasing misuse of developing social skills to avoid participating in learning situations. When given a task above their current level of understanding, younger subjects would simply protest and refuse to watch the hiding sequence; older DS infants, by contrast, would typically attempt to divert the experimenter away from the task in hand into social interaction. The "social" behaviours involved were often highly stereotyped and inflexible and could in no way be described as truly interactive. A frequent ploy, for example, was to catch the eye of the experimenter and then simply to stare or smile fixedly at her, refusing to watch the hiding sequence or to interact in any productive way. Sometimes infants would resort to party tricks – clapping hands, blowing raspberries or "dancing" at some inappropriate moment in testing. This counter-productive behaviour – surely a form of cognitive avoidance – proved to be closely tied to difficulty level. It was not simply due to poor attentional capacity, fatigue or a generalised low level of motivation: a change to a more developmentally appropriate task would quickly restore attention and lead to rapid search, even though the new task involved thc samc toy and occluders as the previous task.

Poor engagement was also evidenced when tasks which had previously been mastered were re-presented in later testing sessions. Although infants would appear to be sufficienty motivated and would quickly search for the toy, they frequently made errors and often did not bother to correct these errors. Search strategies adopted were typically either random or low-level (e.g. always picking the side corresponding to the preferred hand). There was little sign of the higher-level strategies previously used to solve these tasks. Success rates were low, far below those achieved at the time of initial acquisition of that particular stage in understanding, and yet the DS infants seemed unconcerned at this lack of success. Introduction of a tangible reward for success – chocolate – would sometimes lead to a sudden "revival" of success but this tactic was less reliably effective with infants further into the post-acquisition stage of the task in question. By then, poor performance seemed genuinely to reflect a competence that had deteriorated beyond retrieval, not simply poor motivation and low engagement.

These patterns of avoidance of more difficult learning situations and of failure to consolidate recently acquired steps in understanding could help to explain the increasing gap which appears in developmental progress between DS and non-handicapped children as they grow older. Normative and control data indicate that non-handicapped infants show no such narrowed cognitive engagement, working well at all ages on all levels of object concept task, whether above, below or at their current developmental level. Our previous research has shown that the developmental sequence underlying object concept development is normally closely integrated and hierarchical. By failing to consolidate each new step in development, DS children must thus be putting themselves at a further disadvantage, losing the opportunity to build effectively on that knowledge.

Results from the older children tested also suggested that consolidation is possibly a major problem in DS (see Table 2). Performance on all levels of tasks was very poor in the first testing session, much poorer paradoxically than in younger DS subjects. Performance improved very rapidly over sessions, however, far too rapidly for it to be explained simply in terms of rapid acquisition of new skills: non-handicapped children, after all, take nearly two years to develop the understanding necessary to pass the highest level of task. It seems more likely that the older DS children were in fact *re*-acquiring the object concept, re-tuning

Table 2. Success rates on tasks 2, 3 and 4 in older DS subjects over six testing sessions (N = 12)

Testing Session	1	2	3	4		5		6	
Task 2:	5	11	12	8	(+2)	11	(+1)	10	(+1)
Task 3:	5	9	10	12		11		11	
Task 4:	2	3	4	4		5		7	
Combined Totals:	12	23	26	24	(+2)	27	(+1)	28	(+1)

Notes: Numbers in parentheses represent the number of children scored as failing deliberately – "false fails" (see Wishart, 1987a).

Task 1 was used only as a warm up task with older subjects; no child refused or was unable to search under one cup.

earlier learning which had been inadequately consolidated at the time of initial acquisition. This data and its developmental implications are discussed more extensively in Wishart (1987a,b). It is worth noting, however, just how poorly a single testing session measured competence in this older DS group: had this first testing session been the only session given, cognitive ability in these children would have been seriously underestimated.

In summary then, two things are evident from the object concept data:

1) there are important differences in the way the DS child learns
2) early mental ability is higher than would be inferred from later levels of performance.

OPERANT LEARNING STUDIES

Although the object concept studies indicate the presence of considerable potential early in development in DS children, this early potential would appear to be put increasingly at risk by the behaviour of the DS infant himself: by the second half of the first year, he is not only making inefficient use of ability that he clearly has but is also avoiding difficult learning situations, effectively contributing to his own already existing handicap. The operant learning studies were designed to investigate these early counter-productive learning patterns more directly and included infants younger than those involved in the object concept study.

Operant learning – learning the relationship between what one does and what effect it has – is paradigmatic of most human learning. Research has shown that in a laboratory setting, infants can detect a contingency between their actions and events by at least two months of age; regular exposure to high levels of contingency improves that ability (Watson, 1972). Detection of a contingent relationship between behaviour and events is considerably more difficult in the real world, however: a behaviour may not always be sufficient to cause the particular effect, may not always be necessary for that effect (other people can also cause the same effect) or may produce the effect only after a delay (particularly in the case of social reinforcement – see Watson, 1984). For children with DS, this difficulty is compounded by several other factors. Most obvious are the physical and cognitive limitations on the DS infant's ability to produce the appropriate response at the appropriate time. This low responsiveness and its often ambiguous quality must adversely affect chances of producing the desired effect, particularly in interactions with caretakers (Berger & Cunningham, 1983; Gunn, 1985). The reinforcement schedule experienced in DS is consequently likely to be a combination of low levels of partial reinforcement with high levels of non-contingent reinforcement, a mix that can hardly facilitate early learning. This early learning experience may be critical in establishing subsequent learning patterns.

The operant tasks we are using have been designed to encourage exploratory learning activity but require minimal motor skills. The infant sits securely and comfortably strapped into a baby chair, with the head, if necessary, supported by soft padding and both legs free to move easily. He/she sits in semi-darkness, in front of a translucent screen; an infra-red beam crosses in front of the baby in such a way that any leg movement triggers a one-second movement of a brightly coloured acetate mobile, placed behind and projected onto the rear of the screen. This set up is suitable for use with even very young DS infants and will therefore allow us, at a later stage in the research, to investigate whether providing positive learning experience in early months could be beneficial.

In the present studies, we are using a number of different reinforcement schedules, varying the amount of control that the infant has over the situation (80% v 100%) and introducing small percentages (10%) of "free", non-contingent reinforcement into the schedules. By varying schedules, we hope to identify which particular schedules of reinforcement best promote learning effort in children with DS and which encourage better consolidation of that learning once it has been achieved; we also intend to investigate any developmental changes in response to differing schedules.

As in the object concept studies, age at entry to the study is staggered, with subjects entering at three-month age intervals between 3 months and 2 years. All subjects return for repeat testing, again at three-monthly intervals, thereby providing maximum information on the developmental course of learning behaviour while allowing investigation of the effect of amount and timing of prior task experience on performance. Both non-handicapped and DS infants are being tested, with performance being compared both at matched chronological and at matched mental ages. Previous research has shown that young non-handicapped infants respond well when given less than perfect control in a learning task (Watson, 1984). Our initial control data are consistent with these findings. Both younger and older non-handicapped subjects seem more highly motivated in such situations, exploring different timings of responses and lasting longer in the experimental situation. They seem intrigued both by the occurrence of the rewarding event in the absence of any activity on their part (the 10% free conditions) and by the less-than-perfect contingency in the 80% conditions. Initial results also suggest that young DS infants respond reasonably well in these conditions, although taking longer on average to detect the contingency. Older DS subjects, however, seem to make little attempt to explore and master this kind of task, even in early testing sessions. In both the 100% and 80% conditions, they settle happily for the small percentage of free reward, even though a much higher rate is potentially available if they were to exert their own control over the situation (Figure 2).

The semi-longitudinal design of this study should give us some insight into whether the counter productive learning patterns observed in older DS subjects in these preliminary results (and in the study of object concept development) are themselves learned or whether they are a restriction on learning inherent to DS. Avoiding difficult learning situations and settling for low success rates rather than risking errors would be an understandable response to the adverse success/failure rates which must typically be experienced by the DS infant in learning situations. An increasing awareness of low personal efficacy may well be allowed to generalise to areas of comparative or untested strength – a kind of learned helplessness. With appropriately timed and carefully structured intervention, it might be possible to counteract this decline.

CONCLUSION

Assessing deficits in learning and identifying processes which impede learning are prerequisites of any attempt to generate training procedures which might improve that learning. A recurrent theme in DS appears to be learning acquired and then learning lost. While early ability is surprisingly high, poor use is made of this ability and newly acquired cognitive skills appear to be inadequately consolidated: instead of building on skills, the DS child seems simply to allow recently acquired skills to deteriorate. The studies reported here provide consistent evidence of important differences in the way non-handicapped and DS infants respond to learning situations, differences in their natural learning styles. Any attempt to help early development will need to take these

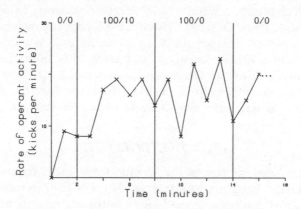

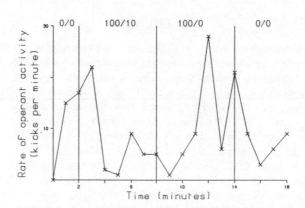

Figure 2. Operant learning: Figure 2 compares performance of a nine-month-old infant with DS (upper graph) with performance on the same operant learning task one year later (lower graph). The reinforcement schedules in operation in each of the four time sections were:

1. 0/0 – 0% contingent reinforcement for kicks
   0% "free", computer-generated reinforcement (base period)
2. 100/10 – 100% contingent reinforcement for kicks
   10% "free", computer-generated reinforcement
3. 100/0 – 100% contingent reinforcement for kicks
   0% "free", computer-generated reinforcement
4. 0/0 – as 1.
   (Extinction period)

At 9 months, the infant performed well under both reinforcement schedules. When older, however, he quickly gave up kicking when 10% free reinforcement was provided even though his subsequent performance showed clearly that he was capable of producing higher levels of reinforcement for himself.

differences into account. Teaching strategies which work with non-handicapped children may have little effect on progress in handicapped children (Morss, 1984; Duffy & Wishart, 1987) and any over-emphasis on the development of compensatory social skills may actually be doing more harm than good. There would still seem to be room for optimism that early intervention in DS could be beneficial. If, however, early developmental potential is to be realised, both the content and methods of intervention programmes may need fundamental re-thinking.

ACKNOWLEDGEMENTS

This research was supported by grants from the Medical Research Council of Great Britain (Project grant No. G8703875N) and from the Scottish Down's Syndrome Association (Lothian Branch). Many thanks are extended to all the children who took part in these studies.

REFERENCES

Berger, J. & Cunningham, C. C. (1983) Early social interactions between infants with Down's Syndrome and their parents. *Health Visitor*, **56**, 58–60.

Buckley, S. (1985) Attaining basic educational skills: reading, writing and number. In: D. Lane and B. Stratford (eds), *Current Approaches to Down's syndrome*. pp. 315–343. Holt, Rinehart & Winston, London.

Cunningham, C. C. (1986) Patterns of development in Down's Syndrome. Paper read at International Down's Syndrome Congress, Brighton, April (Proceedings to be published by Wiley, London, 1988).

Duffy, L. & Wishart, J. G. (1987) A comparison of two procedures for teaching discrimination to Down's Syndrome and normal children. *British Journal of Educational Psychology*, **57**, 265–278.

Gibson, D. & Fields, D. L. (1984) Early infant stimulation programs for children with Down's Syndrome: A review of effectiveness. In: M. L. Wolraich and D. K. Routh (eds), *Advances in Developmental and Behavioral Pediatrics*, *Vol. 5*. JAI Press, Greenwich, Conn.

Gunn, P. (1985) Speech and language. In: D. Lane and B. Stratford (eds), *Current Approaches to Down's Syndrome*. Holt, Rinehart & Winston, London.

Kearsley, R. B. (1979) Iatrogenic retardation: a syndrome of learned incompetence. In: R. B. Kearsley and I. E. Sigel (eds.), *Infants at Risk: Assessment of Cognitive Functioning*. pp. 153–180. Erlbaum, Hillsdale, N. J.

Morss, J. R. (1983) Cognitive development in the Down's Syndrome infant: slow or different? *British Journal of Educational Psychology*, **53**, 40–47.

Morss, J. R. (1984) Enhancement of object-permanence performance in the Down's Syndrome infant. *Child: Care, Health and Development*, **10**, 39–47.

Morss, J. R. (1985) Early cognitive development: differences or delay? In: D. Lane and B. Stratford (eds), *Current Approaches to Down's Syndrome*. pp. 242–259. Holt, Rinehart & Winston, London.

Patterson, D. (1987) The causes of Down Syndrome. *Scientific American*, **257**, 42–48.

Piaget, J. (1955) *The Construction of Reality*. Routledge & Kegan Paul, London (original French edition, 1937).

Rynders, J. E., Spiker, D., & Horrobin, J. M. (1978) Underestimating the educability of Down's Syndrome children. *American Journal of Mental Deficiency*, **82**, 440–448.

Seligman, M. E. P. (1975) *Helplessness*. W. H. Freeman, San Francisco.

Sloper, P., Glenn, S. M., & Cunningham, C. C. (1986) The effect of intensity of training on sensori-motor development in infants with Down's Syndrome. *Journal of Mental Deficiency Research*, **30**, 149–162.

Watson, J. S. (1972) Smiling, cooing and "the game". *Merrill-Palmer Quarterly*, **18**, 323–339.

Watson, J. S. (1984) Bases of causal inference in infancy: time, space and sensory relations. in: L. P. Lipsitt and C. Rovee-Collier (eds), *Advances in Infancy Research, Vol. 3*, pp. 152–165. Ablex, Norwood, N.J.

Wishart, J. G. (1986) The effects of step-by-step training on cognitive performance in infants with Down's Syndrome. *Journal of Mental Deficiency Research*, **30**, 233–250.

Wishart, J. G. (1987a) Performance of young non-retarded children and children with Down Syndrome on Piagetian infant search tasks. *American Journal of Mental Deficiency*, **92**, 169–177.

Wishart, J. G. (1987b) Early learning in infants and young children with Down's Syndrome. Paper presented at the Scientific Symposium of the National Down Syndrome Society, New York, December, 1987 (to be published in: L. Nadel (ed), *"The Psychobiology of Down Syndrome"*, MIT Press, Boston, 1988).

Wishart, J. G., & Bower, T. G. R. (1984) Spatial relations and the object concept: a normative study. In: L.P. Lipsitt and C. K. Rovee-Collier (eds.), *Advances in Infancy Research: Vol. 3*. pp. 57–123. Ablex, Norwood, N.J.

Zigler, E., & Balla, D. (eds) (1982) *Mental Retardation: The Developmental-Difference Controversy*. Erlbaum, Hillsdale, N.J.

Sustained Attention in Mentally Retarded Persons

P. D. Tomporowski

Department of Psychology, University of Alabama,
Tuscaloosa, AL 35487, USA

Retarded and nonretarded adults performed four, 60-min visual vigilance tasks in which single digits were presented sequentially and successively at either a fast rate (30 events per min) or a slow rate (15 events per min). The target event in all tests was a "skipped" digit. During two tests, the event rate experienced during the initial 30 min was shifted without warning to the alternate event rate. A vigilance decrement was observed of retarded observers during both event rate conditions. Retarded adults detected fewer targets and made more false alarm responses than did nonretarded adults; also, the false alarm responses of retarded observers were related to shifts in event rate. The sustained attention of retarded adults is believed to be influenced by the memory demands present in vigilance tasks.

Educators have suggested that the poor attentional processes of mentally retarded individuals comprise the main barrier to their general functioning ability. Considerable efforts have been made by researchers to assess factors which underlie short-term selective attentional processes of retarded individuals; however, relatively little systematic research has been conducted on the capacity of retarded individuals to perform tasks that demand long-term, sustained attention. Considering the importance of vigilance behavior in many activities performed by retarded individuals, it is surprising that the phenomenon has not received more attention by researchers. There are numerous educational and work activities that retarded individuals must perform which necessitate the allocation of sustained attention. The present paper will evaluate research studies which have been conducted to assess the sustained attention of retarded individuals. We will also describe findings obtained in our laboratory and discuss the results of these studies in context of current theories of sustained attention.

Most laboratory studies of sustained attention have been based on the vigilance task paradigm introduced in 1948 by Norman Mackworth. In the typical vigilance task, stimuli such as lights or tones serve as background events (nonsignals) and critical events (targets). Stimuli are presented at near-threshold, or just noticeable, levels and the observer is required to make judgments based upon differences in physical characteristics of stimuli such as size, intensity, or duration. Tasks that employ stimuli presented at near-threshold levels place perceptual demands upon observers and are referred to as "sensory" vigilance tasks. Data obtained from sensory-type vigilance tasks have provided the basis for most theories of sustained attention. More recently, vigilance tasks have been developed which employ symbolic stimuli such as alphabetical letters or digits that are presented for inspection at levels well above threshold; these tasks are referred to as "cognitive" vigilance tasks. Relatively little systematic evaluation has been made of the performance of observers during cognitive-type vigilance tasks. We have reason to believe that the factors which influence performance on cognitive-type tasks may differ fundamentally from those controlling sensory-type tasks. As such, current theories of vigilance performance may be limited to a particular type of vigilance task.

The initial studies which evaluated the sustained attention of retarded individuals employed sensory-type vigilance tasks. The data obtained from studies of children by Kirby, Nettelbeck, and Thomas (1979) and Semmel (1965) suggest that retarded children are less efficient than nonretarded children in performing tasks that demand sustained attention. Whereas, studies of sustained attention of adults failed to detect differences in the vigilance behavior of retarded and nonretarded adults. Ware, Baker, and Sipowicz (1962) tested moderately retarded young adults on a 3-hr visual task that demanded the detection of a variation in light intensity, while Kirby et al. (1978) assessed the performance of mildly retarded adults on a 50-min visual task that required observers to detect changes in light intensity and an auditory task that required subjects to detect a change in sound intensity. In both studies the performance of retarded observers did not differ from the performance of nonretarded observers and there was no difference in the decline of performance between the IQ groups. These data were interpreted by Warm and Berch (1985) as indicative of a developmental delay of sustained attention in retarded individuals. It was suggested that by the time retarded individuals reach late adolescence they achieve parity with nonretarded individuals on task that demand sustained attention.

We propose an alternative explanation for the failure of Ware et al. (1962) and Kirby et al. (1978) to find differences in the sustained attention of retarded and nonretarded adults. The tasks employed by these researchers placed demands upon observers that were primarily perceptual in nature. We hypothesize that vigilance tasks that placed information-processing demands on observers will result in IQ related differences in performance. A study recently conducted in our laboratory (Tomporowski & Allison, in press) assessed the sustained attention of mildly retarded and nontreated young adults during three, 50 min tests in which visual cues were presented successively on a videomonitor. Significant decrements in target detection were observed in both MR and NMR observers during all tests and the vigilance decrement was unrelated to intelligence level. The target detection ability of retarded and nonretarded did not differ on a recognition task that required the identification of the letter "x" from other alphabetical symbols. However, the retarded observers detected significantly fewer target events than did nonretarded observers on two tasks requiring judgment to be made on the basis of a remembered standard; one task demanded the detection of a square slightly larger in size than background cues and the other task demanded the detection of a change in the order of a sequence of numbers. Based upon these data we believe that the sustained attention of retarded adults will differ from that of nonretarded adults on tasks that place demands on the memory abilities of observers; whereas, the sustained attention of retarded adults will not differ from nonretarded adults on vigilance tasks that assess the ability of observers to make simple perceptual discriminations.

The following study was conducted to address the memory-load hypothesis. The sustained attention of retarded and nonretarded adult observers was evaluated under conditions where memory demands were varied systematically by manipulating the rate which stimuli were presented. Background event rate, or the frequency that nontarget stimuli are presented during a vigil, is known to influence target detection performance. Event rate has a particularly important role during vigilance tasks which have memory demands. Dornic (1967) and Davies and Parasuraman (1982) propose theories of vigilance which suggest that the memory for target stimuli is built and consolidated during a vigil, however, memory ability is degraded by interference effects produced by repeated background events. While the effects of background event rate have been measured during several sensory type vigilance tests, there have been no studies of the effects of background event rate on the performance of cognitive-type vigilance test in which memory demands were placed upon observers.

METHOD

Subjects

Thirty-two adults participated in the study. Sixteen individuals comprised the group designated as mentally retarded (MR). The mean CA was 28.93 years and ranged from 23–42 years. The mean IQ score of the MR group was 64.75 with a SD of 5.71 and a range of 56–79 IQ points. Thirteen of the subjects in the MR group were diagnosed as cultural-familial retarded and three were diagnosed as Down's syndrome. Sixteen students were recruited from university introductory psychology classes on a voluntary basis and they served as the group designated a nonmentally retarded (NMR). The mean CA was 18.69 years and ranged from 18 to 20 years. Subjects in the MR group were paid $5.00 upon completion of each of four test sessions; those in the NMR group received extra course credit for their participation. All participants were advised they could withdraw from the study without penalty.

Procedure

Four 60-minute vigilance tasks were administered individually to each subject at the same time of day on separate days within a seven day period. The order of testing was counterbalanced. Each test was a counting task in which individual digits, 3.0 cm in height, were presented serially and repetitively from 1 to 9. The target event was a missing or "skipped" digit (e.g., 1, 2, 3, *5, 6, 7, 8, 9, 1 . . .) while all other digits constituted background events. At the beginning of each test session, a set of written instructions appeared on the screen. The instructions were read aloud by the experimenter who was present throughout each test session. The test required subjects to monitor a computer controlled videoscreen and detect target events from nontarget events. A trial was defined as the presentation of a digit followed by an interval during which the monitor was blank. Subjects responded by pressing the spacebar on the computer keyboard. A response was considered a "hit" if it occurred following the onset of a target event. A response following a background event constituted a "false alarm".

Each of the four test sessions consisted of two 3-min. practice periods and a 60-min. vigilance test period. The first practice period was designed to ensure the subject's ability to perform the task; digit stimuli were presented for 1-s each with a 2-s interstimulus interval (ISI) and target events occurred on 10% of stimulus presentations. Verification of a subject's ability to discriminate target events from background events was determined via a perceptual sensity measure, $P(\overline{A})$, a nonparametric measure similar to d' (Pollack & Norman, 1964). Subjects were required to attain a $P(\overline{A})$ score of ≥ 0.80 to continue the test. All subjects met this criteria on their initial attempt. The second 3-min practice period was designed to prepare subjects to anticipate testing conditions that would be encountered during the main vigilance task; event rate and target probability were identical to the initial 30-min. of the test. The four vigilance tests varied with respect to background and event rate (30 or 15 events per min.) and the presence or absence of an unsignalled shift in

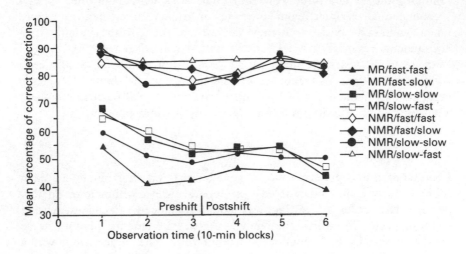

Figure 1.   Percentage of target events detected by retarded and nonretarded
adults during 60-min. vigilance sessions.

event rate following 30 min. of observation. During event rate shift
conditions, subjects received a high or low background event rate during
the first half of the vigil (preshift) and experienced either the same or the
alternate event rate during the second half (postshift) of the vigil. In the
high event rate, digits were presented individually for 1 s with a 1-s ISI; in
the low event rate condition, digits were presented for 1 s with a 3-s ISI.
In all test conditions, 15 target events were presented randomly in each of
six 10-min. time blocks, with the stipulation that target events could not
be presented on successive trials. Measures of each subject's hit rate, and
false alarm responses were recorded for each 10-min. period of the vigil.

RESULTS

An inspection of the target detection responses of MR and NMR
observers revealed clear differences in sustained attention. As seen in
Figure 1, the target detection performance of NMR was superior to that
of MR observers. An evaluation of the performance of NMR observers
revealed a ceiling effect; as such, a parametric analysis comparing the
performance of the two IQ groups was not conducted. A Friedman
Analysis of Variance by Ranks nonparametric analysis of the hit rate of
the two groups did reflect a significant difference in target detection (X^2

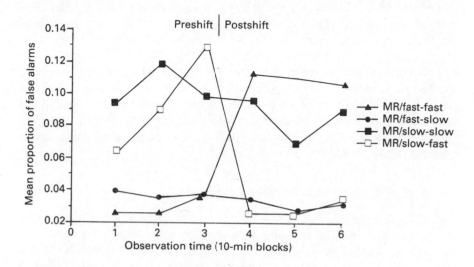

Figure 2. Proportion of false alarm responses made by retarded adults during 60-min. vigilance sessions.

(5) = 30.51, $p < 0.001$). An analysis of the target detection performance of MR observers was conducted with repeated measures ANOVAs. An analysis of hit rate during the initial 30 min of the vigil, collapsed across tests in which subjects experienced a high or low background event rate, revealed a significant decrement in the number of targets detected ($F(2,60) = 13.75$. $p < 0.001$) but no difference in detection as a function of event rate ($F(1,30) = 1.63$, $p > 0.001$) and no interaction between event rate and time ($F < 1$). An analysis of subject performance during the final 40 min. of the vigil revealed that a shift in event rate did not significantly affect target detection.

The average proportion of false alarm responses made by MR subjects is shown in Figure 2. False alarm responding by NMR subjects was negligable throughout the test period and these data were not analyzed nor graphed. The performance of MR subjects during the initial 30 min. of the vigil was collapsed across test conditions in which subjects experienced a high or low event rate; an analysis of these data revealed a significant difference between the two event rate conditions ($F(1,30) = 8.73$, $p < 0.01$) with no significant change in performance across the first three time periods ($F(2,60) = 1.96$, $p > 0.05$) and no significant interaction between event rate and time periods ($F(2,60) = 1.50$, $p > 0.05$). False alarm responses were significantly affected by changes in background event rate. Analysis of false alarm responding during the final 40 min. of the vigil revealed a significant main effect for event rate conditions ($F(3,43) = 4.09$, $p < 0.02$) and a significant event rate by time period interaction ($F(9,135) = 7.06$, $p < 0.001$) with no changes in response over time periods ($F(3,45) = 1.38$, $p > 0.05$). Analysis of changes in false alarm responding from the third time period (preshift) to the fourth time period (postshift) revealed that under the condition where event rate shifted from a high rate to a low rate, there was a significant increase in the number of false alarm responses ($t(15) = 2.59$, $p < 0.05$) and under the condition where there was a shift from a low rate to a high rate, there was a significant decrease in the number of false alarm responses made ($t(15) = 3.68$, $pf1 < 0.01$).

DISCUSSION

Our research provides evidence that the sustained attention of retarded adults differs in two ways from nonretarded adults during cognitive type vigilance tasks that possess memory demands. Retarded observers fail to detect target events and they respond incorrectly to nontarget events more often than nonretarded observers. Further, the frequency that false alarm responses are made by retarded observers is related to the rate which stimuli are presented during the vigil.

The analysis of the performance of mentally retarded adults on discrimination or recognition tasks is typically limited to errors of omission. Educational and training programs often rely entirely on the measurement of change in error rate to mark task acquisition. False alarms or errors of omission are seldom evaluated during training sessions. In our study, the analyses of the effects of stimulus presentation rate indicated that a fast or slow presentation rate had little effect on target detection; however, event rate was related to the frequency of errors of omission made by retarded observers. The longer delay interval between the presentation of stimuli produced greater numbers of false alarm responses than during the short delay interval. These findings differ from those obtained from research conducted with sensory-type, nonmemory vigilance tasks.

It is hypothesized that the frequency of false alarms committed under the low event rate conditions by retarded observers occurred because of the longer time period required of observers to hold information in short-term memory. This interpretation is similar to explanations of decrements in target detection in delayed-recognition memory tasks as the delay interval between stimuli increases (Kinchla & Smyzer, 1967) and performance in repetitive counting tasks (Healy & Nairne, 1985).

It appears that the efficiency of retarded adults to monitor vigilance tasks in which stimuli are presented successively may depend upon the individual's memory abilities. Given that retarded persons are often placed in cognitive-type education or work settings in which information is presented in a successive fashion and which demand sustained attention, the findings of the present study have important practical implications and may help to explain the errors of omission and commission made by retarded adults.

REFERENCES

Davies, D. R., & Parasuraman, R. (1982) A nonparametric analysis of recognition experiments. *Psychonomic Science*, **1**, 125–126.

Dornic, S. (1967) Expectancy of signals and the memory trace. *Studia Psychologica*, **9**, 87–91.

Healy, A. F., & Nairne, J. S. (1985) Short-term memory processes in counting. *Cognitive Psychology*, **17**, 417–444.

Kinchela, R., & Smyzer, F. (1967) A diffusion model of perceptual memory. *Perception and Psychophysics*, **2**, 219–229.

Kirby, N. H., Nettelbeck, T., & Bullock, J. (1978) Vigilance performance of mildly mentally retarded adults. *American Journal of Mental Deficiency*, **82**, 394–397.

Kirby, N. H., Nettelbeck, T., & Thomas, P. (1979) Vigilance performance of mildly retarded children. *American Journal of Mental Deficiency*, **84**, 184–187.

Pollack, I., & Norman, D. A. (1964) A nonparametric analysis of recognition experiments. *Psychonomic Science*, **1**, 125–126.

Semmel, M. I. (1965) Arousal theory and vigilance behavior of educable mentally retarded and average children. *American Journal of Mental Deficiency*, **66**, 647–650.

Tomporowski, P. D., & Allison, P. (in press) Sustained attention in mentally retarded adults. *American Journal of Mental Retardation*.

Ware, J. R., Baker, R. A., & Sipowicz, R. R. (1962) Performance of mental deficients on a simple monitoring task. *American Journal of Mental Deficiency*, **66**, 647–650.

Warm, J. S., & Berch, D. B. (1985) Sustained attention in the mentally retarded: The vigilance paradigm. In N. R. Ellis and N. W. Bray (Eds.), *International review of research in mental retardation: Vol. 13*. New York: Academic Press.

Discourse, in an Integrated School Setting, between Six- and Seven-year-old Non-handicapped Children and Peers with Severe Learning Difficulties

A. Lewis and B. Carpenter

Department of Education, University of Warwick,
Coventry CV4 7AL, England

The objective of the research reported here was to examine some aspects of discourse between non-handicapped (NH) six and seven year olds, and peers with severe learning difficulties (SLD). It was hypothesised that talk by the NH children to SLD partners would contain characteristics found in talk by NH children to younger NH children. This hypothesis was supported. Talk to SLD peers, by the NH children, contained a high proportion of action requests and few prompts, monitoring or question utterances. Approximately one quarter of all utterances by NH children to SLD partners were either repeated unchanged or reformulated within speech topics. This indicates a considerable degree of persistence in attempts by NH children to communicate with SLD partners. Three-way ANOVA demonstrated that session had a more significant effect on the discourse than did identity of either SLD partner or NH child. The study raises questions about the preparation of both NH and SLD children for integration experiences.

Children with severe learning difficulties (SLD) are increasingly receiving part of their education in ordinary schools. A recent survey (Jowett *et al.*, 1988) indicated that 80.0% of schools for children with SLD had links with mainstream schools. It appears, from HMI reports on individual schools, that the greatest degree of integration for pupils with SLD is occurring in the early years of schooling. It is therefore relevant to consider the nature of interactions between young non-handicapped (NH) children and classmates with SLD. These interactions form the basis for children's roles as citizens in an integrated community.

THE SPECIAL SCHOOL CONTEXT

The special school, from which the children with SLD in this study came, caters for 75 children (ages 2–19). A variety of functional links have been established between the school and area mainstream schools and, to date, twenty-three integration programmes have been set up. Integrated work, covering all age ranges in the school, focuses on particular curricular areas. These are identified, for individual SLD children, through an analysis of their learning programmes. Initially, the "open" areas of the curriculum (Ainscow and Tweddle, 1979) were selected as the focus for integrated work. They offered a broad spectrum of learning experiences and enabled all children to participate. Shared learning activities took place successfully in art, craft, cookery, music, P.E. and woodwork. This exploration of shared learning in "open" curricular areas led to the development of similar work in "closed" areas (literacy, written language, mathematics and science).

Preliminary planning meetings have been held prior to each integration project. Children in mainstream nursery and infant schools have been prepared for the integration of SLD classmates through the use of stories and videos about children with SLD. Handicap awareness courses have been devised for older mainstream pupils. Any initial anxieties of mainstream pupils were dispelled through the positive relationships which emerged between NH and SLD children.

THE RESEARCH CONTEXT

There have been a number of studies concerned with non-verbal interaction between NH and SLD children in integrated settings (for example, Sebba, 1983; Pieterse and Center, 1984). Results have been equivocal but indicate that given certain provisos positive interaction between the groups can be promoted at the infant school level. It is surprising, given the active research interests in both integration of children with special needs and work in the burgeoning field of discourse analysis, that very little published research has addressed the issue of the nature of verbal interaction between NH and SLD children.

The research reported here was designed to assess the nature of talk between six to seven year old NH children and peers with SLD in structured integration sessions. It was hypothesised that this talk would contain characteristics associated with talk by young children to younger siblings and tutees. These characteristics include shorter utterances; fewer complex instructions, questions or politeness markers; more attention getting devices, imperatives, and repetitions, compared with speech to peers or older children; and step by step instructional strategies (Cooper *et al.*, 1980; Terrell, 1985; Ervin-Tripp and Gordon, 1986). The few published studies which have examined talk between NH and handi-capped children (Guralnick and Paul-Brown, 1977; 1980; 1984) support these hypothesised characteristics in talk by NH children to classmates with SLD.

METHOD

The setting for the data collection was an integration project (reported in Carpenter *et al.*, 1986; Moore *et al.*, 1987) in which nine children (mean age 6:6) from a Midlands' first school were paired with the corresponding age group (mean age 6:1) from the area school for children with SLD. Seven of the SLD group had Down's syndrome and the remainder had unknown causes of SLD. Children chose their partners; the NH-SLD pairs varied between sessions but remained constant within the recorded segment of each session.

Integration sessions took place fortnightly in an afternoon. The sessions were held in the first school and were run alternately by special and mainstream school staff. Activity in the integration sessions focussed on children working in NH-SLD pairs on cooperative common tasks. Activity focused on a joint art and craft task in all except one of the sessions.

A comparison session took place at the end of the school year. In this session (referred to as the "M5 session") the NH children involved in the integration sessions were paired with four and five year old NH children, randomly chosen, from the mainstream school. The structure and type of activity in the M5 session resembled those in the integration sessions as closely as possible.

During the integration and M5 sessions, NH children wore jackets containing micro-recorders. Leads and microphones were partially concealed in piping on the jackets. Discourse was recorded during the cooperative paired activity segment of integration sessions over one year. The microphones were sufficiently sensitive to pick up vocalisations from both the NH wearer and his/her SLD/M5 partner.

The language samples collected for analyses consisted of all recorded speech spoken by, or addressed to, individual NH children during the part of the integration sessions in which NH and SLD children worked in NH-SLD pairs on a common task. Similarly speech addressed by or to the NH children during the corresponding part of the M5 session provided comparison data.

Appropriate units and classification systems for discourse analyses have been widely debated (Stubbs, 1983) Garvey, 1984; Edwards and Westgate, 1987). The selection of units for analysis and coding systems in this study reflected the specific research context and three aspects of recorded discourse (integration and M5 sessions) were coded: utterance functions, reformulations/repetitions and exchanges.

Results for utterance functions, reformulations and repetitions were based on sub-samples calculated by excluding the first one minute of recorded discourse and then using the first 50 utterances by the NH child to SLD/M5 partner in each recorded session. Where total utterances to SLD/M5 partner numbered less than 50, the total sample was used. Exchanges were infrequent and coding of these was based on the total discourse sample.

Utterance functions (adapted from Dore, 1986) were sub-divided into: requests for action (e.g. "Colour it in now") prohibitions (e.g. "Don't do that"), prompts (e.g. "Shall we do it red then?"), monitors (e.g. "It's going blue"), evaluatives (e.g. "That's good"), affirmatives (e.g. "Oh yeh OK"), questions (e.g. "Where d'you want to go?") (sub-divided into open and closed questions), explains (e.g. "It's wet because you dropped the jar"), self-maintains (e.g. "Get off that's mine") and uncoded (e.g. "sing-song" utterances without any clear function in the discourse).

Codings were also made of reformulations and repetitions of utterances within speech topics. An utterance did not count as a reformulation or repetition of a prior utterance unless this occurred within the same speech topic.

For example: Colour in the red shape.
              Colour in the red shape. REPETITION
              Colour it in red.   REFORMULATION
              Colour it red.   REFORMULATION

Reformulations were classified according to type of reformulation made. Interest was in how utterances were reformulated as this may have indicated beliefs held by NH children about SLD partners. Each single utterance could incorporate more than one type of reformulation. The broad types of reformulation were: adding, deleting or moving an attentional (for example: "Come here"› "Susie come here"); clarifying (for example: "Let's go"› "Let's stop now and go over there"); focusing (for example: "Give me that"› "Give me the pencil"); simplifying (for example: "Do the green all round there"› "Green there"); making more polite (for example: "Sit down"› "Please will you sit down") (tonal cues were used to clarify whether or not a reformulation came into this category); and, developing the topic of the utterance (for example; "Come and play nurses"› "Come and play nurses and we'll be the nurses and doctors and wear white coats").

Exchanges were coded based on McTear's (1985) classification. This was supplemented with a "no response" category as it was anticipated that there would often be instances when a NH child spoke to an SLD partner directly but received no response.

Measures of inter-rater reliability were carried out on 8.7% of the transcripts from integration sessions for (a) accuracy of transcription, (b) segmentation of utterances, and (c) classification of utterance functions.

Agreements were high for all three categories: accuracy of transcription, mean agreement 90.23% (s.d. 3.5); segmentation of utterances, mean agreement 94.3% (s.d. 1.5), kappa (mean) = 0.85, s.d. = 0.07; classification of utterance functions, mean agreement 82.3% (s.d. 6.2), kappa (mean) = 0.71, s.d. 0.14.

RESULTS

Eleven integration sessions took place over the year and these were distributed across all three school terms. Duration of recordings of discourse from the nine NH-SLD pairs during the cooperative paired activity segments of integration sessions over one school year totalled 1,632.5 minutes. Mean duration of recording for each NH child for each integration session was 23.2 minutes. In addition, recordings of discourse in the comparison M5 session totalled 310.0 minutes (mean per target child, 34.4 minutes).

Functions of utterances

The mean percentage of utterances in the major functional categories in S sessions (grouped) and the M5 comparison session are given in Table 1. This table shows that requests were an important discourse feature in speech to SLD partners and that the use of requests with SLD partners was statistically significantly higher than in the M5 comparison session. Prohibitions were used infrequently with SLD partners but not at all with M5 partners. Monitoring, questioning and self-maintaining utterances were all used significantly more with M5 than with SLD partners.

Reformulations and repetitions

Over one fifth of all utterances addressed to SLD partners were a reformulation or repetition of an utterance within the speech topic. Both reformulations and repetitions were more frequent in integration sessions than in the M5 comparison session. The difference in the percentage use of repetitions in the two setting was statistically significant.

Between one third and one half of reformulations and repetitions by individual NH children to SLD partners were part of a string of reformulations or repetitions within a speech topic, that is the NH children were repeatedly amending or reiterating an utterance to SLD partners in an attempt to communicate. This was not the case for speech to M5 partners.

The most frequent type of reformulation to SLD partners was a simplification of the utterance with approximately half (mean: 49.2% of all reformulations to SLD partners being of this type. This type of

Table 1.   Mean percentages, standard deviations and paired t tests (2 tailed) for major discourse features in 50 utterance sub-samples for S (grouped) and M5 sessions

	S Sessions (grouped)		Comparison M5 session		Paired t test (2-tailed, df=8)
requests for action	42.9%	(12.7)	24.2%	(13.5)	t = 3.03, p<.02
prohibitions	4.8%	(2.2)	0%	(3.7)	t = 6.40, p<.001
prompts	6.5%	(3.7)	5.6%	(4.4)	t = 0.46, NS
monitors	21.5%	(6.2)	48.5%	(18.0)	t = −3.81, p<.01
questions	7.6%	(1.8)	14.5%	(6.8)	t = −3.06, p.<.02
self-maintains	0.2%	(0.4)	3.8%	(2.8)	t = −3.49, p<.01
reformulations	11.1%	(5.1)	7.1%	(6.2)	t = 0.81, NS
repetitions	11.1%	(4.3)	4.7%	(4.1)	t = 3.27, p<.02

reformulation often involved omitting non-essential elements (for example, "Oh look shall we go and do this"> "Shall we go and do this"). Thus the SLD partner had, in the reformulated utterance, something which was probably both easier to interpret and required a shorter memory span than the initial utterance. There were too few reformulations to M5 partners to make reliable comparisons of types of reformulations between S and M5 sessions.

Exchanges

One of the most striking points concerning exchanges in the integration sessions was the extent to which the NH children responded to utterances made by their partners. Only 5.0% of utterances by SLD children were initiations by them which received no response from NH partners. Similarly relatively few initiations by SLD children were effectively ignored by being succeeded by an initiation by NH children (8.3% of all utterances by SLD children). This contrasted with the position in the M5 comparison session in which 26.8% of initiations by partners were either ignored or followed by an initiation by the NH child.

Successful dialogue might be regarded as that which involves a sequence in which each member responds to the other until the speech topic is exhausted. From this point of view dialogue between the NH children and children with SLD appeared to be more successful than discourse between the two NH groups. The percentage of total exchanges for each session type which were of a response-response type were 37.9% for S sessions (grouped) compared with 28.2% in the M5 session.

DISCUSSION

The results support the hypothesis that talk by six to seven year old NH
children to peers with SLD will contain features posited in the research
literature as characteristic of talk by NH children to younger children.
These features include: attention-getting devices, a high proportion of
directives many of which were in the imperative mood, few questions and
repetitions. In general, comparisons with talk by six to seven year old NH
children to mainstream four and five year olds showed that these features
were more pronounced with SLD children than with M5 partners. In
other words, if use of these "young listener" features operates on a
continuum then one may hypothesise that the NH children perceived
SLD partners as being even younger than four/five years in spite of the
normal size for chronological age of most of the SLD children. It is
interesting that the NH children's talk to SLD partners was more
appropriate for their actual developmental levels (linguistic ages c.2–3
years) than for their hypothesised ages (c.5 years, given by NH children
in attitude interviews, Lewis and Lewis, 1987).

In a number of studies which have explored "young age listener"
features in the speech of children under seven years old, listener cues
relating to age of listener are confounded with cues concerning ability,
familiarity, and/or sociometric status. For example, a study of how young
children tutoring younger children adapt to the perceived linguistic needs
of the listeners could be reflecting adjustments to one, or several, of the
sets of listener cues mentioned. Is a six year old tutor working with a four
year old tutee sensitive to only one of the cues (e.g. age) or responding
differentially to the various sets of cues? It may be that each cue elicits
similar behaviour, for example, that young children elicit from older
children a high proportion of directives, that less able children elicit from
same age children a high proportion of directives and that unpopular
children also elicit a high proportion of directives from peers. A study by
Masur *et al.* (1978) concerning four year old boys tutoring "high verbal"
and "low verbal" two year olds provides some indication that both
listener age and listener ability cues influenced tutors' speech.

The NH children involved in this study were generally unable to
integrate conflicting cues. Consequently some NH children could not
accept the apparent dual standards of work and behaviour operating in
the integrated classroom. Other NH children resorted to explanations for
the behaviour of SLD children which over-rode one set of cues, for
example, that the SLD children were very young (despite their normal
size for chronological age) and therefore unable to understand instructions (Lewis and Lewis, 1987; Lewis and Lewis, in press). The
explanations adopted of SLD have implications for the ways in which
young NH children address classmates with SLD.

One implication from this research concerns the models of SLD which are presented to young NH children when children with SLD are integrated (either wholly or partially) into the class. If children with SLD are portrayed as young, either implicitly through being given a lot of help, addressed using motherese and with less strict discipline; or explicitly, through teacher requests to NH children to help SLD children with routine tasks (such as removing coats) then the NH children are likely to respond by intensifying use of a style of talk used with younger children. This may well be inappropriate and to the detriment of the linguistic development of both SLD and NH children.

Conversely if teachers of young NH children involved in integration projects such as that described here, can give NH children a realistic and coherent explanation for SLD, more productive linguistic strategies may be developed by both NH and SLD children. For the NH children the infant school years are, as Robinson and Whitaker (1986) make clear, the period during which NH children are developing the rules of communicative competence. However young mainstream children do not, in the school context, generally receive the type of linguistic feedback which promotes this communicative competence. Conversational partners, such as children with SLD, who do not conform to linguistic conventions may provide a rare and valuable impetus for developing the conversational skills of NH partners.

REFERENCES

Ainscow, M. & Tweddle, D. (1979) *Preventing Classroom Failure – An Objectives Approach*. Wiley, London.

Carpenter, B., Lewis, A. & Moore, J. (1986) 'An Integration Project involving young children with severe learning difficulties and mainstream first school children'. *Mental Handicap* 14(4), 152–157.

Cooper, C., Ayers-Lopez, S. & Marquis, A. (1980) *Children's discourse in cooperative and didactic interaction: developmental, patterns in effective learning*. Texas University, Austin.

Dore, J. (1986) The Development of Conversational Competence in R. L. Schiefelbusch (ed) *Language Competence: Assessment and Intervention*. pp. 3–60. Taylor and Francis, London.

Edwards, A. D. and Westgate, D. P. G. (1987) *Investigating Classroom Talk*. Falmer, London.

Ervin-Tripp, S. & Gordon, D. (1986) The Development of Requests. In R. L. Schiefelbusch (ed) *Language Competence: Assessment and Intervention*. pp. 61–95, Taylor and Francis, London.

Garvey, C. (1984) *Children's Talk*. Fontana, Oxford.

Jowett, S., Hegarty, S. & Moses, D. (1988) *Joining Forces*. NFER-Nelson, Windsor.

Lewis, A. & Lewis, V. (1987) The Attitudes of Young children towards peers with severe learning difficulties. *British Journal of Developmental Psychology*. **5.3**. 287–292.

Lewis, A. & Lewis, V. (in press) Young children's attitudes, after a period of integration, towards peers with severe learning dificulties. *European Journal of Special Needs Education*.

McTear, M. (1985) *Children's Conversation* Blackwell, Oxford.

Moore, J., Carpenter, B. & Lewis, A. (1987) "He can do it Really" – Integration in a First School, *Education 3–13*. **15.2**. 37–43.

Pieterse, M. & Center, Y. (1984) The integration of eight Down's syndrome children into regular schools. *Australia and N.Z. Journal of Developmental Disabilities*. **10.1**. 11–20.

Robinson, E. J. & Whittaker, S. J. (1986) Learning about verbal referential communication in the early schools years. In Durkin, K. (ed) *Language Development in The School Years*. pp. 155–171, Croom Helm, London.

Sebba, J. (1983) Social interactions among pre-school handicapped and non-handicapped children. *Journal of Mental Deficiency Research*. **27**. 115–124.

Stubbs, M. (1983) *Discourse Analysis: The Sociolinguistic Analysis of Natural Language*. Blackwell, Oxford.

Self-Talk in the Institutionalized Retarded: Naturalistic Observations

V. A. Binzley, P. Polomsky and P. Shah

Warrensville Developmental Center, Warrensville Township, Ohio 44128, U.S.A.

Self-talk or private speech is thought to play a significant role in the development of thinking and self-regulation. Yet few studies have focused on this phenomenon in the retarded even though lack of self-regulation is a major problem with this group. The present study surveyed the populations of a developmental center and two community workshops to determine the extent and nature of self-talk and if the self-talker differed significantly from the nonself-talker. In addition, ten self-talkers were studied during a motor task to determine the function of self-talk in a structured task situation. Self-talkers were found not to differ from a random control group on certain biosocial parameters. More self-talkers were identified in the developmental center than the workshops but in both settings self-talk tended to be affective-emotional in nature. During the task situation most utterances were descriptive and uttered during the execution of the task. Suggestions are made for additional observations as well as controlled clinical interventions to use self-talk to promote self-regulation.

Self-talk or private speech is a well-known and hotly debated phenomenon in developmental psychology (Zivin, 1979). It refers to speech spoken aloud by children that is addressed either to the self or no one in particular (Berk, 1985). Piaget was one of the first theorists to study this behavior which he claimed constituted 40–70% of the spontaneous speech of children 5–6 years of age (Kohlberg *et al.*, 1968). According to Piaget, this speech was presocial and a manifestation of the young child's immature or egocentric thought development. Others have confirmed the existence of self-talk in children but at lesser rates and still others have disagreed with Piaget's interpretation of this behavior (Zivin, 1979).

Most notable among those who have taken issue with Piaget's interpretation is the Russian psychologist, Vygotsky (1962). He thought self-talk had its origin in social communication and that in the young child it served a self-regulatory function. According to Vygotsky, children use self-talk to verbalize emotions and frustrations, to plan and guide problem-solving activity, to inhibit impulsive behavior and to structure analytically the perceptual field (Diaz, 1986). Self-talk, in this view, is a way station towards inner thought and therefore declines with age as the child develops the cognitive capacity for verbal thought. As to frequency of self-talk, Vygotsky found it varied according to the situation.

Vygotsky's explanation of self-talk has generated a great deal of interest and research, much of which tends to support his theory. However recent research has also pointed out the complexity of the phenomenon. Meichenbaum and Goodman (1979) have suggested that private speech is not a unitary phenomenon. Variation in terms of different developmental trends for different categories of self-talk is even more apparent, they point out, when variables such as mental age, situational factors and cognitive style are considered. That is, higher IQ children produce self-talk earlier than children of average IQ and the incidence of self-talk decreases whenever the possibilities for social interaction are reduced.

Notwithstanding the lack of agreement on this phenomenon, it is surprising that no one has looked for it in the retarded adult in view of the importance of self-talk in the development of self-regulation. Given the many reports of aggression and other maladaptive behavior in this group (Kessler *et al.*, 1984), it would seem that lack of self-regulation is a problem. Luria (1963), reported that the regulatory function of speech is seriously disturbed in certain subgroups of the retarded and he has made suggestions for improving self-regulation by first using instruction and then self-talk. Berk (1985) suggests that children with special learning problems may need to use audible private speech for a longer developmental period. Current research indicates the developmental trend of private speech is more clearly paralleled by mental age than chronological age (Meichenbaum & Goodman, 1979). Assuming this to be so, it should not be unusual to find self-talk occurring in retarded adults who by definition are developmentally delayed. However, a review of the literature found only one report of self-talk in the retarded (Bender, 1980). This study reported on the private speech of six children with Downs' syndrome in three different settings: structured school, unstructured school, and home. The study found 13% of the children's utterances to be self-talk and of these, 49% functioned as regulatory/ descriptive, 33% as affective and 10% as fantasy. Based on these data, Bender concluded that self-talk seldom functioned as controlling or regulating in this group, thus confirming Luria's observation on self-regulation in some retarded individuals.

Given the developmental delay and the poor self-regulation noted in some retarded adults, the present study was undertaken to determine if the developmental phenomenon of self-talk occurs in this population. The specific questions addressed were:

1. Does the phenomenon of self-talk occur in the retarded adult?
2. Under what circumstances does it occur?
3. What is the nature of the spontaneous self-talk?
4. What is the nature of self-talk in a structured task situation?
5. Does the self-talker differ from the nonself-talker on certain biosocial parameters?

METHOD

The populations of a developmental center and two community workshops were observed for two weeks by habilitation team members to determine the extent and nature of self-talk. Although there are many methodological problems yet to be worked out in studying private speech (Meichenbaum & Goodman, 1979), our intent was simply to note the occurrences and content of self-talk in the natural environment. In order to achieve this, habilitation staff were asked, in the course of their usual routine, to observe their clients for the occurrence of self-talk. To assist them, they were given both a description of the phenomenon and an observation form for data collection. The observation form required the observer to identify, when possible, the situation, the antecedents, the consequences and the content of the self-talk.

During the data collection period, the investigators met semi-weekly with habilitation staff to monitor data collection. In some individuals, the frequency of self-talk was so high that habilitation staff found it impossible to accurately detect separate episodes of self-talk. Staff also reported the content of self-talk to be repetitious in these clients. Therefore data collection was modified. For these individuals, once the content had been noted, staff were only required to note the occurrence thereafter during periodic observations.

After the number of self-talkers was computed for the developmental center, data processing staff were asked to randomly generate, from the center's census, a list of the same number. These two groups were then compared on factors which might affect self-regulation in some way. The factors compared were age, social age, IQ, occurrence of seizures, psychiatric illness and behavioral problems. This information was obtained by searching resident records. A psychiatric illness was defined as a mental disorder identified by a psychiatrist and a behavioral problem required the identification of such by the habilitation team.

Lastly, ten residents identified in the developmental center as frequent self-talkers were observed in a structured task situation using a coding format devised by Kohlberg *et al.* (1968) and procedures suggested by Meichenbaum and Goodman (1979). Observers were psychology staff

Table 1.   Biosocial characteristics of groups

Group	N	Social age	Seizure	Psychiatric problem	Behavioral problem
Self-talkers	70	7.3	25.7%	44%	65.7%
Control	70	7.1	35.7%	38.5%	58.5%
Study	10	8.4	36%	36%	54%

trained in the coding format but naive with respect to the theoretical expectations. Subjects were presented with two drawing tasks of differing complexity. Order of presentations was counterbalanced and observations were done in a quiet area either in the resident's cottage or in a classroom.

RESULTS

Among the developmental center's population, 70 self-talkers were identified. These 70 residents were found not to differ significantly from the randomly generated control group in terms of age, social age, IQ, percentage of seizures, psychiatric illness or behavioral problems. These data are presented in Table 1. The task study group was not included in any statistical comparison because of the small number of subjects involved. Although the two groups do not differ on the factors examined, the relatively low incidence of psychiatric illness indicates that this cannot account for all the self-talk seen in these adults. The high incidence of behavioral problems confirms Luria's (1963) observation that self-regulation is deficient in some retarded individuals.

In Workshop I, 33 self-talkers were identified as compared with 11 in Workshop II. The two workshops differed both in size and living arrangements of their workers which probably accounts for the difference in the number of self-talkers. Workshop I had 231 workers, 55% of whom lived in an institution whereas Workshop II had only 165 workers, all of whom lived in a community setting of some sort: group home, own apartment or familial home. These numbers, it would seem, are a reflection of our placement process whereby those with the better self-control are placed in the least restrictive setting. These data are depicted in Table 2 as percentage of self-talkers as a function of setting.

In Workshop I, 9 of the self-talkers (27%) had a psychiatric diagnosis whereas in Workshop II, no one had a psychiatric diagnosis. Residents from the development center attend Workshop I and of this group, 14 (78%) who self-talked in the center also did so at work. Among the three groups of self-talkers, 15 individuals were observed to engage in self-talk

Table 2.   Percentage of self-talkers as
a function of setting

Setting	Percentage
Developmental center	30
Workshop I	14
Workshop II	6

Table 3.   Timing and category of self-talk

Time	Word play	Outer directed	Descriptive	Question	Self-guidance	Emotion	Misc.
Before	1	1	2	0	0	0	6+
During	0	10	14	6	3	5	7+
After	0	1	2	1	0	0	3+

almost continuously and because of this, it was impossible to compute an average frequency score. At the workshop, self-talk was noted to occur in all settings: on the assembly line, in the classroom, in the cafeteria and in the lounge area. In all settings, what was observed was excitatory and emotional. Often a person appeared to be reliving an emotional exchange with someone, or repeating what someone had previously said to them. This latter phenomenon was particularly noticeable in two self-talkers who otherwise had no functional speech.

In the structured task situation, there was not a lot of self-talk but what there was occurred primarily during the motor act itself. This would seem to indicate that speech is not yet controlling behavior. According to Vygotsky, self-talk must occur before or at the beginning of an activity to have any obvious directing or planning function (Rubin, 1979). Out of 62 utterances, 45 occurred during the drawing, 10 before and 7 afterwards. A chi square for frequency was done on this data to test the null hypothesis of no relationship between time, task and number of utterances ($X^2 = 38.6$, *df* 1, $p < .001$). Utterances during the motor task were also categorized as suggested by Kohlberg *et al.* (1968). These data are shown in Table 3.

Kohlberg *et al.* (1968) have suggested a five-level developmental hierarchy for self-talk beginning with presocial and self-stimulating language and ending with silent speech or inner thought. When the utterances are arranged according to this developmental hierarchy, most of the self-talk is at level II. This is immature speech but consistent with Bender's (1980) findings in children with Down's syndrome.

DISCUSSION

The relatively high incidence of self-talk not accounted for by psychiatric illness established the possibility that it is the developmental phenomenon of self-talk. If this is so, then the behavior should not be ignored or discouraged but worked with to promote self-regulation and perhaps even cognitive growth. Such is already being done in certain clinical but nonretarded populations (Meichenbaum & Goodman, 1979) and is being suggested for use in the preschool setting (Berk, 1985).

Although more data are needed on the nature of spontaneous self-talk to determine if there is a difference in self-regulation associated with etiology of retardation as Luria (1963) suggests, clinical studies need to begin. The most obvious application is to attempt to improve self-regulation by substituting calming self-talk for what is now excitatory talk and frequently a prelude to acting out behavior. We have begun to do so on a case by case basis.

What is not so obvious is how to use self-talk to promote cognitive growth which supposedly is the function it serves naturally in the nonretarded. If Vygotsky is correct in assuming that self-talk develops out of incorporating the adults' instructions, then perhaps we should be looking at the kind and quality of verbal instruction the retarded are receiving from caretakers in order to promote cognitive growth. Some recent American studies on mother-child interaction have provided support for this notion. Preliminary results indicate that although children can learn to do things by observation, verbalization during adult-child interaction is associated with superior cognitive growth (Fuson, 1979). Perhaps if we try accompanying our skill training with verbal instruction, particularly with those who already exhibit self-talk, we may find it as potent a tool as the right reinforcer for promoting skill acquisition. For as it has been noted, speech early in the mastery of a voluntary act serves a useful guiding function.

REFERENCES

Anastopoulos, A. & Krehbiel, G. G. (1985) The development of private speech: A review of empirical evidence addressing Vygotsky's theoretical views. *Paper presented at the Biennial Meeting of the Society for Research in Child Development*, Toronto, Canada.

Bender, N. N. (1980) Private speech of Downs' syndrome children in the school and home. *Paper presented at the meeting of American Educational Research Association*, Boston, MA.

Berk, L. (1985) Why children talk to themselves. *Young Children*, **40**(5): 46–52.

Bruning, J. L. & Kintz, B. L. (1968) Computational Handbook of Statistics, pp. 195–209, Scott, Foresman and Company, Illinois.

Diaz, R. M. (1986) Issues in the empirical study of private speech: A response to Frawley and Lantolf's commentary. *Developmental Psychology*, **22**(5): 709–711.

Fuson, K. C. (1979) The development of self-regulating aspects of speech: A review. In G. Zivin (Ed.) The Development of Self-Regulation Through Private Speech. pp. 135–219, Wiley, New York.

Kessler, J. W., Binzley, V. A., Arendt, R., Polomsky, P., & Shah, P. (1984) Dynamic analysis of aggression in an institutionalized mentally retarded population. In J. M. Berg (Ed.) *Perspectives and Progress in Mental Retardation, Vol. II, Biomedical aspects*. pp. 309–319. University Park Press, Baltimore.

Kohlberg, L., Yaeger, J., & Hjertholm, E. (1968) Private speech: Four studies and a review of theories. *Child Development*, **39**: 691–736.

Luria, A. R. (1963) *The Mentally Retarded Child*. Pergamon Press, New York.

Meichenbaum, D. & Goodman, S. (1979) Clinical use of private speech and critical questions about its study in natural settings. In G. Zivin (Ed.) *The Development of Self-Regulation Through Private Speech*. pp. 325–360, Wiley, New York.

Rubin, K. H. (1979) The impact of the natural setting on private speech. In G. Zivin (Ed.) *The Development of Self-Regulation Through Private Speech*. pp. 265–294, Wiley, New York.

Vygotsky, L. (1962) Thought and Language. MIT Press (Original work published 1934), Cambridge, MA.

Zivin, G. (1979) Removing common confusions about egocentric speech, private speech and self-regulation. In G. Zivin (Ed.) *The Development of Self-Regulation Through Private Speech*. pp. 13–50, Wiley, New York.

Theory into Practice: Inculcating Initial Notions about Language Intervention with Children with Mental Handicap

D. M. Walker

School of Clinical Speech and Language Studies,
University of Dublin, Trinity College, Dublin, 2, Ireland

This paper describes the establishment and initial results of a programme to enhance the communication skills of mentally handicapped non-verbal children using a combination of group and individual treatments. The children and parents attended weekly sessions at which therapy was administered by trainee speech therapists under the supervision of a speech pathologist and a psychologist. Specific objectives were determined for each participant and progress towards these was carefully documented. Activities were devised, implemented and evaluated and some were recorded on video. Parental interest was high and involvement with therapy was encouraged. Results, after two years, are reported in terms of the steps individual children appeared to traverse in the initial stages of acquiring an interest in and a limited facility with communication skills.

Over the past decade or so, emphasis has been placed on early intervention. Much of this has focussed on early intervention with mentally handicapped children.

Bricker & Schiefelbusch (1984) identify four guidelines for communication intervention.

Guideline 1. Early intervention is indicated if

a) the infant is thought to be in an environment that will not elicit and support the type of interactive behaviours required for normal language acquisition or

b) the infant's handicapping condition is sufficient to cause concern about the acquisition of early extra- and para-linguistic responses such as voice feature contrasts (i.e. angry-friendly; familiar-unfamiliar) and different intonation contrasts.

Guideline 2. An intervention program for infants should also be a training program for the adult care giver.

Guideline 3. During early intervention, stimulation should be provided in the form of mutual, reciprocal play.

Guideline 4. Early communication training should accommodate the infant who cannot use speech.

It will be shown later that the intervention in this project fitted well into some or all of these guidelines.

Many programmes now have recognised the importance of early intervention. Such programmes as The Portage Project; the McConkey Programmes: Let's Talk; Let's Play; and the Gilham Programme: The Early Words Programme, are well documented. Speech therapists have recognised the need for working with children at a pre-school level, and indeed, the majority of the work with children with language problems would be at this level. Cooper, Moodley and Reynell in 1978, highlighted the need for therapy in the pre-school years, in order to reduce the communication problems for the child in school.

A significant change in therapy over the past decade or so, has been the move away from individual therapy sessions to group sessions. This change in techniques was made for several reasons.

1. It encourages children to talk to each other (Belkin 1983)
2. Activities can be child oriented rather than adult oriented (Belkin, 1983)
3. Group instruction of the severely handicapped in many cases can result in faster learning than one to one instruction (McCormack and Goldman, 1984)

Nevertheless, there are potent factors to consider which favour individual instruction.

1. Therapy can be individualised to the patient's communicative needs.
2. Behaviour problems can be dealt with more effectively.
3. A strong bond can be made between therapist and patient.
4. Parents can identify more easily with the aims of the session.

In this project we were fortunate to be able to combine both individual and group therapy and thus utilise the beneficial aspects of both types of therapy.

PARENTS AND SIGNIFICANT OTHERS

Byers Brown (1984) identifies four ways the practising speech therapist may choose to work.

1. She carries out treatment herself.
2. The speech therapist defines the problem and asks other people to use their skills to remedy it.
3. She combines her skills with those of other professionals to produce programmes which may then be administered by any one of the professional workers.
4. She breaks the tasks down into a series of subtasks and then instructs others in the use of subskills to attack the subtasks.

The role of the speech therapist is changing. It is not possible and indeed in many instances, not desirable for the speech therapist to be the designer of the programme and also responsible on a day-to-day basis for its delivery.

In the area of services for the severely developmentally learning disabled, where progress is slow, and the work is repetitious, it would be a mis-use of the speech therapist's skills to be the person responsible for the daily service delivery. Fitzgerald and Karnes (1987) comment that "parental implementation does not take place in a vacuum, without benefit of professional expertise and guidance." They further state "the speech pathologist serves as a consultant and a team member responsible for the individualised programs for each child."

Fey (1986) supports a strong case for parental involvement. He states that it is sensible to search for intervention approaches that are time effective with regard to the clinician. It also is economically viable and enables the clinician "to treat more children at a significantly lower cost per child." Leaving these two aspects aside, is it an effective procedure for both parents and child? It allows for a greater generalisation of therapy given in the clinic to other (and arguably more important and motivating) aspects of the child's life. Too often "clinic" language bears little relation to the language the child needs and wants to use. Parents can be a helpful information source and indeed as clinicians we should remember that they, and the child, if possible, should be consulted at all stages of the programme as to its appropriateness.

Fey (1986) identifies various roles for the parents.

1. As Aides – where they reinforce the treatment provided in the clinic. The rationale for this being, that more of the same should result in greater effectiveness.
2. As *Primary Intervention Agents* – the parents being trained to take on the role of teacher. It must be remembered in this approach that many parents do not see "teaching" as their role; it upsetting the balance between child and parent.
3. As *A Child Oriented Approach* – here the child acts as the

programme catalyst and the parent takes the lead from the child's activities, capitalizing on language opportunities.
4. As *A Hybrid Approach* – this also offers significant advantages of opportunising on natural events and contexts: the clinician designed activities being reinforced in naturalistic settings of environment, play etc.

These last two approaches have been the ones utilised in this project.

In our programme, there was yet another component, the students, and their involvement will be discussed later.

THE PROJECT

In October 1986, it was decided to give group therapy to a small group of children who were severely developmentally learning disabled. Monitoring of the group's progress and evaluation of the procedures, although carried out on a regular basis, tended to be ad hoc and informal. However, this led the therapist and psychologist involved in the group to ask themselves questions.

1. What was the purpose of the group?
2. Who was the "client" in this case?
3. How do we or can we evaluate effectiveness?
4. What are the parents' perceptions of the group?
5. What are the students learning about service provision for these children?
6. How can we improve the quality of our service?

The clinic in the School of Clinical Speech and Language Studies in Trinity College, Dublin exists primarily to train student speech therapists. It functions during the academic year (i.e. October to late May) with a break during the summer months.

When the group reassembled in October 1987, we felt able to attempt to answer some of these questions, and to identify some ways of evaluating what we thought we were doing.

The group existed for two main reasons:

1. to train student speech therapists in the management of mental handicap.
2. to provide an intervention programme. This programme had two main facets,
   a) the service to the child itself.
   b) the facilitation of the parents as the programme deliverers.

Therefore to answer question two that we posed, the clients are both the parents (and families) and the child himself.

Taking this as a starting point, we identified our programme stages.

In October 1987, the five children ranged in ages from four years to seven years. Four of the children were Down's Syndrome and one (aged six years and seven months) Rubinstein Taybi Syndrome. This child was learning LAMH – a signing system developed in Ireland, for the mentally handicapped. The children were all assessed informally for levels of symbolic play and parents were asked to complete check lists and questionnaires at home.

These consisted of lists of activities and attempts to communicate; times when communication was at its peak; topics of communication; vocabulary; language and communicative interactions. From this data, a useful base line of communication was obtained and this was used to determine therapy. Formal test were not attempted in the main, except with one of the older children (aged seven years), when the Zimmermann Pre-School Language Scale and the Boehm Test of Pre-School Concepts were attempted. The results in the latter case were treated with caution due to the extended nature of testing (two sessions) and behaviour problems during testing.

The Group Session

The programme for the group sessions concentrated on pre-linguistic skills such as listening, attention, eye contact and turn taking and on vocabulary, position in space, auditory/visual sequencing. Video recordings were made of the group in the early stages.

Individual Sessions

These sessions were tailored to the needs of each child. An example of some of the aims would be: Comprehension of names and functions of objects; categorisation; putting two words together; imitation of sounds; syllable closure; specific aspects of phonology; putting two signs together etc. The accompanying parent would be involved in the individual session.

Timetable of Activities

Originally, the children met for group activities for approximately twenty minutes at the start of the session, and for ten minutes at the close of the session, with individual sessions comprising the centre position of the time. This was changed, at the students' suggestion.

The timetable now is: Individual   twenty minutes
                      Group   twenty minutes

Individual   ten minutes
Group   ten minutes

This has worked well. At the first individual session, any new work is presented, the children being more alert at this time. Also it prevents disruption of group activity should any child arrive late. The second individual session allows for the student clinician to consolidate the work of the preceding session, and the final group session is a time when more familiar aspects of the group session are re-presented, thus allowing for a successful conclusion to the group.

THE ROLES OF THE SESSION PARTICIPANTS

The Students

The students role with child and parent is that of therapy provider. She identifies the session aims and plans and presents the procedures. She also discusses with the parents any problems that have arisen during the preceding week. She works with the parent ensuring that all aspects of the therapy are understood, and discusses the "task sheet" for the next week. This task sheet is a written sheet of ideas that will promote the aims of the session and it is left to the parent to incorporate them into the child's day.

The Child

The child's role is that of service recipient. All aspects of the group and individual sessions are geared to each individual child's needs.

The Parent

The parent's role is that of advisor and client. The purpose of each aspect of therapy is identified and the parent is involved in planning activities. The parent's role is that of educator (with respect to their child and family) and educatee (with regard to learning the how and the why of assisting their child's communication).

The Psychologist and the Speech Therapist

Their role is to bring their particular professional skills to bear to the greatest benefit of child, parent and student. The psychologist works closely with the parent, advising and helping them with their problems. The speech therapist is more involved with the children and the students during the session. A second very important role the psychologist and speech therapist have, is as facilitators to the discussion of each session that is held with the students. At the close of each group session, a seminar is held, where all aspects of the session are under discussion, and from this, any changes in approach or therapy are planned.

At intervals during the year, parents attend without the children to review and plan future strategies.

THE RESULTS AND DISCUSSION

Results are subjective. All students report increased attention, turn-talking and listening skills. Parents are enthusiastic about the usefulness of the group and report progress in their child's attempts to communicate. One child now no longer requires group therapy, so arrangements have been made for her to receive individual therapy from now on. Her mother still wishes to attend the parent group discussions, so this will be arranged.

Two children have left the group – one because of the birth of a new baby which posed difficulties in attending, and one becuase of other parental commitments. These places have been filled during the course of the year.

The check lists provide some indication of progress.

As these two tables show, there have been changes both in communication topics and vocabulary size. The type of sentences used was also noted but as these showed such a wide variation, they have not been tabled. Nevertheless two and three element utterances are developing and use of prepositions of size, space and quantity are noted.

The results of this project are encouraging. Whether the improvements were as a result of specific intervention cannot be determined as this project was not and indeed not intended to be, a controlled study, but rather an attempt to evaluate therapy with a small group of children with mental handicap. What can be stated is: that the children communicate more, and about more topics; it also is possible to identify what they want to communicate about; that the parents and students contribute considerably to the implementation of the programme and that it provides a good learning experience to all involved.

REFERENCES

Belkin, A. (1983) Facilitating Language in Emotionally Handicapped Children in Winitz H. (Ed.) *Treating Language Disorders for Clinicians by Clinicians.* pp. 121–141. University Park Press, Baltimore.
Bricker, D. & Schiefelbusch, R. L. (1984) Infants at Risk. In McCormick, L. &

Table 1.   Communication topics

Communicates about	Oct. '87				May '88			
	Always	*Usually*	*Sometimes*	*Never*	*Always*	*Usually*	*Sometimes*	*Never*
Food or drink	3	2			4	1		
Toys	1	2	1	1	3	1	1	
Clothes	1	2	3		4		1	
Pets	2	1	2		2	2	1	
Other things			3	2	2	1	1	1
Parents	4	1			4	1		
Brothers & sisters	3	1	1		3	1	1	
Relatives	3		2		3	1	1	
Friends		2	1	2	1	1	2	2
Neighbours		2	3	1			2	2
Teacher	1	1	2	1	1	1		1
Babysitter		1	4	1		1		3
Other people		1	4	1				3
Eating	1	1	2	1	2	1	2	
Toileting	1	2	1	1	1	1	3	
Playing	1		3	1	1	1	1	2
Going for a ride	4		1	1	2	1	1	1
T.V.		1	3	1	2	1	1	1
Listening to music	1	1	2	1		2	3	
Other activities			2	3	2		3	

Table 2.   Vocabulary

	Oct. '87	April '88
Rachel	–	44
Gerard	16	26
Cathal	12	30
Aine	6	9

The fifth child's vocabulary is extensive
and therefore not included.

Schiefelbusch, R. L. (Eds.) *Early Language Intervention*. pp. 244–265.
Merrill, Columbus, Ohio.

Byers-Brown, B. (1984) Working through other People in Warner, J. A. W.
Byers-Brown, B. & McCartney, E. (Eds.) *Speech Therapy – a clinical
companion*. pp. 149–156. Manchester University Press, Manchester.

Cooper, J., Moodley, M. & Reynell, J. (1978) *Helping Language Development*.
Arnold, London.

Fey, M. E. (1986) *Language Intervention with Young Children*. Taylor and
Francis, London.

Fitzgerald, M. T., & Karnes, D. E. (1987) A parent-implemented language model
for at-risk and developmentally delayed pre-school children. *Top Language
Disorders* **7**(3), 31–46.

McConkey, R. & Price, P. (1986) Let's Talk. *Learning Language in Everyday
Settings*. Souvenir Press, London.

McCormick, L. & Goldman, R. (1984) Designing an Optimal Learning Program.
In McCormick, L. & Schiefelbusch, R. (Eds.). *Early Language Intervention*. pp. 202–241. Merrill, Columbus, Ohio.

The Role of Iconicity in Augmentative and Alternative Communication–Symbol Learning

L. L. Lloyd[1] and D. R. Fuller[2]

[1]*Purdue University, SCC-E, West Lafayette, Indiana 47907 USA*
[2]*Conway Human Development Center, 150 Siebenmorgan Road,*
Conway, Arkansas, 72032, USA

The paper discusses the role iconicity plays in the initial acquisition of augmentative and alternative communication (AAC) symbols. The preponderance of data suggests that iconicity has a facilitative effect on the learning of aided and unaided AAC symbols for several populations. This finding is true for all studies of comprehension and for most studies of production. For those symbols having little or no relationship to their referents, elaboration or enhancement is suggested as a means of aiding acquisition. Several areas of further research are also enumerated.

Over two decades ago, clinicians and educators working with disabled individuals began using augmentative and alternative communication (AAC) symbols and approaches. Through clinical experience, professionals formulated several hypotheses to explain why persons with severe disabilities were successful in acquiring visual AAC symbols while the learning of acoustic symbols (i.e., spoken words) proved to be unsuccessful. These hypotheses have been popularly referred to in the literature as symbol selection considerations (for a review of these considerations, see Lloyd & Karlan, 1984). While some selection considerations have been subjected to scientific inquiry, most of them are based upon clinical/educational observation and experience. The major focus of symbol characteristics research has been on the variable of iconicity.

Iconicity can be defined as the visual representation of a symbol to its referent. This variable can take one of two forms: transparency or translucency. A number of investigators (Bellugi & Klima, 1976; Brown, 1977, 1978; Doherty, 1985, 1985/1986; Fristoe & Lloyd, 1977, 1979;

Lloyd, Loeding & Doherty, 1985; Luftig, 1983) have offered a definition for these two entities as they relate to unaided symbols (e.g., manual signs and gestures) which in turn can be generalized to aided symbols (e.g., Blissymbols, pictographs, and Sigsymbols). A transparent symbol is one in which the shape, motion, or function of the referent is depicted to such an extent that the meaning of the symbol can be readily guessed in the absence of the referent. Transparency is operationally defined as "guessability." A translucent symbol is one in which the meaning of the referent may or may not be obvious but a relationship can be perceived between the symbol and referent once the meaning is provided. Translucency is operationally defined by subject ratings of the degree or amount of relationship of the referent perceived to be present in the symbol. There is an overlap between transparency and high translucency because symbols which are easily guessed are also naturally perceived as having a great degree of relationship to the referent. Opaque symbols are those in which no relationship is perceived even when the meaning of the symbol is known.

Several investigators have hypothesized that iconicity facilitates the learning of AAC symbols. More specifically, it has been proposed that AAC symbols possessing a strong visual relationship to their referents would be easier to learn than symbols having a weak or no visual relationship Brown, 1977, 1978; Fristoe & Lloyd, 1977, 1979). This hypothesis has been subjected to extensive investigation with both unaided and aided AAC symbols. Table 1 provides a summary of studies which have investigated this hypothesis for unaided symbols, while Table 2 lists the studies that have included aided symbols. It should be noted that the vast majority of this research has investigated the translucency aspect of iconicity. In part, this may be partially due to the belief that translucency is more psycholinguistically valid than transparency (Griffith, 1979/1980; Griffith & Robinson, 1980). Furthermore, for experimental purposes the translucency variable provides a better range of values than transparency.

Since Doherty (1985) has written an excellent review of the effect of iconicity on the comprehension and production of unaided symbols, only a brief summary (with some more recent research not covered by Doherty) will be provided here. For these symbols, the iconicity hypothesis has been tested with cognitively normal, cognitively impaired, and autistic individuals. Except for one case, the iconicity hypothesis has been supported with cognitively normal children and adults, and autistic persons who performed comprehension and/or production tasks (Brown, 1977, 1978; Doherty, 1985/1986; Konstantareas, Oxman, & Webster, 1978; Luftig & Lloyd, 1981; Mandel, 1977). The one exception is Doherty's (1985/1986) unpublished dissertation which investigated the

Table 1. Iconicity learning studies using unaided symbols (in chronological order)

Investigators	Subjects	Task	Results
Rogers, 1975	Mod/Sev MR	Production of iconic versus noniconic signs	No differences found
Brown, 1977, 1978	Normal children	Comprehension and production of ASL signs with correct vs incorrect labels	Ss remembered signs having correct labels
Mandel, 1977	Normal adults	Comprehension of iconic vs noniconic signs	Ss comprehended iconic signs
Konstantareas, Oxman, & Webster, 1978	Autistic/ MR	Comprehension and production of iconic vs noniconic signs	Ss learned iconic signs better
Snyder-McLean, 1978	Severe MR	Comprehension and production of iconic vs noniconic gestures	Ss learned iconic gestures better
Griffith,[a] 1979/1980 Griffith & Robinson, 1980	Mod/Sev MR	Comprehension of iconic vs noniconic manual signs	Ss learned iconic signs better
Polzer, Wankoff, & Wollner, 1979	Mod/Sev MR	Comprehension and production of iconic vs abstract[b] Signed English signs	Subject learned iconic signs better
Kohl, 1979/1980[a] Kohl, 1981	Severe MR	Production of iconic vs abstract[b] manual signs	No differences found
Luftig & Lloyd, 1981	Normal college students	Comprehension of high-iconic vs low-iconic manual signs	Ss recalled high-iconic signs better
Doherty & Lloyd, 1983	Mild/Mod MR	Production of high-iconic vs moderate-iconic manual signs	Ss acquired high-iconic/ one-handed signs better

Continued

Table 1 – continued

Investigators	Subjects	Task	Results
Goossens', 1983/1984	Moderate MR	Comprehension of manual signs	Learning data correlated with iconicity data from Ss and from adults
Luftig, 1983	Mod/Sev MR	Production of high-iconic vs low-iconic signs	Ss required less time to acquire high-iconic signs
Doherty, 1985/1986	Normal preschool children	Production of iconic vs noniconic signs	No differences found
Thrasher,[a] 1984/1985 Thrasher & Bray, 1984	Sev/Prof MR	Production of iconic vs noniconic signs	No differences found

[a] Contrary to typical APA publication style the reference for the complete dissertation has been included when the study has been published in a refereed journal to encourage further scholarship in this area through the use of the complete doctoral thesis.
    [b] "Abstract" can be assumed to mean "noniconic".

effects of translucency and motor difficulty on the production of signs by cognitively normal preschool children. Although more high translucency signs were learned than low translucency signs, the difference did not reach statistical significance.

In considering the population of individuals with cognitive impairments, the finding is less clear depending on whether the focus is on comprehension tasks or production tasks. When one considers comprehension of translucent signs, the facilitation hypothesis gains support (Goossens', 1983/1984; Griffith, 1979/1980; Griffith & Robinson, 1980; Konstantareas, Oxman, & Webster, 1978; Polzer, Wankoff, & Wollner, 1979; Snyder-McLean, 1978). However, inconsistent results have been obtained when production tasks have been used. Only Kohl (1979/1980, 1981), Rogers (1975), and Thrasher (1984/1985; Thrasher & Bray, 1984) found no iconicity effect in the production of manual signs. Other investigations involving production tasks (Doherty & Lloyd, 1983; Konstantareas, Oxman, & Webster, 1978; Liftig, 1983; Polzer, Wankoff, & Wollner, 1979; Snyder-McLean, 1978) have supported the hypothesis that iconicity facilitates the learning of unaided AAC symbols. The disparity in results for production tasks may be due in large part to the severity of cognitive impairment. For those investigations which did not support the iconicity hypothesis, subjects exhibited predominantly severe

Table 2. Iconicity learning studies using aided symbols (in chronological order)

Investigators	Subjects	Task	Results
Yovetich & Paivio, 1980	Normal adults	Comprehension of high-iconic vs low-iconic Bliss-like symbols	Ss learned more high-iconic than low-iconic symbols
Goossens', 1983/1984	Moderate MR	Comprehension of Blissymbols and Rebus symbols	Learning data for Rebus symbols correlated with iconicity data, but not for Blissymbols
Luftig & Bersani, 1985	Normal college students	Comprehension of high-iconic vs low-iconic Blissymbols	Ss learned high-iconic symbols better
Fuller, 1987/1988	Normal adults and children	Comprehension of high-iconic vs low-iconic Blissymbols	Both groups of Ss learned high-iconic symbols better
Mizuko,[a] 1985/1986 Mizuko, 1987	Normal children	Incidental learning of Blissymbols, PCS symbols, and Picsyms	Ss learned the transparent symbols

[a] Contrary to typical APA publication style the reference for the complete dissertation has been included when the study has been published in a refereed journal to encourage further scholarship in this area through the use of the complete doctoral thesis.

to profound retardation. On the other hand, in the studies which supported the facilitation hypothesis subjects exhibited mild to severe retardation. Methodological aspects of these studies also need to be examined. Two of the three papers have not yet been published in refereed sources, and the one published in a refereed journal (Kohl, 1981) has been questioned in terms of how iconicity was determined (Lloyd, Loeding, & Doherty, 1985).

As can be seen in Table 2, iconicity research has only relatively recently included aided AAC symbols. Within this research the aided symbols selected have been almost exclusively Blissymbols. In every study, translucency was found to be an important variable in the learning of aided AAC symbols (see Fuller, 1988 for a more detailed discussion). Luftig and Bersani (1985) and Fuller (1987/1988) reported that translucency had a facilitative effect on the learning of Blissymbols by cognitively normal adults. Furthermore, the data from Fuller (1987/1988) supported the iconicity hypothesis for cognitively normal children as young as four and one-half years of age. Yovetich and Paivio (1980)

Figure 1.   Example of the modification of a highly pictographic representation
          of "bird" to a lesser iconic, stylized Chinese character.

determined that representativeness (a concept very similar to translucency; for a discussion see Fuller & Stratton, 1990) facilitated the
incidental and paired-associate learning of Bliss-like symbols by normal
adults. Mizuko (1985/1986, 1987) also found iconicity to be a factor in the
incidental learning of Blissymbols by normal preschool children.

It could be concluded with reasonable certainty that iconicity (i.e.,
translucency) enhances the learning of AAC symbols for individuals
having normal cognitive abilities but severe physical impairments, and for
individuals having a mild to moderate degree of mental retardation.
Ideally, for these individuals the clinician/educator should consider
teaching an initial lexicon containing highly iconic symbols. Of course,
other factors must also be considered, such as the functionality of the
symbols and their acceptance by both the user and communicative
partners. Therefore, when choosing an initial lexicon the clinician/
educator should evaluate all necessary criteria for selection and choose
highly iconic symbols in as much as they meet as many of the other
selection criteria (e.g., functionality) as possible. If the clinician/educator
followed these guidelines, it could be conceivable that an initial lexicon
would contain a large proportion of highly iconic symbols with a lesser
proportion of symbols having lesser degrees of iconicity. What should the
teacher do to enhance the acquistion and retention of those symbols
which are not highly iconic? For these symbols, the answer lies in the
ability of the clinician/educator to manipulate iconicity through the
enhancement or elaboration of those features which serve as the basis for
the symbol's iconicity.

The concept of symbol elaboration or enhancement is not new. In fact,
for several graphic symbol systems the symbols have historically evolved
from more pictographic representations to the highly stylized and
relatively noniconic symbols which exist today. For example, Figure 1
illustrates hypothetically how the graphic Chinese symbol for "bird" may
have evolved from an iconic pictograph to a less iconic, highly stylized
character.

Figure 2. Enhancement of Blissymbols through the *Picture Your Bliss* (McNaughton and Warrick, 1984) method (reproduced from Vanderheiden and Lloyd, 1986, p. 101). The Blissymbolics used herein derived from the symbols described in the work, *Semantography*, original copyright see K. Bliss, 1965 Exclusive license, 1982 – Blissymbolic Communication Institute, 350 Rumsey Road, Toronto, Ontario, Canada M4G IR8.

Several attempts have been made to enhance the iconicity of both unaided and aided symbols so that learning would be facilitated. One example of unaided symbol elaboration is the Amer-Ind gestural system based upon American Indian handtalk (Skelly, 1979). Many symbols in this system were created specifically with elaboration in mind. Additional information is provided through the pantomiming of certain actions or by outlining the salient features of objects, thus strengthening the associational link which aids in retrieving the meaning of the symbol. A recent example of enhancement for aided symbols is the *Picture Your Bliss* technique (McNaughton & Warrick, 1984). This method is illustrated in Figure 2. The clinician/educator employs the use of added graphic information for symbols not possessing a high degree of iconicity so that the learner can make the associational link necessary to acquire and retain the symbols. Of course, the elaboration/enhancement of symbols to increase iconicity has been done for other symbols. Miller and Miller (1968, 1971) have demonstrated how traditional orthography can be modified or enhanced to aid in learning vocabulary words (see Figure 3).

A question immediately comes to mind in considering elaboration and/or enhancement techniques. Do methods creating or increasing iconicity facilitate or hinder the learning of AAC symbols? More specifically, how do these techniques affect individuals exhibiting various impairments? For example, two recent papers have considered the efficacy of symbol enhancement or modification and have obtained conflicting results. Diech and Hodges (1979) reported that they experienced difficulty in teaching Premack symbols (which are opaque) to individuals exhibiting mental retardation. The symbols were then modified to make them more pictographic. The result was an improve-

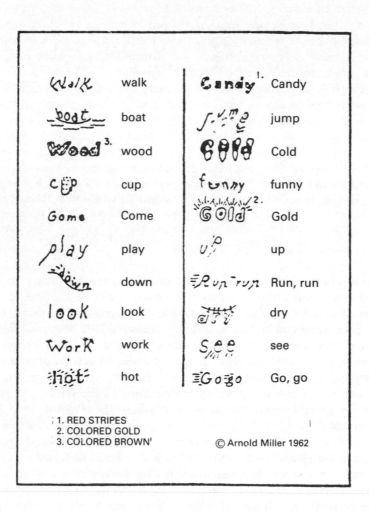

Figure 3.   Enhancement of traditional orthography through accentuation of words (Miller and Miller 1971) (reproduced from Clark and Woodcock, 1976, p. 565).

ment in learning for these individuals. On the other hand, Doherty and Lloyd (1983) conducted an identification task in which cognitively impaired adults were required to provide the meanings of a sample of Amer-Ind gestures. They found that elaboration did not help their subjects in identifying the gestures; for some subjects the elaboration even detrimentally affected identification. It is clear from these two reports that this aspect of iconicity has received very little empirical attention. Therefore, future research should focus to some extent on how the manipulation of iconicity affects the learning of AAC symbols for different symbol sets and systems and for individuals having various physical, cognitive and/or emotional impairments.

There are several other areas of iconicity research which need to be addressed in the future as well. For example, although evidence exists that iconicity data obtained from cognitively normal adults can be generalized to cognitively normal children and to individuals with mild to moderate mental retardation (e.g., Fuller, 1987/1988; Goossens', 1983/1984; Griffith,1979/1980; Griffith & Robinson, 1980; Konstantareas, Oxman, & Webster, 1978), it is not known if this trend will continue for individuals having severe to profound cognitive impairments. What it the extent to which adult translucency values will predict the learning of AAC symbols in these and other populations? Is there an age or cognitive level at which iconicity (as judged by adults with normal cognitive abilities) no longer aids in the acquisition and retention of symbols? These questions remain to be answered and future research should address these issues.

Another area of iconicity research which should receive some attention is the contextual learning of symbols. Dunham (1985/1986, 1989) investigated the effect of linguistic (i.e., two-sign combinations) and nonlinguistic (i.e., background locales) context on the ability of moderately cognitively impaired subjects to guess the meanings of manual signs. Her findings indicated that these individuals did not use contextual information to determine the transparency (or guessability) of manual signs. Dunham discussed her findings in terms of stimulus overselectivity. It is clear that this aspect of iconicity research is in dire need of additional empirical investigation.

Finally, to date there has not been a study reported in the literature that has examined the metalinguistic aspect of iconicity. Evidence is overwhelming that iconicity facilitates the learning of AAC symbols, but presently it is not understood exactly *how* iconicity aids in the acquisition and retention of symbols. What are the cognitive bases for determining iconicity, and how does iconicity act to mediate between symbol and referent? These questions are not going to be easy to answer, but they should be considered once we have progressed to the stage that metalinguistic processes can be analyzed with any degree of reliability.

Obviously, iconicity is still open to much empirical investigation. Many questions remain to be addressed. As research progresses to a point that these issues are resolved, we will finally understand how to manipulate iconicity to its maximal advantage so that our cognitively impaired students will learn and retain AAC symbols in the most effective and efficient manner.

ACKNOWLEDGEMENTS

The authors would like to thank the members of the Purdue Augmentative and Alternative Communication Research Group for their suggestions
during the development of this paper. The preparation of this paper was
partially supported by grants from the Office of Special Education and
Rehabilitation Services, United States Education Department
(G008630079). However, the contents do not necessarily represent the
policy of that agency and endorsement by the federal government is not
to be assumed.

Requests for reprints should be addressed to Lyle L. Lloyd, Professor
of Special Education and Professor of Audiology and Speech Sciences,
Purdue University, SCC-E, West Lafayette, Indiana 47907, USA.

REFERENCES

Bellugi, U., & Klima, E. (1976) Two faces of sign: Iconic and abstract. In S. R.
    Harnad (Ed.), *Origins and evolution of language and speech*. New York:
    Annals of the New York Academy of Sciences, Vol. 280, pp. 514–538.
Bliss, C. K. (1965) *Semantography*. Sydney: Semantography Publications.
Brown, R. (1977, May–June). *Why are signed languages easier to learn than
    spoken languages?* Keynote address at the National Association of the Deaf
    Symposium on Sign Language Research and Teaching, Chicago.
Brown, R. (1978) Why are signed languages easier to learn than spoken
    languages? Part two. *Bulletin of the American Academy of Arts and
    Sciences*, **32**, 25–44.
Clark, C. R., & Woodock, R. W. (1976) Graphic systems of communication. In
    L. L. Lloyd (Ed.), *Communication assessment and intervention strategies*.
    Baltimore: University Park Press.
Diech, R. F., & Hodges, P. M. (1979) *Language without speech*. New York:
    Brunner/Mazel, Inc.
Doherty, J. E. (1985) The effects of sign characteristics on sign acquisition and
    retention: An integrative review of the literature. *Augmentative and
    Alternative Communication*, **1**, 108–121.
Doherty, J. E. (1986) The effects of translucency and handshape difficulty on sign
    acquisition and retention by preschool children. (Doctoral dissertation,
    Purdue University, 1985). *Dissertation Abstracts International*, **46**, 3317A.
Doherty, J. E., & Lloyd, L. L. (1983, May). *The effects of production mode,
    translucency and manuality on sign acquisition by retarded adults*. Paper
    presented at the 107th Annual Conference of the American Association on
    Mental Deficiency, Dallas.
Dunham J. (1986) The transparency of manual signs in a linguistic and an
    environmental nonlinguistic context. (Doctoral dissertation, Purdue
    University, 1985). *Dissertation Abstracts International*, **47**, 146A.
Dunham, J. K. (1989, in press) The transparency of manual signs in a linguistic
    and an environmental nonlinguistic context. *Augmentative and Alternative*

Communication.

Fristoe, M., & Lloyd, L. L. (1977, March) *The use of manual communication with the retarded*. Paper presented at the Tenth Annual Gatlinburg Conference on Research in Mental Retardation and Developmental Disabilities, Gatlinburg, TN.

Fristoe, M., & Lloyd, L. L. (1979) Nonspeech communication. In N. R. Ellis (Ed.), *Handbook of mental retardation: Psychological theory and research* (2nd ed.). New York: Earlbaum Associates.

Fuller, D. R. (1987/1988) *Effects of translucency and complexity on the associative learning of Blissymbols by cognitively normal children and adults*. (Doctoral dissertation, Purdue University, 1987.) *Dissertation Abstracts International*, **49**, 710B.

Fuller, D. R. (1988) Further comments on iconicity. *Augmentative and Alternative Communication*, **4**, 180–181.

Fuller, D. R., and Stratton, M. M. (1990, in press) Representativeness versus translucency: Different theoretical backgrounds, but are they really different concepts? *Augmentative and Alternative Communication*, **6**.

Goossens', C. A. (1984) The relative iconicity and learnability of verb referents differentially represented as manual signs, Blissymbolics, and Rebus symbols: An investigation with moderately retarded individuals. (Doctoral dissertation, Purdue University, 1983). *Dissertation Abstracts International*, **45**, 809A.

Griffith, P. L. (1980) The influence of iconicity and phonological similarity in the perception of American Sign Language by retardates. (Doctoral dissertation, Kent State University, 1979.) *Dissertation Abstracts International*, **40**, 5398A.

Griffith, P. L., & Robinson, J. H. (1980) Influence of iconicity and phonological similarity on sign learning by mentally retarded children. *American Journal of Mental Deficiency*, **85**, 291–298.

Kohl, F. L. (1980) The effects of motoric requirements on the acquisition of manual sign responses trained directly and indirectly and the generalized acquisition of verbal responses by severely handicapped students. (Doctoral dissertation, University of Illinois, 1979). *Dissertation Abstracts International*, **40**, 4527A.

Kohl, F. L. (1981) Effects of motoric requirements on the acquisition of manual sign responses by severely handicapped students. *American Journal of Mental Deficiency*, **85**, 396–403.

Konstantareas, M. M., Oxman, J., & Webster, C. D. (1978) Iconicity: Effects on the acquisition of sign language by autistic and other severely dysfunctional children. In P. Siple (Ed.), *Understanding language through sign language research*. New York: Academic Press.

Lloyd, L. L., & Karlan, G. R. (1984) Nonspeech communication symbols and systems: Where have we been and where are we going? *Journal of Mental Deficiency Research*, **28**, 3–20.

Lloyd, L. L., Loeding, B. L., & Doherty, J. E. (1985) The role of iconicity in sign acquisition: A response to Orlansky & Bonvillian. *Journal of Speech and Hearing Disorders*, **50**, 299–301.

Luftig, R. L. (1983) Manual sign translucency and referential concreteness in the sign learning of moderately/severely mentally retarded students. *American Journal of Mental Deficiency*, **88**, 279–286.

Luftig, T. L., & Bersani, H. A. (1985) An investigation of two variables infiuencing Blissymbol learnability with nonhandicapped adults. *Augmentative and Alternative Communication*, **1**, 32–37.

Luftig, R. L., & Lloyd, L. L. (1981). Manual sign translucency and referential concreteness in the learning of signs. *Sign Language Studies*, **30**, 49–60.

McNaughton, S. & Warrick, A. (1984). Picture Your Blissymbols. *The Canadian Journal of Mental Retardation*, **34**, 1–9.

Mandel, M. (1977) *Iconicity of signs and their learnability by non-signers*. Paper presented to the National Symposium on Sign Language Research and Training, Chicago.

Miller, A., & Miller, E. E. (1968) Symbol accentuation: The perceptual transfer of meaning from spoken to printed words. *American Journal of Mental Deficiency*, **73**, 202–208.

Miller, A., & Miller, E. E. (1971) Symbol accentuation, single-tract functioning and early reading. *American Journal of Mental Deficiency*, **76**, 110–117.

Mizuko, M. I. (1986) Iconicity and initial learning of three symbol systems in normal three year old children. (Doctoral Dissertation, University of Wisconsin, 1985). *Dissertation Abstracts International*, **47**, 159B.

Mizuko, M. I. (1987) Transparency and ease of learning of symbols represented by Blissymbolics, PCS, and Picsyms. *Augmentative and Alternative Communication*, **3**, 129–136.

Polzer, K. R., Wankoff, L. L., & Wollner, S. G. (1979, April–May) *The acquisition of arbitrary and iconic signs: Imitation versus comprehension*. Paper presented to the New York State Speech and Hearing Association.

Rogers, G. (1975) The effects of iconicity on the acquisition of signs in Down's Syndrome children. Unpublished manuscript, Boston University.

Skelly, M. (1979) *Amer-Ind gestural code based on universal American Indian hand talk*. New York: Elsevier.

Snyder-McLean, L. (1978, November) *Functional stimulus and response variables in sign training with retarded subjects*. Paper presented at the 53rd Annual Convention of the American Speech and Hearing Association, San Francisco.

Thrasher, A. W. (1985) Effects of iconicity, taction, and training modality on the initial acquisition of manual signs by the severely and profoundly mentally retarded. (Doctoral Dissertation, University of Alabama, 1984). *Dissertation Abstracts International*, **45**, 2344–5B.

Thrasher, K., & Bray, N. (1984, March) *Effects of iconicity, taction, and training technique on the initial acquisition of manual signing by the mentally retarded*. Paper presented at the Seventeenth Annual Gatlinburg Conference on Research in Mental Retardation and Developmental Disabilities, Gatlinburg, TN.

Vanderheiden, G. C., & Lloyd, L. L. (1986) Communication systems and their components. In S. W. Blackstone (Ed.), *Augmentative communication: An introduction*. Rockville, MD: American Speech-Language-Hearing Association.

Yovetich, W. S., & Paivio, A. (1980) Cognitive processing of Bliss-like symbols by normal populations: A report on four studies. *Proceedings of the European Association for Special Education*, Helsinki, Finland.

Section VI

Educational Issues

Curricula Used with Handicapped Students in Developing Countries: Issues and Recommendations

D. Baine

Educational Psychology, University of Alberta, Edmonton, Alberta, Canada T2G 2G5

Various issues are discussed that are common to curricula used with handicapped students in Developing Countries. The issues reviewed include: a) the emphasis on memorization and examination rather than on comprehension and application of learning; b) the failure to relate curricula to the social, cultural, economic, political and geographic characteristics of the natural environment and c) the lack of ecological validity resulting from the adoption of Western curricula. Recommendations for improving curricula include: a) relating academic skills to functional tasks in the natural environment; b) using ecological inventories to develop curricula teaching functional skills required in students' contemporary and future environments and c) the integration of school and community.

Based on extensive on-site, mail and literature reviews, the paper discusses a number of issues common to curricula used with handicapped students in many Developing Countries. A number of recommendations for improving curricula are made.

In numerous Developing Countries, "special education curricula" are merely "watered-down" versions of regular education curricula. Some of the more difficult tasks have been replaced by simpler craft activities and/or a limited number and type of life skills. Because regular and special education share many common characteristics (Csapo, 1987), both types of curricula are reviewed in the discussion that follows.

In many cases, both regular and special education curricula are based on colonial models of education (Duminy, 1973, Mohanti, 1973, Sarr, 1981, Socrates, 1983). The major emphasis is on rote memorization of academic content and passing examinations (Buchanan, 1975; Duminy, 1973; Mbilinyi, 1977; Neufeldt, 1986; Rao, 1983). Much is gained from passing examinations that grant prestige and permit entrance to higher levels of instruction, employment and economic security, regardless of the skills learned. As a result, there is generally less concern with the content of curricula than there is with passing examinations (Rao, 1983). Little, if any, attention is given to comprehension, application and evaluation of knowledge and skills. Functional, life-skill training is usually minimal or nonexistent.

In India, for example, it is reported that educational institutions are generally oblivious to the problems and characteristics of their environments, especially those of disabled persons. Students and teachers are isolated from the realities of socio-cultural life and the world of work (Common Trust, 1985). As a result, many hours are spent teaching handicapped students skills they cannot master and cannot use. Many intellectually handicapped students never learn to read, write or do arithmetic well enough to use these skills in a functional way. In addition, since these students are not taught essential life-skills, following training, they are unable to function adequately in their everyday lives (Baine, 1986).

The situation is more serious in rural areas in which the majority of people live. Some of the subjects taught in rural schools bear little relationship to village environments (Mukherjee and Singh, 1983, Rao, 1983). Rural children often discover that their curricula, materials, and examinations are designed by and for people from more prosperous urban environments (Hawes, 1979). In South Africa, for example, it is reported that the highly academic curriculum provides poor preparation for life on the land or for the many early school leavers (Csapo, 1986; Hawkins, 1980; IIEP, 1977).

Problems are also found in vocational training programs. In East Africa, for instance, the training offered to people with mental handicaps in some vocational centres is not relevant to the needs of the community (Chege, 1984). In many countries, students are taught unmarketable vocational skills like basket making, pottery, and weaving. Unfortunately, the availability of attractive, and long-wearing synthetic fabrics, and inexpensive, mass produced, aluminium, stainless steel and plastic pots have reduced the need for weavers and potters. Unable to find employment, graduates of some of these programs sell their tools and turn to begging (Moriyama, 1982). Chege (1984) recommended that no vocational program should be planned without a careful assessment of current and projected community needs.

Many Developing Countries have adopted curricula designed for handicapped persons in North America and Europe. A number of problems arise when these curricula are used in Developing Countries. Developmental curricula, norm referenced to average children in average North American environments are not ecologically valid for use in

Developing Countries. These curricula teach a number of skills not required in Developing Countries and fail to teach a number of skills that are required. Nevertheless, these curricula are often used as universal standards of child development. For example, if a child, five years of age, living in a rural area of a Developing Country, is found to be unable to stack five rings on a peg in order of size, because the task is usually performed by North American children at approximately three years of age, a remedial program will be developed to teach the child to perform this task. Stacking rings on a peg is not an essential task; there is little demand in the natural environment to perform this task. The skills that underlie this task, e.g., size discrimination, eye-hand coordination, etc. are essential. However, to teach these underlying skills in a form that is different from that in which they must be performed in the natural environment, inhibits generalization and maintenance of the skills. Skills should be taught in the same form in which they must be performed in the natural environment. Because a child living in New York or London is unable to trap crayfish in a stream, get milk from a coconut or identify a ripe plantain (skills commonly performed by children living in rural fishing villages in Jamaica) is not sufficient reason to develop a remedial program to teach the child to perform these tasks, even if the underlying skills are essential (Baine, in press).

Frequently, Western curricula teach readiness or preacademic skills such as: building a tower of blocks, putting pegs in a pegboard, completing an interlocking picture puzzle, and putting geometric shapes into a formboard. These tasks are thought to be prerequisite to higher levels of development because average North American and European children are typically able to perform the tasks before they can perform higher level skills. Unfortunately, according to the research evidence, instructing children to perform these readiness tasks frequently does not result in an improvement in the performance of higher level tasks such as reading and writing. A number of researchers have concluded that rather than teach readiness and preacademic skills, academic skills should be taught directly, in the form in which they must eventually be performed (e.g., Bailey and Wolery, 1984; Hammill, 1982; Sippola, 1985; Velluntino et al., 1977). When a skill is taught directly in the form in which it must eventually be performed, no generalization is required. Unfortunately, teaching readiness skills not only fails to result in an improvement in academic skills, it also results in a waste of valuable instructional time in which academic skills could have been taught directly. Efficient teaching is crucial to handicapped students whose development is already behind that of their peers.

In the discussion that follows, recommendations are made for improving curricula used by handicapped students in Developing Countries.

RECOMMENDATIONS

1. Steps should be taken to change the attitudes of policy makers, administrators, teachers, curriculum developers and parents regarding the purpose of schooling. Academic skill training should be directly related to the common daily task demands students are required to perform in the environments in which they currently live or in which it is anticipated they may live in future. The careful blending of academic and practical skill training should have the following goals: a) acquisition of a sufficient number, level and type of academic skills to permit the student to achieve the highest level of academic training of which she/he is able to benefit; b) acquisition of basic life skills required to function effectively in home, school, community, and vocational environments, now and in the future; c) acquisition of a broad spectrum of skills, e.g. social, emotional, recreational, vocational, communication, etc. required to function adequately as an adult; d) acquisition of the skills required to adapt to environmental changes resulting from factors such as increased industrialization, technological change and migration from a rural to an urban area.

2. The community and the school should be integrated. Students should be taught in both the school and the community. Community people with specialized skills and equipment (e.g., local craftsmen, artisans, medical and agricultural personnel) should be brought into classrooms to advise teachers and to assist in teaching specific skills to students. In addition, students could be taught child care at the local nursery school, animal and plant care at the community farm, and carpentry and tinsmithing at the village workshop (Mbilinyi, 1977). Initial instruction of some skills may begin in classrooms. As students become more proficient, teaching may alternate between communities and schools. As students approach mastery, teaching may be conducted primarily in the community. Community-based teaching may be made possible by involving skilled people from the community in each phase of both community and school instruction. Bergmann (1985) provides an excellent discussion of how agriculture can be taught meaningfully at the primary level of school. He also describes the problems systems of education have to face when agriculture is included in the syllabus. Bergmann refers to several school programs in Africa in which agriculture has been included.

3. Curricula should be built following a study of the economic, social, political and cultural characteristics of the particular environments within which students live (Hawkins, 1980; Csapo, 1987; Ahmed, 1983). The skills taught in the curriculum should fulfill the immediate and long-range needs for individuals, the family and the community

(IIEP, 1977). The specific skills and knowledge taught will vary according to the locality in which the students live and will be different from region to region (Joshi, 1981). Vocational training should be offered in occupations that will be needed far into the future (Chege, 1984; Moriyama, 1982). All training in crafts should be closely related to the post primary vocational training the student will receive later (Csapo, 1987).

4. The Life Skills, Basic Needs and Non-formal Education programs (e.g., Botti, Carelli and Saliba, 1978; Mbilinyi, 1977; Saunders and Vulliamy, 1983, Tietze, 1985; Unesco-Unicef, 1978) designed for school dropouts, underprivileged children, regular elementary and secondary school children, and adults teach the type of skills that should be included in the curricula of handicapped children in Developing Countries. Examples of some of these skills are listed below.

   a. Reading, writing and arithmetic are related directly to real life situations in areas, such as, agriculture, health and nutrition.
   b. Communication: receptive and expressive language (reading, writing and speech) in applied settings e.g., social conversations and specific language functions in the home, community, and vocational environments.
   c. Recreation: individual, group and team; physical, cultural and social; at home, school and in the community; as participant or observer.
   d. Agriculture: soil cultivation, fertilization, irrigation; seed planting, using insecticides, controlling weeds; harvesting, transporting, storing, and marketing.
   e. Home management: food: selection, storage and preparation; nutrition; safe water collection, storage and use; waste disposal; safe and effective insect and rodent control; child training and care; budgeting; clothing selection, repair and cleaning; conflict management.
   f. Health care: communicable disease prevention, identification, treatment, and referral; prevention and treatment of injuries; personal physical hygiene: teeth, menstruation, etc.
   g. Vocational skills: e.g., agriculture, fishing, carpentry.

5. It is recommended that ecological inventories (Brown et al., 1979) be used to identify the common, daily, functional tasks nonhandicapped and handicapped persons in particular environments are required to perform. Curricula based on ecological inventories are ecologically valid for specific cultural, economic and geographic, urban and rural environments in Developing Countries. These curricula list functional

routine daily tasks as well as academic, recreational, communication and social skills. These skills are required in current and future home, community, school and vocational environments. Application of ecological inventories to Developing Countries is described in Baine (in press, 1986).

6. Preacademic and readiness tasks, such as those described in Baine (in press and 1986) should not be taught. It is recommended that functional skills should be taught directly in the form in which they must eventually be performed in the natural environment.

7. When curricula designed for other countries, for example, North America and Europe are being considered for adoption, tasks should be identified that will not be functional in Developing Countries. Note should also be made of tasks that are essential to Developing Countries and that are not listed in the curriculum. Essential skills that are taught in the curriculum in a different form or application than is commonly required in Developing Countries should also be noted.

REFERENCES

Bailey, D. and Wolery, M. (1984) *Teaching infants and preschoolers with handicaps*. Charles E. Merrill, Columbus, OH.

Baine, D. (1986) *Testing and teaching handicapped children and youth in Developing Countries*. Unesco, Paris.

Baine, D. (In press) *Assessment, Curriculum and Instruction of Handicapped Students in Developing Countries*.

Bergmann, H. (1985) Agriculture as a subject in primary school. *International Review of Education*, **31**, 155–174.

Brown, L., Branston, M.B., Hamre-Nietupski, S., Pumpian, I., Certo, N. and Gruenewald, L. (1979) A strategy for developing chronological age-appropriate and functional curricular content for severely handicapped adolescent and young adults. *Journal of Special Education*, **13**(1): 81–90.

Buchanan, K. (1975) *Reflections on education in the Third World*. Spokesman Books, London.

Chege, W. M. (1984) Vocational training for the mentally handicapped: Guidelines for a curriculum. *Special Education Bulletin for Eastern and Southern Africa*, **2**: 12–14.

Common Trust. (1985) *The True Challenge – A policy perspective: to integrate the disabled*. Karnataka Parents' Association for the Mentally Retarded Citizen, Bangalore, India.

Csapo, M. (1986) *Perspectives in education and special education in Southern Africa*. Centre for Human Development and Research, Vancouver, Canada.

Csapo, M. (1987) Special education in Sub-Saharan Africa. *International Journal of Special Education*, **2**: 41–67.

Duminy, P. A. (1973) *African pupils and teaching them*. L. Van Shaik Ltd, Pretoria, South Africa.

Hammill, D. (1982) Assessing and training perceptual-motor skills. In D. Hammill and N. Bartel *Teaching children with learning and behavior problems*. Allyn and Bacon, Boston.

Hawes, H. (1979) *Curriculum and reality in African primary school*. Longman, England.

Hawkins Associates. (1980) *The physical and spatial basis for Tanskei's first, five year development plan*. Salsbury, Zimbabwe.

Hulley, P. M. and Templer, S. L. (1984) The importance of prevocational training for handicapped children. *Special Education Bulletin for Eastern and Southern Africa.* **2**: 5–7.

IIEP, (1977) *Learning needs in rural areas: Case study of Kwamsis Community School Project*. International Institute for Educational Planing RP/243, 7–9 rue Eugene-delacroiz, 75016, Paris.

Joshi, S. (1981) *Educational Rehabilitation*. Kulapath, Sri Balakrisha Joshi Educational Foundation, Madras, India.

Karugu, G. K. (1984) Preparing the handicapped for the world of work and independence. *Special Education Bulletin for Eastern and Southern Africa*, **2**: 8–11.

Mbilinyi, M. (1977) Primary school education: Aims and objectives of primary education. In *The young child study in Tanzania: Age 7–15*. Tanzania National Scientific Research Council. P.O. Box 4302, Dar Es Salaam, Tanzania.

Moriyama, A. (1982) *The education of the handicapped for life in Developing Countries*. Publisher not identified.

Mukherjee, H. and Singh, J. S. (1983) The new primary school curriculum project: Malaysia. *International Review of Education*, **29**: 247–257.

Neufeldt, A. H. (1987) Poverty complicates disability issues. *The Association for Persons with Severe Handicaps: Newsletter*, **1**: 3.

Rao, S. V. (1983) *Demand for education and its implications for reform at the village level*. International Institute for Educational Planning. Paris.

Sippola, A. E. (1985) What to teach for reading readiness – A research review and materials inventory. *The Reading teacher*, **39**: 162–167.

Unesco-Unicef. (1978) *Basic services for children: A continuing search for learning priorities*. Unesco, Paris.

Velluntino, F. R., Steger, B. M., Moyer, S. C., Harding, C. J. and Niles, J. A. (1977) Has the perceptual deficit hypothesis led us astray? *Journal of Learning Disabilities*, **10**: 375–385.

Designing Appropriate Environments for People with Profound and Multiple Learning Difficulties

J. Ware

*University of London Institute of Education, Department of Educational
Psychology and Special Educational Needs, 24–27 Woburn Square,
London WC1H 0AA*

Over the years a number of aspects of the environment provided for
adults with profound and multiple learning difficulties (PMLDs) have
been investigated. Two studies into two aspects of the school
environment for children with PMLDs are reported: organization and
staff:pupil interactions. The effect of Room Management was particularly investigated.

The results suggest that adults divide their time more evenly between
more and less handicapped children, and that all children experience a
more positive interactive environment when Room Management is
operating.

The implications of these results for designing environments for
people with PMLDs are discussed.

INTRODUCTION

Over the four decades during which psychological research has been
carried out with people with profound and multiple learning difficulties,
there has been a gradual shift in the focus of investigation. Initially,
following Fuller's historic conditioning experiment (Fuller, 1949), the
chief concern was with the extent to which operant techniques would
enable profoundly handicapped people to be taught new skills. During
this period a volume of work was amassed demonstrating the success of
such methods with at least some profoundly handicapped people. (See,
for example, the reviews by Switzky *et al.*, 1982, and Presland, 1980.) The
realization that such laboratory-based research was having little impact on
the lives of the great majority of profoundly handicapped people led to a
greater interest in the environments provided for severely and profoundly
retarded persons.

Over the years a number of different aspects of the environment have been investigated including: location and size of the facility, furnishing and occupational materials, training and numbers of staff, organization, and the types of interaction which take place between staff and clients. Some general conclusions can be drawn from these studies; for example, that the provision of occupational materials tends to result in a decrease of stereotyped and self-injurious behaviour (Berkson and Mason, 1963a & b; Sturmey *et al.*, 1984); that there is a greater amount of interaction between staff and clients in highly structured environments; and, most pervasively and importantly, that it *cannot* be assumed that all clients in the same facility actually experience the same environment, with more handicapped clients being less occupied and receiving a smaller proportion of adult time (Repp *et al.*, 1987). Advice to teachers of children with PMLDs on the type of classroom environment to provide for their pupils is often based on these findings. (For example, the dissemination of Room Management as part of the EDY programme (McBrien *et al.*, 1981).) However, with very few exceptions, these studies have been conducted in residential environments for adults.

This paper reports the results of two observational studies which we conducted into the school environment for children with PMLDs. Two major aspects of the environment were studied in depth, together with the interrelationship between them: organization and staff:pupil interactions.

METHOD

For each study two classes were selected from a wider survey of provision for children with PMLDs (Evans and Ware, 1987) which were providing structured environments, and had staff-ratios approximately equal to the modal value in S.E. England of around 1:3.

For each study, data were collected using two separate observation schedules: a detailed schedule using theoretically derived behaviour categories to observe individual children, and an attention/engagement schedule modified from the PLA-check (Planned Activity Checklist) (Risely and Cataldo, 1973). The detailed observation schedule categorized all adult and child behaviours in a mutually exclusive and exhaustive fashion. The evidence that profoundly handicapped children make few, if any deliberate initiations and the view taken in much of the mother-infant interaction literature, that mothers treat young normal babies 'as if' their behaviours are initiations, persuaded us that no attempt should be made to categorize child behaviours according to whether or not they represented deliberate initiations. Child behaviours were therefore simply divided into three types: vocal, non-vocal and play. Adult initiations were divided into two types: allows for dialogue (AD), and does not allow for dialogue (NAD). Initiations which allow for dialogue are those in which the adult approaches the child in such a way as to allow for a response; the essential element is that the adult leaves time for the child to respond after making the initiation. Initiations which do not allow for dialogue, by contrast, are those in which the adult approaches the child in such a way as not to give the child an opportunity to make a response. Child and adult responses were both divided into three types, positive, negative and none. Each child was observed individually for approximately 100 minutes in 10 minute sessions over about four months. Engagement/ attention data on the whole class was collected for 20 minutes at regular intervals throughout each study. In addition, at the end of the observation period in each Class, each child was assessed using the Uzgiris and Hunt Scales (Uzgiris and Hunt, 1975). Fuller details of the method adopted in these studies including the derivation and development of the categories used in the detailed observation schedule can be found in Ware and Evans, 1988 (copies of both the detailed observation schedule and the attention engagement schedule can be obtained from the author).

Reliabilities

The attention/engagement schedule had inter-observer reliabilities (in Studies 1 and 2 respectively) comparable to those obtained for the original PLA-check at 88.4% and 93.6% for engagement, and 97.6% and 95.0% for attendance. Agreement for adult attention was 90.4% and 100% and for the combination of attention and engagement 83.5% and 90.9%.

Reliabilities for the detailed observation schedule were somewhat lower, which reflects the more complex nature of the instrument. For the main categories of behaviour of concern in the two studies reported here, person initiating the interaction, adult initiations and adult responses, percentage agreements were respectively 89.8%, 75.8% and 97.2% for Study 1 and 87.3%, 70.4% and 98.3% for Study 2.

STUDY 1

Physical Environment

The two classes (Classes A and B) in the first study were situated in two schools for children with moderate and severe learning difficulties at opposite ends of the same town. The two schools were both about 10 years old, purpose-built and designed by the same architect, thus the physical environment in the two classes was fairly similar; both classrooms were light, reasonably spacious, and provided with a curtained-off area for individual work and a teachers' cupboard; both had direct access to an enclosed outside yard.

Staff and pupils

Both classes had an overall staff:pupil ratio of 1:3, but in Class A there were nine pupils with three staff (a teacher and two assistants) and in Class B there were six pupils with two staff (a teacher and one assistant). All the children in both classes had profound and multiple learning difficulties; no child obtained more than 33 items in total on the six Uzgiris and Hunt Scales and only five (three in Class A and two in Class B) were independently mobile. Chronological ages ranged from 64–152 months in Class A (mean 104.3) and from 126–193 months in Class B (mean 173.7).

Organizational Environment

Both classes provided structured environments: in Class A the children were divided for much of the day into three small groups with each staff member being responsible for one group, while in Class B a modified system of Room Management was in force (one member of staff worked individually with each child in turn while the other 'managed' the five remaining children, with roles alternating regularly between staff).

RESULTS

Data obtained using the attention/engagement schedule showed that on average children in both Classes A and B were involved in interaction with an adult about once every 12 minutes (once every 11.4 minutes in Class A; once every 12.3 minutes in Class B). In both classes by far the greatest number of interactions lasted one minute or less (56.7% in Class A and 38.5% in Class B). However, there were considerably more lengthy interactions in Class B than in Class A (Class A mean length of interaction 1.84 minutes; Class B mean length of interaction 3.49 minutes).

General analysis of the data collected using the detailed observation schedule showed that staff generally took the leading role in interactions, being the initiator on significantly more occasions than the child (Wilcoxon Test N = 13 T = 10 p < .005). There was no difference between the two classes in the extent to which interactions were initiated by staff and children.

More detailed analysis of data from the detailed observation schedule showed that in addition staff in both classes ignored the great majority of child behaviours (95.6% in Class A and 87.1% in Class B). However, when the time that an adult was with the child was considered separately, a rather different picture emerged, with staff in Class B responding to over half the children's behaviours (54.5%) while staff in Class A only responded to about one-eighth. This difference was significant (Mann Whitney $U = 0$ $p < 0.01$). Staff in Class B were also significantly more likely to respond positively to children's behaviours than staff in Class A (Mann Whitney $U = 5.5$ $p < 0.5$).

Individual children

Analysis of the data at the level of individual children showed that in both classes, as might be predicted from the adult studies, more handicapped children were less likely to receive positive patterns of interaction (see Table 1). Here, too, there were differences between the classes, particularly in the distribution of staff time between children, which was significantly associated with degree of handicap in Class A but not in Class B.

STUDY 2

Physical Environment

The two classes in the second study (Classes C and D) were situated in two schools in the same LEA, but in towns about 15 miles apart. School C was a purpose-built school for children with severe learning difficulties and about 13 years old, while school D was an ex-junior training centre at least 20 years old. Classes C and D both occupied more than one room in their respective schools, but in both one large room was used for the majority of classroom activities. Neither Class C nor Class D had areas specifically designed for individual work, but both used an adjacent 'spare' classroom for this purpose. Neither class had adequate cupboard space; in Class C this meant that bulky equipment was stored in a corner of the classroom, while in Class D such equipment was housed in an adjacent empty room while not in use.

Staff and pupils

There were 12 children and four staff (a teacher, two nursery nurses and one assistant) in Class C for the majority of the study, giving an overall staff:pupil ratio of 1:3, and eight children and three staff (a teacher, a nursery nurse and an assistant) in Class D, giving an overall staff:pupil ratio of 1:2.7. All the children in both classes had profound and multiple learning difficulties; no child obtained more than 39 items on the Uzgiris Hunt Scales and only one child in each class was mobile without

Table 1. Association (Kendall's TAU) between severity of handicap and patterns of interaction in Classes A and B

	% of AD inits. received	% of responses to AD inits.	% of time adult was present
Class A	0.43	0.67[a]	0.76[a]
Class B	0.86[b]	0.86[b]	0.60

[a] significant at p < 0.05
[b] significant at p < 0.01

assistance. Chronological ages ranged from 85–197 months in Class C (mean 124.1) and from 75–219 months in Class D (mean 130.9).

Organizational Environment

Both classes used a Room Management procedure for the majority of the day, operating with a room manager, a mopper-up and two individual workers in Class C, and a room manager, a mopper-up and one individual worker in Class D.

RESULTS

Results from the attention/engagement schedule for the Classes C and D were remarkably similar overall. On average children were engaged in interaction with an adult once every 14.8 minutes in Class C and once every 13.2 minutes in Class D. As in Classes A and B, in Classes C and D the most common duration for interactions was less than one minute (55.7% in Class C and 52.1% in Class D). The mean length of interaction was virtually identical in the two classes (2.42 minutes in Class C and 2.40 minutes in Class D).

Overall levels of engagement were lower in Classes C and D than in Classes A and B (5% in Class C and 24% in Class D) but despite this the general picture which emerges from Study 2 is very similar to that found in Study 1, with children who are on average unlikely to be engaged unless they are receiving adult attention (see Table 2).

The overall picture which emerges from the analysis of the detailed observation schedule is also similar to that found in Study 1. As in Classes A and B, staff in Classes C and D generally took the leading role in interactions, being the initiator on significantly more occasions than the child (Wilcoxon Test n = 20 T = 0 p < .005). Staff in Classes C and D also ignored the majority of child behaviours (94.7% in Class C and

Table 2.　Mean engagement and attention in Classes C and D

	% eng.	% att.	% att. eng.	% non-att. eng.
Class C	25.4	23.8	49.6	17.6
Class D	24.0	28.3	47.5	16.7

Table 3.　Association (Kendall's TAU) between severity of handicap and patterns of interaction in Classes C and D

	% of AD inits.	% of responses to AD inits.	% of time adult was present
Class C	0.51^b	0.26	0.39^a
Class D	0.18	0.40	0.76^b

[a] significant at $p < 0.05$
[b] significant at $p < 0.01$

92.4% in Class D). However, when the time that an adult was with the child was considered separately, Classes C and D were more similar to Class B than to Class A with staff in both classes responding to children's behaviours between one-quarter and one-third of the time. Staff in Classes C and D were also more likely to respond positively to children's behaviours when they did respond.

Individual children

Once again analysis of data at the level of individual children showed that more handicapped children were less likely to receive positive patterns of interaction (see Table 3).

Interrelationship between interactive and organizational environments

Comparison of the results of the two studies suggests that there may be some effects of organization on interactive patterns; in particular children in the three classes using Room Management were more likely to receive responses, and responses which were positive, to their behaviour, than children in the small groups class. When Room Management and Non-Room Management sessions in Classes C and D are compared the impression of a relationship between organization and interactive patterns

Table 4. Mean length of interaction engagement and attention under R-M and non-R-M in Classes C and D

		Mean length in mins.	% eng.	% att.	% att. eng.	% non-att. eng.
Class C	RM	2.79	34.0	29.1	46.7	28.1
	NRM	2.06	18.4	19.4	53.1	10.0
Class D	RM	1.70	18.7	20.7	42.3	16.4
	NRM	2.88	28.8	33.3	49.6	20.8

is strengthened, particularly with regard to the interactive environment experienced by individual children.

Table 4 shows results from the attention/engagement schedule for Room Management and Non-Room Management sessions in the two classes. It is clear that whereas in Class C, mean length of interaction, engagement, individual attention and a crucial measure – engagement while not receiving individual attention – are all higher during Room Management sessions, the position is reversed in Class D. This curious effect is probably due to the fact that Non-Room Management sessions were very different in the two classes. In Class C most Non-Room Management sessions observed were singing or signing sessions conducted immediately before lunch, while in Class D most Non-Room Management sessions took place when a member of staff was absent from the classroom for some reason (for example a child's case conference). On these occasions the remaining staff in Class D would agree among themselves to abandon the mopper-up and individual worker roles and both concentrate on keeping the children engaged. During Non-Room Management in Class D, therefore, there were to some extent two Room Managers operating.

Closer examination of Table 4 shows that the two classes were similar in one important and curious way. As can be seen from Column 4 of this Table, the mean percentage of time children are engaged while they are receiving adult attention is lower during Room Management than during Non-Room Management. Since Room Management is intended to alter the nature of staff attention so as to increase engagement (Porterfield and Blunden, 1978) it appears from this finding that Room Management is not working as intended in these two Classes. However, examination of the results for individual children suggests a rather different picture. Under Room Management in both classes attention is more evenly divided between children than when Room Management is not operating. Under Non-Room Management more handicapped children receive only half the amount of adult attention received by less handicapped children, while under Room Management they receive over three-quarters of the amount received by less handicapped children. The view that it is this more even division of adult attention amongst the children which is responsible for the mean percentage engagement being lower during Room Management is supported by the fact that under both Room Management and Non-Room Management conditions more handicapped children were engaged for only about one third of the time even when they were receiving attention. It seems therefore that under Room Management more handicapped children receive a larger share of adult time, but that this adult attention is *not* particularly successful in increasing the extent to which these children are engaged.

When data collected using the detailed observation schedule were divided between Room Management and Non-Room Management sessions, due to children's absences there were only sufficient data to compare the two types of organization for 17 of the 20 children (11 in Class C and six in Class D). Comparison of the percentage of staff behaviours which were initiations and responses under the two conditions enables the hypothesis that adults are more responsive to children when Room Management is in force to be tested. A significantly higher proportion of staff behaviours were responses under Room Management than under Non-Room Management and this difference was significant (Wilcoxon's Test $N = 17$, $T = 17.5$ $p < 0.05$).

By contrast with the more even division of adult time between children and the greater responsiveness of adults under Room Management than under Non-Room Management, there were no systematic differences between Room Management and Non-Room Management sessions in the extent to which AD adult initiations were received. However when the extent to which the percentage of AD initiations received was correlated with severity of handicap under Room Management and Non-Room Management conditions there was a tendency for the correlation to be less strong when Room Management was in force (see Table 5). In fact the association is negative in Class D and only significant in Class C under Non-Room Management.

CONCLUSION

The results of the two studies reported here suggest that there is a complex interrelationship between the organizational and interactive environments provided for children with profound and multiple learning difficulties within a school setting. In general the highly structured form of organization known as Room Management resulted in a more positive interactive environment, with more comparatively extended periods of interaction with adults and a greater degree of responsiveness from adults

Table 5. Association (Kendall's TAU) between severity of handicap and percentage of AD initiations received in Classes C and D under R-M and non-R-M

	RM	NRM
Class C	0.30	0.56[a]
Class D	-0.47	-0.33

[a] significant at $p < 0.01$

to children's behaviours. In addition Room Management seemed to reduce the extent to which more handicapped children within the group received less positive patterns of interaction with adult time being more evenly distributed between children when Room Management was in force. Arguably, then, Room Management was particularly beneficial to the more handicapped children.

There are two important implications for the design of environments for people with profound and multiple learning difficulties. First that environmental manipulations need to be carefully evaluated in terms of their effects on individuals as well as the group as a whole. Secondly and most importantly, that it is possible to create environments which are comparatively positive in terms of their potential for promoting development in even the most handicapped individuals, and that at least some of the variables which contribute to such positive environments can be identified and manipulated.

REFERENCES

Berkson, G. and Mason, W. A. (1963a) Stereotyped movements of mental defectives III Situation Effects. *AJMD* **68**: 409–412.

Berkson, G. and Mason, W. A. (1963b) Stereotyped movements of mental defectives IV The effects of toys and the character of acts. *AJMD* **68**: 511–524.

Dunst, C. J. (1980) *A Clinical and Educational Manual for use with the Uzgiris and Hunt Scales of Infant Psychological Development*. University Park Press: Baltimore.

Evans, P. and Ware, J. (1987) *Special Care Provision: The Education of Children with Profound and Multiple Learning Difficulties*. NFER-Nelson, Windsor.

Foxen, T. and McBrien, J. (1981) *The EDY In-Service Course for Mental Handicap Practitioners. Training Staff in Behavioural Methods*. Manchester University Press, Manchester.

Fuller, P. (1949) Operant conditioning of a vegetative human organism. *Am. J. Psych.* **62**: 287–290.

McBrien, J. A. and Foxen, T. H. (1981) *The EDY In-service Course for Mental Handicap Practitioners: Instructors' Handbook*. Manchester University Press. Manchester.

Porterfield, J. and Blunden, R. (1978) Establishing an Activity Period and individual skill training within a day setting for profoundly mentally handicapped adults. *Research Report No. 6*. Mental Handicap in Wales Applied Research Unit, Cardiff.

Presland, J. (1980) Educating 'Special Care' Children: A Review of the Literature. *Educ. Res.* **23**: 20–38.

Repp, A. C., Felce, D. and de Kock, U. (1987) Observational Studies of Staff working with Mentally Retarded Persons: A Review. Research in Developmental Disabilities **8**: 331–350.

Risley, T. R. and Cataldo, M. F. (1973) *Planned Activity Check: Materials for Training Observers*. Unpublished paper, Centre for Applied Behavior Analysis. Kansas.

Sturmey, P. and Crisp, T. (1984b) The effects of Room Management on stereotyped and self-injurious behaviour in six profoundly mentally handicapped young adults. *Bulletin of the British Psychological Society* **37**: A22.

Switzky, H. N., Haywood, H. C. and Rotatori, A. F. (1982) Who are the severely and profoundly retarded? *Educ. and Train Ment. Ret.* **17**: 268–272.

Uzgiris, I. and Hunt, J. McV. (1975) *Assessment in infancy: Ordinal scales of psychological development*. University of Illinois Press: Urbana.

Ware, J. and Evans, P. (1988) Allowing for dialogue? – Observing Interactions between Children and Staff in 'Special Care' Classes. Submitted for publication.

A Model for Integrating Processing Strategies and Curriculum Content

A. F. Ashman and R. N. F. Conway

Fred and Eleanor Schonell Special Education Research Centre,
University of Queensland, St. Lucia, Queensland 4067 Australia

This paper describes a teaching strategy developed as a method of integrating information processing theory within the regular curricula topics of the classroom. It assists students and teachers to work systematically toward solving curriculum tasks by providing a framework for task solution. This framework involves the use of plans and coding strategies which students learn to use as an integral part of the curriculum. Rather than being an after-thought or an additional teaching unit that is presented independently of curriculum content, the teaching strategy overlays teachers' usual instructional methods and techniques.

Cognitive psychology has become a prominent theoretical foundation for research into learning problems. The study of memory strategies and super-ordinate processes has been linked with academic skills and cognitive deficiencies manifested by learning and intellectually disabled students (Das, Bisanz, & Mancini, 1984; Logie & Baddeley, 1987; Waters, Bruck, & Seidenberg, 1985). During the past five years, several instructional approaches have demonstrated the value of cognitive instructions including metacognition in reading, mathematics and spelling instruction (Brown & Palincsar, 1982; Logan & Barber, 1985; Wong, 1986). However, concern for the incorporation of both strategy and meta-strategy training in the classroom led to the development of a model called Process-Based Instruction (PBI). This model grew from the recognition of a need to develop teaching and learning procedures that are relevant to various curriculum areas and topics (Conway, 1986).

In the first section of this paper, we outline the foundations of the instructional method. In the second, we describe the procedure and techniques, and in the third section, we summarize key features of the model which have contributed to its success.

LINKING THEORY WITH INSTRUCTION

Problem solving and planning are the basic elements of the teaching-learning process. Problem solving involves the interrelationship of knowledge, strategies and planful activity, and the execution of appropriate goal-oriented actions (Anderson, Greeno, Kline, & Neves, 1981; Fredericksen, 1984; Simon, 1980). For intellectually disabled students to develop problem solving competence and to transfer newly acquired skills to activities outside the training setting, they must learn how to adapt these skills to new situations. Hence, the focus of instruction is not only the use of strategies appropriate for the task at hand, but also the development of an understanding of how effective problem solving occurs.

While planning and problem solving are closely related terms, the former has an independent research heritage in several domains including intellectual abilities (Berger, Guilford, & Christensen, 1957), information processing theory (Hayes-Roth & Hayes-Roth, 1979; Miller, Galanter, & Pribram, 1960) and neuropsychology (Luria, 1973). Planning is the process involved in making judgments about goals, determining task demands, establishing the available information upon which decisions are made, evaluating the most expedient means of achieving the goal, enacting procedures, and monitoring performance. However, translating cognitive concepts (such as strategies, planning and problem solving) into classroom practice requires consideration of learner (knowledge, skills, ability) and instruction (ecological, content, and teaching) variables (Marsh, Price & Smith, 1983).

COMPONENTS OF CLASSROOM INSTRUCTION

The current model recognizes the interaction between students' processing competence, teaching strategies employed by the teacher, and the curriculum content. It is a premise of Process-based Instruction that these four components are interdependent and of equal status (Ashman & Conway, in press). There are four main components.

Plans

An effective plan provides a structured action sequence that leads to the successful completion of a curriculum task by a student who possesses the prerequisite information and skills. Plans are not the same as task analyses. Task analysis is the process of breaking complex behaviour into components and links (the what-to-teach) to determine the teaching objectives. Teaching objectives must be sufficiently well-defined so that they can be achieved by the student during instruction. Plans enable students to complete examples during learning of the teaching objective.

Coding

Coding refers to the input, storage and retrieval of information. It relates to the individual's method of deriving meaning from the information being presented. Two forms of coding have been identified. One form is called concurrent processing (it also has been called holistic, quasi-spatial, simultaneous, synthetic-appositional or parallel-multiple processing by various researchers). The second is called serial (or successive, sequential, or analytic-propositional).

In some cases, success on a task can occur from the use of one coding strategy only. For example, serial coding would assist a student to blend sound "chunks" when reading words aloud. In other curriculum tasks, competence in both concurrent and serial coding may be required for success. For instance, a mental arithmetic calculation requires both concurrent and serial coding; serial coding helps students keep the information "active" in their minds while concurrent coding enables them to seek the relationship between the elements of the problem and the elements in the number knowledge base. Plans and coding competence act interdependently to provide the information processing skills necessary for achievement.

Cooperative teaching and learning

In any classroom, the teacher is responsible for the selection of the academic content, the teaching sequence, and the organization of the daily and weekly schedule. These responsibilities are extended in PBI to include the initial development of plans and the identification of appropriate coding strategies for curriculum tasks. In introducing PBI, the teacher must develop effective plans as models for the students. However, the responsibility for learning does not rest solely with the teacher. It is the shared responsibility of both teacher and students to evaluate the effectiveness of teaching and learning. From this perspective, students are full members of the teaching-learning process, regardless of their level of ability. The requirement to use plans and coding strategies encourages students to become more involved in the learning activity.

Cooperative teaching and learning strategies are important academically as they lead to a decrease in the amount of "dead time" in which students receive no direct instruction (Polloway, Cronin, & Patton, 1986). At the same time, they provide the teacher with an alternative to individualized instruction which is difficult to achieve in large classrooms (Zigmond, Levin, & Laurie, 1985). Greater peer interaction results in better reasoning skills for all group members and increases the likelihood of the transfer of skills (Johnson, Flanagan, Burge, Kaufman-Debriere, & Spellman, 1980). Furthermore, cooperative teaching and learning leads to improved social acceptance while ensuring that students are not disadvantaged academically (Madden & Slavin, 1983).

One of the more important outcomes of peer group interactions is the initiation of student language during the teaching-learning process. In PBI, student language and elaboration (that is, putting the plans and problem solving activities in students' own words) are the bases of integrating the new content and the new learning strategies. The learning process then takes on added meaning for the student and is more likely to be retained and generalized.

Curriculum content

The final factor in the teaching-learning equation is curriculum content. In the present model, curriculum topics are analyzed in terms of their coding demands, and plans are devised (first by the teacher, later by the students) which lead to successful learning and problem solving. Cognitive concepts and teaching strategies are integrated into curriculum areas and topics rather than being complementary or supplementary to the regular classroom activities.

A MODEL OF CLASSROOM INSTRUCTION

The current teaching model involves five phases. Each of these will be described briefly.

Phase One

The essence of mixed ability instruction is to be found in this first phase, *Assessment*, which refers only to entry skills. When a student confronts a specific curriculum task, three element (curriculum knowledge; coding competence; existing problem solving skills) are evaluated by the teacher and three possible categories of learners emerge in regard to a specific task.

Category A learners have a knowledge base which is both consolidated and automated. Information is retrieved easily in terms of content, coding strategies, and plans. For the task at hand, the learner is proficient and may continue on the same task as a Category A learner (for example, attempting additional examples at the same level of difficulty), or may proceed to a higher level task in the task analysis. Category B learners require assistance in obtaining a solution to the current task as coding, planning or curriculum content elements may not be sufficiently developed for task completion. An instruction sequence is necessary to augment existing skills and strategic behaviour to enable the student to solve the task. Finally, Category C learners do not have the knowledge base needed for task completion. The task is beyond the ability of the learner and is not appropriate at this time.

For a specific curriculum task, only Category B learners need to engage in the PBI sequence. Being capable of solving the task, Category A learners may be assigned a more sophisticated or higher level activity within the task analysis, or if the conditions are appropriate, act as peer tutors to Category B learners (or Category C learners in a lower level task). As students become proficient in the use of coding strategies and plans, they become Category A learners.

Phase Two

In the *Orientation* phase, the teacher introduces (or reviews, in later PBI sequences) the relevant plans, coding strategies, and curriculum content. The teacher's role during this phase is to focus attention on the value of developing effective plans as a means of working systematically towards solving the curriculum task. Plans are defined, described, and exemplified so that the students understand how they are used, why they are used, and where they can be used to help solve problems and to learn. Students also are introduced to the concept of coding, and emphasis is given to the importance of dealing with information either concurrently or serially. In others words, students learn how information is presented and how they may capitalize on their existing skills to help them deal with new content.

Phase Three

This is the *Strategy Development* or teaching phase in which the teacher emphasizes how content and teaching strategies are integrated. This involves a three-step cycle. When new content is introduced, the teacher states the plan to be used (emphasizing the content, coding requirements and prerequisite skills), the students enact that plan, and then restate the plan. The teacher repeats the cycle until students are able to demonstrate their ability to use the plan and appropriate coding strategy (e.g., on blackboard or worksheet examples). The teacher also determines the level of proficiency required to move to the next phase of instruction.

Whenever it is appropriate, the teacher refers to examples of plans and coding already known to the students. Later in the teaching-learning sequence, students generate their own plans when the content becomes familiar. The class or small group works through a sample task using the plan and coding strategy and students learn to internalize plans by describing them in their own words.

Phase Four

Transfer and generalization are defined in terms of the application of plans and strategies to different aspects of the curriculum. Transfer relates to the correct use of plans and coding strategies in tasks that are related in terms of specific skill application. For example, a plan for adding the suffix "ing" to a verb in which the final consonant is doubled would be equally appropriate for tasks involving the addition of "ed". These activities belong to the same task cluster and are taught as part of the *Intra-task Transfer*.

To ensure that students can apply plans and coding strategies beyond the demonstration plan and tasks, the teacher provides additional examples within the task cluster. The importance of this phase lies in the deliberate move away from the teacher generated plan by requiring students to develop plans for similar tasks. Cooperative teaching and learning strategies are important during this phase as they highlight the roles of student language, and the elaboration of personal plans.

Phase Five

This phase, *Consolidation and Generalization*, has two components. Consolidation refers to proficiency within the task cluster when students are able to reduce their reliance on all steps of the plan to solve the task. Merging steps within the plan is a result of usage, experience and teacher guidance, as measured by on-going assessment. An abbreviated plan may be developed by individual students, groups of students, or the whole class. The aim is to incorporate plans and coding strategies related to the focus curriculum task so that students move to Category A status.

Generalization refers to the application of plans and coding strategies to other task clusters. For example, a plan for completing two column addition with carrying might be used by a student when calculating how much money to tender for the purchase of three items at a local store. These arithmetic tasks belong to different task clusters. Students must perceive the need to use a plan and the appropriate coding strategy in a situation where the knowledge base alone is insufficient for task solution. The knowledge of plans, coding and content gained during the current teaching sequence becomes part of the consolidated knowledge base and to be used in a new curriculum task.

KEY FEATURES OF THE MODEL

Process-Based Instruction has been trialled in several teaching settings. An early version of PBI was developed as a resource room instruction model in which students with mild intellectual disabilities were withdrawn from their regular classroom activities for three 20 minute periods each week (Ashman, 1985). The focus of the intervention was to develop information processing skills without specific reference to curriculum content. While several studies indicated the value of the prototype, the application to whole classrooms of students with varying intellectual competencies was the goal of the project.

Currently, the model outlined above has been the basis for instruction in several classrooms containing students with mild intellectual disabilities or learning difficulties. The change in students' performance has been recorded and the results show significant gains over peers who receive regular instruction without PBI. Statistically significant gains were recorded across a range of academic tasks including reading accuracy and comprehension, and mathematics operations, applications, and knowledge. Significant improvement was also noted on information processing tasks. The model has also been used in a mainstream high school class with a similar degree of success.

There appear to be several factors which have contributed to the success of Process-Based Instruction: The first is from the application of information processing theory and concepts to classroom activities and curriculum content. Relevance and efficacy are two principles which apply across the age and ability dimensions.

The second key to the success of PBI is the identification of students for whom the current academic task is appropriate. Only when the academic task is appropriate is it possible to effect change. The awareness of Category A, B, or C learners sensitizes the teacher to select appropriate materials and activities for individual students or for small groups.

The third key is the student's ownership of plans and appropriate coding strategies. One of the important benefits of the transfer from student to teacher is the acceptance of responsibility for learning. Students will accept this responsibility only if they have a positive attributional belief system.

The fourth key to success is the explicit division of transfer and generalization. It is in the consolidation and generalization phase, when plans are streamlined, that students come to understand the value and importance of generalizing beyond the training task cluster.

The final key to success is the willingness of the teacher to adapt current teaching strategies to include PBI. While the terminology used to describe PBI may be "new", teachers may recognize that the principles are neither novel nor necessarily innovative. PBI is essentially appropriate student oriented teaching practice and is consistent with the methods used by many teachers. However, PBI is more than just good practice. It combines logical and consistent teaching practice with procedures that have been derived from sound educational and psychological research.

REFERENCES

Anderson, J. R., Greeno, J. G., Kline, P. J., and Neves, D. M. (1981) Acquisition of problem-solving skills. In J. R. Anderson (ed), *Cognitive Skills and their Acquisition* (pp. 191–230. Hillsdale, N.J.: Erlbaum.

Ashman, A. F. (1985) Process-based interventions for retarded students. *Mental Retardation and Learning Disability Bulletin*, **13**, 62–74.

Ashman, A. F., and Conway, R. N. F. (In press) Cognitive Strategies in Special Education. London: Routledge.

Berger, R. M., Guilford, J. P., and Christensen, P. R. (1957) A factor-analytic study of planning abilities. *Psychological Monographs* **71**, Whole No. 435.

Brown, A. L., and Palincsar, A. S. (1982) *Inducing strategic learning from texts by means of informed, self-control training* (Tech. Rep. No. 262). Champaign, ILL: University of Illinois at Urbana-Champaign, Center for the Study of Reading.

Conway, R. N. F. (1986) Teaching strategies in special education: A continual challenge in all learning environments. *New South Wales Journal of Special Education*, **6**, 11–16.

Das, J. P., Bisanz, G. L., and Mancini, G. (1984) Performance of good and poor readers on cognitive tasks: Changes with development and reading competence. *Journal of Learning Disabilities*, **9**, 549–555.

Fredericksen, N. (1984) Implications of cognitive theory for instruction in problem solving. *Review of Educational Research*, **54**, 363–407.

Hayes-Roth, B., and Hayes-Roth, F. (1979) A cognitive model of planning. *Cognitive Science*, **3**, 275–310.

Johnson, J. L., Flanagan, K., Burge, M. E., Kaufman-Debriere, S., and Spellman, C. R. (1980) Interactive individualized instruction with small groups of severely handicapped students. *Education and Training of the Mentally Retarded*, **15**, 230–237.

Logan, G. D., and Barber, C. Y. (1985) On the ability to inhibit complex thoughts: A stop-signal study of arithmetic. *Bulletin of the Psychonomic Society*, **23**, 371–373.

Logie, R. H., and Baddeley, A. D. (1987) Cognitive processes in counting. *Journal of Experimental Psychology: Learning, Memory, and Cognition*, **13**, 310–326.

Luria, A. R. (1973) The Working Brain. Harmondsworth, England: Penguin.

Madden, N. A., and Slavin, R. E. (1983) Mainstreaming students with mild handicaps: Academic and social outcomes. *Review of Educational Research*, **53**, 519–569.

Marsh, G. E., Price, B. J., and Smith, T. E. C. (1983) *Teaching Mildly Handicapped Children: Methods and Materials*. St. Louis: C. V. Mosby.

Miller, G. A., Galanter, E.H., and Pribram, K. H. (1960) *Plans and the Structure of Behavior*. New York: Holt, Rinehart, and Winston.

Polloway, E. A., Cronin, M. E., and Patton, J. R. (1986) The efficacy of group versus one-to-one instruction: A review. *Remedial and Special Education*, **7**, 22–30.

Simon, H. A. (1980) Problem solving and education. In D. T. Tuma and R. Reif (eds), *Problem solving and education: Issues in teaching and research.* (pp. 81–96. Hillsdale, NJ: Erlbaum.

Waters, G. S., Bruck, M., and Seidenberg, M. (1985) Do children use similar processes to read and spell words. *Journal of Experimental Child Psychology*, **39**, 511–530.

Wong, B. Y. L. (1986) A cognitive approach to spelling. *Exceptional Children*, **53**, 169–173.

Zigmond, N., Levin, E., and Laurie, T. E. (1985) Managing the mainstream: An analysis of teachers' attitudes and student performance in mainstream high school programs. *Journal of Learning Disabilities*, **18**, 535–541.

Establishing Basic Reading Skills in Moderately Retarded Children

F. R. Hoogeveen and P. M. Smeets

Behavior Analysis Unit, Department of Psychology, Leiden University,
Hooigracht 15, 2312 KM Leiden, The Netherlands

The present study describes a project to develop and evaluate
instructional procedures for teaching moderately retarded children basic
reading skills. The project involved four studies on teaching letter-sound
correspondence, phonemic awareness skills (blending and segmentation), and decoding. The studies indicate, that these skills can be
effectively taught to moderately retarded children.

INTRODUCTION

Reading is an important skill for mentally retarded persons to
independently participate in society. Reading requires at least two skills:
letter-sound correspondence and phonemic awareness (Chall, 1983;
Bateman, 1979). Letter-sound correspondence refers to the ability to
respond to graphemes with appropriate phonemes. Phonemic awareness
involves phoneme blending, that is, responding to a sequence of isolated
speech sounds by pronouncing the words they constitute, and phoneme
segmentation, that is, isolating the sounds of a spoken word. Research
evidence suggests that blending and segmentation are causally related to
success in reading instruction (Perfetti *et al.*, 1987; Wagner & Torgesen,
1987; Williams, 1980).

The present paper describes a project to develop and evaluate
instructional procedures for teaching moderately retarded students the
aforementioned skills required for independent reading. The project
involved four studies.

PROCEDURES FOR ESTABLISHING BASIC READING SKILLS IN MODERATELY RETARDED CHILDREN

Letter-sound correspondence

Mentally retarded students may have difficulties with learning to respond to graphemes (Smeets & Lancioni, 1984). Studies with non-handicapped and difficult-to-teach children have shown that the training of letter-sound correspondence can be improved by using concrete, meaningful connectives that link the stimulus and response terms in memory (Ehri *et al.*, 1984; Lancioni *et al.*, 1981). Two kinds of procedures involving pictures as mnemonics have been used, *first-sound mnemonics* and *action sound mnemonics*. First-sound mnemonics (Ehri *et al.*, 1984; Lancioni *et al.*, 1981; Marsh & Desberg, 1978) involve the use of pictures the names of which begin with the sound to be trained (e.g., a picture of a *flower* for the grapheme *f*). Action sound mnemonics (e.g., Coleman & Morris, 1978; Marsh & Desberg, 1978) involve pictures of objects associated with typical action sounds (e.g., the "oo" sound of an owl) identical to the corresponding phoneme of the target letter. These studies indicate that for mnemonics to be effective, (a) the letter should be a distinctive component of the picture (for example, the digraph *oo* as the eyes of an owl) (Ehri *et al.*, 1984; Lancioni *et al.*, 1981), and (b) the switch from the pictorial prompts to the letters should be graduated (Marsh & Desberg, 1978).

Two studies were carried out to evaluate the use of mnemonics with moderately retarded students. In a first study, a first-sound mnemonic procedure was used for teaching letter-sound correspondence (Hoogeveen *et al.*, 1988). Four students with IQs ranging from 47 to 68 (M=58) participated. The letters appeared as salient features of visually portrayed common objects (e.g., an ice cream with the embedded grapheme *Y* [in Dutch pronounced as "i"], or a goose with the embedded grapheme *G*; see Figure 1). The training procedure consisted of four steps. The first step was designed to establish imitative control of the required verbalizations, that is, a self-cueing response (i.e., naming the portrayed object while prolonging or re-iterating the initial phoneme) followed by the repetition of the initial phoneme (e.g., "iiiiice-i", or "g-g-g-g-goose-g"). The second step was designed to transfer the control from the modeled responses to the pictures. The subjects were to emit the same responses in the presence of the visual cues, but without help. The third step was aimed at shifting the control from the pictures to the graphemes. Figure 2 shows how the pictorial elements were gradually eliminated without changing the embedded graphemes. The fourth step was the same, except that self-cueing responses were no longer allowed. For example, when presented the letter *Y*, the subjects were now to respond with "i" rather than with "iiiiice-i".

Figure 1.   Examples of first-sound mnemonics for *Y* (*ice*) and *G* (*goose*).

All subjects successfully completed the program. However, the error rates were high, particularly in Steps 2 (M=36.6%) and 4 (M=43.3%). The elimination of vocal cues in Step 2 frequently resulted in simply naming the picture (e.g., "ice" instead of "iiiiice-i"),. or the name of a picture plus another inappropriate phoneme (e.g., "ice-o"). Similar problems were observed in Step 4, when subjects were required to respond only with phonemes. These data indicated that the first-sound mnemonic procedure was an effective but not an efficient procedure for teaching letter-sound correspondence.

In a second study an action sound mnemonic procedure was used for establishing letter-sound correspondence (Hoogeveen *et al.*, 1987). It was speculated that since this procedure does not require phoneme segmentation and allows the sounds to be meaningful, some of the problems encountered in the first study (see above) might not occur. Seven children with IQs ranging from 27 to 43 (M=37) served as subjects. Each grapheme was presented as a distinctive and accentuated feature of a drawn common object (see Figure 3). The training consisted of four steps. The first step was to establish imitative control of phonemes within the context of a short story together with the picture of the object (e.g., a story of a dog, shown on a picture, tired of running and breathing heavily "h"). The second step was the same except that the experimenter no longer modeled the action sound (phoneme) of the object. The third step was aimed at shifting the control to the pictures (no story). The fourth step was directed at shifting the control from the pictures to the graphemes. As in the previous study (Hoogeveen *et al.*, 1988), this was achieved by fading out the pictorial elements, while keeping the dimensions of the (embedded) graphemes the same. All subjects learned the target behaviours in a nearly errorless fashion. The percentages of correct responses in Steps 1 to 4 averaged 91.1.

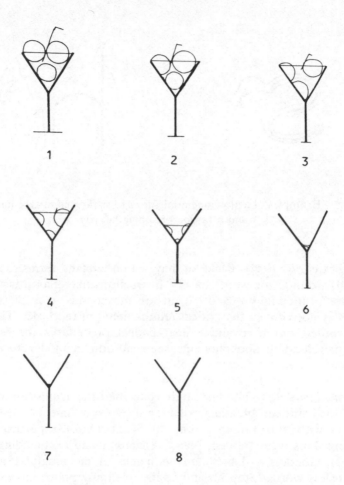

Figure 2. The gradual reduction of the pictorial prompt for *Y*.

Phonemic awareness

Children may also have difficulties with blending phonemes into words and segmenting phonemes from a larger vocal chain (Liberman, 1973; Liberman & Shankweiler, 1985). These difficulties may be related to several variables. First, phonemes pronounced in isolation do not bear much resemblance to blended phonemes. Phonemes are not discrete but coarticulated units of the soundstream (Liberman *et al.*, 1967). Second, nonreading children seldom if ever use individual phonemes, and hence may be totally unfamiliar with isolated speech sounds (Lewkowicz, 1980). Finally, commonly used instructions may be inadequate (Backman, 1983;

Figure 3.   Examples of action mnemonics for *s* (a snake making the hissing sound
"s") and *h* (a dog breathing heavily "h").

Stanovich *et al.*, 1984). Children may not understand terms such as (first
or final) "sounds" or word "parts". Instructions like "Say it fast" or "Put
together" ("blending"), and "What are the sounds in . . ." (segmentation) may not convey the critical requirements of the tasks. Two studies
were carried out to evaluate instructional procedures for establishing
phoneme blending and phoneme segmentation in moderately retarded
children.

Phoneme blending.   The first study concerned the acquisition training of
increasingly difficult blending skills (Hoogeveen & Smeets), 1988). Seven
children with IQs ranging from 30 to 51 (M=43) participated. Six
blending skills were trained, blending words (Step 1), blending syllables
(Step 2), blending syllables and phonemes of meaningful (Step 3) and
meaningless words (Step 4), and finally, blending phonemes (V-C, C-V)
of meaningful (Step 5) and meaningless words (Step 6). All steps
consisted of multiple substeps and involved procedures to gradually
increase the pauses between verbal stimuli (words, syllables, phonemes)
from 0 sec to 1.5 sec. In Steps 1, 2, 3, and 5, pictures were initially used
and then withdrawn for prompting the designated blending responses.
For example, in Step 3, subjects were to blend items such as "ca . . . t"
and "bu . . .s". The first substep of this step was directed at establishing
imitative control of the required (blending) responses (0-sec pause
between components). Each trial, the experimenter presented four
pictures representing target words (e.g., cat, pig, bed, sun) and modeled
the correct (blending) response (e.g., "cat"). The subject was to imitate
the modeled response and point to the corresponding picture. Substeps 2,
3, and 4 were the same, except that the pauses between word components
(CV-C) were extended to 0.8, 1.1, and 1.5 sec, respectively. The two final

substeps were the same as Substep 4 (1.5 sec pauses between components), except that in Substep 5 picture pointing was no longer allowed and in Substep 6 no pictures were used.

The program resulted in all subjects learning the target behaviours. In addition, several other relevant findings were obtained. First, training of some steps resulted in substantial improvements in pretraining performance in all or some subsequent steps. Second, the training data provided empirical support for the facilitative effect of the pictorial prompts. Elimination of these prompts (Substep 6), however, frequently resulted in a marked decline in performance. Finally, the data revealed a continuous shift from failures to blend (e.g., "ca . . .t" instead of "cat") to blending errors (e.g., "mat" instead of "cat") to correct blending ("cat"). This finding suggests that the acquisition of blending skills occurred in two phases, one in which the subjects acquired the concept of blending, that is, came to understand the nature of the task; and one in which they learned to demonstrate these skills accurately and reliably.

Phoneme segmentation

The effect of a training program for teaching moderately retarded students to isolate final consonant phonemes of CVC-words was assessed in a subsequent study involving two experiments (Hoogeveen *et al.*, 1988). Experiment 1 assessed whether the subjects' failure to isolate final phonemes was due to the inadequacy of the verbal instruction ("What is the final sound in . . .") and the lack of familiarity with isolated speech sounds. Experiment 2 evaluated the effects of a time-based stimulus manipulation procedure for teaching the students the segmentation task. Sixteen students with IQs ranging from 35 to 72 (M=52) participated.

In Experiment 1, subjects were taught to repeat the last of two sequentially presented consonants (e.g., "What is the final sound in /k . . .t/") (experimental condition), or to point to pictures representing CVC-words (control condition). Most subjects initially had problems with repeating only the last phoneme, indicating that, at first, they did not understand the instructions. The successive training of this task, however, did not help the subjects with isolating the final phonemes of CVC-words.

In Experiment 2, subjects were randomly assigned to one of two conditions. In one condition, subjects were trained to isolate final phonemes of meaningful CVC-words. The training comprised five steps, involving the gradual reduction of pauses between components (CV-C; e.g., "boo . . k", "ca . . .r") from 1.5 sec to 0 sec ("book", "car"). The other condition was the same, except that (components of) meaningless CVC-words were used (e.g., "ri . . .v"). Both conditions resulted in all subjects reaching criterion performance, although there was some indication that the semantics interfered with learning. This interference, however, was only temporary.

Decoding

The study by Hoogeveen and Smeets (1988) also showed that skill in letter-sound correspondence and phonemic awareness is a necessary but not a sufficient condition for word reading. Although the subjects had acquired both prerequisite skills for reading, they still had difficulty with reading two- and three-letter-words. This finding is in accordance with the 'limited attention capacity' model proposed by LaBerge and Samuels (1974). This model implies that unless the accurate performance of each component skill requires limited attention, their concerted performance is bound to fail due to limited attention capacity. Empirical evidence supports this view. Farmer *et al.* (1976) demonstrated that letter-sound correspondence and sound blending training did not help young students to improve their reading performance until they could sound out letters effortlessly (through overtraining). In the Hoogeveen and Smeets (1988) study, letter-sound correspondence and sound blending training enabled the students to correctly read 70% and 20% of the two- (CV, VC) and three-letter-words (CVC), respectively. Additional training was successful in improving the subjects' performance above the 90% level.

CONCLUSION

Until about 20 years ago, virtually no reading research was conducted with moderately retarded children. According to Singh and Singh (1986), this was mainly due to the prevailing notion (e.g., Kirk, 1972) of these children lacking the cognitive prerequisites to benefit from reading instruction.

Even now, few papers on reading research deal with the problems of the mentally handicapped (Singh & Singh, 1986). Moreover, most programmes developed for these children have used a whole-word approach for teaching simple word-recognition skills. Although successes have been reported (e.g., Smeets *et al.*, 1984) Worrall & Singh, 1983), this approach does not provide the child with the basic skills that are required for independent reading.

Present studies indicate, however, that these skills can be effectively taught to moderately retarded students. Although this finding is encouraging, much additional research is clearly needed for developing programmes that are effective in teaching mentally retarded persons to read.

ACKNOWLEDGEMENT

The studies described in this paper were supported by the Praeventiefonds (Research Grant 28-1063).

REFERENCES

Backman, J. (1983) The role of psycholinguistic skills in reading acquisition: A look at early readers. *Reading Res. Q.* **18**: 466–479.

Bateman, B. (1979) Teaching reading to learning disabled and other hard-to-teach children. In: L. B. Resnick and P. A. Weaver (eds), *Theory and practice of early reading*. vol. 1, pp. 227–259. Earlbaum, Hillsdale.

Chall, J. S. (1983) *Learning to read: The great debate*. 2nd ed. McGraw-Hill, New York.

Coleman, E. B. and Morris, G. (1978) Generalization tests: A terminology that focusses attention on fixed-effect restrictions. *J. Reading Behav.* **10**: 377–392.

Ehri, L. C., Deffner, N. D. and Wilce, L. S. (1984) Pictorial mnemonics for phonics. *J. Educ. Psychol.* **76**: 880–893.

Farmer, A. R., Nixon, M. and White, R. T. (1976) Sound blending and learning to read: An experimental investigation. *Brit. J. Educ. Psychol.* **46**: 155–163.

Hoogeveen, F. R., Smeets, P. M. and van der Houven, J. E. (1987) Establishing letter-sound correspondences in children classified as trainable mentally retarded. *Educ. Train. Ment. Retard.* **22**: 77–84.

Hoogeveen, F. R. and Smeets, P. M. (1988) Establishing phoneme blending in trainable mentally retarded children. *Remed. Spec. Educ.* **9**: 46–53.

Hoogeveen, F. R., Smeets, P. M. and Lancioni, G. E. (1988) Teaching moderately retarded children basic reading skills. *Res. Deve. Disabili.*, in press.

Hoogeveen, F. R., Birkhoff, A. E., Smeets, P. M., Lancioni, G. E. and Boelens, H. H. (1988) Establishing phoneme segmentation in moderately retarded children. Submitted for publication.

Kirk, S. (1972) *Educating exceptional children*. 2nd ed. Houghton Mifflin, New York.

LaBerge, D. and Samuels, S. J. (1974) Toward a theory of automatic information processing. *Cogn. Psychol.* **6**: 293–323.

Lancioni, G. E. (1981) Avviamento alla lettura tramite insegnamento programmato. *Psicologia e Scuola* **17**: 16–27.

Lewkowicz, N. (1980) Phonemic awareness training: What to teach and how to teach it. *J. Educ. Psychol.* **72**: 686–700.

Liberman, A. M., Cooper, F. S., Shankweiler, D. P. and Studdert-Kennedy, M. (1967) Perception of the speech code. *Psychol. Rev.* **74**: 431–461.

Liberman, I. Y. (1973) Segmentation of the spoken word and reading acquisition. *Bulletin of the Orton Society* **25**: 65–77.

Liberman, I. Y. and Shankweiler, D. (1985) Phonology and the problems of learning to read and write. *Remed. Spec. Educ.* **6**: 8–17.

Marsh, G. and Desberg, P. (1978) Mnemonics for phonics. *Contemp. Educ. Psychol.* **3**: 57–61.

Perfetti, C. A., Beck, I., Bell, L. C. and Hughes, C. (1987) Phonemic knowledge and learning to read are reciprocal: A longitudinal study of first grade children. *Merrill-Palmer Quarterly* **33**: 283–319.

Singh, N. N. and Singh, J. (1986) Reading acquisition and remediation in the mentally retarded. In: N. R. Ellis and N. W. Bray (eds), *International review of research in mental retardation.* vol. 14, pp. 165–199. Academic Press, Orlando.

Smeets, P. M. and Lancioni, G. E. (1984) Acquisition of non-vocal communication and discrimination learning in severely handicapped children. In: J. Dobbing, A. D. B. Clarcke, J. A. Corbett, J. Hogg and R. O. Robinson (eds), *Scientific studies in mental retardation.* pp. 375–392. MacMillan, London.

Smeets, P. M., Lancioni, G. E. and Hoogeveen, F. R. (1984) Effects of different stimulus manipulations on the acquisition of word recognition in trainable mentally retarded children. *J. Mentl. Defic. Res.* **28**: 109–122.

Stanovich, K. E, Cunningham, A. E. and Cramer, B. B. (1984) Assessing phonological awareness in kindergarten children: Issues of task comparability. *J. Exp. Child Psychol.* **38**: 175–190.

Wagner, R. K. and Torgesen, J. K. (1987) The nature of phonological processing and it's causal role in the acquisition of reading skills. *Psychol. Bull.* **101**: 192–212.

Williams, J. P. (1980) Teaching decoding with an emphasis on phoneme analysis and phoneme blending. *J. Educ. Psychol.* **72**: 1–15.

Worrall, N. and Singh, Y. (1983) Teaching TMR children to read using integrated picture cueing. *Am. J. Ment. Def.* **87**: 422–429.

Encouraging Contingent Responding in Children With Severe and Profound Learning Difficulties

S. M. Glenn and Y. O'Brien

School of Psychology, Lancashire Polytechnic, Preston PR1 2TQ, England

This paper discusses different approaches to the study of infant development and the implications of these for work with infants with learning difficulties. Contingency responding research is seen as particularly relevant as it has provided the earliest demonstrations of infants' actions on their social and object environments. Further it is argued that for infants with profound and multiple learning difficulties intervention using microcomputer controlled artificial contingencies may be beneficial.

Preliminary work developing equipment and an experimental paradigm for contingency research is described, together with initial results for non-handicapped infants.

THEORIES IN DEVELOPMENTAL PSYCHOLOGY AND ASSESSMENT/INTERVENTION

1. The question of whether it is appropriate to use developmental models based on normally developing children to guide work with children with learning difficulties has been widely debated in the literature and we do not propose to dwell on this other than to note that:

a) The most explicitly developmental theory is Piaget's and there is little disagreement with his description of the sequence of stages of sensori-motor development in children with severe and profound learning difficulties.

b) Even those researchers who argue that comparative work is conceptually and methodologically unsound, will use theoretical models taken from the normal literature to guide their endeavours (e.g. see Kopp and Krakow, 1983).

Our particular interest and work is in the early developmental period (0–12 months), and there is a large amount of information available in the general literature.

345

2. Two major theorists with widely differing views are Piaget and J. J. Gibson. Piaget (1952) for example has argued that the new-born infant is egocentric, unable to distinguish between self and non-self, and conceiving of the world in an entirely subjective way. The infant only develops understanding via its actions on the environment and the information these provide; it has no direct perception independent of action. Gibson (1979) in contrast, would argue that the very young infant has the ability directly to perceive complex perceptual information.

   Research in recent years (reviewed for ex. by Harris, 1983) has confirmed that Piaget had considerably underestimated the perceptual abilities of infants. Nonetheless, even if infants' direct perception is far more sophisticated than we had supposed, it still seems that they have to learn how to act appropriately in accordance with their perceptions. In relation to this a further point should be made: infants are not solitary actors – many of their early actions take place within a social context, where they are considerably helped by the "scaffolding" provided by parents or more able peers (Bruner, 1985).

3. The relevance of the views of both Gibson and Piaget were apparent in research we carried out to investigate auditory perceptual competencies of infants with learning difficulties (Glenn and Cunningham, 1984a and b). Infants could touch one of two boxes to produce auditory stimuli in a free choice play situation, and their choices were monitored. Results included:

   (a) From 6 months level infants of all ability levels (including those with profound and multiple learning difficulties – PMLD) chose consistently between ensuing pairs of auditory stimuli.

      This suggested that certain stimuli are more salient than others to infants, (including those with learning difficulties), and may be more appropriate for use in intervention programmes.

   (b) An additional result seen particularly in children with profound learning difficulties was a positive motivational and affective effect. They spent significantly longer than other children playing with the boxes, responding very positively to being able to control their auditory environment.

   (c) Below 6 months level infants (including non-handicapped) would respond to the boxes, but showed no consistent preferences even if nothing came from one box and a highly salient stimulus from the other.

The last two results focused attention on the role of action in promoting understanding (knowing how and where to act) and motivation. This is not to say that research on perceptual competencies is unimportant. Even with children with PMLD the few studies there are suggest that they too are more perceptually competent than had been assumed (e.g. Shepherd and Fagan, 1981). Our own research however changed direction at this point to concentrate on the study of action on the environment, and on one of the earliest developments seen viz contingency responding.

CONTINGENCY RESPONDING RESEARCH

Studies of contingency learning have a long history of Psychology; from the earliest work of Pavlov contingency in one form or another has been of major interest. Operant conditioning work has concentrated on the nature of the relationship between responses and reinforcement, whereas cognitive views emphasise the perception of the relationship between an organism's response and environmental events. In particular the detection of and belief in causality and the effects this has on subsequent behaviour has been important in infant studies. Piaget (1952) sees the onset of contingency responding at around 3–4 months of age, and uses its appearance as one source of evidence of development from primary to secondary circular reactions. Watson (1984) argues that the capacity for contingency analysis is probably present from birth, in so far as infants of a few weeks of age can be shown to respond appropriately in artificial laboratory contingency situations, but agrees that they do not do so in the natural environment until 3–4 months of age. He comments that "research on general task variables that affect the likelihood that the infant would perceive his causal efficacy has been limited in scope". Yet it is just this type of research which we need to inform intervention efforts with developmentally very young children, particularly as we consider how to move from an initial demonstration of ability to respond to contingency to a consideration of how they can be helped to use this in their everyday lives.

Contingency awareness has been stressed by many researchers as a secondary motivational effect of successful contingency responding. However the notion has been most used in relation to the perception of non-contingency and the resulting state of "learned helplessness" (Seligman, 1975). The argument put forward is that prolonged exposure to non-contingency during early childhood will have as potentially adverse cognitive, motivational and affective consequences. Thus environmental stimulation not linked to contingency will have as potentially bad effects as lack of stimulation per se. It has to be said that there is only relatively limited support for this notion in both the experimental literature (e.g. Watson & Ramey, 1972, Finkelstein and Ramey, 1977, De Casper and Carstens, 1981) and in more real life studies (e.g. Sroufe, 1985). Nonetheless many workers in the field of learning difficulties have adopted this stance, and indeed it seems hard to argue that increasing the possibility of contingent action on the environment could be other than beneficial. Thus Dunst *et al.* (1987) argue "Contingency interactions lead to the infants acquisition of three very important developmental consequencies: contingency awareness, controlability and predictability."

Social Contingencies

Again it is important to note that social interactions may provide the child with many of his or her first contingency experiences in the natural environment and many researchers (e.g. Vygotsky, 1978, Bruner, 1985) emphasise the primary importance of social factors in development.

Both Vygotsky and Bruner argue that many abilities are initially seen in a social setting, in the context of dyadic interaction, and only later are used by the child alone (cf. Vygotsky's notion of development from the intermental to intramental plane). This would imply the need for reciprocal, responsive and sensitive interactions between child and caregiver from the earliest days.

Furthermore Ainsworth *et al.* (1978) have highlighted the connection between such interactions in the first year of life and children who are securely attached and more confident in exploring both the object environment and other social relationships. In the social context a child's initial sense of control of the environment will come about partly through his or her ability to affect the behaviour of other people. However Yoder (1987) for example has demonstrated that infants with severe learning difficulties give different social signals from non-handicapped infants, and that these are difficult even for trained observers to interpret. Marfo (1984) notes distortion in social interaction patterns in handicapped infant/mother dyads. This effect on the reciprocity of interactions would be expected to be associated with effects on attachment, and a review by Blacher (1984) confirms this; she notes that most studies show delayed, dulled or complete lack of attachment behaviours in many children with PMLD. Intervention in this area has been influenced by the need to sensitise caregivers to infants' behaviours and hence increase the likelihood of detection of social contingencies on the part of the child (e.g. Anderson and Sawin 1983, McCallum 1984). In a school context Nind and Hewett (1988) have recently argued that social interaction should be the central focus of the curriculum for PMLD children.

It seems clear that where children are showing social behaviour then this should be a major focus for intervention programmes. However some children have multiple difficulties and appear to show little response to social stimuli. In such instances it would seem appropriate to use microelectronic and computer controlled equipment to aid the possibility of contingency awareness developing and increasing motivation.

Artificial Contingencies using Microelectronic Technology

Dunst *et al.* (1985) have argued that encouragement of response-contingent learning using microtechnology is an important form of intervention with children with PMLD who may otherwise be regarded as 'ineducable', 'incapable of learning'. They argue that as well as potential secondary motivational effects on the child there are also positive effects on parents' perception of children, enjoyment of them and attempts to stimulate them.

Warren and Horn (1987) in contrast have argued that computer application with very young infants can only be limited as children at that stage of development need natural environmental interaction. However, as stated previously this type of intervention may be useful in children with multiple difficulties with very limited behavioural repertoires and very little social responding. Thus Watson and Hayes (1982) worked with an 8 month old infant with a developmental level of 1.5 months, presenting her with a stimulus (rotating mobile) contingent on her kicking a pillow. She learned this response and began smiling at the mobile and then at her mother for the first time. Subsequently more general intervention programmes were implemented.

If contingency responding is demonstrable from a few weeks of age then it should be possible to assist this in infants with PMLD, and also research the question of the generalisation of this ability to more natural environmental circumstances. In the final section preliminary work on the study of contingency responding using computer controlled contingencies will be described.

A PARADIGM FOR INVESTIGATING CONTINGENCY RESPONDING

In order to develop a reliable paradigm initial work was carried out with non-handicapped infants of 12–16 weeks of age. We wished to ensure that a) we could demonstrate contingency responding in this group, b) the emotional and motivational effects previously described (although usually only anecdotally) in the literature could be replicated. A review of the literature however (see O'Brien *et al.*, 1988a) revealed inconsistent reports of learning in non-handicapped infants and methodological variability in the studies. These included: different criteria for learning, different settings, different responses, fixed versus variable session lengths, use of non-contingent comparisons. This may partly explain why some studies (e.g. Millar 1972, Lewis *et al.* 1985, and in his later work, Watson 1985) have found little evidence of learning in young infants. It seems crucial in intervention directed studies to adopt the paradigm most likely to lead to contingency responding (and hence the possibility of contingency awareness), and all the foregoing variables need investigation directly for effects on learning. We have started investigating some of these.

Equipment

Full details of this are given in O'Brien *et al.* (1988b). It consists of a three-sided unit in which is housed an infant seat. Approximately two feet in front of the seat is a vertical stand on which a visual stimulus (a smiling face surrounded by four rotating 'arms') is positioned. Directly underneath the visual stimulus is a loudspeaker which delivers the auditory stimulus (currently a repetitive nursery rhyme chorus). Along each side of the unit, parallel to both sides of the infant seat, are eight infrared transmitters and their corresponding receivers. When the beam generated from one of these transmitters is broken (e.g. by an infant's leg movements) both stimuli are activated simultaneously for a pre set time. Computer control is implemented by a BBC microcomputer, which presents stimuli and monitors responding.

Phase 1

This study investigated the effect of setting on infants' responses, as most consistent evidence of learning in previous studies came from infants in their own home cot. Twenty infants aged from 12–16 weeks, matched for sex, length of gestation, birth order and type of birth were tested in a counterbalanced design over 2 sessions, one in the home and the other in the lab. Both sessions were contingent with no fixed session lengths; sessions were terminated when an infant fussed for 30 seconds or did not attend to the stimulus. To receive stimulation infants had to kick through the light beam, a one-minute baseline phase was incorporated at the beginning of each session.

Results included a) No significant effect of setting over 8 measures used, and subsequent studies have been conducted in the lab. b) Over the group of infants there was a significant increase in responding over trial blocks. c) On individual measures of learning on session 1, 8/20 subjects showed a significant increase in leg kicks over time. However it could be argued that this was an increase in activity caused by the arousing effect of stimulation. Arm movements were also monitored: if these increased also then this would be a sign of general activity increase. Of 8 subjects with an increase in leg movements, 5 did show an increase in arm movements also. Note that this is not necessarily a sign of non-learning; it could be that these infants were still in Piaget's stage 2 sensori-motor and had understood that some activity caused the onset of stimulation, but did not know specifically which activity.

Phase 2

The next study was carried out on 20 infants 12–16 weeks old matched on the same variables as previously. It involved one contingent session and looked at the effect on responding of giving additional tactile feedback (a rubber band was stretched directly under the light beam).

Results included a) a significant increase in responding over trial blocks for the group; b) 11/20 showed a significant increase in leg movements on individual measures; c) of these, 64% showed a significant increase for leg movements only, compared to 38% in phase 1. It thus seemed that tactile feedback did produce more evidence of Piaget's stage 3 responding than kinaesthetic feedback alone.

Phase 3

In phases 1 and 2 there was high individual subject variability in emotional responses. In order to study this more systematically a within subjects design was used comparing both contingent and non-contingent sessions. This also enabled an extra check on the relationship between increase in activity and level of stimulation. In the non-contingent session, the computer activates stimuli in the identical pattern from a yoked subject in a contingent session. At present data are available on 13 subjects in the contingent/non-contingent condition, and 13 subjects in the non-contingent/contingent condition.

Results include:

a) Significant evidence of an increase in responding over the group in the contingent condition, but not for the non-contingent condition.
b) A significant increase in motivation and positive effect in the contingent condition.
c) Some evidence that initial experience of non-contingency may depress subsequent contingent responding including motivational and emotional responding.

In conclusion this seems to be a reliable paradigm for the demonstration of contingency responding. Contingency awareness is indicated by the fact that non-contingency following contingency produces a significant reduction in smiling and time in the experiment, and a significant increase in fussing. Contingency following non-contingency does not show the reverse effects. Setting has no demonstrable effect on learning. Tactile, as well as kinaesthetic, feedback promotes more advanced responding.

Work is now ongoing with infants with PMLD.

REFERENCES

Ainsworth, M. D. S., Blehar, M., Waters, E. & Wall, S. (1978) *Patterns of Attachment*, Erlbaum.

Anderson, C. J. & Sawin, D. (1983) Enhancing responsiveness in mother infant interaction. *Infant Behaviour & Development*, **6**, 361–368.

Blacher, J. (1984) A dynamic perspective on the impact of a severely handicapped child on the family. In Blacher, J. (Ed) *Severely handicapped young children and their families*, Academic Press.

Bruner, J. S. (1985) Vygotsky: A historical and conceptual perspective. In Wertsch, J. V. (Ed) *Culture Communication and Cognition: Vygotskian Perspectives*, Cambridge University Press.

De Casper, A. J. & Carstens, A. A. (1981) Contingencies of stimulations: Effects on learning and emotion in neonates. *Infant Behaviour and Development*, **4**, 19–35.

Dunst, C. J., Cushing, P. J. & Vance, S. D. (1985) Response-Contingent Learning in Profoundly Handicapped Infants: A Social Systems Perspective. *Analysis and Intervention in Developmental Disabilities*, **5**, 33–47.

Dunst, C. J., Lesko, J. J., Holbert, K. A., Wilson, L. L., Sharpe, K. L. & Liles, R. F. (1987) A Systematic Approach to Infant Intervention. *Topics in Early Childhood Special Education*, **7**, 19–37.

Finkelstein, N. W. & Ramey, C. T. (1977) Learning to control the environment in infancy. *Child Development*, **48**, 806–819.

Gibson, J. J. (1979) *The ecological approach to visual perception*. Boston: Houghton Mifflin.

Glenn, S. M. & Cunningham, C. C. (1984a) Selective preference to different speech stimuli in infants with Down's syndrome. In Berg, K. (Ed) *Perspectives and Progress in Mental Retardation*, Vol. 1. Baltimore: University Park Press.

Glenn, S. M. & Cunningham, C. C. (1984b) Selective auditory preferences and the use of automated equipment by severely profoundly and multiply handicapped children. *Journal of Mental Deficiency Research*, **28**, 281–296.

Harris, P. K. (1983) Infant Cognition. In Haith, M. M. & Campos, J. J. (Eds) *Handbook of Child Psychology: Infancy and Developmental Psychobiology*. Vol. 2. New York: Wiley.

Kopp, C. B. & Krakow, J. B. (1983) The Developmentalist and the study of Biological Risk: A view of the past with an eye toward the future. *Child Development*, **54**, 1086–1108.

Lewis, M., Sullivan, M. W. & Brooks-Gunn, J. (1985) Emotional behaviour during the learning of a contingency in early infancy. *British Journal of Developmental Psychology*, **3**, 307–316.

McCallum, J. A. (1984) Social interaction between parents and babies: validation of an intervention procedure. *Child: Care, Health & Development*, **10**, 301–315.

Millar, W. S. (1972) A study of operant conditioning under delayed reinforcement in early infancy. *Monog. Soc. Res. Child Dev.*, **37**, (2, Serial no. 147).

Nind, M. & Hewett, D. (1988) Interaction as Curriculum: A Process Method in a

School for Pupils with Severe Learning Difficulties. *British Journal of Special Education* (in press).

O'Brien, Y., Glenn, S. M. & Cunningham, C. C. (1988a) Factors affecting the demonstration of contingency responding and awareness in infancy (in preparation).

O'Brien, Y., Pollard, P. & Mullin, C. (1988b) Computer-Controlled Equipment for the study of Contingency Learning in Infancy (in preparation).

Piaget, J. (1952) *The Origins of Intelligence in Children*. New York: International University Press.

Seligman, M. (1975) *Helplessness: On Depression, Development and Death*. San Francisco: Freeman.

Shepherd, P. A. & Fagan, J. F. (1981) Visual pattern detection and recognition memory in children with profound mental retardation. *International Review of Research in Mental Retardation*. (N. R. Ellis) (Ed) **10**, 31–60.

Sroufe, L. A. (1985) Attachment classification from the perspective of Infant-Caregiver relationships and infant temperament. *Child Development*, **56**, 1–14.

Vygotsky, L. S. (1978) *Mind in Society: The Development of Higher Psychological Processes*. Cambridge: Harvard University Press.

Warren, S. F. & Horne, M. (1987) Microcomputer Applications in Early Childhood Special Education: Problems and Possibilities. *Topics in Early Childhood Special Education*, **7**, 72–84.

Watson, J.S. (1985) Contingency Perception in Early Social Development. In Field, T. M., Fox, N. A. (Eds) *Social Perception in Infants*. Ablex pp. 157–176.

Watson, J. S. (1984) Bases of causal inference in infancy: time, space, and sensory relations. In Lipsitt, L. P. & Rovee-Collier, C. (Eds) *Advances in Infancy Resarch*, **Vol. 3**. Ablex pp. 152–165.

Watson, J. S. & Ramey, C. T. (1972) Reactions to response-contingent stimulation in early infancy. *Merrill-Palmer Quarterly*, **18**, 219–227.

Watson, J. S. & Hayes, L. A. (1982) Response contingent stimulation as a treatment for developmental failure in infancy. *J. Appl. Developmental Psychology*, **3**, 191–203.

Yoder, P. J. (1987) Relationship between degree of infant handicap and clarity of infant cues. *Amer. J. Mental Defic.*, **9**, 639–641.

The Integration of Children with Intellectual Disability into Regular Schools: Results from a Naturalistic Study

J. Ward and Y. Center
*Special Education Centre, Macquarie University,
New South Wales, 2109, Australia*

This paper reports data from the first stage of a study designed to evaluate the effectiveness of a policy of integrating intellectually disabled (ID) and other children with disabilities into regular classrooms. It also aims to identify those factors associated with child, classroom and school which may relate to the success or failure of such placements. Twelve primary age ID children (moderate/mild range) were studied by means of a naturalistic approach, involving a wide range of instruments and observational techniques. The data, as represented by indices of academic, social and physical integration, and validated by all concerned with the children's education, indicate a marginal level of successful integration. Success did not appear to be associated with age or severity of disability, but was related to appropriateness of resource support, teachers' instructional style and total school commitment to integration.

INTRODUCTION

Children with intellectual disabilities comprise much the largest group of those targetted for programmes of integration or mainstreaming. Many have been traditionally placed in segregated special schools or classes, a practice considered to be socially discriminative and educationally questionable since it has been unable to deliver an educational experience demonstrably superior to that available in the regular classroom. (Carlberg and Kavale, 1980, Semmel *et al.*, 1986; Wang & Baker, 1985). The result has been a growing research effort to develop the procedures necessary for placing even the most severely disabled children in regular classrooms (McCarthy and Schultz, 1987; Taylor, 1984; Thomason and Arkell, 1980).

In Australia there has been a movement towards integration similar to that in Europe and North America, although there are considerable differences among the individual States both in policy and practice (Gow *et al.*, 1987; Gow *et al.*, 1988; Fulcher, 1986). This has stimulated a number of researches into the main problem areas of integration. For example several studies have been carried out into the attitudes of educationists (Center and Ward, 1987; Ward *et al.*, 1987). Data from these have indicated that, generally speaking, the attitudes of school principles, teachers, resource teachers and school psychologists are positive, although the degree of acceptance depends in large part upon the nature of the child's presenting disability or problem, the demands these make upon the classroom teacher's skills and time, and the availability of resources. Other researches have examined the achievement and adjustment of disabled children in regular classes e.g. children with cerebral palsy, (Center and Ward, 1984); groups with Down Syndrome who have been integrated following early intervention programs (Pieterse and Center, 1984, Hudson and Clunies-Ross, 1984) and other disability groups (Westwood, 1982; Andrews and Elkins, 1981).

The above have provided an interesting commentary but, apart from the Westwood study, they have not addressed the day-to-day practices of integration or identified the factors associated with the success or failure of an integrated placement. Thus research, which can provide greater insights into the logical structure of policy and its implementation, is being advocated strongly (Sadler, 1985; Jenkinson, 1987).

AIMS OF THE STUDY

The following, therefore, describes data from the preliminary stage of a research study designed: 1) to provide representative data about the quality of the educational and social experiences of children with disabilities who, as a result of a policy decision are placed and maintained in regular primary school classes and, 2) to determine factors relevant to child, classroom and school which are associated with successful academic, social and physical integration. These include *child factors* e.g. type of disability, cognitive level, social adjustment etc.; *classroom factors* e.g. instructional style, time management, classroom climate etc. and *school factors* etc. school ethos, support services, staff attitude etc. The account will include summary data and brief reviews of cases which, by the criteria adopted, could be regarded as successful, marginally successful and unsuccessful; some general conclusions which are suggested by the data, comparisons between data from this and other disability groups and conclusions based upon the results derived from the first stage of the research.

Design of the Study

The design of the study involved a mixed naturalistic approach using both qualitative and quantitative methods. The design evolved from consideration of a range of approaches (cf. Hegarty and Evans, 1985), its purpose being to permit intensive case studies of a small sample of children across all disability groups in both urban and rural primary schools. This paper, however, is primarily concerned with the mainstreaming of a sub-sample of children in the study defined as intellectually disabled.

Sample

Twelve children with intellectual disabilities, comprising five with Down Syndrome, five with mixed aetiology, one with hydrocephalus and one with P.K.U., were included as part of a larger group of children with disabilities (n=43). Seven of the children were from metropolitan schools while the remaining five were from schools in three country regions. The sample was distributed almost equally between infants and primary grades. As a result of government policy only approximate information was available regarding the cognitive development of each child, but the general intellectual level was in the moderate to mild range of retardation.

Instrumentation

(A detailed list of instruments is presented in the appendix.)

The instruments, which were designed to assess child, teacher and school variables, consisted of both quantitative and qualitative measures. *Quantitative measures* included norm and criterion-referenced tests of scholastic achievement, sociograms, observation schedules, self-report inventories, questionnaires and interviews with all persons concerned with the child's education as well as with the child and a representative peer group. *Qualitative measures* included observations of all aspects of the child's educational environment in both the classroom and playground. The measures relating specifically to the child were designed to assess both scholastic achievement and social status as well as academic progress and social adjustment over time. Pre and post tests on academic and social measures were conducted in the child's entire class group and a parallel class with no disabled child was also tested on academic measures to ascertain whether the presence of a child with disabilities impeded academic progress. The extent to which physical integration occurred, i.e. free movement around the classroom and playground, academic withdrawal and general participation in school activities was also recorded for each target child.

Classroom measures were designed to assess those pre-instructional, during-instructional and post-instructional factors which research (Brophy, 1979; Crisci, 1981; Gage, 1978; Rosenshine; 1979) has indicated are associated with successful mainstreaming. Finally, those *school measures* which were assessed related to the quantity and quality of resource support provided, the way in which principals perceived their role, school ethos and general school attitudes to integration.

Observational Procedures

Six observers, representing two metropolitan and three country regions, spent approximately two weeks in each school. Prior to this observation period all researchers received training to establish reliability on the observational schedules. Estimates of reliability using every combination of research staff ranged from 87% to 100%, with the exception of a single low rating of 77% for an analysis of the questioning pattern of teachers.

ANALYSIS OF DATA

The academic, social/emotional and physical access measures obtained for the target children, through direct testing, observation schedules and teacher/parent ratings from questionnaires and interviews were recorded separately to establish three discrete indices of integration. The index of academic integration for each child consisted of 7 components measuring:

teacher's rating of academic status, parent's rating of academic status, child's academic progress during 6 months in reading relative to the class group, appropriateness of class curriculum for child, degree of curriculum modification for child, child's time on task in basic skill areas;

The index of social integration for each child consisted of ten components measuring:

teacher's rating of social acceptability, parents' rating of social acceptability, peers' rating of social acceptability on a sociogram, change in child's social acceptability over 6 months, teacher's ranking of child's social status relative to the class group, observed playground interaction, teacher's rating of playground interaction, observed classroom behaviour, teacher's ratings of classroom behaviour, extension of school friendships outside school hours;

The index of physical integration related to the child's:

free movement around the classroom and playground, amount of academic withdrawal and general participation in school activities.

In order to establish the independence of the three indices, Cronbach alphas were calculated, obtaining values: .63, .86 and .51 respectively. These indicated that each index was conceptually valid and could therefore be examined independently within a case study analysis. The results of factor analyses performed on the academic and social scales indicated that only one factor was subsumed by each scale. The three indices of integration were also totalled in order to obtain a *total index of integration*. The three discrete indices and the total index of integration were validated, against a separate, non-experimental measure labelled the *total validation index* which reflected the degree of satisfaction expressed for present and continued integration by all concerned with the child's education and the child.

The three indices of integration and the total integration index became the dependent variables for each child in the study. The predictor variables included the child's disability, cognitive level, age, grade and school region, as well as all measured and observed classroom and school factors. All the predictor variables relating to teachers' classroom strategies and to school measures were cross-correlated and scaled to obtain the most economical and efficient group of independent variables. Mult-factorial anovas and multiple regression analyses were also undertaken in order to estimate the best linear combination of independent variables for predicting successful mainstreaming.

RESULTS

The data in Table 1 indicate that, as a group, children with intellectual difficulties appear to be integrated at a marginally successful level. However, the important feature of the results is not the mean integration index of the group but its variability, since fifty percent of the sample could be considered as extremely well integrated.

To identify the factors which may explain these differences both quantitative data and case study were required.

An examination of Table 1 indicates that neither type nor degree of disability differentiated the successfully integrated group (Cases 4, 7, 13, 21, 24 and 41) from those less successfully placed. Furthermore, both groups were located in infants/primary grades in exactly the same proportions, which suggests that, in this sample, effective mainstreaming was neither grade nor age dependent. What does emerge however, is the greater degree of appropriate support which was provided to the children designated as successful. In each of the six cases the mean was higher (87.7%) than that for the total group (70.3%) and for 4/6 cases highly appropriate resource provision was indicated. However, appropriateness of support was confounded by teacher's instructional skills, so that Case 21 was actually receiving exemplary assistance without support from

Table 1. Integration of children with intellectual disabilities

Case no.	Disab'ty	Grade	Indices of Integration				Valid'n index %	Approp. support %	Instruct'l style %
			Academic %	Social %	Physical %	Total integ %			
4	Down s.	4	90.0	88.3	88.9	89.1	100.0	75.0	50.0
6	Intell d.	5	58.3	81.7	77.7	71.8[a]	85.0[a]	50.0	43.0
7	Down s.	3	76.7	96.7	100.0	89.7	100.0	81.3	43.0
12	Down s.	3	63.3	75.0	100.0	76.3[a]	85.0[a]	50.0	55.0
13	Down s.	2	91.7	83.3	88.9	87.8	97.5	93.8	47.0
17	Intell d.	5	80.0	71.7	100.0	81.4+	67.0+	25.0	46.0
21	Hyd'ceph	6	96.7	86.7	94.4	92.3	100.0	93.8	59.0
23	Intell d.	4	78.3	78.3	77.7	78.2[a]	60.0[a]	50.0	54.0
24	Intell d.	2	81.7	98.3	77.7	87.2	95.0	87.5	52.0
34	P.K.U.	3	66.7	55.0	55.6	59.6[a]	90.0[a]	75.0	49.0
41	Down s.	2	81.7	95.0	100.0	91.0	95.0	87.5	51.0
43	Intell d.	1	71.7	76.7	100.0	80.1[b]	70.0[b]	75.0	50.0
Means			78.1	82.2	88.4	82.0	87.1	70.3	49.9

Down s. = Down syndrome   Intell d. = Intellectual delay
Hyd'ceph = Hydrocephalus   P.K.U. = Phenylketonuria
[a] denotes less than effective integration
[b] denotes marginally effective integration

a resource teacher. Thus it appears that when teachers' possess effective instructional strategies demands on resource personnel are reduced. For such teachers, an aide, under their direction, would probably be the best resource provision.

In the two remaining successful cases (4 and 7) where appropriate levels of support were lower and teachers did not use highly structured instructional strategies, an additional factor appeared to contribute to success. Both these schools had strong commitment to the policy and practice of integration which was clearly demonstrated by the attitudes and comments of their principals and staffs. One interesting observation was, that in the most highly committed school, where use of structured strategies was minimal, the academic integration index of the target child was actually low, but the validation index remained extremely high, indicating a lower priority for academic outcomes in a very compassionate learning environment. The success of these students reflects themes that recur throughout the case study analyses. If teachers feel they have the skills needed to integrate lower ability children either intrinsically or through appropriate resource support, then the success of the placement is likely to be assured. However, if a de-emphasis of academic skills is part of the ethos of a strongly committed school, integration can still be successful, even with less effective support.

By contrast, the four cases whose total integration scores fell below the accepted criterion for success (Cases 12, 6, 23, and 34) and the two marginal cases (17 and 43) differed essentially in the poorer quality of assistance they received (mean appropriate support = 56%) although they were also mainly in primary grades. Incidentally, while grade level alone does not appear to militate against successful integration it may do so in more academically pressured classrooms when appropriate resources are not available. It is interesting to observe that for most of this group the absence of appropriate support far outweighed the influence of teachers' instructional style. Thus when the resource issue relevant to these four cases was examined, the critical factor appeared to be the inappropriate deployment of resource personnel, whether they were resource teachers or teachers' aides. In one case, although the child participated three days per week in an effective, task-analysed reading program devised by the resource teacher, there was no coordination between resource room and classroom so that no assistance was provided directly to the teacher. As a result the child spent most of his class time off-task in basic subjects, because his conceptual level in these was two grades below the class average. This reduced the teachers' confidence in her ability to teach such students so that she felt that a regular class was not the most advantageous placement for this child. This is not an uncommon reaction, despite some research evidence to the contrary

(Carlberg & Kavale, 1980), it can only be modified by resource teachers spending more time in the classroom.

Another example of inappropriate resource support occurred in a different classroom where an aide was provided for the target child for two mornings per week. Neither supervision nor programming assistance was provided by the resource teacher; the aide withdrew the child to follow a program devised by herself, which was independent of the classroom program. Despite good social skills, the child's subsequent inability to fit into the classroom's academic program reinforced the teacher's anxiety about the placement. Incidentally, this pattern of inadequate supervision was found in several country schools, when teachers with no training in instructional strategies were required to instruct untrained aides for withdrawal work with disabled children. However, teachers were concerned about the over-dependence of the children upon aides produced by withdrawal since it reduced independence in the home classroom. Consequently, despite the provision of resource personnel, many teachers and pupils were not receiving the type of assistance which could enhance the quality of their educational environment.

In summary, it appears that all children with intellectual disabilities present challenges since they will generally need some modification of the classroom program. In the presence of appropriate in-class support these can be satisfactorily met so that mainstream placement not only becomes a positive academic and social experience for the child but can improve the regular class teacher's instructional competence. In these circumstances regular teachers will also become more skilled at coping with "normal" children who are failing to achieve academically or interact socially within a regular classroom. If however, teachers without the necessary instructional skills do not receive effective resource support from qualified staff, the integration of children with intellectual disabilities will suffer as the anxiety levels of staff members increase. Teacher aides are seen to be a valuable support to regular teachers, but to be effective they must be supervised by trained personnel i.e. either qualified resource teachers or regular classroom teachers versed in appropriate instructional technology. The aim must always be to integrate the child's program more efficiently with the class program and to increase both academic and social independence.

Comparisons with other disability groups

At this stage of the research study children with intellectual disabilities appear to occupy a marginal position with respect to their suitability for mainstreaming. Certainly their placements have been much less successful than the Physical Disability Group (n=10) and the Sensory Disability Group (n=8) which together contained only one ineffective placement. They present somewhat fewer difficulties however, than the groups of Behavioural and Emotional Difficulties (n=5) and Multiply-Disabled (n=3) which had only one clearly successful placement.

CONCLUSIONS

The foregoing data provide tentative evidence that children of primary school age with moderate to mild intellectual difficulties can, provided that some basic requirements are met, be realistically placed in regular school classes. The samples described in this paper and the preliminary report of the research Center *et al.* (1988) are not large but will be considerably augmented in the second phase of the project, thus enabling more intensive analyses of the factors relative to successful integration. Thus far the project has necessitated some review and modification of the instruments used (Ward *et al.*, 1988) and a recognition of the extreme complexity of the problem area. Therefore, the second stage of the research will use the refined instruments and methods with larger samples. The data from this should permit a number of hypotheses to be tested in the areas of systems organisation and policy as well as the instructional techniques required for successful placement. Indeed, a feature of the research is the trialling of a limited form of data base to permit further developmental and policy oriented studies. Further accounts of this research will be available in due course.

ACKNOWLEDGEMENTS

The authors wish to acknowledge generous financial support and collaboration of the New South Wales Department of Education, the N.S.W. Crippled Children Society, the Spastic Centre of N.S.W., the Macquarie University Program for children with Down Syndrome, the Catholic Education Commission of New South Wales, also the work of the principal collaborators Drs Lyn Gow, Phil Foreman, Robert Conway and Ken Linfoot, together with the research staff, particularly Cecile Ferguson and Vanessa Jackson.

Finally they would wish to acknowledge the help and co-operation of the many school principals, teachers, resource staff, children and parents, without which the study would not have been possible.

REFERENCES

Andrews, R. J. and Elkins, J. (1981) *The Management and Education of Children with Spina Bifida and Hydrocephalus*. E.R.D.C. Report No. 32 Canberra: F.P.S.

Brophy, J. (1979) Teacher behaviour and its effects *Journal of Educational Psychology*, **71**, 733–750.

Carlberg, C. and Kavale, K. (1980) The efficiency of special versus regular class placement for exceptional children. A meta-analysis. *The Journal of Special Education* **14**, (3).

Center, Y., Ferguson, C. and Ward, J. (1988) The integration of children with disabilities into regular classes; a naturalistic study. Stage 1 Report. Sydney, Australia. Special Education Centre, Macquarie University.

Center, Y. and Ward, J. (1984) Integration of mildly handicapped cerebral palsied children into regular schools. *The Exceptional Child* **31**, 104–113.

Center, Y. and Ward, J. (1987) Teachers' attitudes towards the integration of disabled children into regular classes. *The Exceptional Child* **32**, 149–161.

Crisci, P. E. (1981) Competencies for mainstreaming: problems and issues *Education and Training of the Mentally Retarded* **6**, 175–182.

Fulcher, G. (1986) Australian policies on Special Education: Towards a sociological account. *Disability, Handicap and Society* **1**, 19–52.

Gage, N. (1978) *The Scientific Basis of the Art of Teaching*. New York, Teachers College Press, Columbia University.

Gow, L., Snow, D. and Ward, J. (1987) Contextual influences on integration in Australia: overview of a report to the Commonwealth Schools Commission, Part 1. *The Exceptional Child*, **34**, 159–171.

Gow, L., Ward, J., Balla, J. and Snow, D. (1988) Directions for Integration in Australia. Overview of a report to the Commonwealth Schools Commission, Part 2. *The Exceptional Child*, **35**, 5–22.

Hegarty, S. and Evans, P. (1985) *Research and Evaluation Methods in Special Education: quantitative and qualitative methods in case study work* London: NFER – Nelson.

Hudson, A. and Clunies-Ross, G. (1984) A study of the integration of children with intellectual handicaps into regular schools. *Australian and New Zealand Journal of Developmental Disabilities*, **10**, 165–177.

Jenkinson, J. C. (1987) School & Disability: Research and Practice in Integration. ACER, Hawthorn, Victoria.

McCarthy, E. F. (1987) with Schultz, M. Integration of students with severe disabilities in Madison Metropolitan School District in M. S. Bernes and P. Knoblock (Eds) *Program Models for Mainstreaming – Integrating students with Moderate to Severe Disabilities*, Rockville, Maryland, Aspen Publications, Inc.

Pieterse, M. and Center, Y. (1984) The integration of eight Down Syndrome children into regular schools. *Australian and New Zealand Journal of Development Disabilities*, **10**, 11–20.

Rosenshine, B. (1979) Content, Time and Direct Instruction in P. Peterson and H. Walberg (Eds). *Research on Teaching: Concepts, findings and implications*. Berkeley, C. A. McCutchan.

Sadler, D. Royce (1985) Evaluation, policy analysis and multiple case studies: Aspects of focus and sampling. In *Educational Evaluation and Policy Analysis*, **2**, 143–149.

Semmel, M. I., Lieber, J. and Peck, C. A. (1986) Effects of special education environments: Beyond mainstreaming. In C. J. Meisel (Ed.), *Mainstream-*

ing handicapped children: Outcomes, Controversies and New Directions (pp. 165–192. Hillsdale, New Jersey: Lawrence Erlbaum.

Taylor, S.T. (1984) *Making Integration Work: Strategies for educating students with severe disabilities in regular schools*. Syracuse, N.Y. Syracuse University, Special Education Resource Centre.

Thomason and Arkell (1980) Educating the severely/profoundly handicapped in the public schools: a side-by-side approach. *Exceptional Children*. **47**, 114–122.

Wang, M. C. and Baker, E. T. (1985) Mainstreaming programs: design effects and features. *Journal of Special Education* **19**, 503–521.

Ward, J., Center, Y. and Ferguson, C. (1988) Integration of Children with Disabilities: Design of a Naturalistic Study, A. F. Ashman (Ed). Integration 25 years on. *Monograph No. 1. The Exceptional Child*. Fred and Eleanor Schonell Educational Research Centre. pp. 249–259.

Ward, J., Parmenter, T. R., Center, Y. and Nash, R. (1987) Principals' attitudes towards the integration of children with mild intellectual disabilities into regular classes in J. M. Berg (Ed). *Science and Service in Mental Retardation*. London, Methuen.

Westwood, P. S. (1982) *Integration of handicapped children in South Australia*. Monograph Supplement, South Australian College of Advanced Education.

APPENDIX

Child Measures

1. Macquarie University Special Education Centre Maths Tests Grades Grades 2–6. Available from Special Education Centre, Macquarie University, North Ryde, N.S.W. 2109, Australia.
2. ACER Primary Reading Survey Tests. Word Knowledge and Comprehension Forms R & S. Available from Australian Council for Educational Research, Frederick Street, Hawthorne, Victoria, 3122, Australia.
3. Perception of social Closures Scale (Horne, 1977).
4. A Modified Sociogram based on Moreno (1934) for Grades 1 & 2.
5. Teacher's Ratings of Social and Behavioural Adjustment.
6. Parents' Ratings of Social and Academic Progress.

Classroom Measures

1. Adapted from the Observer Rating Scale (Larrivee, 1985).
2. Questioning Pattern Observation Form (Larrivee, 1985).
3. Child/Teacher Time Management Form (Larrivee, 1985).
4. Intervention Strategy Record (Larrivee, 1985).
5. Survey of Teachers' Opinions Relative to Mainstreaming (Hudson & Clunies Ross, 1984).
6. Intervention Strategy Inventory (Larrivee, 1985).

School Measures

1. School Priorities Scale (devised for study).
2. Teacher and Observer Ratings of Appropriateness of Support Provision.

The Relative Efficacy of Cognitive and Behavioural Approaches to Instruction in Promoting Adaptive Capacity

L. P. Gow,[1] J. Balla,[2] and E. Butterfield[3]
[1]*Hong Kong Polytechnic, Hung Hom, Kowloon, Hong Kong*
[2]*City Polytechnic of Hong Kong, Mongkok, Kowloon, Hong Kong*
[3]*Department of Educational Psychology, University of Washington,
Seattle, Washington, 98195, U.S.A.*

We compared the effects on adaptive capacity of three cognitively-oriented instructional approaches – Reciprocal Teaching (RT), Self-Instruction Problem-Solving (SIPS), and Simultaneous/Successive Processing (SSP) – with the effects of a behavioural approach using three groups of mildly intellectually disabled children (n=44). RT and SIPS approaches promoted significantly greater adaptive capacity than the behavioural approach for some of the far generalisation tasks, while no significant differences were found between the SSP approach and the behavioural approach. Discussion focuses on the need to program for adaptive capacity.

INTRODUCTION

Relatively little research with people with intellectual disabilities has been done to test ways of promoting transfer of training, generalisation, or as we call it adaptive capacity. Instead, the emphasis has been on behaviour change, without regard to whether it generalises (see Gow, 1986; Gow et al., in press; Ward & Gow, 1982). Perhaps as a result, our students have learned to react with a desired response only to the extremely limited experiences offered in the training situation (Gow et al., 1985; Maker, 1981).

More effective ways of promoting adaptive capacity are needed for persons with intellectual disabilities, whose performance is characterised as rigid, context dependent or as blind rule following (see Brown et al., 1983; Brown et al., 1977; Gow, 1984a; Gow & Ward, 1985). The most widely used methods of teaching people with intellectual disabilities are behavioural. The instructional design of such methods emphasise task analysis of the defined curriculum objectives and identification of a set of the component skills and their assumed pre-requisites. Small, sequential steps to task completion are identified and taught, and progress is monitored carefully, with changes in programs based on daily evaluation of specific objectives (see Baine, 1986). These behavioural approaches let the instructor select the learners' goals and the means of reaching them and they emphasise content. Probably as a result, these approaches have not provided the learner with internalised strategies for (or confidence in) approaching new tasks. The now classic challenge of Baer Wolf & Risley (1968) that: "generalisation should be programmed rather than expected or lamented" (p. 86) is not met by these approaches, and failures to promote adaptive capacity have been rampant.

Partly because of shortcomings with behavioural approaches, interest in cognitive approaches to instruction has burgeoned during the past fifteen years. The focus has been on identifying and teaching cognitive strategies (see Belmont & Butterfield, 1969; Brown & Campione, 1982; Gow & Ward, 1985; Padawer et al., 1980; Pressley, 1979) in ways designed to promote their effective and independent use. Such approaches shift the educational emphasis from task content to processes a person must use when solving problems, including perception, learning, memory, reasoning, and decision making.

Many have argued that cognitive instruction can enhance adaptive capacity by providing students with a framework of information and skills (Belmont et al., 1982; Cherkes-Julkowski, 1986; Feuerstein, 1979; Gow & Butterfield, in press; Sternberg, 1981). Nevertheless, successes have so far been limited to increasing task specific performances. Like behavioural instruction, cognitive instruction has rarely produced generalised learning strategies that are used in new situations (Borkowski & Cavanaugh, 1979; Gow, 1984a; Gow et al., in press). Several explanations for this have been offered, ranging from a fundamental deficit in some students' adaptive capacity, to incomplete experimental analyses of adaptive behaviour measures (Belmont & Butterfield, 1977; Borkowski & Cavanaugh, 1979; Gow et al., in press). Another explanation is that cognitivists too have failed to meet the long-standing challenge of Baer et al. (1968) that "generalisation should be programmed rather than expected or lamented" (p. 86).

Three cognitive approaches have taken the programming of adaptive capacity as their goal: Simultaneous/Successive Processing (Das et al., 1979), Reciprocal Teaching (Brown & Palinscar, 1986) and Self-Instruction Problem-Solving (Gow, 1987). Each has had some success at promoting adaptive capacity (see Conway, 1985; Gow, in press; Brown & Palinscar, 1988). The aim of our study was to examine the relative efficacy of these approaches with a behaviourally-oriented approach, typically adopted for use with intellectually disabled populations, in

teaching arithmetic skills to a sample of mildly intellectually disabled
children. Our hypothesis (in the null form) was that there would be no
differences in adaptive capacity exhibited by subjects instructed by a
cognitive approach as compared to a behavioural approach. A more
detailed description of the procedures and findings is provided by Gow *et
al.* (submitted).

SUBJECTS

Potential subjects were 48 children from three special units for the mildly
intellectually disabled in regular urban primary schools in the eastern
states of Australia. As a result of the erratic attendance of four of the
children, the final sample consisted of 44 children. The chronological age
range of the sample was from 8 years 2 months to 11 years 10 months,
with a mean age of 10 years (s.d. 1 year 1 month), and their I.Q.s
(WISC) ranged from 66 to 79 with a mean of 72.8 (s.d. 4.3).

APPROACHES TO INSTRUCTION

Four approaches to instruction were implemented in teaching arithmetic.
In each unit, a behaviourally-oriented approach was compared with one
of the following three cognitively-oriented approaches.

1. Reciprocal Teaching (RT)

RT (Brown & Palinscar, 1988) is an expert-led group learning procedure
based on the interactive concept of expert scaffolding (Vygotsky, 1978).
Learners pattern their behaviour after that of an instructor (expert) who
gradually withdraws from the learning situation as the learners (novices)
become more competent. Components of the approach are:

i.   Teaching occurs in groups and discussion is encouraged;
ii. A teacher models – overtly, explicitly and concretely – underlying
     processes such as summarising [self review], formulating potential
     test questions, clarifying occasions of ambiguity, and predicting
     future content;
iii. Underlying processes are modelled in appropriate contexts, not as
     isolated decontextualised skills;
iv. Novices are taught the need for strategic intervention and the
     useful ranges of particular strategies;
v.   Novices are shown that strategies work for them; and
vi. Responsibility for an activity is transferred to students as soon as
     they will take it, but transfer is gradual so that learners continually
     face comfortable challenges.

RT is metacognitive. Novices are fully informed of the nature of the strategies, their efficiency and their range of utility. Its heart is trial-and-error by learners and guidance by a teacher who is sensitive to their skill development. The teacher serves as a sympathetic coach whose goal is for the novice to adopt essential skills more fully. Successful coaching requires constant monitoring of the cognitive status of the novice.

2. Self-Instruction Problem-Solving (SIPS)

Based on the work of Luria (1961) and Vygotsky (1978), the assumption behind SIPS is that learning is progressive internalisation of explicit, language-based, overt self-instructions. The goal is to teach learners to verbally and explicitly program their own thinking (Gow, 1987; Gow, in press).

The verbalisation component of SIPS derives from self-instruction as practised by Meichenbaum (1977). Self-verbalisations are either general or specific. The general ones focus learner attention on a task ("What do I have to do?") and prompt problem definition and planning ("How am I going to do it?"), leading to specific verbalisations that guide the learner through a task. Combining general and specific verbalisations seems to promote greater adaptive capacity (see Gow & Ward, 1985).

The SIPS training program is comprehensive and incorporates a range of principles of instruction (see Gow, in press). These are:

i.   Encourage learners to decide their own goals.
ii. Intervene only when necessary. Transfer learning control and responsibility to the learner by facilitating the development of self-management problem-solving skills such as independent goal setting, self planning, self monitoring and self evaluation.
iii. Teach general rules or principles and when and how to use them.
iv. Enhance motivation by using any one, or a combination, of the following strategies:
     a. Select topics of intrinsic interest to the learner;
     b. Minimise the number and type of external rewards and encourage self-reinforcement and self-regulation; and
     c. Ensure the active participation of the learner.
v.   Ensure the learning context is relevant to the learner and to the task.
vi. Give explicit feedback to learners about the purpose and usefulness of using cognitive strategies and help them make a link between means and goals.
vii. Use group instruction where peers facilitate the learning of each other.

3. Simultaneous and Successive Processing (SSP)

Das *et al.* (1979) derived their SSP training from Luria's (1966) description of cortical integrative processes. Simultaneous strategies are considered to involve synthesis of sensory inputs into wholes which are often spatially organised, while successive synthesis requires integration of stimulus information, distributed over time, and may not be organised spatially. Either or both of these strategies may be employed by an individual on any one task, depending both upon the person's habitual mode of processing information, or "cognitive style", and on the cognitive demands of the task. Combined with the use of planning skills, these strategies provide a method of processing any task. Das *et al.* (1979) argue that learning effectiveness may partly depend on the appropriate selection of processing strategies by the learner.

Simultaneous and successive strategies are taught with "content free" tasks having no academic counterparts in order to permit the teaching of processing strategies, free of the constraints and negative connotations of academic task remediation. The three training steps involved "dynamic interaction" (Conway, 1985) between teacher and learner in which verbalisation is encouraged.

  i)   Each strategy is taught separately using relatively "content free" training tasks to ensure that the processing strategy is fully understood;

  ii) Following acquisition of the strategy using the "content free" tasks, the pupil attempts to alternate "content free" tasks as examples or measures of "near transfer" at the executive level rather than the task level; and

  iii) The pupil attempts content-specific tasks in subjects such as reading and mathematics as "far transfer" applications of the processing strategy.

4. Behaviourally-oriented approach

Basic characteristics of the behaviourally-oriented approaches adopted in this study were that the arithmetic skills to be taught were defined in terms of observable, measurable behaviours, environmental conditions, and standards of performance (Snell, 1983). These skills were task analysed into their essential subskills that were then organised into carefully arranged instructional sequences. Behavioural instructional techniques of shaping, prompting, stimulus control, reinforcement and chaining were used to teach the skills. Prompts and external reinforcement were systematically faded from use. Data on students' responses were recorded continuously, and modifications to the program were made to suit individual needs (see Haring *et al.*, 1980). Following the recommendations of Stokes & Baer (1977), generalisation was programmed for by using multiple exemplars and teaching across settings wherever possible.

TEACHERS AND AIDES

The teacher of each of the units, with the assistance of an aide, conducted the study. The three teachers conducted all of the training, while the three aides, who were blind to the experiment, collected the data. All of the teachers were working towards degrees in education and had a minimum of four years' teaching experience with children of similar ability. None of the aides had received prior training in special education, although all had been employed as an aide in similar settings for a minimum of two years.

INSTRUMENTS

A score for *arithmetic* performance was obtained from a test of arithmetic ability developed by one of the researchers (see Balla & McDonald, 1985).

The *measure of adaptive capacity* was based upon the successful generalisation or adaptation of learned skills, from one domain (the training domain) to another "near" (closely related to the training domain) or "far" (less related) domain (see Gow *et al.*, 1986). "Near" adaptive capacity was measured by performance on arithmetic material closely related to the training material. Three measures of "far" adaptive capacity were obtained:

(1) performance on novel arithmetic material;
(2) frequency of decision making during a two-hour leisure activity program conducted in the school grounds;
(3) the number of solutions provided to six real-life problems: What do you do when you miss your bus? What do you do when you lose your money? What do you do when you see two children fighting in the playground? What do you do if you become lost in a crowd? What do you do when you see a fire? What do you do when you need to phone for an emergency and you can't find a public phone?

PROCEDURE

To control for individual differences in arithmetic at pre-intervention, subjects in each unit were matched on their performance on the test of arithmetic and assigned to one of the two groups (cognitive approach or behavioural approach). Pre-test scores were obtained on all measures of adaptive capacity. The experiment was conducted during arithmetic lessons in each of the three special units, three times a week for 30 minutes, over a six week period and during two recreation classes. In each unit, the two groups were instructed in arithmetic using either the cognitive or the behavioural approach. All teaching was done by the teacher, while the aide took the other group for reading. Subjects in RT and SIPS samples were taught in groups for the duration of the study, while SSP subjects and all those in behavioural groups were predominantly taught individually. It has been argued that cognitive instruction takes longer than behavioural, and may sometimes be more effective for that reason (see Gow, 1984a). That was not the case in this study. With each approach extensive training was used, as recommended by Borkowski & Cavanaugh (1979), and all subjects received the same amount of instructional time. All testing was done individually. One week after completion of initial training, subjects were given both near and far tests of their adaptive capacity.

RESULTS

Due to small sample sizes of the matched groups, the Wilcoxon non-parametric test of significant differences was used. The results of such analyses demonstrated that there were no significant differences between groups of subjects in their performance on the near transfer tests, but that the subjects taught using RT and SIPS were significantly better than those taught with a behavioural approach in solving real-life problems and that those taught using RT were significantly better than those taught using the behavioural approach in solving novel maths problems.

DISCUSSION

Our hypothesis that cognitive approaches would promote significantly greater adaptive capacity was supported for two of the three cognitive approaches (RT and SIPS) for at least one of the far generalisation tasks (real-life problems and novel maths problems). The finding of a differential effect of cognitive approaches compared with a behaviourally-oriented approach in promotion of adaptive capacity is illuminating when the three cognitive approaches are analysed.

At least since the seminal paper of Stokes & Baer (1977), there has been much discussion in the literature regarding the need to program directly for the promotion of adaptive capacity. Failure to do this with behavioural approaches has been the major reason advanced to explain problems in promoting adaptive capacity (see review Gow, 1984a). The same criticism could be levelled against the SSP approach which pre-

Table 1. Means, s.d.'s and levels of significance (Wilcoxon) for three pairs of matched groups on post test measures of near and far adaptive capacity

		SIPS n=7	BEH n=7	RT n=7	BEH n=7	SSP n=8	BEH n=8
Near	X	92.4	86.4 N.S.	85.9	80.6 N.S.	89.8	84.9 N.S.
Transfer	S.D.	5.9	9.0	11.6	11.4	6.9	12.8
Novel	X	31.6	24.0 N.S.	39.3	27.3^a	33.1	33.8 N.S.
Maths	S.D.	5.8	7.4	10.3	8.3	9.4	12.9
Leisure	X	8.9	5.7 N.S.	10.9	6.6 N.S.	7.7	8.0 N.S.
Decisions	S.D.	2.0	2.3	5.0	2.7	2.7	3.7
Real	X	17.3	11.1^a	19.9	13.3^a	15.1	14.1 N.S.
Life	S.D.	4.27	3.2	5.5	3.2	4.62	2.93

^{a} p < .05

teaches the processing strategies in the hope that they will generalise to academic skill performance. Content specific performance following SSP training is actually a measure of far generalisation of the processing strategies. This approach is analogous to the train and hope situation described by Stokes & Baer (1977), and thus may provide an alternative explanation to that advanced by Das (1985) regarding failure of his approach to promote far adaptive capacity (see review Conway, 1985). To promote adaptive capacity, it must be programmed for directly. The conclusion can be drawn from this study that cognitive approaches which directly program for promotion of adaptive capacity are superior to a behaviourally-oriented approach which is more typical of the instruction adopted in teaching people with intellectual disabilities.

Another difference between SSP and the behavioural approaches and the other two approaches (RT and SIPS) which could account for the differential effect is that the latter two adopt group instruction and utilise peers as instructors. Students are taught in groups of two to eight in homogeneous or heterogeneous groupings where they are simultaneously or consecutively instructed in the same or different skills and where they are encouraged to assist each other during instruction. For a variety of skills and students, group instruction is an efficient method, not only in terms of teacher time, but also in its potential to enhance adaptive capacity (Alberto, *et al.*, 1980; Conway & Gow, in press; Gow, 1986), largely because the control of the learning situation is more in the hands of the learner.

There are many areas for future research in tackling the complex subject of promotion of adaptive capacity. A major omission in investigations of cognitively-oriented approaches to date has been specification of those aspects of teacher behaviour assumed to be essential for the on-going assessment of implementation. This is a surprising omission given the central role in cognitive approaches of mediated teaching style, and sensitivity to the appropriate time for transferring the responsibility for learning to the learner. Using any one of these cognitive approaches, the teacher must be sensitive to the changing cognitive status of each learner. Teachers must diagnose as they teach, continuously evaluate and revise a theory of each student's competence which must in turn be responsive to their participation capability (Brown & Palinscar, 1988). Optimum instructor direction and the subjectiveness of when to transfer control to the learner and when to intervene are in need of further investigation. Moreover, more efficient ways of monitoring the changing cognitive status of several students at the one time are needed. To enable adequate evaluation of these programs, immediate attention must be given to the area of learner-teacher interaction and to the ease with which these approaches can be acquired by teachers.

While we recognise that research in this area is still in its infancy, from this study we are confident in drawing the conclusion that in teaching intellectually disabled people, highest priority should be placed on using cognitive approaches which program directly for the promotion of adaptive capacity.

REFERENCES

Alberto, P., Jobes, N., Sizemore, A. & Doran, D. (1980) A comparison of individual and group instruction across response tasks. *J. Assoc. Sev. Hand.*, **5**, 285–93.

Baer, D. M., Wolf, M. M. & Risley, T. R. (1968) Some current dimensions of applied behaviour analysis. *J. Appl. Beh. Anal.*, **1**, 91–97.

Baine, D. (1986) Instruction of students with severe handicaps. In: J. Berg, *Perspectives and progress in mental retardation: proceedings of the seventh congress of the international association for the scientific study of mental deficiency (IASSMD)*. pp. 171–178. London, Methuen.

Balla, J. & MacDonald, R. (1985) Latent trait item analysis and facet theory: a useful combination. *Appl. Psych. Meas.* **9**(2), 191–198.

Belmont, J. M., & Butterfield, E. C. (1969) The relations of short-term memory to development and intelligence. In: L. C. Lipsitt and H. W. Reese (Eds.), *Advances in child development and behavior*. Vol. 4, pp. 30–83. Academic Press, N.Y.

Belmont, J. M., Butterfield, E. C. & Ferretti, R. P. (1982) To secure transfer of training instruct self-management skills. In: D. K. Detterman and R. J. Sternberg (Eds.) *How and how much can intelligence be increased?* pp. 147–154. Ablex, New Jersey.

Borkowski, J. G. & Cavanaugh, J. C. (1979) Maintenance and generalisation of skills and strategies by the retarded. In: N. R. Ellis (Ed.), *Handbook of mental deficiency: psychological theory and research.* (2nd Ed.), pp. 569–611. Erlbaum, Hillsdale, N.J.

Brown, A., Bransford, J., Ferrara, R. & Campione, J. (1983) Learning remembering and understanding. In: P. H. Mussen (ed.) *Handbook of Child Psychology, Vol. III*, pp. 77–166. John Wiley, New York.

Brown, A. L. & Campione, J. C. (1982) Modifying intelligence or modifying cognitive skills: more than a semantic quibble? In: D. K. Detterman & R. J. Sternberg (Eds.) *How and how much can intelligence be increased?* pp. 215–130. Ablex, New Jersey.

Brown, A. L. & Palinscar, A. S. (1988) Reciprocal teaching of comprehension strategies: a natural history of one program for enhancing learning. In: J. G. Borkowski and J. D. Day (Eds.), *Intelligence and cognition in special children: comparative studies of giftedness, mental retardation and learning disabilities.* Ablex, New York.

Brown, L., Nietupski, J. & Hamre-Nietupski, S. (1977) The criterion of ultimate functioning and public school service for severely handicapped students. In: M. A. S. Thomas (Ed.) *Hey don't forget about me: education's investment in the severely profoundly and multihandicapped.* Council on Exceptional Children, Reton, Virginia.

Butterfield, E. C. (1988) On solving the problem of transfer. In: M. M. Grunesberg, P. E. Morris and R. N. Sykes (eds.), *Practical aspects of memory (Vol. 2).* Academic Press, London.

Cherkes-Julkowski, M., Davis, L., Fimian, M., Gertner, N., McGuire, J., Norlander, K., Okolo, C. & Zoback, M. (1986) Encouraging flexible strategy usage in handicapped learners. In: J. Berg, *Perspectives and progress in mental retardation: proceedings of the seventh congress of the international association for the scientific study of mental deficiency (IASSMD).* pp. 189–196. London, Methuen.

Conway, R. N. (1985) The information processing model and the mildly developmentally delayed child: assessment and training. Unpublished Doctoral Dissertation, Macquarie University, Sydney.

Conway, R. & Gow, L. (in press). Mainstreaming through group instruction. *Rem. Spec. Ed.*

Das, J. P. (1985) Remedial training and mental retardation. Paper presented at *the Seventh Congress of IASSMD*, New Delhi, India, March.

Gow, L. (1984a) The use of verbal self-instruction to enhance learning in retarded adults: a study of techniques for improving acquisition, generalisation and maintenance. *CORE*, **8**(3), Fiche 5 D10.

Gow, L. (1984b) Cognitive-behaviour modification and its use with intellectually disabled people. *N.S.W. J. Spec. Ed.*, **2**, 24–31.

Gow, L. (1986) Enhancing far generalisation of strategy use. In: J. Berg, *Perspectives and progress in mental retardation: proceedings of the seventh congress of the international association for the scientific study of mental deficiency (IASSMD)*, pp. 345–352. Methuen, London.

Gow, L. (1987) Cognitive strategy training as a means of improving the efficiency of teaching work skills to adults with intellectual disabilities. *J. Prac. Appr. Dev. Hand.* **11**(2), 18–23.

Gow, L. (in press) Self-instruction Problem-Solving: a comprehensive cognitive program for promoting adaptive capacity. *The Hong Kong Journal of Mental Health*.

Gow, L. & Butterfield, E. (in press) Education of People with an Intellectual Disability. in: J. Taplin, G. Maple and T. Miller (Eds.) *An Introduction to Developmental Disability*. Sydney, Williams & Wilkins.

Gow, L., Butterfield, E. C. & Balla, J. (in press) The problem of transfer: are we close to a solution? *The Bulletin of the Hong Kong Psychological Society*.

Gow, L., Butterfield, E. C. & Balla, J. (submitted) An investigation of approaches to promoting adaptive capacity in mildly intellectually disabled children. *Rem. & Spec. Ed.*

Gow, L. & Ward, J. (1985) The use of verbal self-instruction training for enhancing generalisation outcomes with persons with an intellectual disability. *Aust. N.Z. J. Dev. Dis.*, **11**(3), 157–168.

Gow, L. & Ward, J. & Balla, J. (1985) The use of verbal self-instruction training (VSIT) to enhance learning in the mentally retarded: a study of techniques for improving acquisition, maintenance and generalisation outcomes. *Ed. Psych.*, **5**(2), 115–134.

Gow, L., Ward, J. & Balla, J. (1986) The use of VSIT to promote indirect generalisation. *Aust. N.Z. J. Dev. Dis.* **12**(2), 123–132.

Haring, N. G., Liberty, K. A. & White, O. R. (1980) Rules for data-based strategy decisions in instructional programs: current research and instructional implications. In: W. Sailor, B. Wilcox and L. Brown (Eds.). *Methods of instruction for severely handicapped students*. Paul H. Brookes, Baltimore.

Luria, A. R. (1961) *The Role of Speech in the Regulation of Normal and Abnormal Behaviour*. Pergamon, London.

Luria, A. R. (1966) *Higher cortical functions in man*. Basic Books, New York.

Maker, C. J. (1981) Problem Solving: a general approach to remediation. In: D. D. Smith, *Teaching the Learning Disabled*. Prentice Hall, Englewood Cliffs, N.J.

Meichenbaum, D. H. (1977) *Cognitive-behaviour modification: an integrative approach*. Plenum, New York.

Padawer, W. J., Zupan, B. A. & Kendall, P. C. (1980) *Developing self-control in children: a manual of cognitive-behavioural strategies*. Department of Psychology, University of Minnesota.

Pressley, M. (1979) Increasing children's self-control through cognitive interventions. *Rev. Ed. Res.*, **49**(2), 319–370.

Snell, M. E. (Ed.) (1983) *Systematic instruction of the moderately and severely handicapped*. (2nd Ed.). Merrill, London.

Sternberg, R. J. (1981) Cognitive-behavioral approaches to the training of intelligence in the retarded. *J. Spec. Ed.*, **15**(2), 165–183.

Stokes, T. F. & Baer, D. M. (1977) An implicit technology of generalisation. *J. Appl. Behav. Anal.*, **10**, 349–367.

Vygotsky, L. S. (1978) *Mind in Society: The development of higher psychological processes*. Harvard Uni. Press, Cambridge, MA.

Ward, J. & Gow, L. (1982) Programming generalisation: a central problem area in educational psychology. *Educ. Psych.*, **2**(3 & 4), 231–248.

Adapted Physical Education as a Key Issue in Mental Retardation Teacher Training

C. Sherrill

*Texas Women's University, Box 23717, TWU Station, Denton,
Texas 76204, USA*

The purpose of this paper was to acquaint special education and medical personnel with adapted physical education and to stimulate inter-disciplinary, crosscultural, international sharing, particularly in regard to teacher training. Adapted physical education was defined as the body of knowledge that focuses on problems in the motor, fitness, and leisure functioning of all individuals, including the mentally retarded. A brief history of adapted physical education was given, current status described, and the knowledge base explained. Employment practices and research showing the need for adapted physical education concluded the paper.

Internationally and crossculturally, there appears to be little inter-disciplinary sharing in regard to the motor development, physical education, sports/leisure training of mentally retarded children and youth. Physical educators from various countries have become acquainted through the International Federation for Adapted Physical Activities (IFAPA), founded in Canada in 1977. Conferences have been held every other year in Canada, Belgium, U.S.A., England, and Australia, respectively. The 1989 conference is planned for West Berlin, Germany. But these conferences are attended by few individuals outside the disciplines of physical education and recreation. Likewise, international sports gatherings for mentally retarded athletes, like Special Olympics, typically draw together only sports persons and time for sharing is very limited.

The purpose of this paper is to acquaint special education and medical personnel with adapted physical education and to stimulate inter-disciplinary interest and dialogue, particularly with regard to teacher training. In the U.S.A. special education and adapted physical education are very close, with university students who desire to teach mentally retarded children and youth taking courses in both areas. This professional closeness has been stimulated by federal law (Public Law 94–142 in 1975) that mandates that all handicapped children shall receive free, appropriate physical education in the public schools. Appropriateness refers primarily to placement decisions (separate, partially integrated, or fully integrated physical education) and is determined by an interdisciplinary committee, usually chaired by a special educator. The quality of physical education instruction received by mentally retarded students thus often depends on the knowledge and attitudes of members of the interdisciplinary team.

Physical educators, often by virtue of their association with sport teams, are enjoying increased opportunities for travel. For example, coaches from 70 countries interacted in the 1987 International Summer Special Olympics Games which provided competition in 14 sports (78 events) for approximately 5,000 mentally retarded atheletes. There is a growing hunger in the U.S.A. to know what other countries are doing in regard to physical education and sport for mentally retarded populations.

BRIEF HISTORY OF ADAPTED PHYSICAL EDUCATION

The history of adapted physical education, as we teach it in the U.S.A., can be traced to the medical gymnastics movement of Per Henrik Ling (1776–1839) of Sweden and Johann Guts-Muths (1749–1839) of Germany, Ling's teacher (Sherrill, 1988). The first adapted physical education university teachers in the U.S.A. were physicians trained in Ling's medical gymnastics, and the focus of this specialization was health, fitness, and postures (i.e., health impairments and physical disabilities among the normal schoolage population).

Adapted physical education in the U.S.A. did not turn its interests to mental retardation until 1965, when Eunice Kennedy Shriver (the sister of President Kennedy) challenged the profession at a national convention. President Kennedy's and Mrs Shriver's interest and subsequent advocacy were stimulated by a mentally retarded sister. The inclusion of the physical education requirement for handicapped children clause in the PL 94–142 federal legislation is attributed to the influence of the Kennedy family as well as the establishment of many physical education programs for the mentally retarded teacher training workshops in the 1960s and 1970s.

Federal legislation (PL 90–170) in 1967 to provide funding to support university training, research, and demonstration projects specifically in physical education and recreation for handicapped students is also attributed to the Kennedy family. As a result of this legislation and subsequent reauthorization and reappropriation bills, adapted physical education teacher training and research receive approximately 2 million dollars from the federal government each year. This money is divided among approximately 30 universities that have emerged as leaders in adapted physical education teacher training.

CURRENT STATUS OF ADAPTED PHYSICAL EDUCATION TEACHER TRAINING

In addition to university programs funded partially by federal money, many other colleges and universities offer adapted physical education courses and graduate level specializations. Both master's (30–36 credits) and doctoral (about 90 credits) degrees are available in adapted physical education. In fact, doctoral degree specialization in adapted physical education now ranks sixth out of 15 possibilities (Spirduso & Lovett, 1987). The five specializations more popular, in order of rank, are exercise physiology, biomechanics, administration, motor learning/control, and professional preparation.

In regard to teacher training in adapted physical education in other countries, Price (1986) states

> In Britain, there is only one institute of higher education (that being Dunfermline College in Scotland) which offers a post-graduate certificate in sport and recreation for the disabled. There is none which offers a degree (even at the bachelor's level) in therapeutic recreation or adapted physical education. What is more, apart from similarly isolated cases in Norway and (I think) West Germany, this provision is no better anywhere else in Europe. (p. 32)

This statement demonstrates our lack of information about programs in other countries. Physical education is much broader than sport. Nevertheless, seminars and symposia on sport often bring together mental retardation and sport experts and result in published proceedings that can be used as texts in teacher education. Illustrative of such gatherings are the Seminar on Sport for the Mentally Handicapped held in Brussels in 1980, the 1982 Mentally Handicapped Sport Symposium of the Netherlands – USA Bicentennial (Hal, Rarick, & Vermeer, 1984), the first International Medical Congress on Sports for the Disabled in Norway (Natvig, 1980), the UNESCO sponsored International Symposium on Physical Education and Sport Programs for the Physically and Mentally Handicapped in U.S.A. in 1982 (Stein, 1986), the Olympic Scientific Congress Research Sessions on Sport and Disabled Athletes (Sherrill, 1986b), and ReSpo 1986, International Congress on Recreational Sports and Leisure for the Disabled (Vermeer, 1987).

UNESCO (April, 1976) has provided some of the impetus for physical education services for mentally retarded persons in its landmark statement that "the handicapped also have a right to participate in physical education and sport". The United Nations' 1981 International Year of the Disabled and 1986 International Year of Special Olympics have also fostered worldwide understanding of the value of sport and physical education for mentally retarded individuals.

A HOLISTIC APPROACH TO SPECIAL EDUCATION

Adapted physical education, although it appears to have received little attention outside the U.S.A., is a key issue in mentally retardation teacher training. A holistic approach to special education requires application of knowledge in regard to cognitive, affective, and psycho-motor functioning. Adapted physical education is the body of knowledge that focuses on problems in the motor, fitness, and leisure functioning of all individuals, including the mentally retarded. Numerous basic text-books have been published in adapted physical education to present this knowledge in the U.S.A. (well over 30 texts; see Sherrill, 1988, for list), in Great Britain (Groves, 1979); and no doubt in other countries.

THE KNOWLEDGE BASE OF ADAPTED PHYSICAL EDUCATION

Among the best known of the U.S.A. texts are those of Auxter and Pyfer (1985), and Sherrill (1986a). In accordance with subareas within the body of adapted physical education knowledge, most texts include chapters and/or sections on abnormal and delayed motor development; cognitive and affective development as they relate to involvement in play, games, and sport; assessment, including motor performance and fitness tests for use in screening, diagnosis, placement, and instruction; principles and methods for adapting physical education and motor development/control instruction, beginning with infancy; curriculums and sports programs for specific handicapping conditions; behavior management techniques applied to gymnasium, swimming pool, and sports field; and history, philosophy, and current practices in adapted physical education. Most texts include one chapter specifically on mental retardation.

There is a growing trend for chapters to be included on integration because, in the U.S.A., integration of mentally retarded students with nonretarded peers often occurs first in physical education, art, music, homemaking, and industrial arts. This integration thrust is frequently troublesome since mentally retarded students almost always have lower motor skills and less grasp of sports rules and strategies than regular students. Various techniques are being devised to facilitate integration such as pairing mentally retarded and nonretarded students as partners or buddies. The needed additional instruction is delivered by same-age peer models since large class sizes often do not permit sufficient individualized teacher assistance.

These adapted physical education texts are being used in courses for both undergraduate and graduate students. Typically most undergraduate physical education majors (and some special education majors) complete one required general course in adapted physical education. Some states also require undergraduate physical education majors to complete one course in special education. Specialization options in adapted physical education are generally graduate level. In specialization, graduate students take 5 to 15 separate adapted physical education courses. At Texas Woman's University (coeducational at the graduate level) our students complete separate courses in motor development, neurological bases of motor control, adapted physical education survey, mainstreaming or integration, methods for severely/profoundly handicapped, assessment, and administrative issues and concerns in addition to courswork in statistics and research required of all students. Additionally several optional seminars and courses are offered. Many adapted physical education graduate students double major in special education.

EMPLOYMENT PRACTICES AND RESEARCH

The evolution of adapted physical education as separate from regular physical education has been based on both public school employment practices and research findings concerning the special psychomotor needs of handicapped children (Davis, 1986; Henderson, 1986; Hoover & Wade, 1985). Although employment practices vary widely, many public school systems hire one or more adapted physical education specialists. Some specialists provide direct instruction, often driving from school to school. Other specialists work as consultants to special education and regular physical education personnel, focus on assessment and placement concerns, or serve on multidisciplinary teams with physical and occupational therapists.

REFERENCES

Auxter, D., & Pyfer, J. (1985) *Principles and practices of adapted physical education and recreation* (5th ed.). St. Louis: C.V. Mosby.

Davis, W. E. (1986) Development of coordination and control in the mentally handicapped. In H. A. Whiting & M. Wade (Eds.). *Themes in motor development* (pp. 143–155). Hingham, MA: Kluwer-Academic Publishers.

Groves, L. (Ed.) (1979) *Physical education for special needs*. Cambridge, England: Cambridge University Press.

Hal, L. van, Rarick, G. L., & Vermeer, A. (Eds.) (1984) *Sport for the mentally handicapped*. Haarlem, Netherlands: Uitgeverij de Vrieseborch.

Henderson, S. (1986) Some aspects of the development of motor control in Down's syndrome. In H. A. Whiting & M. Wade (Eds.). *Themes in motor development* (pp. 69–91). Hingham, MA: Kluwer-Academic Publishers.

Hoover, J., & Wade, M. (1985) Motor learning theory and mentally retarded persons: A historical review. *Adapted Physical Activity Quarterly*, **2**(3), 228–252.

Natvig, H. (Ed.) (1980) *Proceedings of the First International Medical Congress on Sports for the Disabled*. Oslo, Norway: Royal Ministry of Church and Education.

Price, R. (1986) The status of international activity in recreation, sports, and cultural activities with disabled persons. Part 1. *Palaestra*, **2**(4), 27–32.

Sherrill, C. (1986a) *Adapted physical education and recreation*. Dubuque, IA: Wm. C. Brown.

Sherrill, C. (Ed.) (1986b) *Sport and disabled atheletes*. Champaign, IL: Human Kinetics.

Sherrill, C. (Ed.) (1988) *Leadership training in adapted physical education*. Champaign, IL: Human Kinetics.

Spirduso, W., & Lovett, D. (1987) Current status in graduate education in physical education: Program demography. *Quest*, **39**(2), 129–141.

Stein, J. (1986) International perspectives: Physical education and sport for participants with handicapping conditions. In C. Sherrill (Ed.). *Sport and disabled athletes* (pp. 51–64). Champaign, IL: Human Kinetics.

Vermeer, A. (Ed.) (1987) *Sports for the disabled: ReSpo 86*. Haarlem, Netherlands: Uitgeverij de Vrieseborch.

Section VII

Community Integration, Adjustment, Evaluation and Costs

Planning Sustainable Services: Principles for the Effective Targetting of Resources in Developed and Developing Nations

A. Ager

University of Leicester, Leicester LE1 7RH, England

The concept of sustainability is a vital one in the planning of effective services. Much planning still proceeds without consideration of the factors which will serve to sustain innovation. Work in other fields has much to teach us on this issue. The need to respect the complex ecology of behavioural systems, to build upon existing strengths and to foster participation are all now widely accepted as important in creating lasting change. More sustainable services are therefore likely to be those which are related to a community's existing patterns and concerns.

Many professionals working in the field of mental retardation are involved – to some extent – in the planning and development of services. It is widely accepted that the process of change within services is necessary if the needs of clients are to be met (Mittler, 1987), and it is clearly appropriate that workers directly involved with clients for other purposes play some part in this process. Such changes, however, are infrequently guided by the degree of rigour and prior planning that characterise other aspects of most professionals' work. If resources, often severely limited, are to be effectively targeted in the development of services, it is vital that this state of affairs is altered.

PRINCIPLES OF SERVICE PLANNING

There are a number of principles which could effectively guide the planning of service developments. For the most part, these mirror closely principles which may usefully underly the planning of interventions with individual clients (see Lavender, 1985). Such principles would prompt something akin to the following sequence of activities in the course of service planning:

(a) assessment of need
(b) identification of alternative strategies to meet this need
(c) consideration of these alternative strategies with regard to various
    key factors
(d) implementation of the favoured strategy and
(e) evaluation of the impact of the adopted strategy.

In clinical work with individual clients such a sequence – though perhaps not explicit – will underly the practice of most practitioners. There appear to be adequate grounds, however, to conclude that such a sequence is only rarely followed efficiently in the process of service planning (BABP, 1984; Sartorius, 1984; Kiernan, 1987).

The consideration of alternative strategies prior to implementation is clearly a key stage in such a sequence. To be truly effective, it is vital that such consideration involves an appropriate range of factors. Three factors of prime importance may be identified. Alternative strategies must clearly be assessed through consideration of their *potency*, that is regarding the degree to which they would meet defined needs. They must also be assessed with regards their *cost*, that is regarding the degree of resources their implementation would require. Equally as important as these two, though seldom recognised, is the factor of the *sustainability* of the proposed strategy. However potent and cost effective a strategy is, if the planned service cannot be sustained its ultimate worth is clearly negligible. Whilst this may appear self-evident, it has often been this third factor that has been ignored in the planning of services. A rigorous assessment of service options must include the identification of the mechanisms that will be required to sustain planned service developments.

UNSUSTAINABLE SERVICES

It is not difficult to identify examples where failure to appreciate what would be required to sustain a service development has led to difficulties. Many practitioners will, through their personal experience, have seen examples of planned developments collapsing through the lack of appropriate mechanisms to support them. Perhaps the most common examples involve attempts to change aspects of a service within an institutional setting which fail to take into consideration the complex organisational pressures which act to stultify innovation. Work looking at the systemic constraints on the behaviour of nurses (Cullen *et al.*, 1983; Partridge, 1984; Cullen, 1987) has suggested why traditional interventions within hospital-based services often prove functionally unsustainable.

Evaluations of community-based services have, however, demonstrated similar difficulties in sustaining planned change. For some services initial planning failed to adequately consider the difficulties in recruiting appropriate staff to sustain the service as it developed (Reference Note †). For others, physical integration within the community has falsely been assumed sufficient to sustain social integration, and the degree of community contact achieved by clients has been disappointingly low (Humphreys *et al.*, 1983; Landesman-Dwyer and Berkson, 1984). Dcinstitutionalisation programmes have, in general, been characterised by an underestimate of both the financial and social resources required to sustain someone in the community (Baldwin, 1987). Published work on innovation in staff deployment in day services has indicated that even dramatic increases in client engagement are insufficient on their own to sustain ammended staff behaviour (Jones *et al.*, 1987). Where the effects of early intervention programmes with children with identified developmental delay have initially been encouraging, there has often been little evidence of such changes being sustained over time (Cunningham 1987).

LESSONS FROM DEVELOPMENT WORK

Such difficulties are so ubiquitous that there is a temptation to consider them inevitable, that is unavoidable by any action or forethought at the planning stage. Fortunately this is not the case. The value of considering in advance factors which will serve to sustain innovation is a lesson now well appreciated in other areas of development – notably those involving economic growth and industrial and agricultural change in developing nations.

David Korten, of the Agency for International Development, has identified three generations of such development activity (see Derham, 1988). The 'First Generation' was characterised by the straightforward importation of resources into a needy situation. (Functionally, this is not dissimilar to the previous practice of many mental retardation professionals 'importing' their intervention programmes into an institutional culture where they might meet short-term need, but are unlikely to have any longer-term impact on practice.)

The 'Second Generation' involved small-scale local development, displaying more involvement with people at the 'grass-roots' level, but still attacking the symptoms of need rather than the causes. (Much of our practice within mental retardation seems presently at this level, with attempts being made to meet real needs but – as has been noted – complex factors often leaving such attempts relatively unproductive in the longer term.)

For Korten, though, agricultural and economic development work has now reached the 'Third Generation', concerned with 'sustainable systems development' and the 'integration of local initiatives into a supportive national development system' (see Derham, 1988). Sustainability is the central issue in this era, with community involvement, 'bottom-up' planning and local responsibility the key means of fostering this. There is a growing concensus that such strategies are essential if the errors of the past are to be avoided (Brandt Commission, 1980; Johnson and Bernstein, 1982; Taylor, 1987).

TOWARDS SUSTAINABLE SERVICES

In the area of agricultural and economic development the remnants of unsustained innovation are often painfully visible. The rusty machinery left in parts of Africa from such projects as the British groundnut scheme and the Canadian wheat project (Derham, 1988) are vivid reminders of the worthlessness of developments, which, despite being apparently potent and cost-effective, fail to consider the complex mechanisms required to sustain change. The legacies of failed innovation within mental retardation services may be less publicly visible, but nonetheless to the actual consumers of such services they are no doubt all too frequently apparent.

The question then is, in practical terms, how can we ensure that we develop sustainable mental retardation services? And further, are there any examples of good practice, in this regard, from which we might learn? In fact, there appear to be three key characteristics of service development activity which encourages the establishment of sustainable services. Each may be seen to relate closely to both the lessons learned from general development work noted above, and also the accumulating literature on organisational change.

Respect for Complex Behavioural Ecology

The first characteristic of effective planning for sustainable services is evidence of respect for the complex behavioural ecology of an existing system. As an ecological analysis of biological systems reveals the complex interdependence of organisms, so ecological analysis of behavioural systems identifies the sophisticated interplay of patterns of activity (Willems, 1974; Landesman-Dwyer and Knowles, 1987). Such analyses frequently demonstrate how changing one aspect of a situation can have unexpected consequences in other areas (Milne, 1985). They therefore generally caution against gross interventions which may disrupt subtle balances and counter-controls. Change is made on the basis of building upon existing repertoires of behaviour, and generally with regard to the strengths of the present system (Ager, 1987).

Incremental Change

Associated with the above, a second characteristic of planning for sustainable services will be an emphasis on incremental change. Whilst service situations may frequently appear ripe for gross interventions, the durability of change achieved by such strategics is frequently disappointing (Ager, 1987). The evidence is in favour of more 'minimal' interventions, where potency may be limited but sustainability is high. Such strategies require clear direction and patient adherence if they are to be successful, but their adoption has clear theoretical and empirical support (Georgiades and Phillimore, 1975; Tennant et al., 1981).

Active Participation

Tying together respect for the behavioural ecology of the existing situation and an emphasis on incremental change is the third characteristic of active participation in the planning process by all effected individuals. Participation by consumers in service planning aids the identification of appropriate service goals (Lowe et al., 1986; Jones et al., 1987). Participation by staff involved in a new pattern of service not only fosters morale, but allows detailed 'grassroots' information to be fed into the planning process (Jones et al., 1987). Such mechanisms are vital if ecological factors are to be taken into consideration. Indeed, participation by those effected by developments has been identified as the single most important factor in engineering lasting change in settings as varied as the manufacturing plants of high technology industry and rural communities working towards agricultural reform (Batchelor, 1981; Partridge, 1984). The benefits of 'bottom-up' as opposed to 'top-down' planning are being increasingly recognised (Humphreys, 1986; Derham, 1988).

EXAMPLES OF SUSTAINABLE SERVICES

Considering the above characteristics, it follows that a central feature of a service that takes sustainability seriously is likely to be the manner in which it reflects the general culture and environment for which it is planned. Such services will not be imposed upon a community, but will grow out of its existing patterns and concerns. Few services, if any, will meet this ideal perfectly, but there are now a number of examples of where such an approach has been adopted with commitment, and with promising results.

Using first an example from a developed nation, Jones et al. (1987) describe an evaluation of a service development programme focussed on a small residential and day care unit in South Wales. The central aims of the programme were (i) to involve clients' families, staff and supervisors in identifying aspects of the service which presented problems and (ii) to implement changes based upon the above consultation.

There are numerous features of this programme of relevance to the preceding discussion. Discussions with the various groups involved with the service revealed a surprisingly high degree of unanimity regarding the areas that should be targeted for change. Encouraging families and staff to participate in the planning process along with supervisors effectively mobilised considerable resources for effecting the required changes. With such momentum esatablished, the 'interventions' necessary to prompt change were generally minimal (e.g. establishing discussions, providing written guidelines on procedures etc.). A phased introduction of such discrete interventions resulted in the successful establishment of a number of changes in staff and client behaviour – an outcome that would appear to have been less likely if all interventions had been implemented at once. The timing, nature and extent of such changes indicated the complex ecological relationships between the social environment of the service and staff and client repertoires. Finally, and perhaps most crucially, available evidence suggests that targeted changes not only proved durable over time, but also established foundations for further participative planning in the development of the service (Porterfield et al., 1982).

This work has been built upon with the development of a 'service manager's guide' to involving staff and families in service improvement (Porterfield et al., 1983) and, more recently, through the establishment of 'quality action groups' as a means of prompting participative planning within services (Beyer, 1987). Work in this vein clearly adheres to the principles identified earlier as likely to foster sustainable change. In particular, it provides a useful model of how valuable personal resources – so frequently trapped by the structures of established services – might instead be released to effect development.

A second example of a strategy for service development which encourages sustainability relates to the establishment of a home support service in Zimbabwe. As befits the notion of services growing out of the existing patterns and concerns of a community, the strategy clearly reflects the culture and environment of a developing African nation.

In 1984 the Zimcare Trust, a non-governmental mental handicap agency operating in Zimbabwe, launched a major programme of home support for families with a mentally handicapped child (Mariga, 1984). The programme was structured with respect to the strategy of 'commmunity-based rehabilitation' (CBR), which has been developed through the World Health Organisation primarily as a means of providing services to people with physical and sensory handicaps (Helander et al., 1980). The essential features of a CBR programme are emphases on

(i) work within the natural environment of the handicapped individual, (ii) use of indigenous (unqualified) personnel for family support, and (iii) deployment of professional expertise through training and monitoring (rather than directly therapeutic) roles (McConkey, 1988).

The course of this programme's development again illustrates a number of issues relevant to previous discussion. The programme was established by linking with agencies already operating in the identified catchment districts. Such a policy not only allowed the new service to build upon existing service networks, it also provided access to valuable knowledge regarding the social ecology of communities. Using indigenous personnel also encouraged the development of a pattern of service sensitive to the local culture. With such a foundation, the limited degree of supervision and training available was sufficient to sustain the operation of the support service. Further, an evaluation of the service indicated that home support had encouraged substantial developmental gains in a high proportion of handicapped clients. With training taking place within the client's home setting, the prospect for generalisation and maintenance of such gains is clearly good (McConkey, 1988).

McConkey (1988) notes how this sort of CBR approach is particularly effective in the manner in which it mobilises available resources in a community, rather than taking over responsibility for action from its members. In this regard, he points out that there may be valuable lessons to be learned for the provision of services in developed nations. The professionalisation of services can act as a powerful barrier to the effective delivery of care and support. If services are to be sustainable, they must ultimately receive some sustenance from their host community. While there are sadly at present too few examples from which we can generalise regarding good practice, basic principles holding for both developed and developing nations are suggested. To create lasting change, mechanisms must be identified which will act to sustain innovation. Such mechanisms will reflect the complex behavioural ecology of each individual service setting, and there are therefore likely to be no 'universal solutions' identified. Rather, in respecting the complexity of a situation, in building incrementally upon existing patterns and in encouraging active participation, sustainability must be fostered anew in each unique setting.

ACKNOWLEDGEMENTS

Preparation of this chapter was supported, in part, by a grant from North Warwickshire Health Authority. The assistance of Ms Wendy Ager in compiling bibliographic details was much appreciated.

REFERENCE NOTE

† In 1986 the developing community mental handicap services in North
Warwickshire experienced increasing difficulty in recruiting suitable staff to
new units. As a result, one facility was actually forced to close for a short
period. These difficulties mirrored those experienced by many other rapidly
expanding community services (e.g. NIMROD in South Wales) which
swiftly deplete the available employment pool.

REFERENCES

Ager, A. K. (1987) Minimal intervention: a strategy for generalised behaviour
change with mentally handicapped individuals. *Behavioural Psychotherapy*.
15: 16–30.

B.A.B.P. (1984) *Facing the challenge: common issues in work with people who are
mentally handicapped, elderly or chronically mentally ill*. B.A.B.P. Publications, Rossendale, Lancashire.

Baldwin, S. (1987) Communities to neighbourhoods. *Disability, Handicap and
Society*. **2**(2): 41–59.

Batchelor, P. (1981) *People in Rural Development*. Paternoster, Exeter.

Beyer, S. (1987) Pursuing quality through a quality action group: experiences in
the CUSS Home Support Service. In: L. Ward (ed), *Getting Better All The
Time?: Issues and Strategies for Ensuring Quality in Community Services for
People with Mental Handicap*. King's Fund, London.

Brandt Commission. (1980) *North-South: a programme for survival*. Pan,
London.

Cullen, C., Burton, M., Watts, S. and Thomas, M. (1983) A preliminary report
on the nature of interactions in a mental handicap institution. *Behaviour
Research and Therapy*. **21**: 579–583.

Cullen, C. (1987) Nurse training and institutional constraints. In: J. Hogg and P.
Mittler (eds), *Staff Training in Mental Handicap*. Croom Helm, London.

Cunningham, C. (1987) Early intervention in Down's syndrome. In: G. Hosking
and G. Murphy (eds), *Prevention of Mental Handicap: A World View*.
Royal Society of Medicine Services, London.

Derham, M. (1988) The right kind of development. TEAR Times. **39**: 4–6.

Georgiades, N. J. and Phillimore, L. (1975) The myth of the hero-innovator and
alternative strategies for organisational change. In: C. C. Kiernan and F. P.
Woodford (eds), *Behaviour Modification with the Severely Retarded*.
Associated Scientific Publishers, Amsterdam.

Helander, E., Nelson, G. and Mendis, P. (1980) *Training the Disabled in the
Community: an experimental manual on rehabilitation and disability
prevention for developing countries*. World Health Organisation, Geneva.

Humphreys, S., Lowe, K., and Blunden, R. (1983) *Long-term evaluation of
services for mentally handicapped people in Cardiff*. Annual Report for
1982. Mental Handicap in Wales Applied Research Unit.

Humphreys, S. (1986) Individual planning in NIMROD: results of an evaluation of the system four years on. In: G. Grant, S. Humphreys and M. McGrath (eds), *Community Mental Handicap Teams: Theory and Practice.* BIMH, Kidderminster.

Johnson, H. and Bernstein, H. (eds). (1982) *Third World Lives of Struggle.* Heinemann, London.

Jones, A. A., Blunden, R., Coles, E., Evans, G. and Porterfield, J. (1987) Evaluating the impact of training, supervisor feedback, self-monitoring and collaborative goal setting on staff and client behaviour. In: J. Hogg and P. Mittler (eds), *Staff Training in Mental Handicap.* Croom Helm, London.

Kiernan, C. (1987) Summing up. In: G. Hosking and G. Murphy (eds), *Prevention of Mental Handicap: A World View.* Royal Society of Medicine Services, London.

Landesman-Dwyer, S. and Berkson, G. (1984) Friendships and social behavior. In J. Wortis (ed), *Mental Retardation and Developmental Disabilities: An Annual Review, Vol. 13.* Plenum Press, New York.

Landesman-Dwyer, S. and Knowles, M. (1987) Ecological analysis of staff training in residential settings. In: J. Hogg and P. Mittler (eds), *Staff Training in Mental Handicap.* Croom Helm, London.

Lavender, A. (1985) Quality of care and staff practices in long-stay settings. In: F. Watts (ed), *New Developments in Clinical Pyschology.* BSP with John Wiley, Chichester.

Lowe, K., de Paiva, S. and Humphreys, S. (1986) *Long-term evaluation of services for people with a mental handicap in Cardiff: client's views.* Mental Handicap in Wales Applied Research Unit, Cardiff.

McConkey, R. (1988) Out of Africa: an alternative style of services for people with mental handicaps and their families. *Mental Handicap.* **16**(1): 23–26.

Mariga, L. (1984) *HOPE for the child.* Zimcare Trust, Harare.

Milne, D. (1985) An ecological validation of nurse training in behaviour therapy. *Behavioural Psychotherapy.* **13**: 14–28.

Mittler, P. (1987) Staff development: changing needs and service contexts in Britain. In: J. Hogg and P. Mittler (eds), *Staff Training in Mental Handicap.* Croom Helm, London.

Partridge, K. (1984) *Changing institutions? Quality of care and innovations in hospitals for people with a mental handicap.* University of Birmingham, Birmingham.

Porterfield, J., Evans, G. and Blunden, R. (1982) *Improving mental handicap services: involving client's families and staff in selecting areas for service development.* Mental Handicap in Wales Applied Research Unit, Research Report No. 13, Cardiff.

Porterfield, J., Evans, G. and Blunden, R. (1983) *Working together for change: a service manager's guide to involving staff and families in service improvement.* Mental Handicap in Wales Applied Research Unit, Cardiff.

Sartorius, N. (1984) Mental retardation – a world view. In: J. Dobbing, A. D. B. Clarke, J. A. Corbett, J. Hogg and R. O. Robinson (eds), *Scientific Studies in Mental Retardation.* Royal Society of Medicine and Macmillan Press, London.

Taylor, R. (1987) *The Prisoner and other stories*. Marc Europe, London.

Tennant, L., Cullen, C. and Hattersley, J. (1981) Applied behavioural analysis: intervention with retarded people. in: G. C. L. Davey (ed), *Applications of Conditioning Theory*. Methuen, London.

Willems, E. P. (1974) Behavioural technology and behavioural ecology. *Journal of Applied Behaviour Analysis*. **3**: 131–160.

Designing Individualised Community-Based Placements as an Alternative to Institutions for People with a Severe Mental Handicap and Severe Problem Behaviour

E. Emerson

South East Thames Regional Health Authority Special Development Team,
Centre for the Applied Psychology of Social Care,
Institute of Social and Applied Psychology, University of Kent
at Canterbury, Canterbury, Kent CT2 7LZ, England

The planned closure of larger institutional settings in the UK has resulted in the exploration of alternative strategies for supporting people with a severe mental handicap and severe problem behaviour in community settings. The characteristics of this client group and the services planned for them are described.

INTRODUCTION

It is estimated that 25–35% of people with severe mental handicaps exhibit severe problem behaviours (Jacobsen, 1982). Such behaviours are the major contributor to stress in families (Pahl and Quine, 1984), the main predictor of family decisions to seek residential care (Tausig, 1985) and the most frequently cited reasons for the breakdown of community based placements for adults (Intagliata and Willer, 1982). The needs of people with severe problem behaviour are often neglected. Thus, for example, Oliver *et al.* (1987) report that only 2% of the 596 cases of self-injury they identified in the south east of England had any form of written psychological treatment programme. People with severe mental handicaps and severe problem behaviour are also at significantly greater risk of physical abuse (Rusch *et al.*, 1986).

Services in the UK for this client group have consisted of support from generic educational, health and social services agencies, temporary admission to segregated treatment units and, as a course of last resort, institutionalisation (Blunden and Evans, 1987). Support from local agencies has often been unavailable at either the time or intensity required (Pahl and Quine, 1984), a problem compounded by manpower supply shortages in relevant specialist fields.

The use of segregated treatment units raises a number of problems (Blunden and Evans, 1987; Department of Health and Social Security, 1984; Emerson *et al.*, 1987). At a clinical level concerns include the quality of life experienced by people resident within such units, the social acceptability of the intervention procedures utilised and doubts about the generalisation and maintenance of behaviour changes achieved. At an organisational level the availability of segregated units may, by reducing pressure on the local agency, significantly hinder the development of local services for this client group through enabling local managers and professionals to attend to competing demands for scarce resources. Access to segregated units may also provide incentives to services under stress to represent people as "unmanageable", thus becoming potential dumping grounds for individuals who promote organisational crises.

Recent changes in service ideology and the closure of larger institutions has focused attention in the UK on alternative models of service delivery (Blunden and Evans, 1987; Donnellan *et al.*, 1984; Emerson *et al.*, 1987), including the development of peripatetic specialist teams to provide support in the client's normal living, learning or working environment. The aim of this paper is to present information relating to the planning of community based services for this client group arising from one such development, the South East Thames Regional Health Authority's Special Development Team.

DEVELOPING LOCAL SERVICES FOR PEOPLE WITH A SEVERE MENTAL HANDICAP AND SEVERE PROBLEM BEHAVIOUR

Background

The South East Thames Regional Health Authority (SETRHA) is responsible for the co-ordination and development of publicly funded health services in the south east of England. It funds and supports 15 District Health Authorities with a total population of 3.6 million. The area covered ranges from inner city London to the dormitory and rural centres of Kent and East Sussex. SETRHA policy for the development of mental handicap services over the past decade has reflected an increased commitment to the provision of comprehensive community based services organised at the level of each of the 15 District Health Authorities combined with the closure of all NHS managed mental handicap hospitals.

Within this context regional initiatives for people with severe problem behaviour would need to focus upon two broad objectives: the relocation of residents during institutional closure, and the strengthening of local services to ensure effective support could be provided to people with severe problem behaviour in the future. The establishment of sub-regional residential treatment units was considered an ineffective strategy for meeting the second aim. Indeed, the availability of such services was judged to provide actual disincentives to local managers to develop local initiatives. It was subsequently decided that SETRHA establish an advisory team with the resources to effectively assist agencies develop effective local services for this client group. The Special Development Team, consisting of a Team Leader, Deputy Team Leader and 4 Team Members, was consequently established in 1985 as a 5 year joint project between SETRHA and the Institute of Social and Applied Psychology at the University of Kent at Canterbury.

The Special Development Team was established with two aims: (a) to assist local health or social service agencies develop services for 38 of the most severely behaviourally disordered people with severe mental handicaps, many of whom were currently being contained in institutions scheduled for closure, and (b) to assist in the general development of local services for this client group. These dual aims reflected a commitment to broader based service development based upon the development and dissemination of innovatory demonstration pro-grammes.

Clients

Clients were defined as the 2–3 most behaviourally disordered individuals with a severe mental handicap per District Health Authority. This led to the identification of 29 clients across 13 District Health Authorities, giving an incidence rate for this *particular* level of severity of problem behaviour of 1:100,000 of the general population.

The 29 identified clients include 21 men and 8 women with a mean age of 28.1 years (sd=7.0 years). At the time of referral 83% were living in NHS or private hospital settings, 10% in smaller congregate care settings managed by social services or voluntary agencies and 7% with their natural parents. The 27 clients placed outside of their natural families were first admitted to institutional care with a mean age of 9.6 years (sd=6.8 yrs) and have spent an average of 19.0 years (sd=7.1 yrs) or 67% of their lifespan in some form of social care arrangements.

The incidence of specific severe problem behaviours among the 29 people is given below in Table 1. Severe problem behaviour was defined as behaviour of such an intensity, frequency or duration that the physical safety of the person or others is placed in serious jeopardy or behaviour which is likely to seriously limit or deny access to and use of ordinary community facilities.

Table 1. Incidence of severe problem behaviours among 29 identified clients

Behaviour	n	%
physical assault	20	69
damage to environment	14	48
self-injury	12	41
pica	5	17
severe non-compliance/withdrawal	4	14
absconding	4	14
screaming	4	14
public masturbation	4	14
faecal smearing	3	10
vomiting	2	7
sexual assault	1	3
cyclical obsessional state	1	3

The 29 individuals identified exhibited a total of 74 problem behaviours (average of 2.6 per client) that were of such a severity as to place extreme demands upon direct care staff. Violence towards other people (69%), the material environment (48%) and self-injury (41%) were most common. In all cases members of staff were the major target of aggression. Assault upon other people with mental handicaps was relatively infrequent and only appeared secondary to other forms of violence. The most common forms of assault encountered were scratching, punching, kicking, biting and the throwing of objects (chairs, tables, crockery) at people. Only 2 individuals (7%) had any form of written pyschological intervention programme.

Alternating treatment design (Iwata *et al.*, 1982; Mace *et al.*, 1986) were used with a sub-group of 10 clients to determine whether environmental determinants of such severe problem behaviours could be identified. Clients 1–7 were exposed for 10–15 min on 4 separate occasions to 4 experimental situations analogous to the types of settings in which problem behaviours are likely to occur. The experimental conditions were identical to those developed by Iwata *et al.* (1982). These consisted of: (I) *Social Disapproval* in which staff attention (concern or mild disapproval combined with non-punitive physical contact) was delivered contingent upon the occurrence of the problem behaviour; (II) *Academic Demand* in which the client is taught a novel task, staff demands being withdrawn contingent upon the occurrence of problem behaviours; (III) *Alone* in which the client is alone in a barren environment; (IV) *Unstructured Play* in which staff attention is delivered contingent upon the absence of the problem behaviour. Clients 8 and 9

Table 2. Association between behaviours and analogue conditions for all severe problem behaviours observed within sessions

Client	Behaviour	Analogue condition(s) associated with high rates of observed behaviour
C1	biting/pinching	academic demand
	throwing objects	academic demand
	screaming	academic demand
	public masturbation	alone
	stereotypies	alone
C2	pushing	academic demand
	absconding	academic demand
C3	hitting	academic demand
	screaming	academic demand
	absconding	no relationship
C4	self-injury	academic demand
	pushing/throwing	academic demand
	screaming/shouting	academic demand
C5	self-injury	academic demand
	screaming	academic demand
	absconding	no relationship
C6	no severe problem behaviours observed within sessions	
C7	no severe problem behaviours observed within sessions	
C8	self-injury	academic demand
C9	hair pulling/scratching	staff proximity to client
C10	hitting/spitting	staff interaction with client

were exposed to just one presentation of each condition due to the extremely high rates of self-injury and aggression observed. Client 10 was exposed to modified analogue conditions reflecting their specific problem behaviours.

For 8 of the 10 individuals clear relationships between environmental conditions and the rate of occurrence of at least one of the severe problem behaviours exhibited was apparent (see Table 2). Figure 1 gives illustrative data for clients 1–4. In all instances, other than masturbation, the problem behaviour occurred at a higher rate under the *demand* condition. No behaviours of any client appeared to be maintained by the attention of carers, i.e. could be described as "attention seeking".

That even the most severe problem behaviour may serve social-

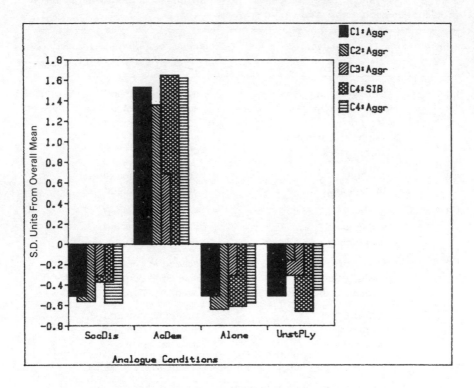

Figure 1. Mean frequency of severe problem behaviours exhibited by clients
1–4 across conditions.

communicative functions leads to the consideration of constructional
intervention procedures based upon the teaching of functionally equivalent communication strategies (Carr and Durrand, 1985). Such approaches
may be more effective by occasioning more reliable generalisation across
settings and maintenance over time of behaviour change (Carr, 1988),
and more ethically acceptable through being less reliant upon the use of
restrictive or punitive procedures (Axelrod, 1987).

Planning Individualised Services

Individual service plans have been developed for 25 of the 29 clients.
These plans identify the resources required to effectively support the
client in integrated community activities. It was considered that effective
services would be individualised, embody systemic constructional programme methods, assure long term flexibility in resource allocation and
be delivered in the least restrictive environment.

Local ownership of the plans was considered crucial to ensuring their adoption, the maintenance of service quality over time and the dissemination of service models and practices within and across agencies (Stolz, 1981). Consequently the development of individual service planning was undertaken as a collaborative venture with local agencies.

The development of an individual service plan typically consisted of a two stage process taking from 2–6 months (Toogood *et al.*, 1988). First, information relevant to planning client support was collected from interviews, searches of agency records, functional analyses of the problem behaviours, observation in the client's natural environment and assessment of adaptive behaviours. Second, the information was used to identify the resources required by alternative service options.

The resulting individual service plan specifies the nature of residential, vocational, educational and recreational services to be provided for the client, including the number and characteristics of other people served, staffing levels, staff characteristics and training requirements of the proposed service and the funding implications for the options.

Salient aspects of the residential component of the proposed plans are given below in Table 3. Of the 21 individuals for whom group living was proposed, it was recommended that 5 live alone for an interim period of 4–18 months. As of September 1988 17 (65%) of the plans developed had been approved by the responsible local agencies, only 1 (4%) had been rejected. Services planned by this process for 11 clients were operative.

DISCUSSION AND CONCLUSIONS

The process of individual service planning raises a number of issues.

1. Individuals with a severe mental handicap who are considered by services the most behaviourally disordered typically exhibit multiple problem behaviours, the most common of which are aggression, damage to the material environment and self-injury. Clear environmental determinants of these behaviours can be demonstrated by brief assessment procedures based upon the use of alternating treatment designs. The major function of such behaviours appears to be one of demand avoidance.

2. Individual service planning represents a viable organisational response to the need to identify and allocate resources for the care of members of the client group. The process of individual service planning has been adopted by 13 of 15 District Health Authorities. Of the plans developed 65% had been accepted, 4% rejected.

3. The process of individual service planning establishes a forum for the discussion of a range of ethical, professional and organisational issues. Central among these are the conflicts between the financial benefits of

Table 3.   Characteristics of individualised service plans for 26 clients

Building	Domestic house (n=19) Domestic apartment (n=7)
Location	Close proximity to generic community facilities (n=26)
Client grouping	Client living alone (n=5) Client living alone in apartment attached to other service (n=2) Client living with 1 other with severe problem behaviour (n=2) Client with 1 other, no problem behaviour (n=3) Client with 2 others, no problem behaviour (n=9) Client with 3 others, no problem behaviour (n=4) Client with non-handicapped co-tenants (n=1)
Transition	Client lives alone for initial period (n=5) Client moves directly to planned service (n=21)
Staffing	Range of 4 to 13.5 whole time equivalent staff
Recurrent revenue costs	Range £27,000 to £105,000 per client.

group living situations, the responsibility of service agencies to minimise the risk of injury to individuals to which it owes a duty of care, and the explicit commitment of many agencies to provide freedom of choice in selection of living situations to service users.

4. Individual service plans developed for members of this client group often involve extensive short-term revenue costs. Common barriers to their adoption by local agencies include: an organisational commitment to maximising the breadth of coverage of limited resources rather than investing in innovation and the establishment of 'centres of excellence'; an organisational focus upon minimising short term cost rather than risking short term investment for medium and longer term benefits; an implicit questioning of the value of people with a severe mental handicap and severe problem behaviour.

5. Commitment to the plans by opinion leaders in local agencies appears central to the chances of successfully overcoming some of the conservative organisational dynamics indicated above. Key factors in

culturing this commitment include: the early identification and recruitment of key local personnel, including professionals whose early input is important in avoiding later issues of professional territoriality; the efficiency of the individual service planning process, which can be enhanced by involving local managers who have executive control over resources and one or two individuals who can contribute a significant amount of time to the process of information collection and analysis; the creation of direct contact between senior managers and the client. Senior managers in health and social service organisations are often ignorant of the conditions under which people with severe problem behaviours are being contained. Arranging for these two groups to meet is often difficult. To date, however, we have found that the results of such encounters are invariably worthwhile.

REFERENCES

Axelrod, S. (1987) Functional and structural analyses of behavior: Approaches leading to reduced use of punishment procedures? *Res. Dev. Dis.* **8**: 165–178.

Blunden, R. and Allen, D. (1987) *Facing the Challenge: An Ordinary Life for People with Learning Difficulties and Challenging Behaviour*. King's Fund Centre, London.

Carr, E. G. (1988) Functional equivalence as a mechanism of response generalization. In: R. H. Horner, G. Dunlap and R. L. Koegel (eds), *Generalization and Maintenance: Life-Style Changes in Applied Settings*. pp. 221–240. Paul H. Brookes, Baltimore.

Carr, E. G. and Durrand, V. M. (1985) The social-communicative basis of severe behavior problems in children. In: S. Reiss and R. R. Bootzin (eds), *Theoretical Issues in Behavior Therapy*. pp. 219–254. Academic Press, New York.

Department of Health and Social Security. (1984) *Helping Mentally Handicapped People with Special Problems*. Her Majesty's Stationery Office, London.

Donnellan, A. M., LaVigna, G. W., Zambito, J. and Thvedt, J. (1985) A time-limited intensive intervention program model to support community placement for persons with severe behaviour problems. *J. Assoc. Peop. Sev. Hand.* **10**: 123–131.

Emerson, E., Toogood, A., Mansell, J., Barrett, S., Bell, C., Cummings, R., and McCool, C. (1987) Challenging Behaviour and Community Services: I. Introduction and Overview. *Ment. Hand.* **15**: 166–169.

Intagliata, J. and Willer, B. (1982) Resinstitutionalization of mentally retarded persons successfully placed into family-care and group homes. *Am. J. Ment. Def.* **87**: 34–39.

Iwata, B. A., Dorsey, M. F., Slifer, K. J., Bauman, K. E. and Richman, G. S. (1982) Toward a functional analysis of self-injury. *Anal. Int. Dev. Disabil.* **2**: 3–20.

Jacobsen, J. W. (1982) Problem behaviour and psychiatric impairment within a developmentally disabled population: I. behaviour frequency. *App. Res. Ment. Retard.* **3**: 121–139.

Mace, F. C., Page, T. J., Ivancic, M. T. and O'Brien, S. (1986) Analysis of environmental determinants of aggression and disruption in mentally retarded children. *App. Res. Ment. Retard.* **7**: 203–221.

Oliver, C., Murphy, G. H., Corbett, J. A. (1987) Self-injurious behaviour in people with mental handicap: a total population study. *J. Ment. Def. Res.* **31**: 147–162.

Pahl, J. and Quine, L. (1984) *Families with Mentally Handicapped Children: A Study of Stress and of Service Response.* Health Services Research Unit, University of Kent at Canterbury, Canterbury.

Rusch, R. G., Hall, J. C. and Griffin, H. C. (1986) Abuse provoking characteristics of institutionalized mentally retarded individuals. *Am. J. Ment. Def.* **90**: 618–624.

Stolz, S. B. (1981) Adoption of innovations from applied behavioral research: "Does anybody care?". *J. Appl. Beh. Anal.* **14**: 491–506.

Tausig, M. (1985) Factors in family decision-making about placement for developmentally disabled individuals. *Am. J. Ment. Def.* **89**: 352–361.

Toogood, A., Emerson, E., Barrett, S., Cummings, R., Hughes, H., and McCool, C. (1988) Challenging behaviour and community services. 3: Planning individualised services. *Ment. Hand.* **16**: 70–74.

Severe Mental Handicap and Problem Behaviour: Evaluating Transfer from Institutions to Community Care

J. Mansell and F. Beasley

Centre for the Applied Psychology of Social Care,
Institute of Social and Applied Psychology,
University of Kent at Canterbury CT2 7LZ, England

Staffed houses for people with severe and profound mental handicaps who also have very severe problem behaviour were evaluated in terms of how the people served spent their time – whether their lives were characterised by long periods of boredom, doing nothing, in isolation, or whether people engaged in meaningful and adaptive activity. Preliminary results showed that (i) the houses each served many fewer people and had much higher staffing ratios than the other kinds of service, (ii) people in staffed houses received contact from staff for on average 27% of the day, compared with 10% in hospitals, (iii) two people showed markedly increased engagement after moving to housing but two did not, and (iv) increased engagement appears to be related to staff contact delivered as direct verbal or physical assistance rather than as conversation or questions.

This study was conceptualised as an evaluation of the effectiveness of community-based residential services, individually designed for people with severe and profound mental handicaps who also have very severe problem behaviour. The services concerned have been set up by district health authorities with support from a regional Special Development Team (Emerson *et al.*, 1987) as an alternative to continued institutional care; without exception they are staffed houses or apartments. Previous research on community-based residential services has shown that people with severe problem behaviour are most difficult to place and are most at risk of being returned to institutional care (Pagel and Whitling, 1978; Sutter *et al.*, 1980; Landesman-Dwyer and Sulzbacher 1981). Once returned, they are often segregated in special wards; they remain unpopular patients who are avoided by staff (Grant and Moores, 1977;

Raynes, 1980) and may continue to exhibit the behaviour problems to the same extent. The development of effective services for these people is therefore of considerable policy interest (Blunden and Allen, 1987).

The primary focus of the study was how the people served spent their time – whether their lives were characterised by long periods of boredom doing nothing, in isolation, or whether people engaged in meaningful and adaptive activity. This focus on engagement in meaningful activity reflected (i) the service emphasis on a constructional approach (Goldiamond, 1977), which indicates that building desired behaviour may be a more effective strategy for personal development than trying to remove unwanted behaviour, and (ii) evidence that even though problem behaviour persists, adaptive behaviour can continue to develop if services provide the occasion for it to do so (e.g. Conroy and Bradley, 1985).

METHOD

Information has been collected on the experience of 18 of the first 24 people living in large hospitals to be served by the Special Development Team to date; the people excluded from the study were those living far away, where the travelling distance was prohibitive (3 people), or where consent is yet to be obtained (2 people) or where the person would not tolerate the presence of anyone else in the same room (1 person). Descriptions of the adaptive behaviour of each person were collected using the Adaptive Behaviour Scale (Nihira et al., 1974) Part 1; given the well-known problems of reliability and validity of Part 2 (Isett and Spreat, 1979; McDevitt, McDevitt and Rosen, 1977), problem behaviour descriptions were instead elicited by interview.[1]

The principal measure was non-participant observation using a 20-second momentary time-sample (Kazdin, 1978), recording type of activity (none, leisure, personal, using complex equipment, other practical tasks, work or formal education), social behaviour by the person observed, contact received from other people and problem behaviour. Also recorded after the start of the study was the number of staff in the same room as the person observed. In addition, a complete inventory of the physical environment was made and the staff allocation to the living unit ascertained. Information has so far been collected on 5 occasions over two years. Inter-rater reliability was assessed across individuals and data-points; weighted occurrence/non-occurrence reliability has been 91 or 92% on each occasion.

The design of the study was originally conceptualised as a multiple

---

[1] See the paper by Emerson in this volume for subject characteristics; more detailed information is available from the authors on request.

time-series design across subjects (Campbell and Stanley, 1967), in which individuals would form their own controls and staggered transfer to new services would control for confounding variables. A control-group design was not appropriate given the extreme characteristics of the client group and the small number of subjects available. In practice, delays in developing new services to replace a closing institution have created a natural experiment in which some people are transferring from ordinary wards or special wards in institutions to houses, but others are transferring to new institutions as interim arrangements, providing some useful comparisons between ordinary and special wards, new 'campus units' and houses. The results presented here are based on preliminary analyses carried out after the first four subjects moved to staffed houses.

RESULTS AND DISCUSSION

Physical environment

The institutional wards on which people lived at the beginning of the study provided much more space than houses, but this space was often shared with large numbers of people. Institutions – especially the secure wards – also restricted access to rooms (no rooms were restricted in the houses. The material environment was also barren in the institutions; on the wards there was usually literally nothing to do but sit, watch television or walk about. The houses were much richer environments equipped with a wide range of ordinary possessions and furnishings.

Staff and other service users

The staffed housing projects each served many fewer people and had much higher staffing ratios than the other kinds of service. In the houses the individual studied was the only client in the room for 71% of observations, with another person present for the remaining time. Hospital settings had, on average, 3–5 other people present.

Typically there were one or two staff in the same room in the houses. In hospital, service users spent about a quarter of their time – twice as much as in the houses – without staff present, with 1–3 staff present for most of the remaining observations. Since these are group care situations, it may be that individuals are at some risk when left unattended among people who have severe problem behaviour.

Social environment

Higher staffing ratios need to be translated into higher levels of contact to clients if the therapeutic intent of these services is to be realised.

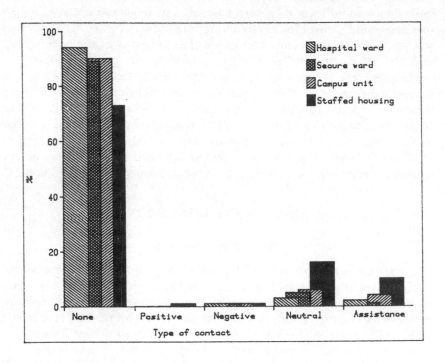

Figure 1.   Distribution of staff contact to individual behaviour in four types of setting.

However, previous research has shown that the relationship between staff ratio and staff performance is not simple (Mansel *et al.*, 1982, Repp *et al.* (in press)).

Figure 1 shows the proportion of the day each individual was receiving contact from staff. The hospital wards and campus units present a similar pattern of no contact for about 90% of the time, which is consistent with other studies of staff-client interaction in hospitals. In the houses, people received staff contact for on average 27% of the day, mainly in the form of neutral contact (e.g. conversation) or assistance in performing a practical task.

For people with severe and profound mental handicaps, high levels of staff antecedents have been suggested to be directly related to high levels of participation in activity (Felce, de Kock and Repp, 1986; Landesman, 1987). This increase is, therefore, encouraging but given the very high staffing levels in the houses it is perhaps surprising that on average people received no contact for three-quarters of their day.

The majority of people studied were never observed receiving contact from other service users. Of the six people who did, it amounts to approximately one-fifth of one percent of time (or about 1.5 minutes in the 11 hour day observed). This reflects the degree of handicap of the people served, and suggests that, for this group at least, the idea that larger facilities provide important social relationships with other handicapped people is mistaken.

Participation in meaningful activity

The point of changing the service environment is to improve the quality of life of the people served; how then does the enriched material and social environment appear to influence these people? Figure 2 shows the level of engagement in meaningful activity at each of 5 occasions over two years for 4 individuals who have moved to houses (from the point at which they joined the study) and, for comparision, two of those who have not. It shows that there is no clear change in level for two of the movers, whereas for two others there are clear increases in engagement – one person doubled and the other quadrupled the amount of time they spent in meaningful activity. The two people still in hospital show no change across the points of transfer.

This preliminary result clearly points to variation in the implementation of the staff performance variables in the houses as a possible area for further work. The general interpretation of variable outcomes in community services which is emerging from ecological studies (Landesman, 1988; Felce, 1988) is that, while they may provide a richer material environment and wider opportunities for constructive activity than institutions, the patterns of staff behaviour which have been shown to be important in manging problems can be overlooked or ignored in the pursuit of 'homeliness'. It is, these authors suggest, the combination of therapeutic objectives, the opportunities created by service design and organisation, and the amount and quality of staff performance which determines the outcomes for the people served. Models for the integration of these components are beginning to be developed (Mansell et al., 1987; Specialized Training Program, 1985).

Some evidence for the importance of staff performance can be found from these results. Figure 3 shows 'a day in the life of' the person who made the greatest gains in engagement after moving to a staffed house. The observations are averaged over 10 minute periods throughout the day, and show engagement by the individual studied, help and other contact from staff.

In the last observation made in hospital, the person was rarely involved in meaningful activity; the three peaks represent breakfast, lunch and tea. There was a small amount of help in the early morning,

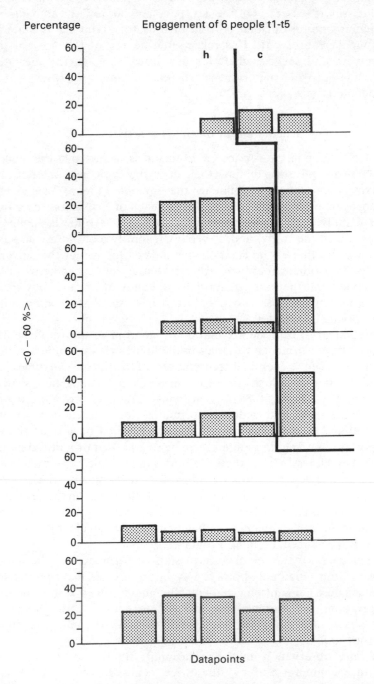

Figure 2. Engagement in meaningful activity by 6 people at 5 points in time.

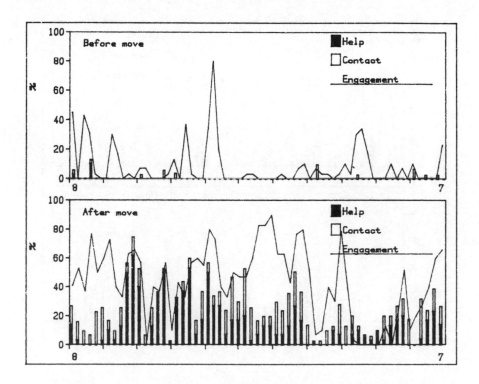

Figure 3. The pattern of one person's day: engagement, help and other staff contact.

and sporadic contact of other kinds from staff through the day. After moving to a staffed house the person received much higher levels of assistance from staff, as well as higher levels of other contact. Her level of engagement shows that she was involved to a greater extent over a much larger part of the day.

This can be contrasted with the experience of one of the people who moved but where there is no clear change in their overall level of engagement (Figure 4). Just before the move, this person lived in hospital and attended day care. They received low levels of contact and help throughout the day and show high levels of engagement, most of which is playing with toys and other leisure activities. After the move, the level of assistance from staff remains low but there are much higher levels of neutral contact. Despite these, there is no change (in fact a slight decrease) in level of engagement.

We think these data capture several important issues faced by the

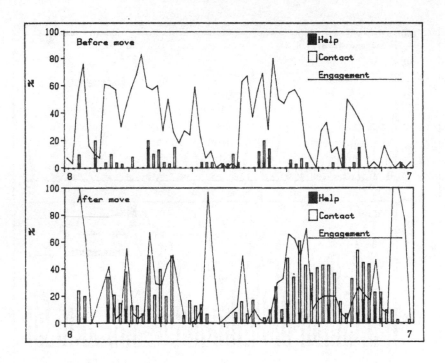

Figure 4. The pattern of another person's day: engagement, help and other staff contact.

Special Development Team. They suggest that the simple enrichment of the social and material environment by transfer from institutions to staffed houses does not of itself ensure greater involvement by the person served in meaningful activity. They also illustrate the importance of the quality of staff contact. The second example is a house where the principle of normalisation has been interpreted to mean that the people served must be offered choices to do valued activities; this is operationalised as making complex verbal requests (even though the people served have almost no receptive or expressive language), and de-emphasising ordinary household activities as sources of possible client involvement. The net result is that staff spend a lot of time asking and cajoling service users who do not respond, so that staff eventually do much of the activity themselves.

This is a perversion of the principle of normalisation (Wolfensberger, 1980), which lays some weight on the 'intensity of relevant programming', as well as a misunderstanding of the nature of choice. It conflicts with the 'active treatment' model of staffed housing developed in the examples referred to earlier. These emphasise client involvement in a full range of household activities to provide a broad base of experience, and provision of structured help and encouragement to maintain involvement; these are seen as the necessary conditions to learn the behaviour of choosing.

Overall, these early results suggest that even for people who, in addition to their severe or profound mental handicap, have very serious problem behaviour, service agencies can provide community-based services which promote engagement in meaningful activity; but that to do so requires attention to the quality of staff performance as well as to basic material and social resources.

REFERENCES

Blunden, R. and Allen, D. (1987) *Facing the challenge: an ordinary life for people with learning difficulties and challenging behaviour*. London: Kings Fund Centre.

Campbell, D. and Stanley, J. (1966) *Experimental and quasi-experimental designs for research*. Boston: Houghton-Mifflin.

Conroy, J. W. and Bradley, V. J. (1985) *The Pennhurst longitudinal study: combined report of five years of research and analysis*. Philadelaphia: Temple University.

Emerson, E., Toogood, A., Mansell, J., Barrett, S., Bell, C., Cummings, R., McCool, C. (1987) Challenging Behaviour and Community Services: 1. Introduction and Overview. *Mental Handicap*, **15**, 166–169.

Felce, D. (1988) Behavioral and Social Climate in Community Group Residences. In Janicki, M. P., Krauss, M. W. and Seltzer, M. M. (Eds) *Community Residences for Persons with Developmental Disabilities*. Baltimore: Paul H. Brookes.

Felce, D., de Kock, U. and Repp, A. (1986) An eco-behavioral analysis of small community-based houses and traditional large hospitals for severely and profoundly mentally handicapped adults. *Applied Research in Mental Retardation* **7**, 393–408.

Grant, G. and Moores, B. (1977) Resident charcteristics and staff behaviour in two hospitals for mentally retarded adults. *American Journal of Mental Deficiency* **82**, 3, 259–265.

Goldiamond, I. (1974) Toward a constructional approach to social problems. Ethical and constitutional issues raised by applied behaviour analysis. *Behaviourism* **2**, 1–84.

Isett, R. and Spreat, S. (1979) Test-retest and interrater reliability of the AAMD Adaptive Behavior Scale. *American Journal of Mental Deficiency* **84**, 1, 93–95.

Kazdin, A. E. (1982) *Single case research designs: methods for clinical and applied settings*. Oxford: Oxford University Press.

Landesman, S. (1987) The changing structure and function of institutions: a search for optimal group care environments. Ch 5 of Landesman, S. and Vietze, P. (Eds) *Living environments and mental retardation*. Washington: American Association on Mental Retardation.

Landesman, S. (1988) Preventing "Institutionalization" in the Community. In Janicki, M. P., Krauss, M. W. and Seltzer, M. M. (Eds) *Community Residences for Persons with Developmental Disabilities*. Baltimore: Paul H. Brookes.

Landesman-Dwyer, S. and Sulzbacher, F. (1981) Residential placement and adaptation of severely and profoundly retarded individuals. In Bruininks, R., Meyers, C., Sigford, B. and Lakin, K. (Eds) Deinstitutionalization and community adjustment of mentally retarded people. *American Association on Mental Deficiency Monograph* **4**, 182–194.

McDevitt, S., McDevitt, S. and Rosen, M. (1977) Adaptive Behaviour Scale Part II: A cautionary note and suggestions for revisions. *American Journal of Mental Deficiency* **82**, 2, 210–212.

Mansell, J., Felce, D., Jenkins, J. and de Kock, U. (1982) Increasing staff ratios in an activity with severely mentally handicapped people. *British Journal of Mental Subnormality*, **28**, 2, 97–99.

Mansell, J., Felce, D., Jenkins, J., de Kock, U. and Toogood, A. (1987) *Developing staffed housing for people with mental handicaps*. Tunbridge Wells: Costello.

Nihira, K., Foster, R., Shellhaus, M. and Leland, H. (1974) *AAMD Adaptive Behaviour Scale*. Washington: American Association on Mental Deficiency.

Pagel, S. and Whitling, C. (1978) Readmission to a state hosptial for mentally retarded persons: reasons for community placement failure. *Mental Retardation* **16**, 2, 25–28.

Raynes, N. (1980) The less you've got the less you get: functional grouping, a cause for concern. *Mental Retardation* **18**, 217–220.

Repp, A. C., Felce, D., de Kock, U., Thomas, M., Ager, A. and Blunden, R. (in press) *Staff:client ratios and their effects on staff interactions and client behaviour in various facilities for severely and profoundly mentally handicapped adults*. Research in Developmental Disabilities.

Specialized Training Program (1985) *Intensive Tenant Support Model*. Eugene: University of Oregon.

Sutter, P., Mayeda, T., Call, T., Yanagi, G. and Lee, S. (1980) Comparison of successful and unsuccessful community placed mentally retarded persons. *American Journal of Mental Deficiency* **85**, 3, 262–267.

Wolfensberger, W. (1980) The definition of normalisation: update, problems, disagreements and misunderstandings. In Flynn, R. J. and Nitsch, K. E. (1980) *Normalisation, social integration and community services*. Baltimore: University Park Press.

Community Reactions to Group Homes: Contrasts between People Living in Areas with and without a Group Home

R. McConkey*

St Michael's House, Dublin, Ireland.
* *Now with the Brothers of Charity Services, St. Aidan's, Gattonside,
nr Melrose TD6 9NN, Scotland*

Over 1,000 people in 23 locations throughout the island of Ireland were individually interviewed; 40% of whom lived in the vicinity of a group home – an ordinary house for persons with moderate to severe mental handicaps. The remaining 60% of people lived in comparable housing estates with no group home.

Information was collected about their level of contact with people from the home, their perceptions of the problems which had arisen or might arise if a group home were to open in the area and their willingness to become personally involved with the home.

Marked differences were found in people's responses from the two types of areas. Discriminant analyses were used to draw up profile characteristics of the people most likely to anticipate problems with group homes and those most willing to become involved in helping.

BACKGROUND

During the last twenty years there has been a revolution in caring for people with mental handicaps. No longer are they placed in large institutions; the majority now grow up with their families. Moreover, ordinary housing in the community is increasingly used to accommodate small groups of children and adults with mental handicap when families are no longer available or able to care. Latterly large numbers of people have been transferred from institutional settings into small-scale living units within the community.

The reactions of neighbours can be crucial to the success of this community housing policy. Local householders have successfully opposed the opening of group homes. In parts of the United States, it has been suggested that as many as half of the existing residences encountered opposition and an unknown number may well have been relocated because of adverse reactions (Seltzer and Litchfield, 1984). Often the neighbour's concerns about the home are unwarranted and in many instances reveal a lack of understanding of mental handicap (M.O.R.I., 1982).

The solution is more and better community education about mental handicap. This would not only reduce irrational opposition but should also help to nurture friendly contacts between the residents of the group home and their neighbours so as to further their integration within the local community (Hogan, 1986).

But this education has to be tailored to the concerns and experiences of the local people. Yet in Ireland, as in many other countries, no systematic information is available about people's reactions to community housing and nor had any attempt been made to document people's experiences of living beside a group home for people with moderate to severe mental handicaps. Indeed the latter exercise has been rarely attempted internationally.

THE PRESENT STUDY

In essence, the present study contrasted the views of Irish people who had the experience of living in the vicinity of a group home with those from a comparable neighbourhood where there was no group home. In all, 1,041 people were individually interviewed in 23 locations throughout the Republic of Ireland and Northern Ireland, making it one of the largest studies ever undertaken in the field of community attitudes. This was made possible through linking with a person from the local mental handicap service who became responsible for all the data collection in their area, using a common questionnaire. The data analysis was handled centrally.

In nine of these locations, there was a group home for an average of five people (range four to twelve) with moderate to severe mental handicaps. All the houses had been open for a minimum of two years and because of the residents' dependency needs, a staff member (or members) was present at all times.

In a further three locations, plans were in hand to open a group home in the future and the data obtained in this study might later be used as a study of change in neighbours' attitudes when the houses opened. The remaining 11 locations were chosen as a 'match' for the neighbourhoods which had a group home. Typically this was another housing estate within a mile or so of the one with the group home. A mix of private and public housing estates was included.

METHODOLOGY

Fifty immediate neighbours of each group home (one per household selected at random from the electoral register), were interviewed on the doorstep by a researcher who introduced themselves as from the University or Local College. Comparable procedures were used in areas with no group home except that where possible, an empty house was used as their 'prospective' group home. Interviews lasted on average 15 minutes.

Of the 1,041 people eventually interviewed (426 in areas with a group home; 615 in areas with no home), 58% were female (42% male), 43% were aged over 40 (57% less than 40 years), 46% had children under 16 years of age (24% were single, 30% were married with no children under 16 years) and 47% had left school at 15 years (30% had taken A levels or Leaving Certificate and 23% had completed a third level course).

The majority of people (70%) lived in private housing estates; with 30% in public housing. Just under two thirds of people (62%) had lived in the area for five or more years; around half (47%) estimated they knew 16 or more of their neighbours by name and 39% of people rated themselves as being frequently in contact with their neighbours (29% stated "some contact" and 32% "occasional contact").

The interview covered the following topics, using a mix of closed and open questions –

* People's knowledge of the group home in their area and contact with residents and staff.
* Second, the problems or difficulties which had arisen or they thought could arise if a group home opened in their locality.
* Third their willingness to help out or become involved with a group home.

RESULTS

Knowing the group home

Surprisingly not everyone living in the vicinity of a group home, knew of its existence or if they did, they found it difficult to name the residents' handicap. Of the 426 neighbours interviewed; 69% knew both the home and correctly named the handicap of the people living there. A further 26% of people knew the house but were unable to identify the residents' handicap correctly and as many as 9% of people were unaware of any house in their locality.

These results confirm previous findings both in Dublin and elsewhere that a significant proportion of the public can be aware of the existence of

Table 1. Local community's contacts with people from the group home

(N.B. Percentages of those knowing home; N=351)		
	With residents	With staff
No contacts	16%	47%
Seen them around	36%	20%
Met with them	48%	33%

a mental handicap facility in their midst (Locker, Rao and Weddell, 1981, McConkey 1987).

Contact with people from the group home

Those people who knew of the group home were then asked five questions regarding their contacts with the people living there, viz "Have you . . . seen them around, . . . talked to them outside, . . . been into their home" etc. The same questions were asked regarding contacts with staff as well as residents, and we further enquired as to who had initiated the contacts.

As Table 1 shows, local people had more contact with the residents of the home than they did with the staff, which is not surprising given that the staff often lived away from the neighbourhood.

Overall 15% of the people interviewed had been inside the group home and 16% had invited a resident from the home, into their house. Also 11% of people reported meeting the residents in pubs, shops or on the bus. In the majority of instances it was the mentally handicapped person or the staff member who had made the approach.

However only 28% of the people interviewed knew at least one of the residents and/or staff by name. (Recall that over half the people said they knew 15 or more of their neighbour's names.) Moreover, only 13% of neighbours had been in contact with a resident or member of staff during the past month (whereas 46% described themselves as being frequently in contact with their other neighbours).

It must be stressed that this information relates only to contacts between people from the group home and their *immediate* neighbours. The residents and staff of the group homes reported more contacts with the wider community.

Discriminant analysis

Who were the people most likely to have had contact with the residents of the group home? A discriminant analysis using the Wilk's stepwise method was undertaken with all the people who knew of the group home (N=386). This analysis identifies the variables which significantly distinguished the people who had met and talked with the residents (N=179) from those who had no contact (N=197) and places these discriminating variables in order of importance. Of the 16 possible discriminators entered into the analysis, seven proved significant (Wilk's Lamba 0.855; Chi Square 58.02, p < 0.0001). The people in this study who were most likely to have had personal contact with residents were –

* Involved in three or more activities within the locality – pubs, churches, school meetings, residents association, sports etc.
* They lived in Tralee and Sligo (contact was lowest in Dublin).
* People who had lived in the area for more than five years.
* Had experience of voluntary work with people who had a mental handicap.
* Females rather than males.
* People who reported they were frequently in contact with their neighbours.
* People under 60 years of age.

These results suggest that levels of contacts between residents and neighbours are more likely in settled, active, non-metropolitan communities.

Problems

Only five people (1.7%) living in the vicinity of one of the nine group homes could think of a problem that had arisen when invited to do so. These were instances of residents' shouting in the street and one person reported "rumours that the men go after younger girls".

By contrast one in eight (12%) people in the areas where there were no group homes thought there could be problems (see later).

Potential problems

In case people found it difficult to think of problems on the spur of the moment or were reticent to state them outright, we went on to ask all the interviewees about nine specific problems that had been mentioned in previous studies (e.g. M.O.R.I., 1982). Four of these problems related to difficulties for mentally handicapped people and five for residents in the neighbourhood. These problems are listed in Table 2 and include all those mentioned spontaneously by the interviewees with one exception, namely that local people had a lack of understanding about mental

Table 2.   Percentage of people perceiving problems

Type of problem	No group home	Group home in area
a) Problems for mentally handicapped people		
They would be teased	46%	16%
They would be victimised/picked on/ taken advantage of	30%	7%
Isolated/kept to themselves	37%	22%
Inadequate professional care and supervision	13%	5%
b) Problems for the neighbourhood		
People embarrassed/don't know how to react	36%	22%
A danger or threat to children	11%	1%
Mentally handicapped people have been violent/irresponsible	10%	2%
The property value of houses would drop	9%	1%
They would be noisy/create disturbances	9%	1%

handicap. For each potential problem, respondents were asked to say whether or not it had been or could be a problem or that they couldn't decide.

In all, 52% of people living adjacent to a group home reported no problems, compared to 22% in areas with no group home. As Table 2 shows, in every instance the percentage of people who reported problems was significantly greater (Chi Square tests; p < 0.001) in areas with no group home than those living in areas with a group home. Likewise the percentages of 'can't decides' was higher in areas with no group home.

Interestingly people tended to express a concern for mentally handicapped people's welfare more often than they did for themselves or their neighbours. The predominant concerns were that mentally handicapped people would be teased or victimised; half of the people (50%) in areas with no group home anticipated this being a problem whereas only 18% in areas with a group home reported this as having happened. Concerns that the people with mental handicap would be violent, noisy or would attack children were expressed by 21% of people in areas with no group home but only by 4% of people where a group home already existed.

The predominant concern in areas with a group home was that mentally handicapped people were isolated and/or not receiving enough professional care and attention (23% of people mentioned this as a problem compared to 41% in areas with no group home).

The foremost concern which people perceived for themselves were feelings of embarrassment in meeting mentally handicapped people – a recurrent theme in past surveys we have carried out in Ireland (e.g. McConkey, 1987). However these were assuaged – although not eliminated – in areas where a group home had opened. There was little overt concern with house values.

Discriminant analysis

Who were the people most likely to anticipate problems arising, especially that residents would cause a disturbance in the neighbourhood – i.e. children attacked or the residents would be noisy or violent? A discriminant analysis using the Wilk's stepwise method was undertaken with 16 possible discriminating variables. Of these, four proved significant and together gave a Wilk's Lamba value of 0.9383 (Chi Square 66.97; $p < 0.0001$).

The distinguishing features of the people who were likely to report or anticipate disturbances for neighbours were, in order of importance –

* Living in an area where there was no group home.
* Aged 60 years and over.
* No local contact with people who have a mental handicap.
* They had lived in the area for less than 5 years.

Although these five variables correctly identified 74% of the people expressing a likely problem, the incompleteness suggests that other factors are involved in people's perceptions of problems which were not covered by this survey. However the above listing may help to identify areas where resistance from neighbours is most likely to be encountered.

Willingness to have contact

Later in the interview, we enquired about people's willingness to be involved with a group home, by listing six possible ways in which they might help and asked them to select one of three possible answers, viz. 'Very interested', 'Perhaps, but wouldn't have the time' or 'Prefer not'. These questions were asked in areas where there was no group home at present, as well as those with a group home, although the wording varied slightly.

Table 3 shows the percentages of people selecting the 'very interested' option for each type of involvement. These have been subdivided for the areas with no group home (or who did not know of the group home in

Table 3. Percentage of people 'very interested' in helping

	Knew group home	No group home
Make a point of talking to them	71	82
Help out in an emergency	69	73
Go along to an Open Day or coffee evening	59	69
Have a handicapped person visit my home	49	60
Go once a week to the home to visit them	35	50
Take a handicapped person on an outing once in a while, e.g. to church, shopping etc.	32	41

their area) and secondly for those people who knew of a group home in their area. As you can see, with the exception of 'helping out in emergencies', people who had no group home in their neighbourhood or who were unaware of its existence expressed themselves significantly more willing to help out (Chi Square tests; p < 0.001) than did those people who already knew of the group home. This is not too surprising. When people have no group home in their area and they don't think it is very likely that a group home will open, it is easy for them to say they would be willing to help, knowing that there is little danger of being asked to help. Such 'socially acceptable' answers are commonly found in attitude surveys. This, however, was not the case for people with a group home on their 'doorstep'. Their answers are probably more indicative of the 'true' willingness of people to get involved. (But even here, people might still refuse when actually asked.)

Significantly, the proportion of people who were unwilling to get involved (i.e. answered 'Perhaps' or 'Prefer not' to all items) was the same for both groups, around one in three (30%).

Discriminant analysis

As before a discriminant analysis based on the Wilk's stepwise method was used in an attempt to discover the characteristics of the people who were most willing to help out. Six variables out of the 16 possible disriminators entered into analysis proved significant and together gave an overall Wilk's Lambda of 0.9339 (Chi Square 73.21; p < 0.0001).

In order of importance, the characteristics of those people who expressed an interest in helping was as follows –

* Past experience of voluntary work with people who have a mental handicap.

* Married with children under 16 years.
* In the past, they have had regular contact with people who have a mental handicap.
* Have a relative living in the neighbourhood.
* Under 40 years of age.
* Female.

This profile may be of use in identifying who best to target when trying to recruit helpers.

IMPLICATIONS

These results have a number of important implications for service planners in both parts of Ireland and beyond.

First, the prospect of a group home opening in an area will give rise to many more *anticipated problems* – both for the mentally handicapped people as well as the residents of the area – than is the reality when a group home has been open for a period of time. The data from this study could be used therefore to reassure residents in advance of a group home opening in their locality. Indeed it has been suggested that an effective way of countering community opposition is for critics to meet with residents from comparable areas where a group home already exists (e.g. Hogan, 1986).

Second, only a small minority of Irish people anticipate problems arising for *themselves* – such as attacks on children or a drop in property values, if a group home were to open in their area. International studies have suggested higher levels although direct comparisons are not valid due to differences in methodologies, populations and so forth. But even within this study there were significant variations within Ireland in the type of problems people anticipated. Hence the need for service planners to carry out their own 'market research' if they are to effectively address neighbours' concerns.

Third, some group homes in the study appeared to be relatively isolated from the local community. Of course this might be true for other householders in those areas, although we suspect that is not so, given the data collected on contact with neighbours (see earlier). Recall also that one of the dominant concerns of neighbours was that the residents of the group home were isolated (see Table 2).

There are many reasons why a group home can remain apart from the local community. It may not have been there long enough, it is supported more by people from outside the immediate vicinity; the staff working in the home live elsewhere and the people resident in the home may not have come from that area. Any or all of these factors could also explain why attempts to involve local people, e.g. through Open days, can meet with little success. Moreover, some agencies may be reluctant to have too high a profile in an area in case they stir up opposition. Our data suggests that this is largely an unwarranted fear.

Fourth, around one third of the neighbours express an interest in becoming more involved with people from the group home. Of course, people's intentions may not translate into action, but that said, it is possible that services have become so specialised that a valuable resource in widening residents' involvement with local people is being overlooked. Greater involvement of people from the community can do much to improve the quality of life of people with mental handicaps and ease the caring burden on the professional staff.

Our data suggests that the initiative for recruiting such helpers has to come from the specialist agency given that many people express embarrassment at the prospect of meeting a person with a mental handicap. Paradoxically though, the handicapped people would appear to be their own best ambassadors because the people in the community who were most likely to see benefits to having a group home in their locality or who were most willing to help, already had experience of meeting and working with people who were mentally handicapped.

Finally, the Irish public's apparent willingness to help their handicapped neighbour augurs well for the further development of community housing for people with mental handicaps in the island of Ireland.

ACKNOWLEDGEMENTS

This study was made possible by the active co-operation of many people. In particular Steve Clarke, University College, Dublin; Frances Smyth, Galway County Association for people with mental handicaps; Dick O'Callaghan, Cork Polio and Aftercare Association and Chris Conliffe, Western Health and Social Services Board (N. Ireland).

St Michael's House Research Trust provided the necessary finance.

REFERENCES

Hogan, R. (1986) Gaining community support for group homes, *Community Mental Health Journal*, **22**, 26–36.
Locker, D., Rao, B. and Weddell, J. M. (1979) The community reaction to a hostel for the mentally handicapped, *Social Science and Medicine*, **13**, 817–821.
McConkey, R. (1987) *Who cares? Community involvement with mental handicap*, Souvenir Press, London.

Market and Opinion Research International (M.O.R.I.) (1982) Public attitudes towards the mentally handicapped: Research study conducted for Mencap, London.

Seltzer, M. M. and Litchfield, L. C. (1984) Community reaction to community residences: A study of factors related to community response. In: J. M. Berg (ed.) *Perspectives and progress in mental retardation, Vol. 1,* University Park Press, Baltimore.

Assessing Post-School Effects of Special Education for Youth with Mental Retardation through Economic Analysis

D. R. Lewis, R. H. Bruininks, M. L. Thurlow and K. S. McGrew

Department of Educational Policy and Administration
136C Burton Hall, University of Minnesota,
Minneapolis, MN 55455, U.S.A

Are the outcomes produced by public school special education for mildly retarded children worth their costs? With the increasing application of benefit-cost analysis to other social service programs, the public has come to expect that similar economic analysis can be applied to special education. This paper reports on such an effort in the evaluation and post-school follow-up of mildly retarded students from a large suburban school district. A formal benefit-cost framework is used to assess the efficacy and efficiency of special education services.

Are the outcomes produced by public school special education for mentally retarded children worth their costs? With the increasing application of benefit-cost analysis to other social service programs, the public has come to expect that similar economic analysis can be applied to special education. This paper reports on such an effort in the evaluation and post-school follow-up of mentally retarded students.

The evaluation of special education program activities has been justified for a number of reasons. The most frequently expressed rationale is the need for improving program effectiveness, which focuses on how well the program is meeting its stated goals and on what changes can be made to enhance the desirable outcomes. A second values oriented perspective focuses on whether special education programs provide appropriate opportunities for handicapped children and youth. This approach may assess the appropriateness of services (e.g., opportunities for integrated learning), or the degree of parent involvement in important educational decisions. A third perspective focuses on the need for fiscal accountability to either the school district or external agencies, and assesses whether allocated funds have been used for their intended purposes. A fourth concern is with the need to determine whether the program itself is "worth its cost" (i.e., whether the program generates outcomes for handicapped individuals that justify the costs of producing them). Although all evaluation perspectives are necessary to assess the full value and results of special education services, this paper deals primarily with only the last perspective; that is, to assess whether the economic benefits of special education services exceed their economic costs. This question has been largely ignored in the special education literature.

Although some recent attention has been directed at examining the costs of special education (e.g., Decision Resources Corporation, 1983; Kalalik *et al.*, 1981; Lewis *et al.*, 1987), no other study has systematically examined the monetary benefit-cost effects of special education. Only a few recent efforts have examined aspects of employment training programs for handicapped populations from a program efficiency or benefit-cost perspective (e.g., Kemper *et al.*, 1981; Kerachsky *et al.*, 1985; Wehman and Hill, 1985). Those readers unfamiliar with the conceptual and technical features of benefit-cost analysis would be well served by reviewing any of these sources.

The use and application of benefit-cost analysis to social and educational programs has been a subject of controversy, due in large part to difficulties in assigning dollar values to program effects. Nowhere is this controversy greater than in the field of special education where traditionally most of the benefits have been assumed to be unmeasurable in monetary or economic terms. This paper attempts to resolve some of these difficulties by examining a specific program area of special education with some preliminary empirical data.

Drawing from data collected in a larger U.S. federally supported follow-up study by Bruininks *et al.* (1987), the authors have been able to identify and value certain costs and benefits from a local suburban school district relating to special education services for a mentally retarded population. The design and data collection methods for the larger study are described in detail in the noted report.

SOURCES AND ESTIMATES FOR COST AND BENEFIT DATA

The data reported were derived from a comprehensive follow-up study of students who graduated or completed twelve years of schooling between the years 1977 and 1984 from two high schools in a large suburban school district in Minnesota. Information from school records and survey outcome information was collected for 311 special education and 698 regular education students who were included in the final sample. The entire special education student population was surveyed, while random sampling techniques were used for the regular student population. The final special education sample with complete follow-up data included 54 mildly retarded (educable mentally retarded) students. The follow-up response rate with complete outcome information was 67% of all mildly retarded students in the sample, equally divided between males and females. The entire sample of mildly retarded students in the larger study was selected as the original sample for this study. However, all eleven 1984 school completers were excluded because of their limited time (i.e., two months) in the community and fifteen other respondents were excluded because their intelligence scores were greater than 80. Thus the final subsample consisted of 28 mildly retarded young adults.

Sources for Estimating Benefits

Earnings

Earnings data were collected from follow-up mail and telephone surveys to all mildly retarded high school completers. Subsequent interviews were conducted with 44 of the 54 respondents. Average annual earned income for all employed mildly retarded respondents in 1984 was $6,475. Average annual earned income for all respondents (employed and unemployed) was $5,319. Life-time earnings were estimated to be $77,115 for all respondents in 1984 present values.

Employment

Eighty-two percent of all the mildly retarded respondents in the sample were receiving earnings under paid employment within one to seven years after completing high school. Of those employed, 17% held part-time jobs. Eighteen percent of the respondents declared themselves as either homemakers or unemployed. Eleven percent of all respondents declared themselves to be unemployed and looking for work. These employment results from the Minnesota sample are slightly more positive, but generally consistent with similar high-school follow-up studies of mildly retarded young adults in other states (e.g., Fardig *et al.*, 1985; Hasazi *et al.*, 1985; Schalock *et al.*, 1986).

Fringe Benefits

The U.S. Department of Labor (1980) estimates that approximately 15 percent of gross wages for low wage earners are paid in fringe benefit compensation.

Taxes

Pechman (1985) estimates the tax rate for low wage earners to be 23 percent of gross income.

Sources for Estimating Costs

Special Education Program Costs

Special education costs for each respondent were determined from actual school use of resources and expenditure and student records (Lewis *et al.*, 1987). The student records reflected actual hourly use of special education services over 16 service areas on an annual basis over the entire 12 or 13 year school history of each student. Through the actual measurement and valuation of all resource components used in each of the 16 service areas, per student hourly cost data were similarly estimated. In 1984 dollars per student average annual special education costs for the mentally retarded students in this study were estimated to be $3,652. When these data were compounded over a 12 year schooling period at 6 percent, 1984 present values were estimated to be $61,609 in total costs for each student.

Regular Education Costs

Regular education costs for the respondents were determined from actual school expenditure and resource use records and were reported in 1984 dollars as averaging $3,418 annually per student. When these cost data were compounded at 6 percent over a 12 year schooling career, 1984 present values were estimated to be $57,658 for each student.

Community Residential Care

Thirteen percent of the mildly retarded respondents in the sample reported living within a group or foster home. Sixty percent reported living with their family; 25% reported living alone or with spouse or friends; and 2% reported institutionalization for medical reasons.

In 1982 the median annual per capita cost of care in 36 Minnesota private residential homes for mentally retarded populations was $20,082 (adapted from primary data in Greenberg *et al.*, 1985). These costs do not include training or cost of capital facilities. When expressed in 1984 dollars these per capita costs approximate $22,030. A recent study by Burchard *et al.* (1986) indicated that there are not significant differences in average income, or type or extent of employment among mentally retarded individuals within different types of community residences.

Institutional Care

Average annual per capita costs of care in Minnesota state-operated residential facilities for people with mental retardation were reported as being $44,986 in 1984 by Lakin *et al.* (1986, p. 29). Bradock *et al.* (1986) reported a similar national average of $42,457 for 1984. These costs do not include capital costs of facilities and are thus underestimated. When these costs were projected over an expected life-span of 44 years and discounted at 6%, institutionalization care costs were estimated to be

$691,885 per capita in 1984 present values.

It is important to note that when an institutionalization is prevented, the state saves the total amount that would have been spent on that person in the institution. However, the costs of board, room and any other basic care must now be paid by someone else within the community, usually the person or their family. Average annual costs in family home care for children were estimated to be $2,346 in 1984 dollars by the U.S. Department of Commerce (1985).

Community Support Services

Participation in community support services for each of the respondents was identified from the follow-up survey and interviews.

Supplemental Security Income (SSI)

Supplemental income from SSI for each respondent was determined through the follow-up survey and interviews. Only 15% of all respondents received SSI with an average of $201 per month. The average for all 54 respondents was only $30 per month.

Medicaid Assistance

Follow-up interview data indicated that 7% of the respondents received medicaid. It was assumed that those individuals who were gainfully employed would not receive medicaid assistance but would purchase private insurance. In Minnesota during 1984 average annual costs for private group health insurance were estimated to be $834 for a single participant. These costs were based on Blue-Cost/Blue Shield monthly rates of $69.50. It was assumed that health benefits from private insurance were comparable to public insurance. Average annual medicaid assistance for all respondents was estimated to be $65.

THE BENEFIT-COST ACCOUNTING FRAMEWORK

As in all benefit-cost analyses, the analyst must first specify the program being evaluated and the comparison against which it will be judged. Second, it is essential to identify all costs and benefits in an appropriate accounting framework. Third, the analyst must value (or measure as best as possible) all costs and benefits for subsequent analysis. Since benefit-cost analysis attempts to assess all alternatives in terms of monetary values, pecuniary measurement becomes an obvious and very challenging hurdle in this form of analysis. This is undoubtedly why no other evaluators of public school special education services have attempted this technique.

The first major problem arises in developing an alternative for comparing the costs and benefits resulting from current special education services. As with most special education services, both law and ethics preclude controlled experimental designs to compare treatment and non-treatment alternatives. In reality, and in most other similar special education situations, only one program is in place with no observable alternatives available for comparison purposes. Consequently, it is necessary to employ a post-hoc non-experimental comparison design with hypothetical rather than actual treatment alternatives.

A conceptual framework for benefit and cost comparisons of special education for former students with mild intellectual retardation can be constructed if it is assumed that appropriate costs and benefits can be measured and valued for a similar hypothetical sample that received no special education services. Such an alternative is incorporated within the framework of Table 1.

The benefit-cost accounting framework as presented in Table 1 draws heavily upon a taxonomy outlined by Thornton and Will (1986). The framework in this illustration compares a school-based special education program for mildly retarded individuals with a hypothetical situation wherein at least one in ten individuals are saved from subsequent institutionalization. This approach also identifies the analytical perspectives of interest to both students and society. It is important to note that this model provides insight into not only those benefits and costs that can be monetized, but also into those effects that cannot be measured in dollars alone. It notes, for example, important other non-monetary benefits such as preferences for work and prospects for increased self-sufficiency, self-esteem and quality of life.

ECONOMIC ANALYSIS OF ALTERNATIVES

In the original study by Bruininks *et al.* (1987) a number of other alternative hypothetical comparison groups were constructed for use within the benefit-cost framework which we have illustrated in Table 1. These hypothetical comparison groups were constructed largely through developing historical and current data to meet differing assumptions. Many of these assumptions and estimates are identified within the section above describing sources and estimates of costs and benefits. Various rates of prevented institutionalization, school dropout, and unemployment were examined as hypothetical comparisons to provision of special education services for our sample of mildly retarded youth. The resulting benefit-cost estimates almost universally indicated the economic efficiency of special education.

When institutionalization was viewed, for example, as the hypothetical comparison with its attendant and exceedingly high costs, the resulting benefit-cost analyses clearly favored special education in the schools (and deinstitutionalization) even if post-school competitive earnings were zero.

Table 1. Benefits and costs of special education for mentally retarded students. Comparison group: current program vs. hypothetical condition of no special education with only regular instruction and subsequent institutionalization at rate of one per ten.

Impacts	Analytical perspective		
	Social	= students	+ rest of society
Benefits			
1) Increased output			
Increased earnings	$8,262	8,262	0
Increased fringe benefits	$1,239	$1,239	0
Increased taxes	0	($1,899)	$1,899
Work preferences	+	+	+
2) Reduced use of alternative programs			
Institutional Care Costs	$70,265	($3,865)	$74,130
3) Other benefits			
Increased self-sufficiency	+	+	+
Increased self-esteem	+	+	+
Improved quality of life	+	+	+
Total benefits	$79,766	$3,737	$76,029
Costs			
1) Program costs			
Special education costs	($61,609)	0	($61,609)
Regular instruction costs	0	0	0
2) Increased use of social services			
Community support services	($43)	0	($43)
3) Increased use of transfer payments			
Increased SSI/medicaid payments	0	$663	($663)
Total costs	($61,652)	$633	($62,315)
Net benefits	$18,114	$4,400	$13,714

1. All data are reported in per student 1984 present values discounted at 6%.
2. All data are from suburban school district follow-up study or sources as noted in paper.

It was noted (and is illustrated in Table 1) that if special education in the schools prevented at least one out of ten mildly retarded persons from becoming institutionalized, special education was cost-beneficial in monetary terms alone. In several other subsequent simulations we assumed that due to technological and occupational changes many mentally retarded individuals would require the benefits specific to special education to be employable in today's competitive labor markets. In one case relative to this latter assumption we had actual data from a comparison group of mildly retarded adults without special education (Burchard *et al.*, 1986). It was found that if special education for mildly retarded students was successful in preventing school dropouts there were likely to be significant economic net benefits to society. Consistent with the early work by Conley (1973, p. 297) wherein he employed different methodology, it was found that "educational services provided to the (mentally) retarded can be justified on the basis of earnings alone."

CONCLUSIONS

This paper has focused on the application of a benefit-cost conceptual framework for estimating the efficiency of a public school program for mildly retarded students. Based on the methodology and data in this study, special education for these students in 1984 appears to be "worth its cost" even if all of its post-school effects are measured solely in monetary terms.

Generalizations from this study are limited somewhat by the absence of a randomly constituted control group design. On the other hand, controlled experimental design, while more elegant, is neither feasible nor desirable for special education student populations. Our society has decided that special education services for children and youth with handicaps is an entitlement not an optional matter. Despite the difficulty of constituting viable control groups, this paper has argued the merits of applying benefit-cost analysis for examining questions of efficiency in special education. Clearly more efforts of this type are needed to expand the evaluation perspectives of services for persons with disabilities.

ACKNOWLEDGEMENT

The research reported in this paper was supported by a grant from the Office of Special Education and Rehabilitative Services, U.S. Department of Education.

REFERENCES

Bardach, E. (1977) The Implementation Game. The MIT Press, Cambridge.
Bradock, D., Hemp, R. and Howes, R. (1986) Direct costs of institutional care in the United States. *Mental Retardation*, **24**: 9–17.
Bruininks, R., Lewis, D. and Thurlow, M. (1987) *Benefit-Cost Evaluation of Local Special Education Programs*. Department of Educational Psychology, University of Minnesota, Minneapolis.
Burchard, S. N., Hasazi, J., Gordon, L., Rosen, J., Yoe, J., Toro, H., Dietzel, L., Payton, P. and Simoneau, D. (1986) *The Community Adjustment and*

Integration of Adults with Mental Retardation Living in Group Homes, Supervised Apartments, and with their Families. Department of Psychology, University of Vermont, Burlington, Vermont.

Conley, R. W. (1973) *The Economics of Mental Retardation.* The Johns Hopkins University Press, Baltimore.

Decision Resources Corporation. (1983) *The Costs of Special Education and Related Services.* Decision Resources Corporation, Washington, D.C.

Fardig, D., Algozzine, R., Schwartz, S., Hensel, J. and Westling, D. (1985) Postsecondary vocational adjustment of rural, mildly handicapped students. *Exceptional Children,* **52**: 115–121.

Greenberg, J., Lakin, C., Hill, B., Bruininks, R. and Hauber, F. (1985) *Costs of residential care in the United States.* In C. Lakin, B. Hill and R. Bruininks (eds), *An Analysis of Medicaid's Intermediate Care Facility for the Mentally Retarded (ICF-MR) Program.* Center for Residential and Community Services, University of Minnesota, Minneapolis.

Hasazi, S. B., Gordon, L. and Roe, C. (1985) Factors associated with the employment status of handicapped youth exiting high school from 1979 to 1983. *Exceptional Children,* **51**: 455–469.

Kalalik, J. S., Furry, W., Thomas, M. and Carney, M. (1981) *The Cost of Special Education.* Rand Corporation, Santa Monica, CA.

Kemper, P., Long, D. and Thornton, C. (1981) *The Supported Work Evaluation: Final Benefit-Cost Analysis.* Manpower Demonstration Research Corporation, New York.

Kerachsky, S., Thornton, C., Bloomenthal, A., Maynard, R. and Stephans, S. (1985) *Impacts of Transitional Employment on Mentally Retarded Young Adults: Results of the STETS Demonstration.* Mathematica Policy Research, Princeton.

Lakin, K. C., Hill, B. K., Street, H. and Bruininks, R. H. (1986) *Persons with Mental Retardation in State-Operated Residential Facilities.* Center for Residential and Community Services, University of Minnesota, Minneapolis.

Lewis, D. R., Bruininks, R. and Thurlow, M. (1987) *Cost Analysis for District Level Special Education Planning, Budgeting and Administrating.* Department of Educational Psychology, University of Minnesota, Minneapolis.

Pechman, J. (1985) *Who Bears the Tax Burden?* Brookings Institution, Washington, DC.

Shalock, R. L., Wolzen, B., Ross, I., Elliott, B., Werbel, G. and Peterson, K. (1986) Post-secondary community placement of handicapped students: A five-year follow-up. *Learning Disability Quarterly,* **9**: 295–303.

Thornton, C. and Will, J. (1986) *Benefit-Cost Analysis and Special Education Programs.* Department of Educational Psychology, University of Minnesota, Minneapolis.

U.S. Department of Labor. (1980) *Employee Compensation in the Private Non-farm Economy.* Bureau of Labor Statistics, Washington, DC.

Wehman, P. and Hill, J. W. (eds). (1985) *Competitive Employment for Persons With Mental Retardation: From Research to Practice.* Rehabilitation Research and Training Center, Virginia Commonwealth University, Richmond.

Dimensions of Community Adjustment among Young Adults with Intellectual Disabilities

R. H. Bruininks[1], M. L. Thurlow,[2]
K. S. McGrew[3] and D. R. Lewis[4]

[1]*Rehabilitation Research and Training Center, University of Minnesota,*
6 Pattee Hall, 150 Pillsbury Drive SE, Minneapolis, MN 55455 USA
[2]*Rehabilitation Research and Training Center, University of Minnesota,*
357 Elliott Hall, 75 East River Road, Minneapolis, MN 55455 USA
[3]*(St. Cloud Public Schools) University of Minnesota,*
355 Elliott Hall, 75 East River Road, Minneapolis, MN 55455 USA
[4]*Educational Policy and Administration, University of Minnesota,*
136 Burton Hall, 178 Pillsbury Drive SE, Minneapolis, MN 55455 USA

About 150 separate items were scaled into 21 measures to assess the personal competence and community outcomes of 239 persons with mental retardation who had been out of school special education programs from 1 to 10 years. Using principal components analysis with varimax rotation, 8 interpretable factors emerged from the analyses. Four of the 8 factors assessed aspects of personal competence, with the remaining four factors assessing important community outcomes. Results from this study argue for a multi-dimensional and interactive perspective in assessing adjustment and quality of life for persons with mental retardation. Although research on community adjustment and quality of life is in a very early stage of development, further inquiry is essential to understand the many and valued forms of living in the community and to promote worthwhile qualities of life for persons with mental retardation.

Recently, a number of studies have examined the community adjustment of young adults with intellectual disabilities who have received educational experiences within regular public school programs and lived in community settings. These recent studies stand in sharp contrast to many previously reported studies of persons who formerly lived in large institutional settings (Goldstein, 1964; Lakin, *et al.*, 1981). While many of these studies have focused on students with a particular disability (e.g., learning disability), several have included former students with a wide range of disabilities. For example, Edgar (1987) reported that school retention was much greater for students with severe mental retardation and related disabilities (12% drop out rate) compared to students with learning disabilities and behavior disabilities (42% drop out rate). Yet, approximately six months after leaving school in 1984–85, 65% of the former students with severe handicaps were not engaged in any substantial daytime activity; 18% were involved in further schooling and 29% were employed. Hasazi, *et al.* (1985) reported that of those students who had left school between 1979 and 1983, approximately 30% were employed. Wehman, *et al.*, (1985) investigated the employment status of 117 transition age adults who had participated in public school programs for persons with moderate, severe, or profound mental retardation who had left school between 1978 and 1983. They reported that approximately 21% were employed (9% in sheltered workshops, 12% in competitive employment, either full-time or part-time).

Most studies of the adult status of individuals who received public school special education services have concentrated on employment outcomes. Yet, many researchers suggest that there is a need for a multidimensional perspective of community adjustment and integration (Brown & Hughson, 1980; Emerson, 1985; Halpern, *et al.*, 1986; Heal, *et al.*, 1978; Irvin, *et al.*, 1979; Lakin, *et al.*, 1981; Mitchell, 1986; Parmenter, 1980, 1986; Ward, *et al.*, 1978, 1986; Whelan & Speake, 1981). Clearly, it is necessary to go beyond employment as the primary measure of community adjustment, to include measures of use of community resources, the establishment of friendships, and other quality of life variables.

Parmenter (1987) has cogently argued for developing models of community adjustment or quality of life that are based on multidimensional research perspectives. In previous analyses of community adjustment and integration, measures have focused primarily on the single perspective of the personal characteristics of individuals in order to identify what needs to be changed. An alternative approach is to consider several different aspects of personal independence. For example, Reiter and Levi (1980) suggest that the skills necessary for successful community and vocational adjustment are different from those skills needed for acquiring and maintaining personal friendships (Edgerton & Bercovici, 1976; Schalock & Harper, 1978; Stanfield, 1973).

Most research efforts have reported the status of persons living within community settings on a limited number of outcomes (e.g., employment, legal infractions), but few studies have been guided by more comprehensive models of community participation and adjustment. A promising conceptual model of personal competence, advanced by Greenspan (1979), views personal competence as composed of physical competence, adaptive intelligence (conceptual, practical, and social), and emotional competence. Recent reviews have provided some support for Greenspan's model of personal competence (Bruininks & McGrew, 1987; McGrew & Bruininks, 1988). In a recent study by Halpern, *et al.*, (1986), support was found for a four-dimensional model of community adustment that includes occupation, residential environment, social support/safety, and client satisfaction. These kinds of conceptual models could productively guide future research efforts.

   Moving out of the school environment to the community is a critical transition for all young adults, particularly those with intellectual disabilities. While increasing numbers of researchers are examining the post-school employment status of students with various disabilities, few have investigated the post-school adjustment of individuals in broader community contexts such as economic independence, recreation/leisure involvement, friendships/social networks, living arrangements, and use of community resources. Aside from a few promising conceptual papers and studies, little research has been conducted to identify statistically reliable dimensions of community adjustment among persons with mental retardation. The purpose of this study was to (a) explore the community adjustment of young adults with mental retardation from 1 to 10 years after completion of high school, and (b) empirically devise a conceptual model of community adjustment.

METHOD

A sample of former students with mild to severe degrees of mental retardation was located after they had left secondary public school programs. Included in the sample were 44 students with mild retardation (IQs 60–79), 91 with moderate retardation (IQs 40–59), and 104 with severe retardation (IQs 20–39). The 239 subjects (126 male, 113 female) included in the samples represented 68% of the potential respondents. The response rate for former students with mild retardation was much lower (45%) than that for former students with moderate to severe retardation (89%).

   In assessing personal and community adjustment, an effort was made to assess the broadest possible range of measures. Two instruments were used to collect data: (a) a detailed interview protocol consisting of 142 questions in 11 areas – employment, education, social participation, support payments, social adjustment and living skills, health/physical status, family/household characteristics, living arrangements, service and program participation, citizenship status, and miscellaneous information, and (b) the *Inventory for Client and Agency Planning (ICAP)*, (Bruininks, Hill, Weatherman, & Woodcock, 1986), a standardized measure of personal functioning including 123 items and scores used for this analysis (e.g., diagnostic status, functional limitations, adaptive behavior, and problem behaviors). Both instruments were used with the respondent, who was either the former student (for subjects in the mild group) or an informed respondent (for subjects with moderate to severe retardation). The *ICAP* was administered first (taking 20–30 minutes) and the project interview second (taking about 45 minutes).

Data analysis consisted of (a) descriptive summary statistics of select outcome variables by degree of retardation, and (b) exploratory factor analysis of selected variables. Exploratory factor analyses were completed on variables extracted from the interview and *ICAP* to determine whether important dimensions of personal competence and community adjustment could be identified for use in future research. Twenty-one variables were constructed for inclusion in these exploratory analyses; each generally included at least three separate assessments of the measure. The 21 variables, described in Table 1, were subjected to principal components analysis followed by varimax rotation. A combination of objective (viz., eigenvalues greater than one; Scree test) and subjective (viz., interpretability of factors) factor extraction criteria were employed.

RESULTS

Post-School Community Adjustment

The description and the summary statistics for each outcome measure are shown in Table 1. Considerable variability is evident across the measures according to level of functioning (mild, moderate, and severe levels of mental retardation). One-way analyses of variance were significant for all but five variables. All adaptive behavior and maladaptive behavior scores were significantly more impaired for the samples with the greater degree of retardation. A similar ordering of significant differences was found for economic independence, earned income, level of income support, extent of independence in living arrangements and daytime activity, the variety of friends, number of support services and need for social support, and number of factors limiting leisure opportunities. Surprisingly, no significant differences were found among groups on physical mobility, need for health care or physical-sensory limitations.

Principal components analysis of the 21 variables followed by varimax rotation revealed six eigenvalues that were greater than one, suggesting that at least six factors should be extracted. The Scree test suggested the presence of seven to eight factors. All solutions were reviewed, with the eight-factor solution considered to provide the most meaningful representation of the data. This solution is presented in Table 2.

In the area of personal competence, four consistent factors emerged. Factor 1 produced a *Personal Independence* or general adaptive behavior

Table 1. Variables in exploratory factor analysis, with values for young adults with mild, moderate, and severe retardation

Variable/Definition		Mild	Moderate	Severe	F
Personal living skills (ICAP cluster)	M (SD)	541.0 (19.7)	509.6 (19.8)	480.8 (30.7)	94.58
	N	45	92	99	p < .001
Community living skills (ICAP cluster)	M (SD)	539.6 (23.6)	493.8 (24.9)	454.1 (29.6)	164.91
	N	45	92	99	p < .001
Social/communication skills (ICAP cluster)	M (SD)	529.7 (26.8)	487.6 (27.8)	451.3 (30.3)	119.80
	N	45	92	99	p < .001
Motor skills (ICAP cluster)	M (SD)	511.3 (31.4)	485.0 (30.4)	454.3 (36.5)	49.52
	N	45	92	99	p < .001
Externalized maladaptive behavior (ICAP index)	M (SD)	1.5 (4.7)	-4.0 (11.1)	-7.1 (11.8)	10.51
	N	45	92	99	p < .001
Internalized maladaptive behaviour (ICAP index)	M (SD)	-1.2 (7.0)	-6.1 (9.5)	-10.1 (10.7)	13.65
	N	45	92	99	p < .001
Asocial maladaptive behavior (ICAP index)	M (SD)	-.9 (8.1)	-8.6 (11.1)	-11.5 (12.0)	14.42
	N	45	92	99	p < .001
Physical mobility (ICAP mobility + arm/hand)	M (SD)	-2.1 (0.3)	-2.1 (0.4)	-2.1 (0.4)	.37
	N	45	91	98	
Need for health care (ICAP health + req. care by nurse/physician)	M (SD)	1.0 (0.2)	1.2 (0.7)	1.2 (0.7)	1.51
	N	35	91	98	
Physical complications (ICAP vision + hearing & frequency of seizures)	M (SD)	-3.1 (0.2)	-3.2 (0.6)	-3.3 (0.8)	1.82
	N	35	91	99	
Economic independence (additive scale of six interview items)[a]	M (SD)	4.2 (1.4)	1.7 (1.4)	1.0 (0.9)	96.27
	N	42	84	91	p < .001

continued

Table 1 – continued

Variable/Definition		Mild	Moderate	Severe	F
Earned income (interview $/month)	M (SD)	510.81 (440.28)	139.17 (156.04)	40.18 (70.84)	67.13
	N	46	81	91	p < .001
Income support (interview soc sec + disability $/month)	M (SD)	33.82 (97.42)	129.01 (133.04)	145.02 (142.11)	11.81
	N	46	81	91	p < .001
Living arrangement (continuum scale created from interview item)[b]	M (SD)	3.5 (1.0)	2.6 (0.7)	2.4 (0.6)	33.82
	N	44	88	100	p < .001
Daytime activity (continuum scale created from ICAP item)[c]	M (SD)	6.8 (0.9)	4.3 (1.9)	3.3 (0.9)	91.16
	N	41	90	98	p < .001
Number of friends (interview reported #)	M (SD)	3.6 (4.4)	3.1 (3.6)	2.2 (3.0)	2.94
	N	47	91	98	
Variety of friends (additive scale of nine interview items)[d]	M (SD)	1.4 (1.8)	2.8 (1.7)	2.2 (1.9)	5.47
	N	16	89	96	p < .01
Recreation/leisure/community social (additive scale of ten interview items)[e]	M (SD)	3.7 (1.5)	4.7 (2.0)	4.4 (2.1)	4.07
	N	47	90	100	
Number of support svcs (count of support svcs currently used from ICAP)	M (SD)	0.1 (0.3)	2.0 (1.3)	2.4 (1.3)	43.50
	N	45	92	99	p < .001
Need for social support (additive scale of five interview items)[f]	M (SD)	4.0 (0.8)	2.5 (1.0)	1.8 (0.9)	85.38
	N	41	80	76	p < .001
Number of limiting factors-leisure (count of limiting factors from ICAP social + leisure)	M (SD)	0.1 (0.3)	1.1 (0.7)	1.2 (0.7)	46.80
	N	45	92	99	p < .001

continued

Table 1 – continued

Note: Prior to factor analysis, all variables (except Income Support) were rescaled so that high values indicated greater competence or community adjustment/integration.

[a] Items: pays income tax; receives medicare/medicaid; receives social security income; puts $ in/out of saving account; has own checking account; employed. Content of this created scale was based on exploratory factor analysis and rational content analysis of a pool of 44 dichotomous interview items.

[b] Living Arrangement Scale: 5=living independently or with friends, spouse; 4=apartment training or half-way house, 3=living with family or relatives; 2=group residence; 1=institution, hospital, nursing home.

[c] Daytime Activity Scale: 7=competitive employment; 6=supervised/supported employment; 5=school or volunteer; 4=sheltered workshop; 3=day/work activity center; 2=day care): 1=no formal program outside home.

[d] Items: has special friends; peer friend; residence staff friend; teacher/boss friend; other friends; romantic friend; regular contact with same age non-handicapped person; visited friend; attended party or dance. Content of this created scale was based on exploratory factor analysis and rational content analysis of a pool of 44 dichotomous interview items.

[e] Items: went out to eat; went to sporting event; went to movie, concert, or play; attended religious service; went to park or on walk; went to club or meeting; participated in sports; went shopping; attended party or dance; visited friend. Content of this created scale was based on exploratory factor analysis and rational content analysis of a pool of 44 dichotomous interview items.

[f] Items: pays by self; dials phone; shops; pays bills; puts $ in/out of savings. Content of this created scale was based on exploratory factor analysis and rational content analysis of a pool of 44 dichotomous interview items.

Table 2. Varimax-rotated factor loadings (eight factor solution) for the personal competence and community adjustment/outcome variables

	1	2	3	4	5	6	7	8
Personal living skills (21)	0.882++	0.188	0.100	0.088	0.149	0.148	0.085	0.101
Community living skills (19)	0.860++	0.214	-0.010	0.076	0.131	0.140	0.293	0.138
Social/communication skills (19)	0.851++	0.272	-0.058	0.048	0.110	0.137	0.178	0.097
Motor skills (18)	0.835++	0.153	0.264	0.121	0.096	0.022	0.069	0.068
Need for social support (5)	0.740++	0.052	-0.056	0.064	0.030	0.173	0.429+	0.120
Economic independence (6)	0.517+	0.092	0.071	0.033	0.097	0.139	0.641++	0.355+
Variety of friends (9)	0.124	-0.108	-0.055	0.106	0.867++	-0.150	0.083	0.043
Number of friends (1)	0.204	-0.025	-0.069	-0.202	0.817++	-0.106	0.065	-0.051
Rec/leis community-social (10)	0.035	0.213	0.106	0.203	0.633++	-0.061	-0.261	0.222
External maladaptive (6)	0.155	0.866++	0.016	-0.080	0.033	0.040	0.107	0.026
Asocial maladaptive (4)	0.143	0.854++	0.019	0.052	-0.103	0.125	0.130	0.017
Internal maladaptive (6)	0.341+	0.704++	0.003	0.016	0.091	0.080	0.106	-0.131
Physical mobility (2)	0.160	-0.094	0.882++	-0.096	-0.031	-0.113	0.066	0.029
Need for health care (2)	-0.014	0.161	0.723++	0.274	-0.024	0.290	0.093	-0.063
Physical complications (3)	0.229	-0.036	0.074	0.913++	0.039	-0.003	0.020	0.017
Number of limiting factors (7)	0.203	0.183	0.089	-0.099	-0.127	0.842++	0.052	0.118
Number of support services (11)	0.223	0.045	-0.010	0.118	0.032	0.715++	0.367+	-0.092
Living arrangement (1)	0.159	0.272	0.065	-0.067	-0.157	0.108	0.766++	-0.184
Earned income (1)	0.367+	0.123	0.098	0.084	0.072	0.176	0.649++	0.334+
Daytime activity (3)	0.453+	0.093	0.150	0.052	0.084	0.223	0.550++	0.362+
Income support (4)	-0.258	0.094	0.044	-0.004	-0.096	-0.003	-0.114	-0.854−

Note: In parentheses following each variable is the number of items that formed the variable.
++ or −− for loadings of .50 or above.
+ or − for loadings of .30 to .49.

factor with primary loadings of the four *ICAP* adaptive behavior domain scores (i.e., Personal Living, Community Living, Social/Communication, and Motor Skills). Other variables with high loadings on this factor included the Need for Social Support and Economic Independence variables, areas consistent with the Personal Independence factor interpretation. Factor 2 was defined by the three *ICAP* maladaptive behavior indexes, and appears to represent a general *Maladaptive Behavior* or emotional competence dimension. Two other factors appeared to represent different aspects of physical competence. Factor 3 was defined by the Physical Mobility and Need for Health Care scales. This factor was labeled *Physical Mobility* since the two defining scales measure the extent to which an individual can move freely about the environment without the need for assistance. Factor 4 was defined by a single loading for a variable created from the *ICAP*; this *Physical Complications* factor appears to reflect the number of an individual's significant sensory-physical conditions and limitations. Although the Physical Mobility and Physical Complications factors are intuitively similar in that both appear to assess aspects of physical competence, these factors failed to merge into a single factor in most solutions.

Four community adjustment dimensions were identified. Factor 5 was called *Community Social/Recreation/Leisure*, with very high loadings by the Number of Friends, Variety of Friends, and active Recreation/Leisure outside the home variables. This factor appears to represent the extent to which an individual has developed an active social network and the extent to which the individual is actively involved in community-based recreation/leisure activities. When a nine-factor solution was extracted (not included in this report), this factor split into separate social (i.e., Variety and Number of Friends) and recreation/leisure (i.e., Recreation/leisure-Community Social) factors. This suggests that if other indicators of recreation/leisure activities had been included in the analysis, separate social and recreation/leisure dimensions may have been identified. This did occur when the recreation/leisure variable was split into two separate subscales.

Factor 6 was created from the *ICAP* and defined primarily by Number of Limiting Factors for Social-Leisure activities and Number of Support Services scales. This factor appears to define a *Social and Service Support* dimension of community adjustment. Finally, Factors 7 and 8 appear to represent *Financial Independence* and *Community Independence/Integration* dimensions. Factor 7 appears to represent the degree to which an individual is self-sufficient and integrated in the community (i.e., *Community and Economic Integration*), since it was defined by high loadings for degree of independence in living arrangements, daytime activities approaching more independent levels (e.g., extent of competitive employment), financial independence (economic independence, earned income), and freedom from social and service support (need for social support, number of support services). Factor 8 appears quite similar to Factor 7 in that it was consistently defined by economic/financial variables. However, Factor 8 is a bipolar factor, defined primarily by the degree to which an individual receives external income support (high negative loading for Income Support), in contrast to positive loadings for variables measuring income earned (Earned Income) during daytime activities (Daytime Activities). Except for the variable assessing absence of external income support, Factors 7 and 8 are highly similar. In a seven factor solution, these two factors of *Financial Independence* and *Community Independence/Integration* merged into a single factor.

DISCUSSION

This study is one of a growing number of conceptual and empirical efforts to identify reliable dimensions of personal competence and community adjustment of persons with mental retardation. Through an extensive review of studies on community adjustment, measures were created or employed that assessed a wide range of personal competence and community outcome variables. These measures relied upon rating scales and extensive interviews. The sample included 239 subjects who had been out of school special education programs from 1 to 10 years. Approximately 150 separate items were scaled into 21 measures of personal competence and community outcomes.

The intent of the study was to identify broader factors to describe the community adjustment of young adults with mental retardation. Using principal components analysis with varimax rotation, 8 interpretable factors emerged from the analyses. Four of the 8 factors appears to assess aspects of personal competence (Bruininks & McGrew, 1987), with the remaining four factors assessing important community outcomes. The descriptive labels chosen to describe these factors appear below:

Personal Competence	*Community Adjustment*
Personal (Adaptive) Independence	Social-Recreation-Leisure
Maladaptive Behavior	Need for Social Support Services
Physical Mobility	Community Economic Integration
Physical Complications	Financial Independence

These findings add to the growing research literature on the community adjustment of persons with mental retardation. One conclusion supported by these results is that functional behaviors and aspects of personal competence are important to community adjustment (Bruininks & McGrew, 1987; Greenspan, 1979; Parmenter, 1987).

A second conclusion is that the expression of personal competence in the community is comprised of a number of identifiable areas. The four personal competence factors identified in this study corroborate three of the four components of Greenspan's (1979) model of personal competence: physical competence, social competence, and emotional competence. The Cognitive Competence component did not appear, probably due to the absence of strong cognitive measures in the study. However, the strong Personal Independence factor is comprised of variables with strong positive relationships to cognitive measures (Bruininks & McGrew, 1987).

The four community outcome factors bear some similarity to the findings of Halpern *et al.* (1986). They identified an occupational factor that also included a measure of integration with non-retarded persons. While measures and samples used in this study differed from those of Halpern *et al.* (1986), the Community and Economic Integration factor included economic variables such as earned income and financial skills with degree of social integration in housing and daytime services. The remaining three factors argue strongly for inclusion of social networks (i.e., friends) along with social-leisure opportunities, service support and absence of income support as major aspects of community adjustment.

The increasing decentralization and attendant community integration of services is providing new impetus for questioning previous constructs of adjustment and quality of life for persons with mental retardation. Results from this study and those of others argue for a multidimensional and increasingly interactional perspective. While these results are promising, there is a clear need for replication and expansion of such studies. The number and variety of measures, the ability range of the sample and the extent of living and daytime activities were expanded from those reported in a few previous studies. Attempts to define community adjustment of persons with mental retardation, however, should encompass a wider range of personal competence and community and personal outcome measures. The search for reliable and valid dimensions of community adjustment must also embrace conceptual models and direct measures that assess extent of satisfaction (Halpern *et al.*, 1986; Heal & Chadsey-Rusch, 1985), environment qualities (King *et al.*, 1971; Raynes, 1988; Landesman & Vietze, 1987), the responses and interactions of persons with their environments (Parmenter, 1987), influences from the community and broader society (Parmenter, 1987) and other personal-affective factors reflecting personal choice, beliefs and aspirations.

Exploring the dimensions of community adjustment and quality of life is in a very early stage of development. Such inquiry is essential for many compelling reasons if we are to extend our understanding of the many varied and valued forms of living in the community and to promote worthwhile qualities of life for citizens with mental retardation.

ACKNOWLEDGEMENT

Preparation of this paper was supported in part by a cooperative agreement with the National Institute on Disability and Rehabilitation Research (#H133B80048) to the Rehabilitation Research and Training Center on Community Integration, University of Minnesota. Follow-up data collection activities were supported in part by grants from the Office of Special Education and Rehabilitative Services (#G008400605 and G008630478) and the National Institute on Disability and Rehabilitation Research (#G008435056).

REFERENCES

Brown, R. I., & Hughson, E. A. (1980) *Training of the developmentally handicapped adult.* Springfield: Charles C. Thomas.

Bruininks, R. H., Hill, B. K., Weatherman, R. F., & Woodcock, R. W. (1986). *Inventory for client and agency planning.* Allen, TX: DLM Teaching Resources.

Bruininks, R. H., & McGrew, K. (1987) *Exploring the structure of adaptive behavior* (Project Report Number 1). Minneapolis: University of Minnesota, Minnesota University Affiliated Program.

Edgar, E. (1987) Secondary programs in special education: Are many of them justifiable? *Exceptional Children*, **53**(6), 555–561.

Edgerton, R. B., & Bercovici, S. M. (1976) The cloak of competence: years later. *American Journal of Mental Deficiency*, **80**(5), 485–497.

Emerson, E. B. (1985) Evaluating the impact of deinstitutionalization on the lives of mentally retarded people. *American Journal of Mental Deficiency*, **90**, 277–288.

Goldstein, H. (1964) Social and occupational adjustment. In H. A. Stevens & R. Heber (Eds.), *Mental retardation*. Carbondale, IL: Southern Illinois University Press.

Greenspan, S. (1979) Social intelligence in the retarded. In N. R. Ellis (Ed.). *Handbook of mental deficiency, psychological theory and research, 2nd ed.* Hillsdale, JF: Lawrence Erlbaum.

Halpern, A. S., Nave, G., Close, D. W., & Nelson, D. (1986) An empirical analysis of the dimensions of community adjustment for adults with mental retardation in semi-independent living programs. *Australia and New Zealand Journal of Developmental Disabilities*, **12**(3), 147–157.

Hazazi, S. B., Gordon, L. R., & Roe, C. A. (1985) Factors associated with the employment status of handicapped youth exiting high school from 1979 to 1983. *Exceptional Children*, **51**(6),. 455–469.

Heal, L. W., & Chadsey-Rusch, J. (1985) The Lifestyle Satisfaction Scale (LSS): Assessing individuals' satisfaction with residential, community setting, and associated services. *Applied Research in Mental Retardation*, **6**, 475–490.

Heal, L. W., Sigelman, C. K., & Switzky, H. N. (1978) Research on community residential alternative for the mentally retarded. In N. R. Ellis (Ed.).

International Review of Research in Mental Retardation, (Vol. 9) New York: Academic Press.

Irwin, L. K., Crowell, F., & Bellamy, G. T. (1979) Multiple assessment evaluation of programs for severely retarded adults. *Mental Retardation*, **17**, 123–138.

King, R. D., Raynes, N. V., & Tizard, J. (1971) *Patterns of residential care: Sociological studies in institutions for handicapped citizens*. London: Routledge & Kegan Paul.

Lakin, K. C., Bruininks, R. H., & Sigford, B. B. (1981) Early perspectives on community adjustment of mentally retarded people. In R. H. Bruininks, C. E. Meyers, B. B. Sigford, & K. C. Lakin (Eds.). *Deinstitutionalization and community adjustment of mentally retarded people*. Washington, DC: American Association on Mental Deficiency.

Lakin, K. C., Bruininks, R. H., & Sigford, B. B. (1981) Deinstitutionalization and community-based residential adjustment: A summary of research and issues. In R. H. Bruininks, C. E. Meyers, B. B. Sigford, & K. C. Lakin (Eds.), *Deinstitutionalization and community adjustment of mentally retarded people*. Washington, DC: American Association on Mental Deficiency.

Landesman, S., & Vietze, P. (Eds.). (1978) *Living environments and mental retardation*. Washington, D.C.: American Association on Mental Retardation.

McGrew, K. S., & Bruininks, R. H. (1988) *Research on the construct of adaptive behavior: Implications for research and practice*. Manuscript submitted for publication.

Mitchell, D. R. (1986) A developmental systems approach to planning and evaluating services for persons with handicaps. in R. I. Brown (Ed.). *Management and administration of rehabilitation programmes*. London: Croom Helm.

Parmenter, T. R. (1980) *Vocational training for independent living*. New York: World Rehabilitation Fund, Inc.

Parmenter, T. R. (1986) *Bridges from school to working life for handicapped youth: The view from Australia*. New York: World Rehabilitation Fund, Inc.

Parmenter, T. R. (1987) An analysis of the dimensions of quality of life of people with physical disabilities. In R. I. Brown (Ed.) *Quality of life and handicapped people*. London: Croom Helm.

Raynes, N. V. (1988) *Annotated directory of measures of environmental quality for use in residential services for people with a mental handicap*. Manchester, England: University of Manchester, Department of Social Policy and Social Work.

Reiter, S., & Levi, A. M. (1980) Factors affecting social integration of noninstitutionalized mentally retarded adults. *American Journal of Mental Deficiency*, **85**(2), 25–30.

Schalock, R., & Harper, R. (1978) Placement from community-based mental retardation programs: How well do clients do? *American Journal on Mental Deficiency*, **83**, 240–247.

Stanfield, J. S. (1973) Graduation: What happens to the retarded child when he grows up? *Exceptional Children*, 548–552.

Ward, J., Parmenter, T. R., Riches, V. & Hauritz, M. (1978) Adjustment to work: A follow-up of mildly handicapped adolescents who have undergone training in a Work Preparation Center. *National Rehabilitation Digest*, **2**, 34–38.

Ward, J., Parmenter, T. R., Riches, V. & Hauritz, M. (1986) A summative report of a work preparation program for mildly intellectually disabled schoolleavers. *Australian Disability Review*, **3**, 7–15.

Job Histories in Open Employment of a Population of Young Adults with Mental Retardation

S. A. Richardson, H. Koller and M. Katz
*Albert Einstein College of Medicine, 1300 Morris Park Avenue,
Bronx, New York 10461*

Reasons for leaving all jobs and reasons for choosing jobs as least and
most liked were examined for a population of mildly retarded young
adults and appropriate comparisons who were not retarded. These
reasons represented the viewpoint of the young adults. Sets of categories
were developed from the responses given. Issues examined included
worker incompetence and working conditions most frequently cited as
reasons for leaving and for liking and disliking jobs. Similarities and
differences between the mildly retarded and comparison workers were
noted.

The job role is central for most of adult life. A person's job history plays
a major part in defining their social and economic status, and the job of
the head of the household largely determines the socioeconomic status of
the entire family. For adults who had been judged mildly mentally
retarded (MMR) during childhood, an important determinant of their
need for adult MR services is whether after leaving school they are able
to obtain and hold jobs. For those who do, the kinds of jobs they obtain,
how long they hold jobs, and how much they are unemployed will
influence the degree to which they can become independent.

MR young people may have problems as they enter the work force.
The intellectual and scholastic incompetence that caused them to be
identified as MR during the school years is likely to be a continuing
difficulty in some job roles which require literacy and numerical skills and
facility in the use of language. The industrial revolution led through a
scheme of "scientific management" to the breakdown of work, with a
maximum decomposition of jobs, a minimization of skills and consequently minimum job-learning time. This provided the basis for
assembly line organization of jobs (Littler & Soloman 1985, p. 86) that

generally did not require intellectual and scholastic competence. A reviewer (Rosenbrock 1985, p. 163) suggested that many assembly line jobs may be more suited to the mentally handicapped. He suggested that "slight mental retardation . . . often enables a person to do tedious work which would handicap a "normal" worker because of the monotony."

The concept of incompetence focuses on the individual, while the changes stemming from "scientific management" focus on the work environment and the characteristics and requirements of the job. We need to consider the interaction between the worker and the work environment, including job performance, the physical setting and other characteristics of each job, the interpersonal relations between the worker and those he or she works with and for, and the circumstances of seeking, leaving and finding jobs. We used this approach in studying the job histories of young MR persons in the years after leaving special school, presenting their point of view and examining what they told us. Specifically, we analyzed their reasons for leaving each job and the reasons they chose a particular job as least or most liked.

METHOD

The study design and methods for examination of the job histories has already been described (Richardson *et al.*, 1988), so these will only be summarized here.

Subjects – 221 MR subjects were selected from the total population born 1951–1955 and resident in Aberdeen, Scotland in 1962 (n=13,842), yielding a prevalence rate of 16 per 1000. Children were selected if they had been placed in any special facility for MR children, an administrative definition. When the study subjects were 22 years of age, a follow-up study was carried out, and data were obtained from 192 subjects. They left school at age 15 or 16 and thus were potentially in the work force for 6–7 years. None of the severely retarded (IQ<50) and 23% of the mildly retarded young people had any job history. The present report deals with those who had some job history – 75 MMR males and 50 MMR females.

Comparison subjects were matched with MR subjects on age, sex, and social class in childhood. For the analysis of the work histories, we limited this matched comparison population to those 33 males annd 19 females who left school without the scholastic attainments needed for entry into further education or the more skilled jobs open to better qualified young people. In this way, they were the most appropriate for comparison with the MR study subjects who also were without scholastic qualifications on leaving school.

MEASURES

Reasons for leaving jobs

The measures used in the present report are based on the young adults' account of their work histories. For each job left, they were asked about their reasons for leaving. For those who had remained in the same job since leaving school the question does not apply. After reading the responses to the question, we developed, after several revisions, a reliable set of categories that spanned the variety of reasons given. The categories vary from specific to general. On conceptual grounds these categories were then grouped under a set of more general classifications. The categories and classifications are shown in Table 1. We defined the category of "functional incompetence" to mean any inability or behavior on the part of the worker that caused them to be fired from the job or any admission by the worker that they were not capable of managing the tasks assigned them. Because people held different numbers of jobs and some gave more than one reason for leaving a job, we used number of reasons rather than number of persons who gave a reason. The average number of reasons given per person is shown in Table 1. The average number of jobs left per year (turnover) did not differ significantly between the MMR and comparisons for either sex (Richardson *et al.*, 1988).

Reasons for choosing particular jobs as least or most liked

Those who had held more than one job were asked to select the job that they liked least and the job they liked most. Study subjects who made these choices were asked for their reasons. Categories were developed into which the response could be reliably placed. These categories were also grouped under broader conceptual classifications. These are shown in Table 2. The categories do not show direction. This must be inferred from whether the reasons were given for a most or least liked job. For example, poor pay may be inferred as a reason for the least liked job and good pay a reason for the most liked job. If several reasons were given, each was coded. The totals refer to numbers of reasons given.

SETTING

The city where the study took place is described in a previous paper (Richardson *et al.*, 1988). At the time and place of the study there were unusually low rates of unemployment. The Youth Employment service provided help in obtaining first jobs for many of those leaving special schools. These young adults did not often receive further help.

Table 1. Reasons for leaving related to jobs left for MMR and comparison males and females

	Males		Females	
	MMR *(n=70)*	Comparisons[a] *(n=33)*	MMR *(n=45)*	Comparisons *(n=17)*
I. Left for job-related reasons				
A. Reasons related to functional incompetence				
a) Unable to cope	5	1	3	0
b) Lacked skills/abilities	7	0	14	0
c) Did not meet physical requirements	2	1	0	0
d) Did not meet time requirements	11	6	9	0
e) Caught pilfering, stealing	4	2	2	0
f) Damaged company property	2	2	1	0
g) Other unacceptable behavior	14	12	5	4
h) Fired, sacked, no reason given	5	3	1	0
Subtotal	50	27	35	4
B. Unrelated to functional incompetence				
1. Left of own accord				
a) Not enough pay	55	32	15	7
b) Disliked the hours	6	8	3	5
c) Disliked physical environment	18	6	11	2
d) Too physically demanding	7	2	8	1
e) Too little to do	0	1	2	0
f) Not treated fairly	4	4	3	3
g) No prospects for advancement	0	1	0	0
h) Persuaded to leave by family	1	0	3	1
i) Generally disliked, fed up	39	21	24	9
j) Got another job	14	19	4	1
k) Entered a training program	3	2	0	0
Subtotal	147	96	73	29
2. Did not leave of own accord				
a) Firm closed	10	3	4	0
b) Seasonal or other layoff	16	5	4	3
c) Change in job operations	6	1	1	0
d) Became too old for job	5	1	0	0
e) Made redundant, no reason given	4	0	0	0

	Males		Females	
	MMR *(n=70)*	*Comparisons*[a] *(n=33)*	*MMR* *(n=45)*	*Comparisons* *(n=17)*
f) Work-related illness or injury	11	6	8	0
Subtotal	52	16	17	3
C. Unclear whether due to functional incompetence				
a) Problems with workmates	5	0	5	1
b) Problems with supervision	9	6	7	5
c) Problems with others at work (unspecified)	0	2	2	1
d) Left as a consequence of a row	8	1	0	1
e) Asked to leave unjustly	3	3	1	1
Subtotal	25	12	15	9
II. Left for reasons unrelated to the job				
a) Sent to prison or other trouble with law	9	2	0	0
b) Sent to MR or psychiatric institution	3	0	2	0
c) Location of job inconvenient	1	0	0	1
d) Became a housewife	–	–	3	6
e) Pregnant	–	–	12	7
f) Illness or injury not job-related	5	2	5	1
g) Other, mainly moved to another community or left because a friend left	26	7	10	6
Subtotal	44	11	32	21
Total I & II	318	162	172	66
Number of reasons/person	4.5	4.9	3.8	3.9

[a] An additional 6 jobs were left by comparison males who completed apprenticeships.

RESULTS

Reasons for Leaving Jobs

To examine whether the MMR left jobs more often than the nonretarded comparisons because of functional incompetence, all categories of job-related reasons were assigned to one of three classifications (see Table 1): IA. functional incompetence, IB. unrelated to functional incompetence,

Table 2.   Reasons given by MMR males and females for choosing jobs as least and most liked

	Males		Females	
Reasons	*Least liked*	*Most liked*	*Least liked*	*Most liked*
A. Physical conditions of the workplace	14	9	4	0
B. Interpersonal relations				
1) Workmates mentioned	0	6	3	2
2) Supervision mentioned	1	4	4	0
3) People at work (general)	0	6	0	4
4) Customers, clients	0	1	0	2
Subtotal	1	17	7	8
C. Characteristics of the job				
1) Interesting/boring	5	9	1	4
2) Variety of things to do	0	1	0	2
3) Autonomy given to employee	0	4	0	2
4) Physical demands on employee	2	2	2	0
5) Pay	2	1	2	2
6) Hours	3	2	0	1
7) Perks	0	1	0	1
8) Lack of job security	1	0	0	0
Subtotal	13	20	5	12
Totals	28	46	16	20

IC. unclear whether or not leaving was related to functional incompetence. In the categories under functional incompetence, all except "unable to cope" were ones in which the worker was fired from the job. These categories included inability to do the job (IA a&b), physical limitations (IAc) and various forms of behavior difficulties (IA d–h). The behavior categories are specific except for "other unacceptable behavior". For males, this consisted largely of either physical or verbal aggression. For females the reasons were diverse.

To test the hypothesis that the MMR left jobs because of functional incompetence more often than comparisons, we used the subtotals of reasons given in the three classifications of leaving for job-related reasons (IA, IB, IC). Because the reasons in IC were unclear whether leaving was due to incompetence, actual incompetence can range from none to all of the reasons. The most conservative test of the hypothesis was to assume that all the reasons for leaving in the unclear classification were functional incompetence. When "Reasons related to functional incompetence" (IA) and "unclear whether incompetence" (IC) were combined and tested against "unrelated to incompetence" (IB), no significant differences were found between the MMR and comparisons for males or females. It should be noted, however, that there would be more functional incompetence among the MMR than comparison females had the categories that were related to incompetence (IA) been examined against the other two classifications (IB&IC). This would not occur for the males.

Within the classification of functional incompetence (IA), the MMR young adults of both sexes were unable to cope or lacked skills/abilities more often than the comparisons but they were less often fired because of unacceptable behavior (categories d–h combined).

We tested the hypothesis that the MMR more often than the comparisons left jobs which were less secure because they were seasonal, or because the firm was less stable. To do this we determined whether, among the job-related reasons unrelated to incompetence (IB), the MMR more often left because of reasons in categories B2 a–e. The hypothesis was confirmed for males (41 v. 147 MMR, 10 v. 96 comparisons, $x^2=7.24$, d.f=1, p<.01), but not for the females.

Within the classification "left of own accord" (IB1), we inspected the categories for differences between the MMR and comparisons. The MMR left twice as often as the comparisons because of dislike of the physical environment of the work setting (males, MMR 12%, comparisons 6%; females, MMR 15%, comparisons 7%). The MMR males left less often than their comparisons in order to get another job (MMR 10%, comparisons 20%). There was no difference for the females. Workers most frequently left of their own accord because of not enough pay and general dislike and being fed up.

The reasons for leaving that were unrelated to the job just left are shown in II, Table 1. For males, the MMR more often left for reasons unrelated to the job (14%) than the comparisons (6%). For the females, more comparisons left for reasons unrelated to the job (32%) than the MMR (19%). The sex difference was due to the females leaving because of pregnancy or to become a housewife.

Reasons for choosing a job as least liked or most liked

The categories of reasons are shown in Table 2. They have been placed under three general classifications of: A. physical conditions of the workplace, B. interpersonal relations, and C. characteristics of the job. There were no differences for either sex in the frequencies of use of these classifications between the MMR and comparisons for the reasons for the least or most liked jobs. Because of this the reasons are only given for the MMR. For the least liked jobs the males mentioned the physical conditions of the workplace (50%) and the characteristics of the job (46%) with similar frequency, whereas interpersonal relations were only mentioned once. The distribution of reasons for the most liked job, on the other hand, indicates the physical conditions of the workplace were the least often mentioned (20%) and more reasons were given pertaining to interpersonal relations (37%). The characteristics of the job received the same attention in describing both the least and most liked jobs.

For MMR females, interpersonal relations were frequently mentioned reasons for the jobs least liked (44%) and most liked (40%). The characteristics of the job were given more emphasis in the most liked (60%) than in the least liked job (31%).

There were also differences between the MMR males and females that may be implied from the results given. For males, reasons related to interpersonal relations were prominent only for the most liked job, whereas for females, interpersonal relations were important in reasons for both least and most liked jobs. In both the least and most liked jobs, males more often than females gave reasons related to the physical conditions of the workplace. Within the categories dealing with the characteristics of the job, the MMR males, in both most and least liked jobs, mentioned intrinsic interest or boredom. For the MMR females this category was the one most used for choosing the most liked job, but not the least liked.

Recurrent Themes

Among the reasons examined in both parts of the results, there were some themes that recurred. We selected three which appeared to be salient. The first was the physical conditions and environment of the workplace (Table 1, IB1C and Table 2 A). We examined the responses that were coded under these categories. For males the conditions described most often dealt with being indoors or out of doors. Some who worked indoors disliked their jobs because they felt shut in and oppressed. They wanted to get outdoors to escape from being tied down in one place. Some with outdoor jobs chose them as most liked because they were not closed in and could move about. While the majority spoke favorably of the outdoors, some spoke of the disadvantages of being out in all kinds of weather and getting wet or cold. Some left or disliked inside jobs because of noise, smell, dirt, heat, cold, damp, and air pollution.

A second recurrent concern dealt with supervision on the job, both negative and positive. Responses may be summarized as follows: 1) too many bosses, e.g., "one person told you one thing, another told you something else," 2) degree of supervision, e.g., "always breathing down my neck," 3) whether appreciation was shown by employers, e.g., "they just took you for granted," or, alternatively, "it really boosts you when they say you're doing great," ands 4) personal characteristics of the supervisor, e.g., sarcastic, moody, talked religion all the time, or alternatively, friendly, treated workers as equals, would lend a hand, or would listen to you.

A third concern was the interest or boredom of the job. It is one of the main reasons why workers left of their own accord (Table 1). When workers found jobs with intrinsic interest this was given as a reason for liking a job (Table 2).

DISCUSSION

The expectation that the MMR workers would show more evidence of functional incompetence on the job was not realized by our results. For the MMR males the proportion of jobs left due to incompetence was almost exactly the same as for the comparisons and constitutes from approximately one fifth to one quarter of all job-related reasons. For the females there was some evidence of more job-related incompetence among the MMR, but when a more conservative measure was used, there was no difference.

When the kinds of functional incompetence were examined, the MMR did leave jobs somewhat more frequently than comparisons because of their inability to master the skills needed for the job, but this was offset by the MMR leaving jobs somewhat less often than the comparisons because of behavior unacceptable to employers.

While some expectations for MMR workers were based on their possible incompetence, some focused on the characteristics of the job and how they may have influenced MMR workers. Some reviewers suggested that mentally retarded workers would not mind the repetition and tedium of industrial jobs. The results show that the MMR workers did frequently have jobs that were boring and tedious, but the MMR disliked these jobs just as frequently as the comparisons. More generally, examination of reasons for liking jobs most and least showed that MMR workers were similar to comparisons in their likes and dislikes.

Of all the reasons for leaving, "not enough pay" was by far the most frequent, and more often given by MMR males than females. This may reflect a time and place where a man needed to be the breadwinner throughout his working life, whereas most women worked until marriage or pregnancy, and then became full time housewives. With changing social and economic conditions this may well have changed.

The physical conditions of the workplace were important criteria by which MMR young people evaluated their jobs. For males it was the most used category in reasons for choosing jobs as both least and most liked. It was also one of the more frequent reasons why they left jobs of their own accord. While the same categories were used by the women, they were used relatively less. This may because women rarely did laboring jobs where the physical conditions may more often be unpleasant.

With increased training and skill comes greater personal autonomy in organizing the job and planning the working day. Workers with few skills have little control over their daily working lives and are more closely supervised. Because of the lack of autonomy given most MMR workers, the quality of supervision is critical in influencing worker satisfaction. Supervision may be an especially important factor for women because they more often have assembly line work than men, who do more general laboring jobs.

Relationships with workmates were also shown to be important. In part these are under the control of supervisors, but there is need for further study of the organization of work to facilitate relationships between workmates in ways that do not interfere with and may enhance the quality and amount of work done. Interpersonal relations were shown to be of equal importance in reasons for both liking and disliking jobs for women. For the men interpersonal relations were virtually absent as reasons for disliking jobs, but were given as a reason for liking jobs as frequently as was given by women. For men physical conditions and unpleasant characteristics of their jobs appeared to overshadow all other reasons.

The results suggest that the MMR, especially the males, had less control over their working lives than the comparisons. In a previous paper (Richardson *et al.*, 1988), we showed that young adults who were MMR more often than comparisons had unskilled jobs and were paid less for jobs with the same level of skill. The present results show the MMR more often were laid off or made redundant, the decision to leave being taken out of their hands. The MMR left jobs more often for reasons unrelated to jobs and less often for another job or training. These differences between MMR and comparison workers may be related to more unemployment found for MMR males (Richardson *et al.*, 1988). In layoffs and redundancy the workers have no lead time to look for another job while still working. The MMR left jobs more often without having arranged for a job to go to. They may also have had more difficulty in planning for job changes, and, with fewer skills to offer employers, may have had more difficulty in finding new jobs.

We have addressed the question of functional incompetence, the extent to which it exists and what obstacles it places in the job careers of young adults who are MMR. If attention is restricted to jobs held, there is little evidence to support a hypothesis that MMR young adults are functionally incompetent. When the focus of attention is broadened to the overall job career, there is indirect evidence of functional incompetence which shows up in their having less skilled and less well paid jobs (Richardson *et al.*, 1988) and less favorable conditions of work. In the process of seeking and negotiating for jobs, and in shifting from one job to the next, the MMR appear to be at a disadvantage, and when they succeed in these transitions, it is often at the price of settling for poorer working conditions. In addition, it must be remembered that this report has dealt with only the MMR young people in the study population who exhibited enough functional competence to enter the labor force. There were some MMR young adults (males 16%, females 23%) who never worked in competitive employment. They must be considered the most functionally incompetent.

Finally, it is important to recall that this report has presented the worker's viewpoint, which has rarely been done. We hope that this phenomenological exploration will encourage other researchers to pursue the topic further.

ACKNOWLEDGEMENT

This study was supported by the Foundation for Child Development, the William T. Grant Foundation, the National Institute of Child Health and Human Development Grant No. HD07907, Maternal and Child Health Training Grant MCJ-000241-22-1, the G. Harold and Leila Y. Mathers Charitable Foundation, the Charitable trust of Mrs Abbey R. Mauze, the Scottish Home and Health Department, and the Social Science Research Council of the United Kingdom. The authors wish to thank Raymond Illsley, Jan McLaren, and the late Gordon Horobin of the British Medical Research Council for their help and support.

REFERENCES

Littler, C. R. & Salaman, G. (1985) The design of jobs. In C. R. Littler (ed.), *The Experience of Work*, Hampshire, Gower Publishing Co. Ltd., pp. 85–104.

Richardson, S. A., Koller, H. and Katz, M. (1988) Job Histories in Open Employment of a Population of Young Adults with Mental Retardation – I. *American Journal on Mental Retardation*, **92**, 6, 483–491.

Rosenbrock, H. (1985) Engineers and the work that people do. In C. R. Littler (ed.) *Op. Cit.*, pp. 161–171.

Mental Handicap, Ageing and the Community

J. Hogg

Hester Adrian Research Centre, The University,
Manchester M13 9PL, England

Increases in the life-expectancy of people with mental handicap coupled with progressive closure of large institutions has, during the past decade, led to a growing interest in the development of services and research concerned with older people with mental handicap. The present paper provides a summary of five contributions concerned broadly with aspects of life in the community for such people and their families. They reflect international interest in this population, contrasts in characteristics of institutional and community populations, the problem of the hidden population of older people with mental handicap *not* known to service providers, and the preparation for the future for families with an older member with mental handicap.

Throughout the twentieth century there has been a progressive change in the age stucture of most societies (See United Nations, 1956; 1973; Reproduced in Hogg, Moss and Cooke (1988)). Both medical and social factors have contributed to this trend. Improved health care has decreased mortality while family sizes have been progressively restricted. Similar trends to those observed in the general population can be determined among people with mental handicap, though as Eyman, Grossman, Tarjan and Miller (1987 p. 1) observe, ". . . recent studies have documented that such trends are not as dramatic as was originally hoped". Nevertheless, an increase there has been and one which has occured at a significant time in the development of services for people with mental handicap. In many countries the large institutions which have

---

Editorial footnote: The problems of ageing are too varied to be addressed comprehensively by the inclusion of isolated papers in this volume. The two moderators of the symposia on ageing have agreed to contribute short reports herein which will be published in detail later by agreement with IASSMD.

traditionally provided a place of resident for such individuals have been replaced by the provision of residential accommodation in the community, with access to the facilities and resources offered in local neighbourhoods.

Both the changing demographic trends and these developments in policy have conditioned much of the research that has been undertaken with ageing people with mental handicap. Demographic studies have or are being undertaken in several countries in both institutional and community settings. In addition, the nature of service provision and the quality of the lives of such people have increasingly received attention (e.g. Seltzer and Krauss, 1987). Bruckmuller (1988) considered the international perspective on the needs of ageing people with mental handicap and their families. She emphasised the commitment of the International League of Societies for People with Mental Handicap to these populations, noting the existence of the League's special committee on ageing and mental handicap and its work, and the need for further work to understand the nature of such people and their families.

A starting point, internationally, for such research has been the many demographic studies that are being undertaken. Given the diversity of residences in which older people with mental handicap find themselves, many of these studies have taken into account the contrasts offered by differing provision. Thus, Badry, Groeneweg, Vbrancic and McDonald (1988) report on a comparison of the service needs of community and institution-based older persons with mental handicap in Canada. Their study considered older persons (age 45 and over) with mental handicaps residing in either community or institutional settings were compared for their current use of and need for social and habilitative services. These comparisons were based on data arising from a province-wide survey of older developmentally handicapped individuals (n=742).

Although there was a disproportionate representation of all individuals in the institutional environment (56.5%), those residing within congregate care settings in the community (i.e. within lodges, extended care centres, nursing homes and auxiliary hospitals) demonstrated significantly higher frequencies of health impairments, e.g. obesity, oedema, paralysis, and musculoskeletal and neurological impairments.

In the area of independence capacity skills (i.e. banking, laundry, public transportation, shopping, telephone usage, and meal preparation), those individuals involved in community-based vocational, residential, or other programs co-ordinated by associations or Social Services, were significantly more skilled than those individuals involved in either institutional or community-based congregate care facilities. Similarly, the former were more competent in self care skills such as grooming and dressing. Overall involvement in activity or leisure programs was greatest for community environments. Correspondingly, access to and involvement with professional services was greatest in the community, as was involvement in social and familial relationships.

An analysis of stated and perceived needs for current and future services was also conducted. These results were discussed in the context of future program design for this population.

A critical concern in such studies in the community is the fact that we know many people with mental handicap are unknown to service providers. Purely administratively based surveys, therefore, inevitably involve an underestimate of numbers and are likely in unspecified ways to result in somewhat distorted data (see Hogg *et al.*, 1988, pp. 67–72). The first two of these authors are at present engaged in a demographic survey in a single administrative (local authority) area in the north west of England. As part of this study an extensive outreach exercise has been undertaken to identify people not known to service providers. This was reported by Horne (1988) who noted that early in the study it became clear that the picture in Oldham was complex and that there was no simple dichotomy between people known and not known to the Community Mental Handicap Team. Preliminary work indicated that the initial setting up of the Community Mental Handicap Team did not result in all people with mental handicap changing from their existing social worker to a member of the Community Mental Handicap Team.

In addition, the Community Mental Handicap Team does not necessarily have contact with (or even know of) people with mental handicap who are living in residential accommodation, attending or receiving day services for elderly people or those with disabilities. A major result of this state of affairs was that the Community Mental Handicap Team was not in a position to provide a comprehensive list of all people with mental handicap known to Oldham Social Services Department. In addition, some individuals whose names were provided by the Community Mental Handicap Team were no longer in contact with the team and locating and collecting information on them became part of the outreach exercise.

In the first stage of the study, contact was made with four broad groups of service providers, notably, general practitioners, social service personnel, health service personnel and those working in the voluntary sector. The purpose of the study was explained, and a descriptive definition of the characteristics of the target population offered.

With respect to GP's, only six people falling within our population not known to the Community Mental Handicap Team were identified, with only a further five people known to the team being reported. It is clear that the GPs, of whom just over 50 per cent responded, overwhelmingly failed to report people with mental handicap over 50 years actually known to the Community Mental Handicap Team.

More success was achieved with social service personnel dealing with generic social work and home care, residential and day services for adults who are elderly, mentally ill, disabled etc. Thirty nine people have so far been identified of whom ten are in current contact with the Community Mental Handicap Team. As yet, returns from the voluntary sector are awaited.

Further individuals originating from Oldham but not known to Community Mental Handicap Team members were identified through a search of records in relevant hospitals. A total of 73 people were found who would now be over 50 years had been admitted, and in some instances discharged, from 1963 onwards. It must be assumed, however, that some proportion of this number must now be dead. A similar check on Oldham SSD records yielded 23 people with mental handicap over the age of 50 years of whom only one was known to the Community Mental Handicap Team.

Taken together, these figures sum to 140 people over the age of 50 years and with mental handicap not known to the Community Mental Handicap Team or not currently receiving services from the team. It should be noted that a proportion of these people are known through records and have not been personally traced. Some correction of the figure for mortality is therefore called for.

The second stage of the procedure is to gather information on identified individuals through use of the Adaptive Behaviour Scales and an appropriate questionnaire. Clearly it will not prove possible to collect information on all individuals given the diversity of contexts in which they now find themselves. To date information has been collected on 20 people, seven of whom live in Oldham SSD residential accommodation for elderly people.

It is, of course, necessary to go beyond the determination of population characteristics and to focus more specifically on the lives of ageing people with mental handicap and their families. This is an area of critical concern as families with whom their offspring still live, age and may become incapable of coping. This particular transition, from home to some other form of residential accommodation has been a central concern in much research. Grant (1988) reported a survey of 190 informal carers of people with mental handicap living in Wales. The mean age of these informal carers was 57 years with their sons and daughters ranging from 2–62 years. Grant noted the diversity of views amongst informal carers regarding the prospects of long-term care for their member with mental handicap, but also emphasised the extent to which attitudes can change over time. Loneliness among carers, socioeconomic class and support from kin, friends and neighbours all provided ". . . reasonably robust markers about predispositions to long-term care", (p. 23) while professional involvement was also a critical issue in this respect. Thus, family reliant carers as against agency reliant carers tended to be less lonely, of lower socioeconomic status, have fewer friends and neighbours in the network, as well as fewer professionals.

Grant also reported qualitative data on specific family situations, as did Richardson who drew on her recently published paper "If you love him, let him go", a moving account of an interview with a single mother of 65 years, whose son, Martin, had moved away from the family home two years ago. Richardson (1988 p. 341) notes that there are two interwoven themes underlying her analysis of the interview; "One is the very distinct nature of the situation faced by parents whose son or daughter has a mental handicap. The other, perhaps surprisingly, is the similarity of their situation to that of all parents, who must at some time undergo the transition of seeing their children leave home."

Study of the field of ageing and mental handicap provides a unique opportunity to consider the interaction of demographic trends and the impact of changing policy on the lives of people in this population. From such analysis can come not only a greater appreciation of the factors that influence the quality of the lives of older people with mental handicap and their families, but also information that is directly relevant to the development of humane and appropriate services for a group who have been described as being in "double jeopardy" from both ageing and mental handicap.

ACKNOWLEDGEMENT

This paper is based on a symposium convened by Hogg on behalf of The International League of Societies for People with Mental Handicap.

REFERENCES

Badry, D. E., Groeneweg, G., Vrbancic, M. and McDonald, L. (1988) A comparison of the service needs of community and institutionally-based older persons with mental handicap, Paper presented at the Eighth Congress of the IASSMD, Dublin, Ireland, August.

Bruckmuller, M. (1988) The International League of Societies for People with Mental Handicap: An international perspective, Paper presented at the Eighth Congress of the IASSMD, Dublin, Ireland, August.

Eyman, R. K., Grossman, H. J., Tarjan, G. and Miller, C. R. (1987) *Life Expectancy and Mental Retardation: A longitudinal study in a state residential facility*, AAMR Monograph No. 7, AAMR, Washington DC.

Grant, G. (1988) Letting go: Tracing reasons for the different attitudes of informal carers towards the future care of people with mental handicap, Paper presented at the Eighth Congress of the IASSMD, Dublin, Ireland, August.

Hogg, J., Moss, S. and Cooke, D. (1988) *Ageing and Mental Handicap*, Croom Helm, London.

Horne, M. (1988) Diverse contacts for ageing mentally handicapped people, Paper presented at the Eighth Congress of the IASSMD, Dublin, Ireland, August.

Richardson, A. (1987) "If you love him, let him go", *LSE Quarterly*, August.

Seltzer, M. M. and Krauss, M. W. (1987) *Aging and Mental Retardation: Extending the continuum, AAMR Monograph No. 9, AAMR, Washington DC.*

United Nations (1956) The Aging of Populations and its Economic and Social Implications, Population Studies No. 26, United Nations, New York.

United Nations (1974) *Demographic Yearbook 19731, 25th Edition*, New York, United Nations.

Service Provision for Aging/Aged Persons with Mental Retardation

M. P. Janicki

Office of Mental Retardation and Developmental Disabilities,
44 Holland Avenue, Albany, New York 12229

Service provision for aging/aged persons with mental retardation was the subject of two symposia composed of speakers from North America, Europe, and the Pacific Rim. The common thread running throughout the presentations was the recognition that in each country there was an emerging concern regarding that nation's population of older individuals with mental retardation, and in particular a need to know who and where were these individuals, and a means to best define an appropriate public policy response that would meet their needs.

The papers in the two symposia were clustered around the following programmatic areas: theoretical models, epidemiological research and service provision.

THEORETICAL MODELS

Anderson noted that the fastest growing group among persons with mental retardation is that represented by the elderly, similar to international growth trends among elderly persons in general. Such increases in longevity are due to a number of factors, including improved health status and improvements in the quality of medical and residential care. The increasing prevalence of older persons with mental retardation is also reflected by their increasing numbers in a variety of residential care settings. The prevalence of chronic health conditions, associated limitations and hospitalizations among those living in facilities licensed by government agencies is similar to or lower than that for elderly persons in general living in the community. A major placement for this population, however, is nursing homes or government operated institutions. Differences between persons in institutional settings and persons in community residential facilities have been found to be largely a function of skill limitations and/or severity of retardation, rather than health-related conditions. Anderson noted that the trend toward an increasingly aged population of individuals with mental retardation is expected to continue well into the future, and that this will present challenges with respect to the development of models of residential care and related services that are both responsive to the needs of an aging population and that address the issue of cost-containment.

Nahemow's perspective on the ecological theory of aging as it relates to elderly persons with mental retardation offers a basis for examining adaptation resulting from aging. The ecological theory of aging states that individuals adapt to a particular functional level depending upon their competence and the "press" of their environment. Normally individuals seek their own level, adapt to it, and over time their competence level stabilizes. Individuals with developmental disabilities are less likely than others to be able to seek their own level of environmental "press". Institutionalization limits choices in this and in many other areas. If a person is socialized in an environment with limited choices and challenges, overtime competence may be reduced thus creating "excess disabilities." Moreover, less competent individuals are highly vulnerable to a mismatch between person and environment. Related to persons with mental retardation, measures using the ecological theory must take into account competence, environmental press, and adaptation level. Since environments, by virtue of their newness, make considerable demands upon the resources of an individual, transitions can be problematic for older persons with mental retardation who have been institutionalized. However, Nahemow noted, if excess disabilities have built up as a consequence of the mismatch between the person and the institutional environment, the result may be not only a higher level of adaptation, but improved competence.

EPIDEMIOLOGICAL ISSUES

Several papers addressed the need to better understand both the scope and structure of a nation's older population of individuals with mental retardation. Hand, Bray & Reid's study provided a perspective on a segment of New Zealand's older disabled population. Their study was designed to gather information about the demographic characteristics, health status, service use patterns and preferences, social resources, and life histories of all older persons with mental retardation in a region of New Zealand. Based upon a preliminary sample of over 200 such individuals, they noted that a wide range of abilities and life-experiences were evident in the study population, both among those who were institutionalized and those who were living in community settings. Most significantly, they found that older individuals expressed unexpectedly high levels of self-esteem and knowledgeable demands for services and leisure activities.

Gow offered insights into the difficulties faced in Hong Kong. She noted that largely for cultural reasons, services for people who are either mentally retarded or ageing are still developing and to date the needs of such individuals have received little or no attention. Her study, the first documented investigation of the population of older individuals with mental retardation, is a work-in-progress survey conducted collaboratively with the Rehabilitation and Elderly sections of the Social Welfare Department. The survey was designed to determine how many mentally handicapped individuals are living in homes for the aged, what services are being provided for this client group and whether these services are considered adequate. The major preliminary finding was that although large numbers of such individuals do exist in Hong Kong, only small numbers could be readily identified.

Moss & Hogg undertook an intensive demographic survey of persons with severe and profound mental retardation over the age of 50 years in Northwest England. More telling than the data findings were the procedures and schedules employed to collect the data. Data collection measures included the *Community Schedule* (designed to collect information on disabled individuals already living in the area, irrespective of their living arrangement), the *Hospital Schedule* (designed for use in the Local Health Authority's two major hospitals), and the *Family Schedule* (designed to be used with family interviews). They collected information on residence, relocation, services, work, retirement, education, leisure, contact with friends and relatives, pastoral input, financial and legal issues, consideration of future plans, experience of aging, state benefits, and informal support networks.

Harper and Jacobson's study was designed to obtain information on a sample of older persons with mental retardation across the United States who were identified as having a mental health disorder. The information gathered characterized their mental health status, identified the extent to which behaviors consistent with impairments of aging or psychiatric conditions were apparent, determined whether residence type differed for persons in concordance with their diagnostic characteristics, and determined the extent to which various psychological and psychiatric services and therapies were available. The mail survey responses indicated that 60% of the individuals were male, 28% were age 55 to 59, 45% were age 60 to 69, and 22% were age 70 to 74 years. Those identified with a "mental health disorder" were functioning in the severe to profound range of mental retardation, but required only low levels of assistance with basic activities of daily living. Some 10% had shown marked behavioral changes over the recent past that could be attributed to aging or dementing processes. It was noted that most clinical services were provided to assist these individuals with maintaining function and to assist in the control and remediation of conditions such as seizure disorders and maladaptive behaviors.

Janicki's study of the characteristics of older persons with cerebral palsy and mental retardation dealt with a cohort of 883 older individuals. The study sample was drawn from an all-ages governmental agency registry population of 7304 persons with cerebral palsy within the state of New York (USA). The study identified 883 persons age 45+, 295 age 60+, and 41 age 75+. Within the sample there was a greater number of males to females irrespective of age; virtually no non-whites in the old-old group; a co-occurrence of mental retardation of 84%, 75%, and 88%, respectively, across three age groups; there were decreases in rates of seizures with age; increases in rate of impairment in sensory and mobility abilities with advancing age; above norm age-specific rates of individuals in institutional settings and marked increases in the rate of institutionalization with advancing age; and generally lesser numbers of individuals in all older age groups indicating earlier age-specific mortality.

SERVICES PROVISION

Papers addressing this topic dealt with a variety of issues related to services. Several spoke to the issue of the nature of quality of care (Brown et al.; Roberts et al.); others covered program models and program development practices (Gordon; Weber & Haines), family attitudes (Heller & Factor), and clinical practices (Kenefick).

Brown, Bayer & MacFarlane reported that the Canadian Rehabilitation Programmes Study, which looked at older individuals with mental retardation within five agencies that carry out rehabilitation in Western Canada, was concerned with examining the quality of care provided by the agencies and the quality of life enjoyed by their clientele. The agencies were concerned with mentally retarded and multiply handicapped persons ranging in age from 18 years upwards. Brown et al. note that the needs spoken to included leisure time participation, community interests, worries and anxieties, and the context of agency programs. Brown et al. noted these needs arose as issues in relation to the development of services of aging handicapped persons and that agencies needed to shift their delivery patterns because of the advancing ages of their clientele.

Roberts et al. reported on a study in the state of Ohio (USA) that dealt with changes brought about by volunteers serving as escorts to individual older persons with mental retardation over a period of two years. Change measures noted physical status, activities of daily living, social skills, personal relationships, use of leisure time, and participation in community activities. Project results showed that significant increases occurred in the number of community activities in which the subjects participated. Further, effective partcipation in generic senior services became the mode, the number of affective relationships increased, and there were increases in language and social skills, and improvements in grooming and overall appearance.

Gordon and Weber & Haines reported program models in which either area-wide community development or site-specific program development techniques were used. Gordon noted the use of government sponsored agent model in the state of Maryland (USA) in which, over a two year period, the agent (designated as "aging specialist") travelled throughout the state and visited with all the state's agencies for the elderly. The focus of the project was to explore and define the relationship between the community's elderly network and the mental retardation agency system. The intent was to determine how best the elderly network could serve the community's elderly with mental retardation. Additional facets of the model included presentations of currently available programs, links with university-based centers on aging, and informational workshops which brought together staff from both systems. The agency also used financial stimuli by awarding grants to agencies for the elderly that were designed to integrate older persons with mental retardation into the regular service network for the aging.

Weber & Haines reported on a project model (social model adult day care) that was designed to provide a day services program in a rural area of the state of Wisconsin (USA) for that area's elderly impaired residents as well as a cohort of older individuals with mental retardation. Select pre-admission measures were first used to determine individual level of functioning and to guide programming for program applicants. The program incorporated design features that included individualized program planning with expanded opportunities for development and growth, encouraging individual decision-making to develop feelings of self-esteem and independence, training opportunities for undergraduate and graduate students in gerontology and mental retardation, and program cost containment through use of volunteers from the community and student interns to supplement and assist professional staff. Weber & Haines concluded that the program demonstrated improved quality of life for the program's participants.

Heller & Factor studied family attitudes to better understand the deterrents to permanency planning and placement and to examine the factors that lessen caregiving burden in the home. Their sample included 100 families of adults with mental retardation age 30 or above living in their natural homes in the state of Illinois (USA). Their findings revealed that the majority of families preferred that their children remain in the family home both currently and after the parents died. Of the 44% who wanted an eventual residential placement, very few had taken any actions to seek such placements. Less than 10% had placed their son or daughter on a waiting list for residential placement. In terms of caregiving burden, Heller & Factor found that family caregivers who had more demands placed upon them and who received fewer informal supports, experienced the most caregiving burden. Indeed, higher caregiving burden led to a greater desire to place adult offspring in a residential program. They noted that families with older caregivers that had higher socioeconomic status and service usage, but fewer informal supports, were also more likely to desire residential placement.

Kenefick's study of oral communication among three groups of elderly persons was intended to identify similarities and differences of interaction patterns, and the communicative strategies that could be used to enhance cognitive processing for elderly persons with mental retardation. The three groups include older age individuals with mental retardation, individuals free of disability, and individuals who are regarded as particularly successful by their age peers in one or more major areas of life activity. Identified patterns were examined from two perspectives: speaker intent and response of other speaker-listeners to determine their effectiveness. Based on these examinations, communicative configurations were selected to assist older individuals with mental retardation in enhancing personal relationships with both disabled and non-disabled age peers. The results led to the development of a number of strategies to promote the acquisition of communicative configurations.

The overall conclusions drawn from the symposia were that there were many common themes related to the aging of persons with mental retardation that emerged across nations irrespective of culture, wealth, or level of program development and provision. Paramount among these was the emerging awareness of the phenomenon of the "greying" of the population of adults with mental retardation and the need to have a much better understanding of the demographics of the population. Secondary was the concern that the quality of life of persons in this "third age" must be an important consideration and that many governments and provider agencies must face the realization that these individuals are experiencing increased longevity and decreased morbidity and that service development must be responsive and contextual with regard to age and need. Third was the agreement that more must be done to effectively make available and exchange information about available research, program models, and clinical practices, and to provide greater support for the growing body of research on the processes of aging (and related effects) among individuals with mental retardation.

REFERENCES

Anderson, D. (1988) Elderly mentally retarded persons: policy issues and trends. (Department of Educational Psychology, University of Minnesota, Minneapolis, MN 55455, USA). Paper presented at VIIIth Congress of IASSMD Dublin, August 24.

Brown, R. I., Bayer, M. B. & MacFarlane, C. (1988) Aspects of quality of life for aging mentally handicapped persons. (The University of Calgary, Rehabilitation Studies, 2500 University Drive, NW, Calgary, Alberta, Canada T2N 1N4). Paper presented at VIIIth Congress of IASSMD, Dublin, August 24.

Gordon, I.A. (1988) Mental retardation program development among agencies serving the elderly in Maryland. (Maryland Development Disabilities Administration, 201 West Preston Street, Baltimore, MD 21201, USA). Paper presented at VIIIth Congress of IASSMD, Dublin, August 24.

Gow, L. (1988) Aging people with mental handicaps in Hong Kong. (Hong Kong Polytechnic, Department of Applied Social Studies, Hung Hom, Kowloon, Hong Kong). Paper presented at VIIIth Congress of IASSMD, Dublin, August 24.

Hand, J., Bray, A. & Reid, P. (1988) Aging and intellectual handicap: A report of a study of intellectually handicapped people born 1939 and prior in one province in New Zealand. (University of Otago Medical School, PO Box 913, Dunedin, New Zealand). Paper presented at VIIIth Congress of IASSMD, Dublin, August 24.

Harper, M. S. & Jacobson, J. (1988) A national study of the mental health status of older persons with mental retardation. (National Institute for Mental Health, Rockville, MD, USA & New York State Office of Mental Retardation and Developmental Disabilities, 44 Holland Avenue, Albany, NY 12229-1000, USA). Paper presented at VIIIth Congress of IASSMD, Dublin, August 24.

Heller, T. & Factor, A. R. (1988) Family caregiving burden and attitudes toward residential placement of older adults with developmental disabilities. (Institute for the Study of Developmental Disabilities, 1640 West Roosevelt Road, Chicago, IL 60608, USA). Paper presented at VIIIth Congress of IASSMD, Dublin, August 24.

Janicki, M. P. (1988) Aging, cerebral palsy and older persons with mental retardation. (New York State Office of Mental Retardation and Developmental Disabilities, 44 Holland Avenue, Albany, New York 12229-1000, USA). Paper presented at VIIIth Congress of IASSMD, Dublin, August 24.

Kenefick, B. A. (1988) Communicative strategies to enhance cognitive processing for elderly persons with mental retardation. (New York State Office of Mental Retardation and Developmental Disabilities, 44 Holland Avenue, Albany, NY 12229-1000, USA). Paper presented at VIIIth Congress of IASSMD, Dublin, August 24.

Moss, S. & Hogg, J. (1988) Determinants of service provision for people with severe and profound mental handicap over the age of 50 years. (Hester Adrian Research Centre, The University Oxford Road, Manchester M13

9PL, England). Paper presented at VIIIth Congress of IASSMD, Dublin, August 24.

Nahemow, L. (1988) Ecological theory of aging as it relates to elderly persons with mental retardation. (Traveler's Center on Aging, University of Connecticut, Storrs, CT 06268, USA). Paper presented at VIIIth Congress of IASSMD, Dublin, August 24.

Roberts, R. S., Sutton, E., Stroud, M., Ayidiya, S. & Davis, D. (1988) Use of quality of life scales to measure outcome of project using volunteers with elderly persons with mental retardation. (Carroll Hall 112, University of Akron, Akron, OH 44325, USA). Paper presented at VIIIth Congress of IASSMD, Dublin, August 24.

Weber, E. & Haines, E. (1988) Quality of life in programming for aging persons with developmental disabilities. (St. Coletta School, W4955 Highway 18, Jefferson, WI 53549, USA). Paper presented at VIIIth Congress of IASSMD, Dublin, August 24.

Additional Submitted Papers given at the Eighth IASSMD Congress

The list below provides professional addresses of the speakers whose submitted papers, shown by title, could not be published in this volume. Each paper was read by an independent reviewer in addition to the Editor and was subject to the scrutiny of the Editorial Board. It is regretted that space cannot be found for publication of these papers.

Agran, M. Facilitating the Work Transition of Students with Mental Retardation by Teaching them to use Self-Instructional Strategies. Department of Special Education, Utah State University, Logan, Utah 84322-6500, U.S.A.

Airaksinen, E. M., Matilainen, R. and Launiala, K. Need of Care, Additional Disabilities and Daily Activities of Nine to Ten Year Old Mentally Retarded Children. Department of Paediatrics, Kuopio University Central Hospital, SF-79210, Kuopio, Finland.

Aitchison, C., Easty, D. L., and Jancar, J. Eye Abnormalities in the Mentally Handicapped. Stoke Park Hospital, Stapleton, Bristol, BS16 1QU, England.

Alexander, D. Prevention of Mental Retardation. National Institute of Child Health and Human Development, National Institutes of Health, Washington, D.C., U.S.A.

Arya, R. P. People with Mental Handicap – As Parents (A Review). 3 Skipton Avenue, Crossens, Southport, PR9 8JP, England

Baum, N. T. Sandplay Therapy with Mentally Retarded Individuals with Severe Emotional or Psychiatric Disorders (Dual Diagnosis). Muki Baum Association for the Rehabilitation of Multi-Handicapped (Adult and Children's Treatment Centres), 111 Anthony Road, (Downsview) Toronto, Ontario, M3K 1B7 Canada.

Baxter, C. Investigating Stigma as Stress in Social Interactions of Parents. Victoria College, Faculty of Special Education and Paramedical Studies, Burwood, Victoria, Australia.

Berney, T. P. and Jones, P. M. Manic Depressive Disorder in Mental Handicap. Prudhoe Hospital, Prudhoe, Northumberland, NE42 5NT, England.

Blackman, L. S. Promises to the Mentally Retarded: History and Illusion. Department of Social Education, Teachers College, Columbia University, 525 W. 120th Street, New York, N.Y. 10027, U.S.A.

Blindert, H. D. A Behavioural Accounting System – Quality Control in Behavioural Programs for the Developmentally Handicapped. Behaviour Clinic, Children's Psychiatric Research Institute, P.O. Box 2460, London, Ontario N6A 4G6, Canada.

Bray, D. A. Social Interaction at Home of Young Children with Down's Syndrome. New Zealand Institute of Mental Retardation (Inc.), University of Otago, Dunedin, New Zealand.

Brinkworth, R. Effective Treatment and Training for the Child with Down's Syndrome – a 20 year Study. National Centre for Down's Syndrome, Birmingham Polytechnic, Westbourne Road, Edgbaston, Birmingham, B15 3TN, England.

Butler, B., Fitzgerald, M., and Kinsella, A. The Burden on a Family Having a Child with Special Needs. Hospitaller Order of St. John of God, Community Service, St. Teresa's, Main Street, Tallaght, Dublin 24, Ireland.

Černá, M. Teacher of Mentally Handicapped (knowledge, skills and attitudes). Charles University, European Information Centre for Further Education of Teachers, Kaprova 14, Prague 1 110 00, Czechoslovakia.

Cherkes-Julkowski, M., Bertrand, J. and Roth, D. Identification of Atypical Infant Development in the Caretaking Context. Department of Educational Psychology, 249 Glenbrook Road, Box U-64, University of Connecticut, Storrs, Connecticut 06268, U.S.A.

Conliffe, C. The Person with Mental Handicap – Preparation for an Adult Life in the Community: Staff roles and experience in Day Centres. Social Service Training Unit, Gortmore Day Centre, Derry Road, Omagh, County Tyrone, Northern Ireland.

Connor, F. P. Education of Medically Fragile Children. Teachers College, Columbia University, 200 4th Avenue, Spring Lake, New Jersey 07762, U.S.A.

Cooke, L. B. Hearing Loss in an Ageing Mentally Handicapped Population: Further Studies. Stoke Park Hospital, Stapleton, Bristol, BS16 1QU, England.

Costa, M. P. R. Prevention in Special Education – A Study of the Educational Intervention. Departamento de Psicologia, Universidada Federal de São Carlos, Rodovia Washington Luiz, Km 235, São Carlos – SP – Brazil 13.560.

Curfs, L. M. G., Schreppers, G., Wiegers, A., Borghgraef, M. and Fryns, J. P. Intelligence and Physiological Profile in the FRA(X) Syndrome: A Longitudinal Study in 20 FRA(X) Boys. Observation Centre De Hondsberg, The Netherlands and Centre for Human Genetics, University of Leuven, Belgium.

Diamond, G. W., Cohen, H. J., Belman, A. L., Harris-Copp, M., and Rubenstein, A. Mental Retardation and Physical Disabilities in

HIV-Infected Children – Implications for Rehabilitation. Rose F. Kennedy Centre, Albert Einstein College of Medicine, 1410 Pelham Parkway South, Bronx, New York 10461, U.S.A.

Dibietz, E. M. Yours or Ours – Developmentally Disabled with Mental Illness. Maryland State Department of Health and Mental Hygiene, Mental Hygiene Admin., 201 West Preston Street, Baltimore, Maryland 21201, U.S.A.

Dinani, S. and Carpenter, S. Down's Syndrome and Thyroid Disorder. Brentry Hospital, Charlton Road, Bristol BS10 6JH, England.

DiPalma, E. Dance/Movement Therapy – Innovations in the Rehabilitation of Persons with Mental Retardation. New York University, P.O. Box 232, Jackson Heights, New York 11372, U.S.A.

Dodson, G. and Alaszewski, A. Developing the Key Worker Model in Barnardo's Croxteth Park Project for Children with a Profound Mental Handicap. Barnardo's, N.W. Division, 7 Lineside Close, Liverpool L25 2UD, England.

Doll-Tepper, G. M. Controversies and Current Tendencies in Physical Education and Sport for the Mentally Retarded – an International Comparison. Institut für Sportwissenschaft, Freie Universität Berlin, Rheinbabenallee 14, 1000 Berlin 33, Federal Republic of Germany.

Drury, M. I., Brennan, M., Murphy, C., Gayer, E. and Keenan, P. Hypothyriodism in Down's Syndrome. Diabetic Day Centre, 48 Eccles Street, Dublin 7, Ireland.

Dunne, T. P. Assertiveness Training with Mentally Handicapped Adults. Psychology Department, Assessment & Child Development Clinic, St. Michael's House, Ballymun Road, Dublin 9, Ireland.

Dupper, M. A. The Effects of a Ten-Week Aerobic Exercise Program on the Physiological, Cognitive, and Behavioural Functioning of Institutionalised Retarded Children. The University of Mississippi (Research and Training Centre for the Handicapped), 304, Old Chemistry, University Mississippi 38677, U.S.A.

Dwyer, C. J. Adoption of Children with Developmental Disabilities: One Recruitment Effort. University Affiliated Cincinnati Centre for Developmental Disorders, Pavilion Building, Elland and Bethesda Avenues, Cincinnati, Ohio 45229, U.S.A.

Dyer, S., Gunn, P., Rauh, H., and Berry, P. Motor Development in Down Syndrome Children – An Analysis of the Motor Scale of the Bayley Scales of Infant Development. James Cook University, Townsville Q4811, Australia.

Farnan, L. Music Therapy within a Transdisciplinary Model. Central Wisconsin Centre for the Developmentally Disabled, 317, Knutson Drive, Madison, Wisconsin 53704, U.S.A.

Feldman, M. A. and Case, L. The Effectiveness of a Child-Care Training

Program for Mentally Handicapped Parents. Parent Education Project, Surrey Place Centre, Toronto, Ontario, M5S 2C2 Canada.

Felix, T. 3 C's Concept. Central Institute on Mental Retardation, Jagathy, Trivandrum – 695 014, Kerala, India.

Fishler, K., Azen, C. G., Friedman, E. G., and Koch, R. School Achievements in Treated PKU Children. Division of Medical Genetics, Childrens Hospital of Los Angeles, 4650 Sunset Boulevard, Los Angeles, California 90027, U.S.A.

Frankish, P. Meeting the Emotional Needs of Handicapped People – A Psycho-Dynamic Approach. District General Hospital, Scartho Road, Grimsby, South Humberside DN33 2BA, England.

Fryns, J. P., Volcke, Ph., Haspeslagh, M., Beusen, L. and van den Berghe, H. A Genetic Diagnostic Survey in an Institutionalised Population of 262 Moderately Mentally Retarded Patients – The Borgerstein Experience. Centre for Human Genetics, University of Leuven, U.Z. Gasthuisberg, Herestraat 49, B-3000 Leuven, Belgium.

Gfeller, K. E., McDonald, D. T. and Svengalis, J. Preschool Programming for the Mentally Retarded Child – Music Therapy as a Sensorimotor Experience. School of Music, The University of Iowa, Iowa City, Iowa 52242, U.S.A.

Gjessing, L. R., Lunde, H. A. and Sjaastad, O. Inborn Errors of Carnosine and Homocarnosine Metabolism. Research Institute for Neuropsychiatry, Dikemark Hospital, Oslo Commune, Asker N-1385 Solberg, Norway.

Gleason, J. J. Underlying Meaning in the Behaviour of Persons with Severe and Profound Mental Retardation and Multiple Handicaps: Implications for Clinical Intervention. Rhode Island College, Providence, Rhode Island, U.S.A.

Gold, H. B., Mahler, A., O'Brien, M., and Knowlton, J. Health Care Utilisation and Costs for Persons with Mental Retardation Residing in Institutions and Community Programs. State of New York Office of Mental Retardation and Developmental Disabilities, 44 Holland Avenue, Albany, New York 12229, U.S.A.

Graf, T. Impact of the Voluntary Movement on Developing Community Services for Mentally Retarded Citizens in the United States. Retarded Citizens/Atlanta, 1687 Tullie Circle, N.E., Suite 110, Atlanta, Georgia 30329, U.S.A.

Grelli-Garrick, F. a) Special Care Unit = Better Health? Mere Coincidence or Real Facts? b) The Nurses!? Nurse, Teacher, Trainer, Therapist? What? Which? Residential Training Unit, Bromham Hospital, Bromham, Nr. Bedford, MK43 8HL, England.

Griffin, J. Overview of a Research Programme Designed to Address Key Issues in the Planning and Delivery of Services for People with

Mental Handicap. Department of Health and Social Security, B605 Alexander Fleming House, Elephant and Castle, London SE1, England.

Grubar, J. C., Colognola, R. M., Gigli, G. L., Ferri, R., Musumeci, S. A. and Bergonzi, P. Sleep and Mental Retardation: The Neuropedagogical Approach (Neurophysiological Aspects). Institut Universitaire de Technologie "B", Education Specialisée, Université de Lille 111, 9 Rue A. Angellier, 59046 Lille Cedex, France.

Guralnick, M. J. Social Competence as a Future Direction for Early Intervention Programs. Child Development and Mental Retardation Centre, University of Washington, Seattle, Washington 98195, U.S.A.

Hayden, F. J. and Tarnopolsky, L. J. Fitness and Lifestyle of International Special Olympians. School of Physical Education and Athletics, McMaster University, 1280 Main Street W., Hamilton, Ontario, L8S 4K1 Canada.

Hobart, A. Z. The Affective-Sexual Development of Persons with Down's Syndrome – Ten Years of Observation and Interviews with the Families and School Teachers. Associazione Bambini Down, Viale delle Milizie 106, 00192 Roma, Italy.

Hughes, M. J. and Segall, A. Quality of Life of Former Residents of a Provincial Institution. University of Manitoba, Winnipeg, R3T 4N4 Canada.

Iivanainen, M. and Lähdevirta, J. Infectious Diseases as Causes of Mental Retardation and their Neurological Sequelae. Department of Neurology, University of Helsinki, Haartmaninkatu 4, SF-00290 Helsinki, Finland.

Irwin, K. C. Teaching Numerical Concepts to Children with Down's Syndrome. Room 11–129, Ontario Institute for Studies in Education, 252 Bloor St., Toronto, Ontario, Canada.

Jancar, J. Fractures in the Ageing Mentally Handicapped Population. Stoke Park Hospital, Stapleton, Bristol BS16 1QU, England.

Jayawardhana, B. Risking it in the Community: New Ways in Which Disabled People Live in the Community. Catholic Social Services, 8815–99 Street, Edmonton, Alberta, Canada T6E 3V3.

Kääriäinen, R. Screening and Prevalence of Severe and Mild Retardation in Two Finnish Provinces. Department of Community Medicine, University of Kuopio, Finland.

Koppe, J. G. Congenital Toxoplasmosis and Long-Term Follow-up of Twenty Years. Department of Neonatology, Academic Medical Centre, University of Amsterdam, Meibergdreef 9, 1105 AZ Amsterdam, Holland.

LaFontaine, L. The Savant Syndrome: A Case Study (1974) and Follow-

Up Report (1987) of a Calendar Calculator. CRS Department, Northeastern University, 203 Lake Hall, 360 Huntington Avenue, Boston, Massachusetts 02115, U.S.A.

Lee, W. Y. and Broad, J. C. The Pandora's Box – A Clinical Perspective in Staff Sexuality Training Issues. Sexuality Clinic, Surrey Place Centre, 2 Surrey Place, Toronto, M5S 2C2 Canada.

Lester, B. M. Early Detection of the Infant at Risk Through Cry Analysis. Bradley Hospital Women & Infants Hospital, 1011 Veterans Memorial Parkway, East Providence, Rhode Island 02915, U.S.A.

Liberoff, M., Feldman, J. and Liberoff, S. P.C.P. Pictographic Communication Programme Applied to Argentine non-speaking Children. Ile, Instituto de Lenguaje y Educacion Especial, Conesa 2051–1428 Buenos Aires, Argentina.

Lindsay, W. R., Fee, M., Baty, F. J. and Michie, A. M. Cue Control to Promote the Extension of the Effects of Relaxation Training. Clinical Psychology Department, Strathmartine Hospital, Dundee DD3 0PG, Scotland.

Little, M. T. Sport and Recreation – a Social Resource in the Community Integration of People with an Intellectual Disability. Australian Sport and Recreation Association for People with an Intellectual Disability. P.O. Box 632, North Adelaide, South Australia 5006, Australia.

Lyster, G. V., and Kinsella, L. Prevalence of Psychiatric Disorders Among a Residential Mental Handicap Population and a Day Attender Group. St. Brigid's Hospital, Ardee, Co. Louth, Ireland.

Malbrán, M. C. and Feoli, I.S. Education for the Mentally Deficient, Evaluating the Quality of the Environment: The Social Acceptance Scale. Departamento de Ciencias de la Education, Universidad Nacional de la Plata, Argentina.

Matulay, K., and Smiešková, A. Remarks on the Findings of Acoustic Brain Stem Evoked Potentials in Mentally Handicapped. Department of Developmental Disturbances, University Children's Hospital and Research Institute of Medical Bionics, Bratislava, Czechoslovakia.

Mavrin-Cavor, L. J. Results of the Application of the Adaptive Behaviour Scale Among Mentally Retarded Pupils in Special and Integrated Educational Conditions. Faculty of Defectology, University of Zagreb, Zagreb, Kušlanova 59a, Yugoslavia.

McCallion, P. The Training School at Vineland: Towards a Second Century of Services and Research. The Training School at Vineland, 1667 East Landis Avenue, Vineland, New Jersey 08360, U.S.A.

McCarthy, E. A. Intangible Barriers to Full Adult Status in the Age of

Transition. Mill Lane Training Centre, Stewart's Hospital, Palmerstown, Dublin 20, Ireland.

McConachie, H. R. What Parents think about Parenting and Teaching. Department of Developmental Pediatrics, Institute of Child Health, Mecklenburgh Square, London WC1N 2AP, England.

McEvoy, M. Study of Lifestyles of Teenagers with Special Learning Needs. Department of Work Training, St. Augustine's School, Blackrock, Co. Dublin, Ireland.

McGinley, P. A Study of the Quality of Life of Formerly Institutionalised People now Living in Community Residences. Woodlands Centre, Renmore, Galway, Ireland.

Moilanen, I., vWendt, L., Myhrman, A. and Rantakallio, P. Education for the Mentally Subnormal. Department of Paediatrics, University of Oulu, SF-90220 Oulu, Finland.

Molony, H. and Taplin, J. Evaluation of Deinstitutionalisation of the Mentally Retarded – the New South Wales Experience. Department of Developmental Disability, Division of Community Health, Prince of Wales Hospital, Randwick, Sydney, NSW 2031, Australia.

Morss, J. R. Cognitive Motivation in the Young Child with Down's Syndrome. University of Otago, P.O. Box 56, Dunedin, New Zealand.

Paul, F. M. A Survey of Intellectual Disability in Singapore Children over a Twenty-Four Year Period. Academy of Medicine, Faculty of Medicine Building, College Road, 0316 Singapore.

Phillipson, R. The Fetal Alcohol Syndrome: Recent International Statistics. Battlefield Heights, Box 659, Berryville, Virginia 22611, U.S.A.

Pollicina, C. and D'Erario, C. Sleep and Learning: An Interdisciplinary Approach (Psychopedagogical Aspects). Department of Psychology, Oasi Institute for Research and Prevention of Mental Retardation, Via Conte Ruggero, 73, Troina, Italy.

Radtke, F.A., and Radtke, J. C. Special Education Methods and Curriculum Design. International Office, The Lutheran Church Missouri Synod, St. Louis, MO 63122, U.S.A.

Rao, J. M. A Population Based Survey of Mild Mental Deficiency in 8–12 year old Children – Preliminary Results. Coleg Meddygaeth Prifysgol Cymru, Department of Psychological Medicine, Ely Hospital, Ely, Cardiff, Wales.

Reiter, S., Tirosh, E., Bar-Tikvah, H. and Adam, D. Are We Stereotyping Parents of Down's Syndrome Children? – Comparison Between Parents of Down's Syndrome Children and Parents of Other Developmentally Disabled Children. School of Education, University of Haifa, Haifa 31999, Israel.

Remington, B., Clarke, S., Goodman, J. and Watson, J. Sign Learning and Sign Use – Aspects of Transfer following Sign Training Procedures. Department of Psychology, University of Southampton, Southampton SO9 5NH, England.

Richardson, M. R. A Community Plan for Individuals who are Mentally Retarded and have Substantial Medical Needs. Child Development and Mental Retardation Centre, University of Washington, Seattle, Washington, U.S.A.

Roberts, R. S. Use of Quality of Life Scales to Measure Outcomes of a Project Using Volunteers with Elderly Persons with Mental Retardation. Kennedy Access Project Counseling and Special Education, The University of Akron, Carroll Hall 127, Akron, OH 44325-5007, U.S.A.

Rowitz, L., Farber, B. and Heller, T. Domestic Cycle of Families with Retarded Offspring. University of Illinois at Chicago, Box 6998, Chicago, Illinois 60680, U.S.A.

Rufas, F. Ma. V. Autistic Syndrome in Children with Mental Deficiency. Licenciado en Pedagogia Terapeutica, San Antonio Ma Claret, No. 30-B 5o 1a 43002, Tarragona, Spain.

Rush, D. Syndrome – Specific Cognitive Patterns in Adolescents with Down's Syndrome. St. Michael's House, Dublin 6, Ireland.

Schreppers-Tijdink, G. A. J., Curfs, L. M. G., Wiegers, A., Kleczkowska, A. and Fryns, J. P. A Systematic Cytogenetic Study of a Population of 1170 Mentally Retarded and/or Behaviourly Disturbed Patients Including Fragile X Screening. The Hondsberg Experience. Observation Centre de Hondsberg, Oisterwijk, The Netherlands and Centre for Human Genetics, University of Leuven, Belgium.

Schumacher, N. C. and Fields, W. S. Psycho-Social Aspects of Epilepsy: The Spider's Net, 10236 Xerxes Ave. So., Bloomington, MN 55431, U.S.A.

Shaddock, A. J. The Use of Video Packages in the Inservice Education of Residential Staff. Department of Behavioural Studies in Education, University of New England, Armidale, N.S.W. 2351, Australia.

Sherrill, C. Sport Training and Competition for Mentally Retarded Persons. Department of Physical Education, Texas Women's University, P.O. Box 23717, Denton, Texas 76204, U.S.A.

Sousa, A. A. A. and Braga, M. E. C. O. Cabeceiras de Basto Project (Answers to the Problem of Disability). Centro Regional de Seguranca Social de Braga, Avenida de Liberdade, 516, 4719 Braga, Portugal.

Spangler, P. F., Gilman, B. and LaBorde, P. R. Frequency and Type of Incidents Occurring in Urban Based Group Homes. Philadelphia Office of Mental Health and Mental Retardation, 1101 Market Street, Philadelphia, PA 19107-2907, U.S.A.

Stammler, A. A Psychotherapeutic Approach to a Bed-Ridden Enceph-
alopathic Child in a Medicopaedagogic Institute. Institut Médico-
pédagogique "Marie Auxiliatrice", 2 Avenue Henri-Barbusee,
91210 Champrosay Draveil, France.

Stodden, R. A. A Study of Secondary School Post-School Training and
Employment Transition for Youth with Handicaps. Department of
Special Education, University of Hawaii at Manoa, 1776 University
Avenue, Wist 208, Honolulu, Hawaii 96822, U.S.A.

Takahashi, O., and Irie, N. Community Medical Care System for
Developmentally Disabled Children and Adults in Higashi-Osaka
City, Japan. 209 Tsunoi, Tottori, Tottori 689-11, Japan.

Toomey, J. F. Bawnmore Personal Development Programme – A Pilot
Study. Brothers of Charity Services, Bawnmore, Limerick, Ireland.

Touwen, B. C. L. Development of the Brain in Mentally Deficient
Children: Conceptual Considerations. Institute for Developmental
Neurology, University of Groningen, Oostersingel 59, 9713 EZ
Groningen, The Netherlands.

Turner, L. A., Hale, C. and Borkowski, J. G. Components of Memory
Performance in Retarded and Non-Retarded Children. Department
of Psychology, Box 154, George Peabody College, Vanderbilt
University, Nashville, Tennessee 37203, U.S.A.

Van Gennep, A. T. G. Quality of Care in Dutch Residential Facilities.
University of Amsterdam, Ijsbaanpad 9, 1076 CV, Amsterdam,
Holland.

Velche, D. A Study of the Difficulties of Travellers with a Mental
Handicap in Urban Areas of France. Syndicat National des
Associations de Parents d'Enfants Inadeptés, 86 Avenue de Saint-
Ouen, 75018 Paris, France.

Walsh, G. F. Views on Residential Facility Options. Mount Oliver
Rolling Acres, 7200 Rolling Acres Road, Excelsior, MN 55331,
U.S.A.

Walsh, P. N. The Horse Comes First: Devising and Evaluating a
Community-Based Curriculum for Persons with Mental Handicap.
St. Michael's House Research, Upper Kilmacud Road, Stillorgan,
Co. Dublin, Ireland.

Webb, A. Y. Toward an Organisational Paradigm: Lessons Learned in
Management of Basic Research – A Case Study, NYS Department
of Mental Retardation and Developmental Disabilities, 44 Holland
Avenue, Albany, N.Y. 12229, U.S.A.

Westling, D. L. The Effect of Single Setting vs. Multiple Setting Training
on Learning to Shop in a Department Store. Department of Special
Education, Florida State University, Tallahassee, Florida, 32312
U.S.A.

Westwood, R. E. and Mitchell, D. R. The Transition of Intellectually

Handicapped Adolescents from School to Adult Living, Work and Post-Secondary Education: A Recent Feasibility Study in New Zealand. Program Coordination Branch, Department of Advanced Education, 11160 Jasper Ave., Edmonton, Alberta, Canada.

Whyte, J. Process Variables in Intervention – A Qualitative Analysis. School of Clinical Speech & Language Studies, Trinity College, Dublin 2, Ireland.

Whyte, J. and Ryan, N. Sign Language and Mentally Handicapped Children: The Evaluation of a LAMH roject. Clinical Speech and Language Studies, Trinity College, Dublin 2, Ireland.

Wickham, E. R. and Blackmore, R. Attitudes of Parents of Developmentally Handicapped Persons Towards Specialised and Generic Services. Faculty of Social Work, Wilfrid Laurier University, Waterloo, Ontario, N2L 3C5 Canada.

Wilgosh, L., Waggoner, K. and Adams, B. Parent Views on Education and Daily Living Concerns for Children with Mental Handicaps. Department of Educational Psychology, University of Alberta, Edmonton, T6G 2G5 Canada.

Wilton, K. Employment and Adjustment of Mildly Retarded School Leavers in New Zealand. Education Department, The University of Auckland, Private Bag, Auckland, New Zealand.

Wohlfarth, R. Profoundly and Multiply Handicapped Persons: Care, Education, Occupations. Anstalt Stetten, Kernen im Remstal, Federal Republic of Germany.

Wu, W-T. Family Environments in Chinese (Taiwanese) and American Families with Mentally Retarded Children: A Cross-Cultural Study. National Taiwan Normal University, Taipei, Taiwan, R.O.C.

Yon, K. Performance with Severely Mentally Handicapped Children: Developing the Expressive-Functional Role of their Helpers. Department of Theatre, Dartington College of Arts, Totnes, Devon TQ9 6EJ, England.

Name Index

Subject Index

Note: DS = Down's syndrome; MMR = mild mental retardation; NH = non-handicapped; PMLD = profound and multiple learning difficulties; SLD = severe learning difficulties